In Praise of Desire

OXFORD MORAL THEORY

Series Editor
David Copp, University of California, Davis

In Praise of Desire

Nomy Arpaly

Timothy Schroeder

OXFORD
UNIVERSITY PRESS

OXFORD
UNIVERSITY PRESS

Oxford University Press is a department of the University of Oxford.
It furthers the University's objective of excellence in research, scholarship,
and education by publishing worldwide.

Oxford   New York
Auckland   Cape Town   Dar es Salaam   Hong Kong   Karachi
Kuala Lumpur   Madrid   Melbourne   Mexico City   Nairobi
New Delhi   Shanghai   Taipei   Toronto

With offices in
Argentina   Austria   Brazil   Chile   Czech Republic   France   Greece
Guatemala   Hungary   Italy   Japan   Poland   Portugal   Singapore
South Korea   Switzerland   Thailand   Turkey   Ukraine   Vietnam

Oxford is a registered trademark of Oxford University Press
in the UK and certain other countries.

Published in the United States of America by
Oxford University Press
198 Madison Avenue, New York, NY 10016

Library of Congress Cataloging-in-Publication Data
Arpaly, Nomy.
In praise of desire / Nomy Arpaly, Timothy Schroeder.
pages cm.—(Oxford moral theory)
Includes bibliographical references and index.
ISBN 978-0-19-934816-9 (hardback : alk. paper)   1. Desire (Philosophy)   2. Ethics.
3. Virtue.   4. Virtues.   I. Title.
B105.D44A77 2014
171'.2—dc23
2013019576

1 3 5 7 9 8 6 4 2
Printed in the United States of America
on acid-free paper

{ CONTENTS }

{ ACKNOWLEDGMENTS }

We owe at least the following people acknowledgments for their generous help on parts or all of this work: Nicolas Bommarito, John Broome, Sarah Buss, Ben Caplan, David Christensen, Rachel Cohon, Justin D'Arms, Stephen Darwall, John Doris, James Dreier, Julia Driver, David Estlund, Thomas Fisher, John Hurst, Christa Johnson, Jaegwon Kim, Niko Kolodny, Han Li, Danny Pearlberg, Philip Pettit, Peter Railton, Richard Samuels, Valerie Tiberius, Vladimir Vlaovic, and Jeremy Weiss.

Julia Driver, Julia Markovits, and Peter Railton were our referees for Oxford University Press, and they provided us with a wealth of valuable feedback in that capacity.

This work also greatly benefited from pieces of it (better: versions of pieces of it) being presented to the philosophers at the Chapel Hill Colloquium, Davidson College, Massachusetts Institute of Technology, the Moral Psychology Research Group, the Practical Reason and Metaethics Conference at the University of Nebraska, Ohio State University, the Ohio Philosophical Association, the St. Louis Annual Conference on Reasons and Rationality, the Society for the Theory of Ethics and Politics, the Stanford ethics reading group (2012–2013), the State University of New York at Albany, the University of California–Davis, the University of Western Kentucky, and the Workshop on Moral Expertise.

The Center for Advanced Study in the Behavioral Sciences at Stanford provided financial support and a wonderful environment for Tim Schroeder to do final revisions.

Much of chapters 1 and 2 is drawn from our 2012 paper, "Deliberation and Acting for Reasons," *Philosophical Review* 121, 209–239. Copyright, 2012, Cornell University. All rights reserved. Reprinted by kind permission of Duke University Press.

Chapter 6 is drawn from our paper, "The Neuroscience of Desire," to appear in D. Jacobson and J. D'Arms (eds.) *Moral Psychology and Human Agency*. New York: Oxford University Press. Appearing here by kind permission of Oxford University Press.

Much of chapter 9 is drawn from Nomy Arpaly's 2011 paper, "Open-Mindedness as a Moral Virtue," *American Philosophical Quarterly* 48, 75–85. Copyright, 2011, *American Philosophical Quarterly*.

Chapter 11 is drawn from our paper, "Addiction and Blameworthiness," to appear in Neil Levy (ed.) *Addiction and Self-Control*. New York: Oxford University Press. Appearing here by kind permission of Oxford University Press.

Introduction

In Praise of Desire is a work in moral psychology. It has two central ambitions, one of which is more modest and the other of which is perhaps less so.

The relatively modest ambition is to show that having the right desires—intrinsic desires for the right or good, correctly conceived—is what makes it possible to act for moral reasons, to act in a praiseworthy manner, and to be virtuous. Having such desires is having *good will*.

The less modest ambition is to introduce and argue for an unabashedly desire-centered moral psychology. The right desires are not just necessary in the life of the reasonable, praiseworthy, and virtuous person. Desires of the right sort underlie all of moral life, from spontaneous kindness to the lengthy deliberations of the person who would see justice done.

I.1 Moral Psychology

Moral psychology is the study of our psychological relationship to morality. It is the discipline that asks what it is to be cruel or kind. It asks whether there is something wrong with us if we find a sexist joke funny. It asks why people sometimes do what they know to be wrong. It asks what is going on in a person who is reasoning about what she should do. It asks what is involved in having "good will toward men."[1]

By being focused on our psychological relationship to morality, moral psychology does something different from other branches of moral theory. Normative moral theory tells us what it is right or wrong to do, and what states of affairs are morally good or bad. Meta-ethical theory tells us what kinds of things rightness, wrongness, goodness, and badness are in the first place. But moral psychology takes for granted that certain things are right or good, and other things wrong or bad. The job of moral psychology is to tell us how, in acting, feeling, and thinking, we end up related to the right and the good, or the wrong and the bad.

At least, the above is the narrowest way of understanding the role of moral psychology. Many philosophers have asked moral psychology to do a great deal more. Aristotle,[2] Hume,[3] Kant,[4] and many of their intellectual descendants[5]

---

[1] Luke 2:14 in the King James edition of the Bible.

[2] In *Nicomachean Ethics*, especially (Aristotle 1999).

[3] In the *Treatise*, especially (Hume 2000).

[4] In the *Groundwork*, especially (Kant 1998).

[5] See Foot (2001), Blackburn (1998), and Korsgaard (1996) for three of the best-known contemporary examples.

asked moral psychology to explain where morality comes from and to explain its content, in addition to explaining how we as acting, feeling, thinking people relate to it.[6]

Our suspicion is that normative and meta-ethical facts are settled in a way that is largely independent of the facts about moral psychology. Facts about irreducible reasons, or irreducible goodness, or the culture, or ideal observers, or something else outside the individual mind establishes that it is wrong to break promises and good to help children who are drowning. Particular people then care, or do not care, about breaking their promises or the fates of drowning children. This is where moral psychology comes in.

Our approach might seem to strip moral psychology of its allure. If we are not going to explain what kind of thing morality is, or its content, it might seem that we are not going to do very much. But in the pages to come we present partial or complete theories of deliberation, thinking and acting for reasons, having mixed motives, habit, emotionally expressive action, love, care, pleasure, desire, praise- and blameworthiness, the psychology of moral side-constraints, virtue and vice, open-mindedness, prejudice, modesty, *akrasia*, inner struggle, and addiction. And perhaps that will prove enough.

Our approach might also seem to ensure we will leave troubling holes in our positions. If we are not going to explain where moral reasons come from, how can we rely on their existence? If we are not going to explain whether it is ever morally permissible to kill an innocent person, how can we say what the virtues are? But this simply leaves us in the position of the philosopher who holds that certain things are true without having a theory of truth, or that certain beliefs cause others without having a theory of causation. At the end of a work in moral psychology, there will be much more to do in moral theory.

I.2 Reason and Appetite

The central thesis of this work is that having a good will, that is, having the capacity to act for the right reasons, in a praiseworthy manner, and out of virtue is just a matter of desiring the right things. Thus, *In Praise of Desire* takes the side of Appetite in the long-standing philosophical dispute between Reason and Appetite.[7] So we should pause for a moment to acknowledge this dispute and note our place in it.

The picture of human beings that we get from Plato and Aristotle is of a divided creature, partly beastly and partly divine. Our animal heritage, the

---

[6] Plato's metaethics seems independent of his moral psychology, but in *Republic* he takes the bold step of asking his moral psychology to explain how our political lives should be arranged.

[7] These are just labels of convenience. If the reader prefers Reason to be contrasted with Passion, for instance, that is not something we see ourselves disputing.

beastly part of ourselves, has the capacities for hunger, craving, and emotion that we can see in other animals. The beastly part of ourselves seeks out food and water, warmth, sex, safety. The beastly part of ourselves gets angry when struck by an equal, and fearful when struck by a superior force. The beastly part of ourselves is, one can say, Appetite. Then there is our divine inheritance, Reason. This divine part of ourselves has the capacity to engage in abstract thought, to understand truth, beauty, and justice, to interpret the past and foresee the future. The divine part of ourselves also carries out plans, leads us to choose what is good over what is merely pleasant in the moment, and controls our feelings until a cooler head can prevail.

There are many ways in which this picture is too crude, both as a picture of the world and as a summary of Plato's and Aristotle's views. For just one illustration, notice that sometimes our strong feelings are the product of complex reasoning: the horror of a scientist who realizes she has just been exposed to a huge dose of radiation might be intense, but it is also the product of insight that is beyond any other animal on the planet.[8] Still, the picture has a certain appeal. The idea that Reason struggles with Appetite inside us is seemingly vindicated every time we wisely judge that we should get out of bed only to be confronted by something that reminds us how sweet a few more moments under the blanket would be.

On this picture, it is natural to hold that good will lies on the side of Reason, not Appetite. Good will is not just a tender feeling engendered by seeing happy infants. Good will often calls on us to go against our beastly natures and to master ourselves in the service of some higher good, something that might not be quite as fun as being beastly would be.

There are other pictures of human beings that we might draw upon, however. According to the picture that we get from philosophers such as Hobbes and Hume, and scientists such as Darwin, people are merely the best abstract thinkers of the animals now living on Earth. Every mammal and bird (at least) is a combination of Reason and Appetite, in that every such animal is a combination of powers to abstractly conceptualize the world, i.e., Reason, and distinct powers to have and prioritize ends, i.e., Appetite. What is special about human beings is not that we have Reason but that we can deploy Reason to grasp things—truth, beauty, justice, and the like—that other animals cannot. And, having grasped them via Reason, we can then be nurtured so that we acquire an Appetite for them. According to this picture, there are not two selves in each person, one beastly and one divine, sometimes struggling for control of action. There is just one self, some of whose concepts and desires are shared with other species, and some of whose concepts and desires are specific to her kind, her culture, or her own particular experience.

---

[8] Aristotle notes that "spirit" is informed by reason in *Nicomachean Ethics*, for example.

There are many ways in which this picture is too crude, even for Hobbes and Hume. For instance, it leaves out the way in which mental performances such as conscious reasoning and intention formation add complexity to our mental lives. That some of this complexity is shared with other animals is increasingly well established.[9] That this sort of complexity can be explained within this second picture is more controversial, but Hobbes and Hume did not particularly despair: perhaps reasoning is but reckoning;[10] perhaps choosing between appealing ends is like serving as a balance that weighs each option.[11] Despite the controversies, this second picture does have a certain appeal. The idea that Appetite, not Reason, is the sole force setting and prioritizing our ends is seemingly vindicated every time we cheer on a favorite sports team, knowing that nothing particularly recommends the team but loving it all the same.

On this second picture, the good will cannot be identified with Reason. Reason enables a person to grasp whether an action would be a breaking of a promise or a saving of a drowning child, but it does not set ends or prioritize among them. Setting ends is the job of desire, that is, Appetite. If a person has a good will, then, it must be that she desires to keep her promises and not allow children to drown.

In contemporary philosophy, Reason and Appetite both have their defenders. Contemporary defenses of Reason in moral psychology include, but are hardly limited to, Anscombe (2000), Darwall (2002), Korsgaard (1996), McDowell (1979), Parfit (2011), and Scanlon (1998). Contemporary defenses of Appetite in moral psychology include, but again are hardly limited to, Blackburn (1998), Driver (2001), Frankfurt (1988), Hurka (2000), Railton (1988), Smith (1994), and Tiberius (2002).

From the defenders of desire, however, one often gets a concessive impression. A few go so far as to defend Appetite by making it almost a form of Reason: making desire a perceptual representation of goodness, for instance.[12] Many others keep Appetite distinct from Reason but hold that desires only

---

[9] For evidence of deliberation in other mammals, consider the work in Johnson and Redish (2007). In these studies, not only did rats in mazes hesitate as though they were trying to remember which way to turn in the maze, but their brains revealed that, while the rats hesitated, they were first recalling going one way down the maze, then recalling going the other way down the maze, before selecting which way to go. This is about as close to a demonstration of deliberation in a nonverbal animal as can be given. For evidence of deliberation in birds, see Taylor et al. (2007) on New Caledonian crows. In this study, seven crows were given a novel task (extracting food from a box using a long stick) that required the crows to plan ahead in order to best accomplish the task (the crows needed to start by using a short stick to acquire the necessary long stick). Two crows solved this task in one attempt, without any trial-and-error learning; six of seven started the task by trying to use the short stick to acquire the long stick, again without any trial-and-error learning. Again, it appears that deliberation has to be invoked—in this case, to explain the sophistication of the initial behaviors.
[10] Hobbes (1994).
[11] Hume (2000).
[12] See, e.g., Stampe (1986), Oddie (2005).

explain acting for the right reasons, praiseworthiness, or virtue insofar as desires are appropriately supplemented. Desires are the "right" sorts of desires, according to these philosophers, when nestled in a hierarchy of desires,[13] or when they would be endorsed on reflection,[14] or held under full information,[15] or when they are derived from beliefs about what it would be rational to desire,[16] or are otherwise limited, managed, contained.[17]

At least one reason for the concessive stance is that plain desires appear to many theorists to be mere impulses to behavior, and as such they appear to have no ability to explain central phenomena in moral psychology. A mere impulse to behavior seems unlikely to be a source of acting on a reason, it seems unlikely to be a praiseworthy motivation for acting rightly, and it seems an unlikely candidate for what it is to have a virtue. A mere impulse might even be a paradigmatically irrational force: a tic, a compulsion, an alcoholic urge, a crazy whim that just pops into one's head. In addition, philosophers have objected to plain desires because they can also seem too much of the moment, too fragile, too much under the control of reasoning, too much a product of (often unhealthy) social influences, and otherwise unsuited to ground moral psychology.

This work will nonetheless defend Appetite by defending the central role held by plain desires. When we act for reasons we act on plain desires. When we act in a praiseworthy manner we act on plain desires. And having a virtue is having a plain desire for the right things. We will reject the supposed need for desires to be restricted before playing these roles, with two important but limited qualifications. The first is that the desires under discussion are understood to be *intrinsic* desires, not instrumental desires or desires merely for specific realizations of ends that are intrinsically desired. The second is that the desires under discussion are understood to have, not merely the right reference, but the right sense as well: they are desires *for the right things,* desired *via the right concepts*. But these are minimal precisifications of the idea. With these minimal precisifications, we will give a wholehearted defense of the above theses regarding the centrality of desire, a package we will call 'Spare Conativism' ('SC' for short) in what follows.

One part of the present work amounts to a defense of Spare Conativism against objections, while another part proceeds more positively, building theories that aim to capture, in a manner respectful of the concerns of the defender of Reason, the phenomena people are familiar with from their own lives as people who act, feel, and think in morally interesting ways. Once Reason and

[13] See, e.g., the essays in Frankfurt (1988, 1999).
[14] See, e.g., Tiberius (2002).
[15] See, e.g., Railton (2003, chapter 1).
[16] See, e.g., Smith (1994).
[17] See also, e.g., Brandt (1979), Hubin (2001; 2003).

Appetite are both properly understood, we hope, our claims about the centrality of desires in moral psychology, and especially about the role of desires in
acting for moral reasons, praiseworthiness, and virtue, will seem able to with-
stand familiar challenges.

I.3 Intrinsic, Instrumental, and Realizer Desires

A distinction is the first thing needed for all that follows: the distinction between
intrinsic desires, instrumental desires, and realizer desires. At least since Plato,
philosophers have made a distinction between ends sought for their own sakes
and ends sought as means to other ends.[18] We see this as the distinction between
what is desired for its own sake (what is intrinsically desired) and what is desired
as a means to some intrinsically desired end (what is instrumentally desired).
To intrinsic and instrumental desires should be added a third category, discussed in depth only more recently: that of realizer desires.[19] Realizer desires
are desires for, not the means to achieve, but specific realizations of, ends that
are intrinsically desired.

In this work the focus will be on intrinsic desires. The possession of the right
intrinsic desires, and acting upon them, is what makes a person moved by the
right reasons, praiseworthy, and virtuous. According to Spare Conativism, the
person about whom we know only his instrumental or realizer desires in acting
is a person about whom we know little or nothing of moral significance. So it
will be worthwhile to say a little about intrinsic desires at the outset and to do
a little more to secure the distinctions among desires.

The things that we want for their own sakes are disputed. The psychological
hedonist holds that people desire only pleasure (and the absence of displeasure)[20] for its own sake; everything else is desired only as a means to secure
pleasure (and avoid displeasure), or because it realizes a state of pleasure (or
avoidance of displeasure). And if the psychological hedonist is right, then it
seems that Spare Conativism must accept the dismal conclusion that no one
acts for the right reasons, no one is praiseworthy, and no one is virtuous—
because whatever the right reasons are to keep promises or save drowning children, they are surely not just that one will feel good.[21]

---

[18] See, e.g., *Republic*.

[19] Schmidtz (1994, 227).

[20] Throughout, we will treat displeasure as the opposite of pleasure. Pain is best understood
as a mixture of displeasure (which might equally have occurred in smelling a skunk or reading
about injustice as in being injured) and nociception, which is a pure perceptual state. See Dennett
(1978, chapter 11) and Hardcastle (1999).

[21] For this reason, contemporary Aristotelians often join Aristotle in rejecting the idea that
the virtuous person acts only for the sake of pleasure, even if "eudaimonia," i.e., happiness, is in
some way the ultimate end of a virtuous person.

Fortunately, it is more plausible that many things are desired for their own sakes: not just pleasure, but also the health and wellbeing of those we love, the success of our favorite sports teams, the discovery of truths that matter to us, the respect of our peers, the doing of what is right, and the bringing about of what is good. Less admirably, it appears that the defeat of those we personally dislike and the attainment of power over others are also things that are often desired for their own sakes: they are pursued by some even when it seems that success will bring little personal happiness and come at a noticeable personal cost.

The arguments for the diversity of the ends that are desired for their own sakes—the ends that are intrinsically desired—are familiar, and we will not repeat them here. This work just assumes their common conclusion.[22]

It often happens that one intrinsically desires something while also having an instrumental desire for that same thing, as Aristotle among others has pointed out.[23] For instance, Nomy might desire that Rice's baseball team win the College World Series for its own sake, as a fan, while also desiring that they win the College World Series as a means to avoiding feeling miserably disappointed—something that she intrinsically desires not to be. The existence of instrumental desires for an end does not in itself demonstrate that the end is not also intrinsically desired.

It sometimes happens that a person thinks she wants something for its own sake only to later understand that she wanted it only instrumentally, and it sometimes happens that a person thinks she is mostly motivated by her intrinsic desire for an end when it turns out that most of her motivation stemmed from the fact that the intrinsically desired end was also a means to something else that was intrinsically desired even more.

Each intrinsic desire generates many instrumental desires. If Tim intrinsically desires that his elderly father be healthy, then he will also instrumentally desire that his father not shovel heavy snow in the biting cold, that his father eat plenty of vegetables, that his father not handle raw asbestos, not play tackle football, and so on. He will also desire certain things that, although they are not instrumental to what he intrinsically desires, are *realizers* of what he intrinsically desires. Tim will desire that his father not have the flu, for instance, but it

---

[22] The best-known of these arguments is perhaps that invoking the experience machine, due to Robert Nozick (Nozick 1974). Blackburn (1998, chapter 5) covers many of these arguments in some depth, sharing our conclusion. Schroeder (2004) weighs the neuroscientific evidence and finds that it favors a large plurality of intrinsically desired ends. A classic multidisciplinary case for altruism is made in Piliavin and Charng (1990); a classic early survey article arguing for altruism in social psychology is Batson and Shaw (1991). A more recent collection of arguments is found in Dovidio et al. (2006). For a more conservative interpretation of the recent literature, see Stich, Doris, and Roedder (2010).

[23] Aristotle (1999, book 1). Of course, Aristotle makes the point in terms of ends, not in terms of desires for ends, since his psychological theory is quite different from ours.

would be odd for Tim to desire this specific state of affairs for its own sake (for him to have not just a specific animus against the flu but against his father's having of the flu). It is more likely because the flu is a condition *realizing* ill health that Tim desires that his father not have the flu.

Imagine that Tim visits his family one winter. Snow starts falling, and his father announces that something ought to be done about that snow on the driveway and sidewalk, before it gets packed down. Tim experiences a sudden motivation: he wants to stop his father from going out to shovel the snow. The desire he has is a new one, but it is instrumental, generated by his pre-existing intrinsic desire that his father be healthy and his belief that if his father goes out to shovel snow it is likely to damage his health. On another occasion, Tim sees his young nephew Noah looking bored at a family gathering, and he experiences a new motivation: he wants to invite Noah to play a game with him. Again his new desire is an instrumental one: its content is instrumental to what he already intrinsically desires, namely, Noah's happiness. Playing with his nephew, Tim experiences conflicting motivations as they kick a ball around in front of a hockey net: he wants both to let Noah win the game (instrumentally, because he intrinsically wants Noah to be happy) and he wants to kick the ball past Noah (as a realizer of his intrinsic desire to win at games). Perhaps he kicks an easy one straight to Noah, and then feels bad for not treating his nephew as up to the challenge of a better-struck ball (since being treated as a big enough boy to handle higher-level play is one of the things that really will make Noah happy, failing to strike the ball better is a realization of a desire-frustrating state of affairs, Tim now sees).

In this little story, Tim has a set of stable intrinsic desires that shape the way he deliberates and acts, and he has a set of instrumental and realizer desires that spring into existence and pull him in various directions, including some impulsive ones that he regrets satisfying as they disrupt the achievement of some of the ends he desires intrinsically. This pattern is widespread. Even a desire to eat a particular peach exemplifies it: people intrinsically desire certain taste experiences, such as sweetness, and certain scent experiences, such as the perfume of the peach, and they intrinsically desire not to suffer, and sometimes it happens that having a particular peach at a particular time –this one, right now!—will be instrumental to having wanted taste and scent experiences, relieving the suffering that is a part of feeling hungry, and so on, and so there is an instrumental desire to now eat the particular peach. We might also desire the peach for the sake of the pleasure it brings, but that pleasure itself would not have been there if we did not desire certain taste experiences in the first place, in the same way that people can have sex for pleasure but the pleasure would not be there if sexual desire were not present too (we say more about desire and pleasure in chapter 5).

Instrumental and realizer desires are generated from intrinsic desires along with beliefs about means-end and realization relationships. If Tim intrinsically desires his elderly father's health, he will instrumentally desire that his father not shovel snow so long as he believes that shoveling snow is bad for his father's health, and he will have a realizer desire that his father not have the flu so long as he believes the flu is a disease, and so a way of having ill health. Perhaps because of this, instrumental and realizer desires do not appear to have interesting lives of their own: they are *mere* manifestations of a person's intrinsic desires and beliefs. If Tim instrumentally desires that his father not attend fitness classes, because he believes that it is unhealthy to subject an older heart to any needless stress, and then he becomes convinced that it is actually healthy for older hearts to be put under occasional higher demands, then Tim's instrumental desire will disappear instantly, the very instant his belief changes. His instrumental desire will not linger, needing to be overridden or eroded away by experience; it will simply vanish. Likewise if Tim has a realizer desire that his father not have bacteria in his gut. When Tim learns that having (the right) bacteria in one's gut is part of what good health consists in—that they are a part of the body's design for successful digestion and disease resistance—then his realizer desire will instantly disappear. Instrumental and realizer desires do not entirely vanish when the old beliefs sustaining them do not entirely vanish (perhaps, despite his substantial change of opinion, Tim suspects that the doctors might be wrong and that exercise is not really good for elderly hearts), but this observation strengthens rather than weakens the point being made about the dependency of such desires upon beliefs and intrinsic desires.

This is in contrast with intrinsic desires, which rarely vanish in an instant and often linger despite changes in our relevant beliefs and other desires. Though Michael Smith (1994) discusses desires vanishing in response to reasoning, it is not the usual course of things. If James comes to the conclusion that he should not eat meat or that he should not seek his mother's approval, it would be quite unusual for the desire for meat or the desire for approval to vanish as an immediate result. Perhaps sometimes intrinsic desires disappear quickly, as when the desire for alcohol goes away after a religious conversion. Usually, however, it would take years of vegetarian habits to get rid of the desire for meat, and a great deal of therapy, or growing older, to get rid of the desire for one's mother's approval, regardless of one's belief that these desires can be no part of a rational life, and regardless of one's desire not to have them.[24] It would not be particularly strange if the desires in question never completely disappeared from James's life, and that he would always be tempted by meat or upset when contemplating actions his mother would dislike.

---

[24] Smith discusses a desire to vote for a certain party disappearing as an immediate result of a change in one's political views through reasoning. Such a desire is unlikely to be an intrinsic desire. It is most likely to be a realizer desire—say, of the desire to benefit Australia or to bring about justice.

Like Smith, Derek Parfit discusses intrinsic (he calls them "telic") desires vanishing in response to changes in beliefs.[25] However, this might be because Parfit does not distinguish intrinsic desires from realizer desires: his example of an intrinsic desire that depends upon belief is a desire "to hurt you ... because I falsely believe that you deserve to suffer, or because I want to avenge some injury that I falsely believe you have done me" (60), a desire that disappears once the false belief is corrected. To us, this appears a desire for something (the other person's suffering) that would realize justice or vengeance. Such a desire is dependent upon the beliefs in question exactly because it is a desire for a realizer of something intrinsically desired, and not an intrinsic desire itself. To intrinsically desire that someone suffer is to have a foundational hatred for the person that is not (except causal-historically) dependent upon any beliefs.

In short, intrinsic desires have lives of their own; instrumental and realizer desires do not, unless one comes to intrinsically desire what was previously just a means or realizer (a possibility we discuss in chapter 4). Hence it is a mistake for a theorist to focus on instrumental or realizer desires, or to develop a theory based on examples that mix instrumental and realizer desires with intrinsic desires. The theorist interested in desire is really interested, in the first instance, in intrinsic desires: their nature, their necessary connections to other things, and their contingent but common causal powers.

This discussion of intrinsic, instrumental, and realizer desires might remind the reader of another distinction, that between dispositional and occurrent desires. It might appear that intrinsic desires here are playing the role of dispositional desires: they are states that sit in the background of the mind, waiting for triggering events. Tim's desire for his father's health might seem to be such a dispositional desire. And it might appear that instrumental and realizer desires are playing the role of occurrent desires: they are processes that are actively at work, shaping actions and feelings. Tim's desire to prevent his father from going out to shovel snow might seem to be such an occurrent desire. But these appearances are misleading. In fact, the two sets of distinctions are independent of one another, and the dispositional/occurrent distinction is not a particularly helpful one for the study of intrinsic desire.

To see that the distinctions are independent, consider that there are also occurrent intrinsic desires and dispositional instrumental and realizer desires. When Tim intrinsically desires his father's health and learns that his father is going to undertake some action that will threaten his health unless Tim says "wait," Tim's intrinsic desire is part of what makes him feel anxious at the prospect, and is part of what causes him to be motivated to say "wait." That is, the intrinsic desire occurrently shapes Tim's feelings and motivations. For an example in the other direction, consider that when Tim instrumentally desires

---

[25] Parfit (2011, 60 and also 129).

that his father not shovel snow, this instrumental desire is likely to persist (so long as beliefs about the harm of snow-shoveling persist) even when Tim is not thinking about his father at all. In the middle of enjoying a summer hike, if Tim would be asked, "does your dad still shovel his own sidewalk?" he could correctly say, "I want him to stay away from shoveling snow!" Before the question was asked, this instrumental desire existed but was merely dispositional, in that it was not doing anything in Tim's mind.

That the distinction between dispositional and occurrent desires is not particularly helpful is somewhat more tendentious. Desires are said to be occurrent when they are occurrently doing something in the mind of the person with the desire, especially doing something that affects the person's consciousness in a transparent way. They are said to be merely dispositional when they are not doing anything. But of a disposition one might ask, what is the categorical basis of that disposition? We hold that the desire is not the disposition but the categorical basis of the disposition. It is having intrinsic desires that makes one disposed to take certain actions (when certain contingencies seem to obtain), to have certain feelings, and even to have one's cognitions influenced in certain ways. Rather than argue for this, the present work will take it for granted. The theory of desire allowing it to be taken for granted will eventually receive a full presentation (chapter 6).

Whims might seem to threaten the general picture we have been painting of intrinsic desires as stable, long-standing, and largely beyond cognitive influence. A person with a whim seems to be a person who desires to do something, for its own sake, but a whim is typically unstable, short-lived, and readily influenced by one's thoughts. A few examples will be helpful.

> On a whim, Anya watches the movie *Jules et Jim*. She has not seen the movie before and has not thought about the movie for years, though her late father used to like it. She had not planned on watching a movie tonight.
>
> Chloe, walking by the river, meets a wild goose. She feels the urge to chase the goose—and so to engage in a "wild goose chase"—and does so.
>
> Rick, an introvert, is at a party when he feels an impulse to tell jokes and be "the life of the party." He has never done it before and will not do it again for quite a while.

Other desire-centered theorists might attempt to explain whims by complicating the sorts of intrinsic desires at the centers of their theories. Spare Conativism offers a simpler answer: in human beings, at least, there are no intrinsic desires that are whims; all whims are instrumental or realizer desires. This does not follow directly from the positive theory of desire for which we will argue, but it does appear to be how human beings work—that is, it follows from our theory of desire as defended in chapter 6 plus the facts about how intrinsic desires work in healthy human beings.

It would be nice to see armchair confirmation of the idea that all whimsical desires are either instrumental or realizer desires, laid out independently of the more empirical arguments that will appear later. Fortunately, this is not so difficult. Think of Anya's, Chloe's, and Rick's experiences. In each case, it is easy enough to imagine credible intrinsic desires that each person might have such that the person's whim is instrumental toward, or a realizer of, the content of the intrinsic desires. Perhaps Anya has an intrinsic desire to see great art, an intrinsic desire to be entertained occasionally, and an intrinsic desire to remember or honor her late father. Then her whimsical desire to watch *Jules et Jim* is for an end that serves these various desires. Chloe might intrinsically desire to fully experience the complexities of language, and to engage in childlike play, and her engaging in a literal wild goose chase serves both of these intrinsic desires. And perhaps Rick intrinsically desires social popularity, but due to various facts about his personality (his extreme aversion to social ridicule, and so on) it is also rare for him to act on his desire for popularity. These sorts of intrinsic desires are both credible in general and the sort of thing one expects in people acting on whims. It is quite a stretch to imagine Anya being moved to watch *Jules et Jim* without there being some larger story to it: that she wanted to watch a movie, that she is intrinsically attracted to good art and has heard that *Jules et Jim* is a good work of art, or some such. And so too with Chloe and Rick.

The question remains, though: if the genuinely explanatory desires in questions are enduring intrinsic desires, why did the individuals in question feel their whims at the particular moments they felt them? There can be at least two kinds of explanation. First, in order to have an urge to do something one needs to have relevant cognitions as well as the relevant intrinsic desire, and it helps that these cognitions be conscious. Most people have a stream of thoughts and images going through their minds on a regular basis, with the stream sometimes proceeding via the flimsiest unconscious associative connections. A stream of associations of this sort could have brought a particular movie to Anya's mind as randomly as in a dream, and once the idea of the movie is there, bringing with it associated ideas of Anya's father's taste in movies, Anya's memory that this particular movie is said to be good art, and so on, the intrinsic desires that might be served by watching the movie can be engaged. If the occasion is suited to watching a movie, and Anya has no competing actions to perform, it can then happen that she has the impulse, seemingly out of the blue, to watch the movie. And while Anya's whim might come to her purely by random chance through the appearance of a particular item in her stream of consciousness, this is hardly the only way for ideas to come to mind. Chloe is presented with the idea of a wild goose chase by meeting the wild goose: she would not ordinarily think much about wild geese. Meeting the wild goose is the occasion for associating to the idea of the wild goose chase, and from there her intrinsic desires for play and to explore language can be engaged, giving her the impulse to try out a wild goose chase of her own.

The ideas that, along with intrinsic desires, can launch whimsical impulses are only part of the story, however. When one calls a state of mind 'a whim,' one normally means to suggest that there was something unusual or out of character or unlikely to be repeated in one's behavior. Since intrinsic desires are stable, enduring entities, there needs to be an explanation of why the whimsical action is so outside of the norm. Part of the reason will be the infrequency of the enabling beliefs—one does not see wild geese on the grass before one every day—but this is not enough. Anya would not describe her impulse to watch *Jules et Jim* as a whim if she routinely watched older artistically interesting movies, even if the specific idea of renting *Jules et Jim* just popped into her head. Nor would Rick find his action so impulsive if he had long been waiting for a chance to be the life of the party, but never before quite found an opening that would permit it.

The missing idea here is that whims are characteristically dependent on what can be thought of as enabling conditions for motivation. Rick might be particularly comfortable with speaking on a particular day because various factors have converged, with each factor contributing to his readiness to speak in a social gathering. He is in a good romantic relationship that started recently, a number of the people at the party are from the same profession as he, he has been drinking wine, and he just heard a good joke. These are the sorts of conditions under which many people become more willing to speak—even people who are not particularly shy find it easier to be lively at a party when their hearts are high (with chemical assistance supplementing other sources of good mood) and the gathering is full of kindred spirits. Similarly, Chloe might have felt a little high-spirited immediately before meeting the goose, making it more likely that she would leap from the idea of a wild goose chase to actual action, and Anya might have been bored, making her more receptive to the idea of the movie. Other enabling conditions are absences: Rick might not have felt his impulse to become the center of attention had his academic nemesis been present in the group; Chloe might not have felt any impulse to chase the goose if she had been in the middle of a conversation; Anya might not have had the urge to watch *Jules et Jim* if she had been occupied planning a trip to the Philippines.

Some of these enabling conditions for motivation are rationalizing conditions: it is particularly reasonable for Anya to watch a movie when she is particularly bored, assuming that watching the right movie is likely to alleviate boredom. To relieve an aversive state, an action only needs a weak rationalization to be better than the current alternative and so to be performed, and so uncharacteristic, unexpected actions are more likely to be performed than at other times. In contrast, a person in the middle of a serious debate over whether to pay for private schooling for the children is unlikely to act on a whim, since there are so much stronger reasons to do other things at that moment. And it is particularly reasonable to do something otherwise whimsical when one has no competing reasons to do something different: when there is no one to judge, no project to interrupt. Other enabling conditions for motivation are not rationalizing: being in high spirits, drinking alcohol, or just witnessing someone else doing what one wishes one could do, is not the sort of thing that gives one a better rationale for action. Nonetheless, such factors can contribute to the likelihood that one acts. (An extreme example: cocaine consumption characteristically increases the impulse to talk, an effect sometimes known as "pressured speech," without changing the strength of one's rationalizations to talk.)[26]

Our theory of desire will make sense of how there could be a motivationally enabling condition that did not contribute to the rationalization of the enabled actions. As the reader will see, it follows from the theory of desire that not every condition that promotes action is an intrinsic desire, and so when we argue for intrinsic desire being at the heart of rationalizing action and of virtue, or when we defend the view that desire is at the heart of love and caring, we are not referring to just every condition that promotes action. But for now, we hope we have at least postponed the objection from whims. For now, perhaps we have done enough to suggest that intrinsic desires are, for the most part, in ordinary and healthy human beings, stable, enduring, and reasoning-independent mental states.

I.4 The Many Guises of the Good

The second qualification placed on Spare Conativism was that the person who acts for the right reasons, in a praiseworthy manner, or out of virtue, must be understood to have and be acting on an intrinsic desire with not only the right reference but also the right sense: the right conceptualization. We will return to this topic (especially in chapter 7), but a little should be said at the outset just to prepare the reader and keep our position clear.

The terms 'sense' and 'reference' are familiar from Frege's work,[27] but there have been many ways of describing the distinction between how a thing is represented (the sense) and the represented thing itself (the reference). At least passingly similar distinctions are made in terms of narrow and broad content, primary and secondary intension, syntax and semantics, individualistic and anti-individualistic psychology, semantic internalism and semantic externalism, conceptualization and the object conceptualized, and so on.[28]

---

[26] Psychiatry's *Diagnostic and Statistical Manual IV* calls this effect "talkativeness" in its characterization of cocaine intoxication.

[27] Famously, "On Sense and Reference." See, e.g., Beaney (1997, 151–71).

[28] Some of these contrasts are between what are understood by their proponents as competing, rather than complementary, theories. But for our purposes this is not important; a person wanting to understand something like the conventional sense/reference contrast could treat these theories as complementary without changing many of their features.

According to Spare Conativism, the person who acts for the right reasons acts on her intrinsic desire for the right or the good; that is why she is praiseworthy, and her intrinsic desire is the ground of her claim (insofar as she has one) to be virtuous. But to say this is to so far stay fixed on the reference, broad content, secondary intension, semantics, anti-individualistic content, external content, or the object of the intrinsic desire. It is not yet to say how the virtuous or praiseworthy person, the one who can act for the right reasons, conceptualizes the right or good.

According to Spare Conativism, the person of good will is the person who conceptualizes the right or the good in the right way. The nature of this "right way" is a question for the true normative ethical theory, whatever that might be. If Millian consequentialism is correct, then the way of saying what she intrinsically desires that best suggests her conceptualization of that end is that she intrinsically desires that happiness be maximized. If Kantian deontology is correct, she intrinsically desires that she treat persons with respect.[29] If some other normative theory is correct, then she intrinsically desires (perhaps) that people be as happy as possible so long as no one need be treated unfairly, or (perhaps) that there be liberty for all, constrained only by voluntary contract. For our purposes, the person who intrinsically desires the right or the good might even need to conceptualize it as achieving personal unification with the One, or as spreading misery for Satan's glory, though we are skeptical about these particular hypotheses. The point is simply that SC has a commitment to intrinsic desires for the right things conceptualized in the right ways, and the right conceptualization of the right thing is picked out by the correct normative moral theory.

This view contrasts with the view that the person of good will is the person who conceptualizes what she does specifically as right or good. This contrasting approach might give a central role to a desire with just this conceptualization of its content, or it might theorize all desires as perceptual or intellectual representations of goodness, rightness, or reasons,[30] or it might give a central role to a cognitive attitude, such as judging an act to be right, while denying that this attitude amounts to a desire.

In our view, any such approach is subject to two sorts of problem cases. In the first sort, a person acts (well or badly) for what she conceptualizes as the right or good, while holding a terrible theory of what is right or good. This person does not strike us as acting for the right reasons, as praiseworthy, or as exemplifying virtue, regardless of the fine details. In the second sort of problem case, a person acts for the sake of what she conceptualizes as maximizing

---

[29] Of course, there is more than one way to interpret the Kantian idea of the right. Just how to capture the Kantian idea that the respectful person does not prefer to kill one innocent in order to prevent five murders is a tricky issue, to which we turn in chapter 7.

[30] This is the approach of Oddie (2005), Scanlon (1998), and Stampe (1986), for example.

happiness, or respecting persons, or whatever is in fact demanded by the correct normative theory of morality—but also sees herself as doing what she conceptualizes as wrong or bad (because of her false moral theory). This person strikes us as acting for the right reasons, as praiseworthy, and as potentially virtuous. And so, when we write that to act for the right reasons, praiseworthily, or out of virtue, one must act on a desire with the right sense (or conceptualization . . .), we mean this latter sort of sense, and not one that (as it were) explicitly presents its object as the right, good, or reasonable.

I.5 The Work to Be Done

It is the aim of this work to offer an approach to desire-centered moral psychology that puts plain desires at its center without apology, and to demonstrate that such an approach can accommodate more complexity and subtlety than it has seemed to friends of desire and foes alike.

We will ultimately argue that having the right desires is what makes a person morally virtuous. In support of this conclusion we will discuss the role of intrinsic desires in acting for reasons, provide a theory of intrinsic desire itself, and then develop a theory of praise- and blameworthy action according to which one is praise- or blameworthy for acting for the right or wrong moral reasons, out of one's intrinsic desires. This long path to a theory of virtue will, we hope, make the very Spare theory of virtue we defend seem as plausible as it can be made to seem. Capping the theory of virtue is a discussion of the role of thought and cognition in the virtuous person, the vicious person, and those of us situated in between. We finish with two related phenomena that present puzzles for the desire-centered moral psychologist: the common experience of inner struggle between Reason and Appetite and the less common experience of drug addiction.

We begin by grasping a loose thread and pulling on it. The loose thread is the nature of deliberation, with the theses that unravel making room for the positive theory to come.

PART I

Reason

{ 1 }

Deliberation

Allan sees that the tea shop has no pastries today and he wonders—deliberates about—where to go instead. He considers various options, and settles on the café up the street. Mira is asked whether she really believes in animal rights or only the moral importance of animal wellbeing, and she starts pondering— deliberating about—the differences between the two, finally concluding that she believes in animal rights. The frequency of deliberation in our lives could be exaggerated, but it is common and familiar.

Moral deliberation is less common than deliberation in general, but still common enough to earn deliberation a central place in a theory of the moral mind. We deliberate about our obligations to the third world, about whether to break particular promises, about the permissibility of laughing at a particular joke. We deliberate in advance of confronting moral quandaries and in the very moment of decision. Sometimes we share or work through our deliberations publicly, implying or asserting their relevance to anyone in similar circumstances.

Desire-centered moral psychology is thought to have an obvious and serious problem with deliberation.[1] Desires are impulses to action, it is said, but deliberation is different: deliberation is a process that allows us to step back from our impulses and bring them into question.[2] When we act *for reasons* we do not simply follow our desires, but rather deliberate and perform the actions which our deliberation endorses. Our ability to deliberate is thus the foundation of our ability to think and act for reasons. This idea has taken many forms.

> To make a reason for doing something the agent's reason for doing it, the reason must enter into a process of practical reasoning.... I do not insist that every stage of the agent's reasoning be consciously carried out. The agent may have developed short-cuts in reasoning, and some

---

[1] Important objections are raised both by proponents of desire in moral psychology and by opponents of it. For objections from the proponents, see, e.g., Frankfurt (1971), Hubin (2001; 2003), and Tiberius (2002). For objections from the opponents, see, e.g., Herman (1993, ch.1), Korsgaard (1986; 1996; 2009), and Watson (1975). Of course, this is just the tiniest sampling of an enormous literature.

[2] This borrows the phrasing used in Korsgaard (1996; 2009).

of these steps can become programmed into his brain and be carried out automatically. (Chan 1995, 140 and fn.10)

[T]here are reasons why animals act as they do, but…only in the most tenuous sense can we say that they *have* reasons for acting as they do. Only a language-using creature can reason and deliberate, weigh the conflicting claims of the facts it knows in the light of its desires, goals and values, and come to a decision to make a choice in the light of reasons. (Hacker 2007, 239)[3]

[O]nce we are aware that we are inclined to believe or to act in a certain way on the ground of a certain representation, we find ourselves faced with a decision, namely, whether we should do that—whether we should believe or act in the way that the representation calls for or not. Once the space of reflective awareness—reflective distance, as I like to call it—opens up between the potential ground of a belief or action and the belief or action itself, we must step across that distance, and so must be able to endorse the operation of that ground, before we can act or believe. What would have been the *cause* of our belief or action, had we still been operating under the control of instinctive or learned responses, now becomes something experienced as a consideration in favor of a certain belief or action instead, one we can endorse or reject. And when we can endorse the operation of a ground of belief or action on us *as a* ground, then we take that consideration for a reason.…[W]e now both can have, and absolutely require, *reasons* to believe and act as we do. (Korsgaard 2009)

[A]n agent [must, to be an agent,] take herself to have good reasons for the option she chooses.…[And her taking herself to have these good reasons] must not change under appropriate reflection. (Tiberius 2002, 343)

In addition to these claims about deliberation, one also often sees related claims about the role of Reason via appeal to judgments of reasons. While these are not appeals to deliberation as such, they are appeals to something in the same neighborhood, with similarly difficult implications for desire-centered moral psychology.

When acting rationally, an agent undertakes to act in light of her belief about what she has reason to do. She chooses her action because it is supported by reasons. In this sense, rational action seems to embody a distinctly rational form of motivation in which the agent guides herself by the thought that an action is recommended by reason. This guiding thought need not always be explicitly articulated. For rational action

---

[3] Cited in Glock (2009).

to be possible, however, the agent must, at some level of awareness, conceptualize the features to which she is responding as reason-giving. (Barry 2007, 232)

For the person [who wants to not have a toothache, and who believes that going to the dentist will cure the toothache] to act rationally, she must be motivated by her own recognition of the appropriate conceptual connection between the belief and the desire. (Korsgaard 1997, 222)

It would appear hard for any desire-centered moral psychology to get off the ground if it were true that deliberation, with its attendant experience of stepping away from our desires, is what founds our ability to act for reasons. Similarly if it were true that judgments about practical reasons founded our ability to act for reasons. Yet these views are very common, and even some theoretical friends of desire seems to accept them.[4] Other theoretical friends of desire have been less than forthcoming about the whys and wherefores of deliberation,[5] which can look a little suspicious; it would be better to confront the problem head-on.

So we start by showing that first deliberation and then judgments about practical reasons are not fundamental to thinking and acting for reasons. In chapter 3 we go beyond this negative conclusion and develop a positive theory of thinking and acting for reasons that gives deliberation its rightful place as a powerful but fallible tool for enhancing our foundational, nondeliberative capacities to think and act for reasons on the basis of our beliefs and intrinsic desires.[6]

1.1 The Nature of Deliberation

The theses we will press about deliberation and reasons are largely unfamiliar ones, and so we begin slowly. This section is devoted to a theory of deliberation

---

[4] Michael Smith (1994) straddles an interestingly intermediate position. Although a self-described Humean and defender of desires against their staunchest foes, Smith also gives desires a subordinate role to beliefs about what one would desire if rational when developing his moral psychology.

[5] Harry Frankfurt's work on alienation and wholeheartedness provides a case study of a brilliant defender of the centrality of desire whose lacunae on the precise nature of deliberation speak almost as loudly as the words on the page. See Frankfurt (1971; 1976; 1987). A prominent exception is found in Peter Railton's work on deliberation, which this chapter relies upon and develops further. See Railton (2004; 2009).

[6] The general topic of interest to us has been treated by a number of philosophers. See, e.g., Arpaly (2003), which touches briefly on the issue, Dreier (2001), which deals in depth with a related issue, and Railton (2004; 2009), in which the first steps of the present argument are taken (in the jargon we deploy later in this chapter, Railton makes the regress argument against a combined version of Present Deliberation and Present Recognition).

that does not presuppose anything particularly controversial, although it reaches some important conclusions.

Deliberation is commonly divided into theoretical and practical deliberation. Theoretical deliberation is primarily concerned with what to believe, while practical deliberation is primarily concerned with what to do. The product of theoretical deliberation is perhaps a new belief (or entrenchment of an existing belief), or a new credence in a possible state of affairs, or a sincere thought about the truth of a proposition, or something similar. The product of practical deliberation is perhaps a new intention (or entrenchment of an existing intention), or an action, or something similar, in which case it is purely practical. Or the product of practical reasoning is a new belief that now taking a certain course of action would be best overall, or a belief that it would be fitting, or something similar, in which case practical deliberation is a subtype of theoretical deliberation. For our purposes, it is not important what, exactly, the product of either sort of deliberation is, so long as the above proposals are not all radically misguided.

Both sorts of deliberation are kinds of actions.[7] They are mental actions, or perhaps mental actions conducted with supplementary nonmental aids (notepaper, calculators, interlocutors, the sound of one's own voice speaking one's thoughts aloud...). We will, however, focus on the mental aspect of deliberation, as mixed cases do not alter the plausibility of the conclusions to come.[8]

The thesis that deliberation is an action is not entirely obvious, and merits a defense. Deliberation is, like other actions, something one can do "at will." To experience the voluntary nature of deliberation, the reader can now deliberate upon the reasons for dwindling membership in trade unions within the United States (for example), if she so chooses. In being the sort of thing that can be performed at will, deliberation is like other mental actions, such as visualizing simple geometric shapes or holding a question in mind, and like overt actions such as reading a book or making a request.

Deliberation also resembles other actions in that it is not *always* possible to perform it at will. When the circumstances are not favorable, one cannot read a book at will (when there are no books present, when the books are in unfamiliar languages...) or even make a request at will (when one is particularly intoxicated, when one is tongue-tied by the beauty of one's interlocutor...). Similarly, there are occasions on which one tries to deliberate but fails, or fails to achieve the end at which one was aiming in deliberation (being terribly drunk, one cannot focus one's thoughts enough to deliberate at all; being

---

[7] For other instances of this claim, see, e.g., Hookway (1999) on epistemic deliberation and Railton (2009) on practical deliberation.

[8] We should note, if only in passing, the existence of arguments that there is no principled difference between "purely" mental actions and "mixed cases." See, e.g., Clark and Chalmers (1998).

deeply puzzled about the nature of knowledge, one cannot reach a firm conclusion about whether knowledge is belief that cannot be mistaken).

It can also be pointed out that deliberation is subject to all of the forms of aberration, distortion, and perversion characteristic of overt action. There are instances of deliberation from which one is alienated ("I could hardly believe I was contemplating covering up my misbehavior"), deliberation conducted for an end that is not transparent to one ("I found myself thinking again about the facts of the case, uncertain as to why my mind was drawn to them but unwilling to stop myself"), and deliberation conducted absentmindedly ("I suddenly realized that, in my mental wanderings, I had started going over all the reasons I had given myself for ending my past romances"). There is even weak-willed deliberation, in which one resolves to cease thinking about what will happen if one loses one's job, but cannot help continuing to estimate how long one's savings would last, how immediately one's children would have to be deprived of their pricier advantages and entertainments, and so on, all to one's dismay.

There is also the fact that private deliberation is treated as an action within the larger social context. Deliberation, like other actions, seems to be the sort of thing one can reasonably demand that another person do ("figure out whether the company has a genuine obligation to continue supporting breast cancer research, and then write up a memo on it") and the sort of thing one can reasonably censure another person for failing to do ("I told you to have something figured out"), or even for doing ("I told you to stop wasting time thinking about our so-called moral obligations; just figure out the legal angle").

Deliberation shows every sign of being an action. So deliberation is an action.

The act of deliberating is carried out by means of performing various mental actions aimed at a suitable end. Both the mental actions performed and the end they are aimed at are important. To be deliberating, one must be performing the right actions with the right end.

For a mental activity to be deliberation, it must be aimed at determining what to think or do.[9] An ecumenical stance can be taken on just what this amounts to, but there are limits to ecumenism. A mental activity aimed only at amusing the subject is not deliberation,[10] nor is a mental activity aimed only at facilitating sleep. Visualizing a particularly funny pratfall is a mental action, and so is visualizing a sequence of sheep jumping over a fence, but these actions are not typically going to be any part of deliberation, because they are not typically undertaken in order to determine what to think or do. Determining what

---

[9] Perhaps there is also deliberation about what to feel, or what to intend, that is distinct from deliberation about what to think or to do, but we are skeptical. In any case, the existence of such deliberation would not substantially change the arguments that follow.

[10] A parody of deliberation is not an act of deliberation itself, any more than a parody of a manifestation of racism is a manifestation of racism.

to think or what to do is a constitutive end of deliberation, in the same way that persuasion is a constitutive end of arguing, or getting coffee is a constitutive end of going for coffee. Deliberation can fail to achieve its end, but it is an activity aimed at achieving that end, perhaps among others.

For a mental activity to be deliberation, it must also be carried out by means of particular kinds of mental acts: bringing to mind—to consciousness—various ideas (general or particular, abstract or concrete) or images (visual, auditory, gustatory...).[11] There are other mental actions one can take to determine what to do or what to believe, but these are not deliberation. As a person with the aim of determining what to do, Maria might be aware that she will decide if she can just enter a state of meditative tranquility. And it might well be true that entering this state is a mental act that Maria can perform, aiming through it to determine what to do. But Maria would not be deliberating if she were to proceed in this way.

Mental acts are not guaranteed to be acts of deliberation even if they bring ideas or images to mind with the goal of determining what to do through filling one's consciousness with them. Perhaps Randa finds that what to believe about a difficult matter comes more quickly to her if she visualizes her fourth-grade teacher sternly asking, "What is the answer, Randa?" This would not make her use of such an image into an act of deliberation. Deliberation requires that one try to bring to mind ideas or images that have some rational relation to the propositions[12] one considers, with the aim of reaching a conclusion. Even this is probably not a sufficient condition,[13] but the full complexities can be set aside. Deliberation, at the least, requires bringing to mind ideas or images meant to have some rational relation to the topic being considered, in the service of reaching a conclusion about what to think or do.

Talk of mental acts that bring ideas and images to mind might be unhelpfully unspecific. Experiences of deliberation suggest a variety of perhaps helpful concrete examples. Consider Harold, who is deliberating about whether to promise to meet his son in Calgary on Tuesday. Harold engages in a mental action known colloquially as "searching his memory" for potentially conflicting promises, a process that itself might involve the mental act of holding in

---

[11] Given that deliberation is an action, we think it reasonable to hold that there is no unconscious deliberation. There might be unconscious inference (indeed, surely there is). But not all inference is deliberation. As Korsgaard and others have emphasized, deliberation takes place from a conscious, first-person perspective.

[12] Or perhaps propositions express or can represent the conclusions of one's deliberation, rather than being identical to them. And perhaps propositions cannot express plans, though plans can be the conclusion of practical deliberations (thanks to an anonymous referee for this point), and so we need to make room for them as well.

[13] For instance, it fails to exclude cases in which one brings to mind a rationally relevant idea in order to convince a mind-reading angel to directly induce a state of being settled on what to think and do. Chapter 3 deals with this issue, but presupposes the work in the present chapter, and so cannot be relied upon in defense of the present argument.

mind the idea of Tuesday, but might not even involve that so much as an effortful attentiveness in Harold's present context. This mental act will produce a
notable nothing in consciousness or some idea or image tied to a competing
promise. Or consider Albert: when he deliberates about the implications of
curved space-time for time travel, he visualizes a warped rubber sheet with a
ball rolling along it, and this image is hoped to be relevant—in the context of
his thinking—to the truth of the claim that a straight line in a curved space-time
is one that could loop back on itself.[14]

We think it important to focus on the most basic acts that make up deliberation. While it can be perfectly correct to say that in deliberating one considered
X, Y, and Z and concluded that P, it would be a mistake to think of this whole
process as an indivisible unit, just as much as it would be a mistake to treat
the act of washing the dishes as a single, indivisible unit. If one is interested in
deliberation as an active, agential process it is important to see that it is made
up of units of activity, and these units are, in each case, acts in which something
with apparent (theoretical or practical) relevance is brought into consciousness
as part of a larger plan to reach a theoretical or practical conclusion. Seen
on this fine-grained scale, deliberation is often a far cruder process than the
step-by-step deductions philosophers enjoy describing. It is common for the
process of deliberation to throw up a fragment—Harold might suddenly say
to himself, "oh, the Planning Council!"—rather than a complete set of ideas
entailing the conclusion—I can't go to Calgary on Tuesday—that is, nonetheless, reached on the basis of the fragment.

Thinking of these basic units of action in deliberation highlights the fact
that extended deliberative actions are made up, not just of these basic exercises of agency over thought, but also of the occurrence in consciousness of
thoughts and feelings that serve as input to deliberation but which are not
brought to consciousness through exercises of agency. When Harold searches
his memory for possible conflicting commitments—a voluntary mental act—it
might result in his consciously remembering that he has committed to going
to a meeting of the Planning Council. This conscious remembering itself is
something that might well happen in Harold as a *result* of something he does
directly without it being something he does directly. The remembering happens in Harold, and having happened, prompts (as it might be) another action,
such as Harold's saying to himself, "Yes, I mustn't forget the Planning Council
meeting. Now, when does that get out?" This act, in turn, might lead to other
nonvoluntary spontaneous thoughts or feelings, or it might lead to another

---

[14] We assume that there is a way of making intelligible the idea that there is a rational relationship between a visual mental image and a proposition. One line of evidence in favor of this
thought is found in the rich literature on the content of sensory perception and imagery (see, e.g.,
Peacocke 1983; Tye 1995). If imagery has content, then that content can stand in rational relations to the contents of beliefs.

voluntary mental act—and so it will go, until Harold settles what to do or gives up (for the moment, at least) on settling what to do.[15] In this way (as in so many others), extended deliberative acts are like extended overt bodily acts: made up of more elementary acts selected, in part, because of the ongoing consequences of working through the extended action.

1.2 The Rationality of Acts of Deliberation

Like any action, deliberation can be more or less reasonable or unreasonable on any given occasion.[16] Sometimes, deliberating would be smart, reasonable, or rational,[17] and sometimes it would be stupid, unreasonable, or irrational. Furthermore, even when it is rational to deliberate, a person can deliberate in a specific way that is rational or in a way that is downright foolish. That is, the specific mental acts making up the process of deliberation will be reasonable or foolish, rational or irrational, in addition to the generic activity of deliberating (about anything at all) at the moment being such. The word "rational" in the expression "rational deliberation" is thus not a redundant one: irrational deliberation is possible.

First, consider cases in which it is either rational or irrational to try to deliberate, regardless of the ultimate path of one's deliberations. Rebecca deliberates on whether she should really be getting off the Interstate highway at exit 33, ignoring the fact that she and her car are already on the off-ramp for exit 33 and situated in swift-moving traffic. The rational thing for Rebecca to do is surely to drive first and deliberate later, perhaps once she has reached a calm surface street. Deliberating about the wisdom of taking exit 33 at just that moment is irrational.

The second sort of case to be illustrated is the case in which the agent is rational to deliberate in general, but in which the particular deliberative acts taken by the agent are either rational or irrational. Suppose that Katie begins to consider the grammaticality of the phrase "I'm loving," and that it is rational for her to be considering this question. If she searches her memory for different uses of the phrase, she is probably proceeding reasonably. Calling to mind

---

[15] Thanks to Peter Railton for pointing out to us the importance of the back-and-forth in deliberation between basic mental acts and the spontaneous thoughts and feelings such acts often engender.

[16] Compare our arguments on this over the next few paragraphs to, e.g., Joseph Raz, who expresses the view that "Reason is inherently normative" (Raz 1999, 68).

[17] We take a rational person to be a person who acts as she does for very good reasons and thinks as she does for very good reasons; we also take it that facts about being smart or stupid, reasonable or unreasonable, are relevant to claims about rationality and irrationality. We do not rely here on the idea that rationality is tied to what is ideal from the perspective of an omniscient outside observer, or anything similar. Newton was rational in holding his theory of universal gravitation, in spite of that theory's falsity, on our way of thinking about these things.

a pop song, an advertising campaign, and sentences uttered by different people will bring to consciousness evidence that the phrase has widespread use, and this is worthwhile evidence to consider when determining what to think about a phrase's grammaticality: in conservative circles the verb "to love" is not used in the progressive, but there might be a linguistic change in progress. But suppose that Katie begins to consider ways to express ongoing enjoyment of something without using the phrase "I'm loving." She calls to mind the phrases "I've been enjoying," "I relish," and others. She says to herself, "no one needs to say he's loving something." Perhaps as a conservative speaker of English she finds the phrase "I'm loving" distasteful, and her distaste is influencing her effort to determine what to believe about grammar. If she proceeds in this way, it seems that Katie's deliberation is now proceeding unreasonably: there is a sort of wishful thinking at work in her. After all, the existence of another way to say much the same thing as "I'm loving" is no evidence one way or the other regarding the grammaticality of "I'm loving" itself. As Katie knows, a phrase can be grammatical even though it is also optional as a means of expressing some idea. Given that her goal is to determine what to think about the grammaticality of the phrase "I'm loving," she has taken a wrong turn. Each time she calls to mind another alternative expression, or declares to herself the inessentiality of the expression "I'm loving," she is acting unreasonably in her deliberation.

Katie's unreasonable deliberation exemplifies just one way in which deliberation can be improperly influenced. In addition to deliberation that is excessively oriented toward what we wish for (i.e., wishful thinking), there is also fearful thinking, antagonistic thinking, disgusted thinking, and the like.[18] These are all forms of "hot" irrationality in action: forms of irrational action caused by emotional states.

To these forms of irrationality can be added "cold" irrationality: irrationality that is not tied to the influence of an emotional state. If Harold is deliberating about whether to promise to meet his son in Calgary on Tuesday, and he is not highly confident that he has no obligations scheduled for the date, then it is probably rationally compulsory for Harold to search his memory (or check his calendar) before promising. But perhaps Harold is very sleepy, and his deliberation surveys only the most obvious issues involved: is the weather good enough for such a trip? Will he have other chances to meet his son in the near future? By failing to investigate the possibility of competing obligations, Harold acts irrationally—in just the way that a driver can act irrationally by failing to look for pedestrians before accelerating through an intersection. In addition to sleep deprivation, there are intoxicating chemicals and many other factors that can bring about irrational actions, both overt and covert, without emotions contributing to the irrationality.

---

[18] A particularly valuable discussion of sources of irrational thought is found in Lazar (1999).

There is a good deal in the philosophical literature about rational deliberation, but irrational deliberation is rarely mentioned. There is talk of people who
deliberate correctly or who deliberate incorrectly, or of people who deliberate
under good conditions ("a cool hour") or under bad conditions, but there is
little mention of deliberating irrationally or unreasonably. Is there, then, some
independent standard for deliberation, failures of which are best called "incor-
rectness in deliberation" rather than "irrationality in deliberation"?

Consider what it is to deliberate correctly. It is not to deliberate in a cool
hour, because incorrect deliberation can be the product of a cool hour (this
sometimes seems to happen, for example, when major economic policies are
designed) and at least some correct deliberation is the product of "hot" hours
(for example, when righteous indignation sharpens thoughts on the subject of
human rights). It is not to deliberate in a manner prescribed by some optimal algorithm for deliberation, because there is no more an algorithm for
good deliberation than for good conversation. Deliberating well or correctly is
deliberating without fallacies and logical errors, as well as without such things
as wishful thinking, fearful thinking, or interference by sleep deprivation or
alcohol, in a way that deploys what we know, suspect, and can figure out, in
a manner suited to determining what to think or do. In other words, correct
deliberation is deliberation in conformity to the requirements of rationality. It
thus appears that incorrect deliberation is simply deliberation in violation of
those requirements. It is, in short, irrational deliberation.

Another approach to showing the rich range of possibilities for more and
less rational deliberation is more *a prioristic*. Philosophers as different from
one another as Anscombe, Davidson, and Korsgaard[19] have held that it is a
necessary truth that every action is done for a reason (or reasons). It need not
be done from overwhelming reasons or even good reasons, but to count as
an action at all it must be done for some reason or other, whether good or
bad or downright foolish. We agree with these philosophers about this feature
of action,[20] and draw the immediate conclusion regarding deliberation. Since
deliberation is an action, deliberation cannot be deliberation without something else rationalizing it, without it being done for some reason or other.[21] And
with the need for rationalization comes the possibility of a rationalization's
being a better one or a worse one: the possibility of deliberating more or less
rationally or irrationally.

---

[19] See Anscombe (2000), Davidson (1980), Korsgaard (1996).
[20] With a caveat to be added in chapter 3 concerning habitual and emotionally expressive
actions.
[21] In chapter 3 we will see the need to amend this claim slightly. An action must always be
a manifestation of one's reasons, but it need not be performed *for* reasons, in the most natural
sense. We will note, however, that deliberation is always done for a reason. An action performed
out of sheer habit cannot be deliberation, as deliberation is always performed in order to figure
out what to think or do.

Nothing so far need be very controversial. Though most philosophers interested in deliberation have not provided us with theories of deliberation or particularly naturalistic examples,[22] most of them have said nothing directly incompatible with the foregoing, which in any case we take to be largely familiar and conservative. And yet following the consequences of this account of deliberation and its relation to reasons leads to some very controversial theses indeed.

1.3 Deliberation and Regress

It is time to discuss the thesis that deliberation is fundamental to thinking and acting for reasons. If our abilities to think and act for reasons are based upon our capacities for deliberation, then each action we take for some reason (however good or bad) is taken for that reason on account of the act's relation to some act of deliberation that happened in the past, some act of deliberation that is happening in the present, or some merely possible act of deliberation. But when the action in question is an act of deliberation itself, all three of these possibilities appear to lead to untenable regresses or infinities.

First, consider the idea that an act of deliberation is an action taken for reasons because it is an action with an appropriate relationship to a previous occasion of deliberation. Call this approach "Previous Deliberation." In the past, perhaps, Harold engaged in some deliberation, at the end of which he embraced the principle that he should not make a promise without considering (i.e., deliberating upon) possible conflicting prior promises. And that is why, when he searches his memory for such promises, he not only does what he has reason to do but does it *for* a reason. His present deliberating for reasons is constituted by his acting in accordance with the conclusion of previous deliberation about how to deliberate in such cases. Or, in a slightly more sophisticated vein, his present acting (i.e., his present searching of his memory) for reasons is constituted as being done for reasons by his acting out of a habit, policy, or virtue that was engendered by his previous deliberative conclusion about how to deliberate.[23]

---

[22] An example of a richly detailed work on deliberation (not so far mentioned) is Seidman (2008), which considers the ways in which caring about subjects rationally informs the shape of deliberation.

[23] The role of habit in making deliberation responsive to reasons appears to be invoked by Chan (1995, 140 and fn.10). It is emphasized by, e.g., Hookway (1999) and Herman (1993). Hookway does not clearly endorse Previous Deliberation, however—perhaps as a result of having a slightly different framing of the issues from the one that concerns us. Railton (2009) also emphasizes the role of habit, but Railton is very clear that he rejects anything like Previous Deliberation.

Suppose that one act of deliberation is made into an action done for a reason by a previous deliberative conclusion, as Previous Deliberation requires.
That previous deliberative conclusion was reached through one or more acts
of deliberation. Consider the previous act of deliberation (assume for simplic-
ity that there was only one) that resulted in the conclusion. To be an act of
deliberation it had to have been done for a reason. If it had not been done for
any reason—if it had not been rationalized, to any extent, by something—it
would not have been an action, and so not an act of deliberation, and would
not have the power to rationalize the present act of deliberation. What, then,
made it true of the prior deliberative act that it was an action done for a reason?
What rationalized it? According to Previous Deliberation, it would have to be
some prior act of deliberation. And so we are set off on a regress. Further, the
regress is a vicious one, for no matter how far back in a deliberating agent's
life we go, we must always find a prior act of deliberation in order to satisfy
the theory: back to childhood, to the womb, and so on without limit. Previous
Deliberation thus fails.

Second, it might be suggested that an act of deliberation is an action taken
for a reason because it is an action with an appropriate relationship to another,
simultaneous act of deliberation. Call this approach "Present Deliberation."
A defender of Present Deliberation might hold that, as we reach deliberative
conclusions, we also embrace the process by which we reach these conclusions.
That is, each deliberative act contains, as it were, a second act of deliberation in
which the first act is deliberated upon and found reasonable—and on this basis,
the first act is performed for a reason.[24]

Present Deliberation, like Previous Deliberation, also begins a vicious
regress. To be an action at all, the second deliberative act required by Present
Deliberation requires that something make it the case that it is an act done for
a reason, and so it requires a third deliberative act; and so on. The viciousness
of this regress lies in its requirement that, to deliberate at all, an agent engage
in infinitely many distinct acts of deliberation simultaneously, with each act
having a distinct goal. Infinitely many implicit beliefs can, perhaps, be stored in
a finite agent. But infinitely many distinct mental actions, each with a distinct
represented goal, cannot be performed at the same time by finite agents.[25]

In the light of the foregoing it might be suggested that an act of deliberation is performed for reasons because it is an action with an appropriate

---

[24] Hacker (2007, 239) and Korsgaard (2009) both appear to endorse Present Deliberation.

[25] A variant of Present Deliberation, suggested in conversation by Gil Harman, avoids the
regress by means of self-reference. The suggestion is that acts of deliberation are undertaken for
reasons just in case the act of deliberation judges itself to be reasonable, in addition to judging
whatever else it judges. The content of e.g., Katie's deliberation might then be: there is an advertising campaign using the phrase "I'm loving" and this is a reasonable thing to be considering.
But Harman's proposal does not solve other problems for Present Deliberation, found in the next
section.

relationship to a merely possible act of deliberation. Call this third approach "Possible Deliberation." Perhaps it is true that, were Harold to deliberate about it, Harold would conclude that he is being reasonable (or unreasonable) in trying to call to mind promises that might conflict with meeting his son in Calgary. And perhaps it is this fact about what conclusion he would have reached that makes it true that Harold's act of trying to call these promises to mind is indeed a reasonable (or unreasonable) act.[26]

Possible Deliberation, like its counterparts, faces a serious regress problem. Suppose it is true that, had Harold deliberated about the reasonableness of calling to mind promises that might conflict with meeting his son in Calgary, he would have reached the (theoretical) conclusion that it would be reasonable of him to do so. But had Harold deliberated he would have done so for a reason; and for this counterfactual act of deliberation to be one that would have been done for a reason, it would have to be true that had Harold deliberated about the counterfactual act of deliberation, he would have come to a conclusion as to how to deliberate about how to deliberate about the reasonableness of calling to mind promises that might conflict with meeting his son in Calgary. That in turn would have had to have been done for a reason, and so on. So Harold's mind, as it actually is, must support infinitely many counterfactuals about the ever increasingly complex processes of reasoning he would have gone through. And Harold, being an ordinary human being, is not capable of guaranteeing that if he had deliberated about how to deliberate about how to deliberate about... about how to deliberate about meeting his son in Calgary, he would have reached a policy about deliberating about deliberating about...If Harold had attempted to engage in this sort of massively complex deliberation, he would have become confused, and given up, and reached no conclusion at all. This is the viciousness of this particular form of regress.

It might be thought that the infinitely many counterfactuals can be simplified, and the regress eliminated, if Harold reviews his evidence in the right way. Suppose that, if Harold had struggled through deliberating about the acceptability of his Nth level of deliberating about deliberating about... deliberating about whether to search his memory, he would have concluded that these Nth level deliberations were performed for good reasons. When the question arises about this very act of deliberation—about his N+1th level of deliberating— could Harold not just say that, since his level N deliberations were undertaken for good reasons, so too must his level N+1 deliberations be for good reasons? And could he not repeat this trick for every level greater than N? If he could, then although infinitely many counterfactuals must be true about Harold, they would all turn out to be simple counterfactuals, not involving excessively

---

[26] Possible deliberation appears to be defended by Tiberius (2002), quoted above. It would also seem to be defended in McGeer and Pettit (2002, 294), on the assumption that believing for a (better or worse) reason is what makes one responsible for one's beliefs.

complex contents. Facts about Harold could make all of these infinitely many counterfactuals true even while Harold remains an ordinary person with an ordinary, finite memory and intelligence.

Though ingenious, this proposal faces a problem. When we imagine what Harold would conclude were he to reason about his Nth level of deliberation, we cannot imagine him saying to himself, "Well, I don't remember what action I was judging here, but I suppose it must have been reasonable enough." That can hardly be the sort of counterfactual deliberation that the advocate of Possible Deliberation thinks grounds acting for reasons. So what must Harold (counterfactually) do? He must bring to mind the details of his Nth level of deliberation, and think specifically about them. He must bring to mind the fact that he was saying to himself, "I can't just take for granted that my memory works well," if that was how his Nth level of deliberation proceeded. But even this is not enough, since Harold can hardly think to himself "well, that was foolish of me!" and thereby make it true, in a way that makes us believe Possible Deliberation, that his Nth level deliberation was conducted for bad reasons. We have to imagine that Harold thinks carefully about his Nth level of deliberation, and to do so he must consciously consider what its purpose was, which was to evaluate an N-1th level deliberative act that was itself . . . and so on, all the way back down to the basic action. In short, if what Harold would conclude about his deliberating is to mean anything—if it is to be the sort of conclusion that can carry the weight Possible Deliberation requires—then it cannot be anything less than a full consideration of all the details of the action being evaluated. And this just restores the problems with there being unboundedly complex actions for Harold to contemplate and no fact about what he would conclude were he to (try to) contemplate them.

A view that combines elements of Present Deliberation and Possible Deliberation is the view that Harold deliberates as he does for reasons if his deliberation stems from an actual mechanism that ensures that he does whatever he would have done had he deliberated. But it is hard to see how this view makes progress over Possible Deliberation. Presumably the combined view holds that Harold deliberates as he does for reasons if his deliberation stems from an actual mechanism that ensures he deliberates as he would have done had he deliberated on how to deliberate, which again would have had to be for a reason. This sets off the regress problem again.[27] We have no objection to the idea that thinking and acting for reasons relies on a mechanism, and one that could be validated by an ideal observer who deliberated about the

---

[27] The combined view is also subject to the problems raised in the next section: that if Katie has foolish views about how she ought to deliberate, views that do not ordinarily come up when she deliberates about this or that, but do come up when she deliberates about how to deliberate about this or that, then this combined view must hold that to deliberate for good reasons in the present she must now deliberate in the manner she would, foolishly, validate upon considering her deliberative process. More on this below.

operations of the mechanism. Indeed, this has to be the case, and we will discuss the key features of this mechanism in chapter 3. But there is a related idea that is unsupportable, and that we reject: the idea that what makes the mechanism one suited to ensure that we think and act for reasons is reducible to facts about counterfactual reasoning about the mechanism.

Possible Deliberation is thus no more tenable than Previous or Present Deliberation. And with it we exhaust our imaginations. There are surely other ways to defend the claim that a deliberative act is performed for a reason just in case it bears the right relation to some other deliberative act. But we have covered the main options and have found no defense that succeeds. It seems that acts of deliberation are performed for reasons (good or bad) in virtue of something other than their relation to deliberation.

1.4 Other Objections

Apart from regresses, there are various other problems for Previous, Present, and Possible Deliberation.

Quite salient is the fact that the experience of deliberating as to how to deliberate is rare and the experience of deliberating about how to deliberate about how to deliberate almost nonexistent. Many people seem to get by in life with a bare minimum of reflection upon their own thought processes. Must it be believed that they have managed at some time or other to have deliberated about how to deliberate in sufficiently broad terms that now their acts of deliberation are all capable of being taken for good (or bad) reasons? This seems required by Previous Deliberation, but unlikely to be true.

Present Deliberation requires an act of deliberation that is not phenomenologically familiar yet that should be as easy to experience as ordinary deliberation itself. At the very moment at which Harold consciously tries to call to mind competing promises that would prevent him from promising to meet his son in Calgary, he is not (if he is anything like us) consciously evaluating the reasonableness of this conscious search of his memory. Yet Present Deliberation requires that there be such an act. So the second deliberative act required by Present Deliberation would seem not to be a conscious act at all—which makes it, not an act of deliberation, but something else.[28]

More problems appear when we turn the discussion from acting for reasons *per se* to acting for *good* reasons: acting rationally or reasonably. Consider the view that acting for good reasons depends on a previous, present, or possible act of deliberation. Problems for these views arise from the possibility of people deliberating about how to deliberate but reaching foolish conclusions.

---

[28] See footnote 36.

For Past Deliberation, consider people who, perhaps as a result of adolescent philosophical discussions, have in the past embraced foolish principles constraining deliberation: for example, to believe nothing in the future without seeing a *proof*; to do nothing without first asking how it will benefit *me*. People who manage to constrain their deliberations in these ways seem less reasonable, not more, in virtue of their conformity to their principles. If they neglect their principles (common sense reasserting itself unnoticed), they deliberate in ways that are more reasonable, yet in violation of their most recent settled policies for deliberation.[29]

Present Deliberation entails, similarly, that an utterly unreasonable deliberation about how to deliberate has the power to make what otherwise appears wholly reasonable first-order deliberation into unreasonable first-order deliberation. If Katie is deliberating about the grammaticality of "I'm loving" and her deliberation has been exemplary in its use of nondemonstrative evidence, but she simultaneously reaches the foolish conclusion that her deliberations about grammar have no evidential value if they do not conclusively prove that "I'm loving" is ungrammatical, then somehow her utterly foolish subjective discontent with her exemplary first-order reasoning is supposed to make that exemplary first-order reasoning unreasonable after all. If this foolish discontent is unable to shake Katie from her modest confidence that "I'm loving" is probably grammatical, modest confidence reached through her exemplary first-order deliberation, then she seems reasonable in the face of foolish meta-considerations, not unreasonably stubborn.

Finally, Possible Deliberation faces these same problems stemming from the possibility of foolish views about deliberation. Katie is, suppose, acting for good reasons when she says to herself, "lots of people seem to say 'I'm loving' without scare-quoting it or anything." She is trying to determine the grammaticality of the phrase, and saying this to herself is rehearsing relevant information, and she has said it to herself for the reason that it is relevant information. But suppose Katie believes that no piece of evidence is worth considering if it is not conclusive. This belief of hers is unreasonable, of course, and normally she does not revise her beliefs in accordance with it (though occasionally she does, especially when this belief spontaneously occurs to her while she is reasoning). But in contexts in which she theorizes about how her reasoning should be conducted, this belief comes to the fore all the time. It seems to us that this scenario is possible. And yet, Possible Deliberation must say it is impossible, because the fact that Katie *would* reject her own deliberative act as unreasonable makes it true, according to Possible Deliberation, that her own deliberative act actually was unreasonable. The mere possession of a foolish belief about what counts as evidence worthy of consideration in deliberation deprives Katie of the capacity

---

[29] Arpaly (2000; 2003, Chapter 2) discusses these cases at length.

to deliberate for good reasons. This goes against what seems the most natural interpretation of the case, which is that Katie can be reasonable in actuality while being counterfactually disposed to reject her own reasonableness. To hold that, under these circumstances, Katie would not actually deliberate reasonably also requires attributing too much power to single meta-theoretical beliefs. Believing that every act is selfish cannot make every act by that agent selfish. Why should beliefs about the nature of deliberation be so much more powerful? Katie can deliberate for reasons even though her deliberation does not conform to her (ill-judged, poorly substantiated) belief about how such deliberation should proceed.

Valerie Tiberius defends her form of Possible Deliberation against this objection.[30] Her defense focuses on making it plausible that an agent who forces herself to conform to a foolish practical principle acts rationally in so conforming. An agent who believes she should consult an astrologer as part of ideal deliberation, and who as a result does not get proper medical treatment for something, acts rationally in not getting the medical treatment (if doing so follows from the astrological advice), according to Tiberius. But Tiberius does not consider the question of whether this same agent would be acting irrationally if she had never deliberated (and so never concluded she ought to start by consulting an astrologer), but had simply acted on her belief that doctors know what to do for people with mysterious pains, plus her belief that she has a mysterious pain, plus her desire to not be in pain. It seems to us that the agent would be acting for a good reason if she were to just spontaneously visit a walk-in clinic as she was walking past one. And if so, there is something wrong with Possible Deliberation. The fact—if it is one—that the agent could undermine her justification for taking this action via reasoning on the basis of a foolish deliberative principle does not change what the agent can do for good reasons in the absence of such misguided deliberation.

One thing to note about all of these arguments about foolish beliefs and deliberation is that they attribute irrationality on the basis of facts that are internal to the person deliberating. The thesis that Harold or Katie is, was, or would be acting irrationally in a given situation by deliberating in a certain way does not require taking an external or ideal perspective on what Harold or Katie should believe, or what an ideal or reliable belief-forming mechanism would do in Harold's circumstances or Katie's. If Katie is trying to determine the grammaticality of "I'm loving" but is deliberating at length on how many ways there are to avoid the phrase then the claim that she is deliberating irrationally is derived, not from the outside perspective, but from the fact that the Katie of our example knows full well that the existence of an alternative phrasing for "X" does not affect the grammaticality of "X." It is just that, whatever

---

[30] Tiberius (2002).

the explanation (whether "hot" or "cold"), Katie is not taking this knowledge into account in her deliberation. Her deliberation is unreasonable from her own perspective even though she is not thinking to herself "I'm being unreasonable" as she deliberates.

1.5 Deliberative Exceptionalism

A defender of Past, Present, or Possible Deliberation might grant that regresses threaten Past, Present, and Possible Deliberation but propose to solve the problem by giving deliberation an exceptional status. One sort of exceptionalism would hold that deliberation does not need to be performed for any reason at all in order to make it the case that other acts are performed for reasons. Although we argued that deliberation is made up of actions and all actions are performed for reasons, it might be thought that there is room to slip away from these constraints: perhaps some deliberation is involuntary and as such not really an action, or not really performed for reasons. Another sort of exceptionalism would hold that, while deliberation does need to be performed for reasons, it is an exceptional sort of action in that something other than deliberation can secure the fact that it is performed for reasons. Every *other* sort of action, in contrast, can only be performed for reasons in virtue of some act of past, present, or possible deliberation.

The problem with deliberative exceptionalism in either of its forms is that it addresses only the regress arguments. It does nothing to show that deliberation can have a special, rationality-granting status in the face of the objections of the previous section. Let it be granted that deliberation can be undertaken without this fact being secured by some other (past, present, or possible) act of deliberation. Even with this granted, the questions that were just raised can be raised again: is there any reason to believe that, for every sort of nondeliberative action people perform, they have in the past deliberated about how to act in the circumstances? If not, then Past Deliberation still fails. Is there any reason to believe that there are acts of deliberation concurrent with all actions? If not, then Present Deliberation still fails. And deliberative exceptionalism does nothing to respond to the arguments from bad deliberative conclusions. Even under deliberative exceptionalism, it is not credible that a person visiting a doctor without first consulting an astrologer is acting irrationally simply because she once (or would have) concluded she should always ask an astrologer before making any decisions about her health.

Because of these problems, we see no advantage to holding deliberative exceptionalism. Even if true, it will not secure any privileged role for deliberation in determining what it is reasonable to think or do. And if there is no advantage to holding it, then we see no reason at all to believe in it. The idea that one can deliberate, an act constitutively performed to determine what to think or do, without deliberating for a reason, strikes us as inconsistent. And the idea that deliberation is performed for reasons that only apply to deliberation strikes us as a metaphysically arbitrary posit. So it seems we are back where we started: with the thesis that deliberation is not what makes it true that we think and act for reasons.

1.6 Is There an Ambiguity?

There must be a way of thinking and acting for reasons independently of and prior to deliberation, and this must be what makes acts of deliberation more or less reasonable as actions. But it is worth asking: are there perhaps two senses of "thinking for reasons" and "acting for reasons," a weaker sense in which deliberation is not necessary and a stronger sense in which deliberation is necessary after all?[31]

There is rarely anything wrong with making distinctions in philosophy, and we see nothing to object to in the present proposal. Let there be one sense of what it is to think or act for a reason, the sense under discussion in this work so far, and let there be another, called "thinking and acting for reasons *par excellence*,"[32] that is only instantiated when the thought or act in question was, is, or would be considered and validated by the thinker or actor's own deliberative processes.

With this distinction made, however, it is worth asking what the status is of beliefs formed and actions performed for reasons *par excellence*. Are these actions the only ones that are properly said to be actions as opposed to mere activities? (Are these beliefs the only ones that are properly said to be beliefs as opposed to mere cognitions?) Are these thoughts and actions the only ones that are properly said to be rational, reasonable, sensible, intelligent (or irrational, not very reasonable, foolish, unintelligent)? Are these thoughts and actions ones that are certain to be more rational than they would have been otherwise? Our answer to all of these questions is "no," for reasons found largely in what has come before. And if the answer to all of these questions is "no," then while we are happy to grant the existence of thinking and acting for reasons *par excellence* we see no special role for this sense of "acting for reasons" in the philosophical literatures with which we are most familiar. It is the sense of thinking and acting for reasons that is not *"par excellence"*—plain thinking and acting for reasons—that has all of the properties we are most interested in when we are interested in thinking and acting for reasons.

---

[31] We thank an anonymous referee for *Philosophical Review* for urging us to consider this possibility.

[32] We borrow the expression from Velleman (1992).

Begin with the question of whether "thinking" and "acting" for reasons in a sense wholly independent of deliberation (not "*par excellence*") really counts as thinking or acting. There are philosophers who distinguish, for example, the "mere activity" of some animals from the full-blooded actions that only people can perform.[33] Perhaps the philosopher interested in thinking and acting for reasons *par excellence* would want to hold, in a similar vein, that being moved by reasons *par excellence* is a necessary condition for being a belief or action. But we argued previously that deliberation is a paradigmatic (covert) action, with all the characteristics of other actions: acts of deliberation can be performed at will, though without any guarantee of success; they are susceptible to the varied faults and sources of irrationality common to all actions; they are performed for better or worse reasons, given the ends they are undertaken with. The evidence that deliberation really is an action is just as good as the evidence that anything is an action. And since deliberation cannot (on pain of regress) always be an action performed for reasons *par excellence*, deliberation serves as a counter-example to the thesis that all genuine actions are performed for reasons *par excellence*.

Moving beyond deliberation, there are all of the apparent actions people perform and the apparent beliefs they form wholly independently of deliberation. If we have any grasp of action, then passing the salt when asked to pass the salt is an action, and is so whether or not one deliberates (as rarely happens, in the case of salt-passing) about whether to pass the salt. Likewise, if we have any grasp of belief, then what typically happens when one opens the fridge and sees everything but butter is that one comes to believe that there is no more butter, and this counts as a belief even in the absence of deliberation on butter's availability. To deny these theses in the cases of ordinary adult language-using human beings (at least) is, it seems to us, to lose any grasp one might have had on what actions and beliefs are.[34]

So thinking and acting for reasons *par excellence* is not required for performing actions or forming beliefs. It is likewise not required for these actions or beliefs to be more or less rational, performed for better or worse reasons. As we wrote earlier, nothing can be an action without being performed for some reason or other, whether a better or a worse one. So if we have shown that there can exist actions that are not performed for reasons *par excellence*, then

---

[33] See, e.g., many of the essays in Velleman (2000). We note that although Velleman's views have a strongly Kantian cast, he need not fall prey to any of the arguments in this chapter. The desire to make sense to oneself, from which all genuine action must stem on Velleman's account, is one that might move one for good reasons in the absence of deliberation upon those reasons.

[34] Someone wishing to nonetheless diminish the status of these putative actions and beliefs by denying them these names could always reserve the words "action" and "belief" for things upon which there has been deliberation—but then the philosophical interest of true beliefs, as opposed to schmeliefs (things just like beliefs except for not having been deliberated upon), and true actions, as opposed to shmactions, becomes open to question.

we have shown that there are actions that are performed for better or worse reasons without being performed for reasons *par excellence*. And the same reasoning, it seems, should hold for belief as well as action.

Even if this much is agreed to, it might still be held that thinking and acting that does not happen for reasons *par excellence* must always be somewhat deficient in its rationality, intelligence, or reasonableness. But this too seems wrong. Consider Oscar Wilde. According to one story, Wilde bragged that he can make a pun on any subject. Presented with the challenge "the Queen" he answered, quickly, "the Queen is no subject." A conversation like this can happen much too fast for any deliberation to take place, and surprise even the pun-maker himself; this is a big part of what makes a great conversationalist. Yet Wilde's answering is a paradigmatic action, and a paradigmatically witty, smart, well-chosen, intelligent action as well. It would have been less witty and a lesser display of intelligence had Wilde deliberated before his quip; this strongly suggests that Wilde's quip strikes us as performed for excellent practical and esthetic reasons, in a way that warrants this kind of praise, without any presumption that deliberation was involved, and so without any presumption that it was performed for reasons *par excellence*.[35] Similar thoughts apply in the epistemic domain. It is a true dullard who only concludes that he is out of butter after deliberating upon the fact that no butter is in evidence in the refrigerator, and after concluding that the absence of visual evidence is a reason to believe in the absence of butter. A more intelligent person would be shown to be more intelligent—would have her rational faculties on full display—in drawing the same conclusion without engaging in any deliberation at all. There are cases in which human beings cannot draw the correct epistemic conclusions for good reasons without relying on deliberation (for example, about complex philosophical matters; see chapter 2) but that such cases exist does not show that every case is one in which the only way to believe something for a good reason is to have first thought it over.

Finally, there is the evidence that theoretical and practical conclusions reached on the basis of deliberation can be less reasonable, less rational, than the theoretical and practical conclusions that would have been reached in the absence of deliberation. The person with a foolish theory of how to deliberate is one who can make herself less reasonable than she would otherwise be. The person whose deliberation about whether or not there is any butter does not rest until a *proof* is at hand is a person whose deliberations are likely to harm his epistemic status, not help it; had he only not deliberated (and so not drawn upon his thesis that all beliefs need proofs for their justification) he would likely have believed what was reasonable on the grounds that made it reasonable. Similarly for his practical counterpart.

---

[35] Arpaly (2003, chapter 2) gives witty conversation as an example of possibly rational action without deliberation.

In short, while there is room for the idea that there is such a thing as responding to reasons *par excellence*, there is no important property that attaches to all and only instances of responding to reasons in this way, in the light of deliberation about one's reasons.

1.7 If Not Deliberation, Then Representation?

Deliberation does not ground thinking and acting for reasons. But there is another way in which Reason could be given a privileged role over Appetite in the explanation of thinking and acting for reasons. The defender of Reason might say that to think or act for reasons we must represent to ourselves that we are thinking or acting for reasons. It might be said that an action is one performed for reasons just in case it is an act that is believed reasonable, consciously believed reasonable, thought to be justified by the reasons before the agent, or otherwise taken (cognitively) to be appropriately licensed. Call this view "Recognition."[36]

Recognition solves the regress problems that faced Past, Present, and Possible Deliberation, because these regresses were based on the fact that deliberation is an action, and so is itself performed for reasons. Recognizing that one has reasons is not an action; it is a belief, a thought, or something similar. But Recognition still seems to give Reason a very special role in explaining how it is that we can think and act for reasons. So the philosopher who wants to make room for a desire-centered moral psychology needs to confront it.

Recognition faces both regress and foolish-attitude problems. They have a slightly different origin from the problems confronting Past, Present, and Possible Deliberation, but their upshot is much the same.

Consider the regresses first. Suppose that Harold is searching his memory for any promise he has made that might conflict with picking up his son in Calgary on Tuesday. This action is one he takes for a good reason, and this is because (according to Recognition) Harold represents to himself the reasonableness of searching his memory in this way on this occasion. Harold's representation of this might have occurred in the past (Past Recognition), it might be contemporaneous with his searching his memory (Present Recognition), or it might be purely counterfactual (Possible Recognition). Whichever it is, however, a regress looms. For whether Harold's representation of the reasonableness of

---

[36] Recognition appears to be endorsed by (among others) Barry (2007, 232), Korsgaard (1997, 222), and Wallace (1999, 225). Niko Kolodny seems to endorse something like Recognition in writing that for a mental transition to happen for a reason, it must result from awareness of the justification for the transition (Kolodny 2005, 520). But in a footnote, Kolodny wants to allow that unconscious, automatic awareness is possible. Since there is no such thing (in our understanding) as unconscious awareness, we find this a bit puzzling, but suspect that the problems do not go away by burying the putative awareness in the unconscious.

searching his memory is past, present, or merely possible, it is itself a belief, and so it is held for a more or less good reason. Being held for a reason, it in turn must be the object of a past, present, or possible representation of it as reasonable, and so on; the same regresses that held for deliberation will appear again.[37]

There is a way out of the regress, but it is not appealing: it is to hold that the beliefs required by Recognition were, are, or would be held for no reason at all. Perhaps this is true. Certainly beliefs can be given up for no reason at all: head injuries can deprive people of beliefs without giving them reasons (even bad ones) to abandon their beliefs. So it is not implausible that beliefs could be gained for no reason at all. (Perhaps a nefarious neuroscientist could induce new beliefs by means of purely anatomical manipulation.) But even if the beliefs required by Recognition can be gained and held for no reason, it is not plausible that this helps. If belief A has as its content that a second belief, B, is held for good reasons, but A itself is held for no reason at all, then this alone does not secure that belief B is indeed held for good reasons. On its own this is, at most, a rather poor reason to hold belief B. And likewise for actions. Since some beliefs are held for good reasons, and some actions are performed for good reasons, an escape from regress that licenses only thinking and acting for bad reasons is not particularly satisfying.

Second, consider the foolish-attitude objection.[38] Foolish approving attitudes would seem unable to make otherwise foolish thoughts or acts into ones for good reasons, or to make otherwise wise thoughts or acts into foolish ones. As before, it would seem that if Katie is getting caught up with thinking of alternatives to the phrase "I'm loving" while deliberating about its grammaticality, then Katie is deliberating irrationally—even if she believes (consciously, unconsciously, in the past, in another possible world...) that she is proceeding very reasonably, or otherwise has a positive cognitive attitude toward her responsiveness to reasons. Her conscious belief is simply mistaken, and her mental action is no more reasonable than it appears to us. And similarly if Katie reaches a reasonable conclusion about "I'm loving" that she judges (in the past, present, or a possible alternative) to be unreasonable because it was not reached via a decisive proof.

A third and final objection asks: how is a belief about one's reasonableness supposed to secure actual reasonableness, as opposed to mere conformity to what reasonableness requires? There is a gap between thoughts and actions that are in conformity to what an agent has reason to think or do and actions that are performed (and beliefs that are believed) *because* of the reasons an agent has to think or perform them. Let it be true that one thinks or does what one has good reason to do, and that one believes that this is the case. How does the latter secure that the former is not just accidentally, luckily, in accordance

---

[37] Something like Recognition is attacked in Dreier (2001), following Carroll (1895).
[38] Wedgwood (2006, 675) raises similar objections to a similar idea.

with rational requirements? We see no hope for answering this question without appealing to some process that is *not* a representation of reasonableness and that *is* sufficient to secure the conclusion that one is thinking or acting for reasons all on its own. And it is just this process that we have been seeking.

Recognition, it seems, is neither necessary nor sufficient for one's thinking or acting for reasons.

1.8 Thinking and Acting for Reasons without Deliberation

One final line of inquiry should be pursued. Most of our arguments so far have been focused upon the proposal that deliberation is what makes our actions reason-responsive, but it might be suggested that some other action is needed to make actions (and thoughts?) reason-responsive. Perhaps someone will suggest that a mental action such as committing to a long-term plan is required in order to make it true that we act for reasons. Or perhaps someone will suggest that an overt action or set of actions, such as engaging in a suitable "form of life," is required in order to make it true that we act for reasons. Is there some way for these alternative theories to succeed where deliberation failed?

Suppose X is some inner or outer action, one that is supposed to secure its being the case that other actions are performed for reasons. Because X is an action, it must itself be performed for some reason or other, however good or bad. And so now the question arises of how it comes to be that X is performed for that reason. It must, it seems, be the case that another action of the same type as X was, is, or would be performed to make it the case that X is performed for a reason. And so it seems that the arguments against Past, Present, and Possible Deliberation will be repeatable. Though the details of the arguments would be different for different particular replacements for X, we do not see any particular action being able to avoid the problems that faced deliberation while also being in any way plausible as the sort of action that must be performed in order for other actions to be performed for reasons.

The main conclusion of this chapter is that deliberation is not what grounds thinking and acting for reasons. And the previous section showed that recognition of reasons is likewise unable to ground thinking and acting for reasons. Now it appears that no voluntary action of any sort will ground thinking and acting for reasons.

Whatever makes it possible for us to think and act for reasons, it must be a process that is nondeliberative, nonrecognitional, and nonvoluntary (an "ND process" for short). This ND process has so far been given only a negative characterization; a positive theory will be developed in chapter 3.

{ 2 }

How Deliberation Works

So far, the discussion of deliberation has been largely negative. After its quick sketch of what deliberation is like, the focus of chapter 1 was on showing that deliberation lacks certain powers. Though necessary, this work might also leave the mistaken impression that as theorists we dislike deliberation, when nothing could be further from the truth. Although deliberation is not able to make it the case that we think or act for reasons, and so is not a foundational ability, it is an incredibly valuable tool.

In this chapter, we discuss the roles played by deliberation. We begin by showing how deliberation is able to enhance our nondeliberative, nonvoluntary, nonrecognitional (ND, for short) abilities to think and act for reasons. From there, we investigate how deliberation works, seeking to understand (so far as possible, from the armchair) how ND processes enable deliberation to proceed. We finish by drawing some basic morals. (A difficult task, that of explaining how, given the nature of deliberation, the experience of struggling with oneself over what to do is possible, is postponed until chapter 10.)

2.1 The Role of Deliberation

We would be remiss not to give deliberation its due, and there can hardly be any doubt that the ability to deliberate is one to which we owe the enormous technological and social gains that we as a species have made in the last 13,000 years.

One role played by deliberation appears to us to be central to these gains, and that is its role in allowing us to compound insights. Deliberation can be used to sequence together a set of ideas, each one of which can be reached without deliberation, in such a way that the sequence can then itself be surveyed and used to reach some further idea that could never have been reached otherwise.

Consider complex sums: faced with the task of adding 3545 to 869, most of us find ourselves unable to see the result directly. But if we focus our attention first on the sum of 5 and 9, and keep in mind that the result ends in 4 (a conclusion that, itself, can be reached without the aid of deliberation), and then sum 1, 4, and 6...and so on, then we can perform a sequence of mental actions with the final result being a correct belief about the sum of 3545 and 869. Each step in this sequence of actions can be performed using only ND abilities to believe for good reasons, but the specific sequence followed is the product of organized mental actions (focusing attention now on one set of numbers, now on another, keeping in mind certain results, and so on) aimed at determining what to believe. And it is only because this sequence, the product of deliberation, is followed that the final result is a correct belief about the sum of 3545 and 869. This is a paradigmatic instance of deliberation enabling us to reach a conclusion not immediately reachable via the deployment of ND abilities, enabling us to reach the conclusion via strategic sequencing and compounding of the deployment of ND abilities.

Whether or not a particular task calls for this sequential compounding treatment depends on the individual's capacity for ND reason-responding: young children require deliberation even for simple arithmetic, most adults require it only for more complex calculations, and a few arithmetical wizards immediately see sums and products that the rest of us must work through with painstaking effort. It also depends on the circumstances: deliberation can suddenly be required for a task not normally requiring it if one is overwhelmed by fear, for instance. And presumably it depends on the nature of the task itself: arithmetic lends itself to algorithms requiring only small steps (relative to our ND capacities), and so does shopping for groceries, but some complex tasks seem not to neatly decompose. Yet even with these tasks that do not decompose so neatly, deliberation often seems tremendously valuable: it is hard to imagine how a human being could develop a good philosophical theory, devise a reasonable scientific experiment, or write a structurally complex short story without it. Similarly, there are morally important actions that are impossible without deliberation, such as running a charity, fighting injustice through activism, or figuring out the right truths to tell in unfamiliar and complex circumstances. These activities are so complex, relative to our native ND abilities to think and act for reasons, that we need to be able to attack them piecemeal, to be able to reduce them, however awkwardly or haphazardly, to collections of simpler problems that are tractable relative to our ND abilities. Deliberation makes this possible.

When it comes to tasks that do not require such treatment, thinking and acting for reasons via ND processes has an impressive role in our lives. But it is also evident that there are obstacles to thinking and acting for the very best reasons using only our ND abilities in even mundane circumstances. Other causal processes are at work within our minds in addition to those that mediate our ND abilities to think and act for reasons. Quick wit and even ordinary grammaticality can suffer from low blood sugar, from background emotional distress, from sitting in view of a distracting display, and more. There is, as a result, room for various interventions to enhance our ND abilities to think and act for reasons. The use of caffeine or a good night's sleep or a bite to eat can be such an intervention but there is also room for the intervention of deliberation as a tool for enhancing reasonableness in thought and action, and it is worth illustrating a few examples of this.

These abilities can be diminished by distraction: a television in the background, noisy children running around, and the presence of a very attractive person can make it hard to maintain witty banter, generate philosophical insight, or do other things displaying ND reason-responding at its best. (They can even make it difficult to act on the reasons one has to use a verb conjugated for the third person singular or to move the fork in one's hand to one's mouth.) One thing people do to enhance their ND abilities to think and act for reasons is to dismiss the distractions: to turn off the television, send the children to play outside, and gaze at the ceiling in preference to the attractive person. But they can also deploy deliberation for the same purpose. In deliberation, one can take mental actions to deal with distraction: one can refocus one's attention onto one's question or the evidence already called to mind, one can use verbal imagery to say to oneself "I need to say something about causation," and otherwise use mental behavior to block the effects of potentially distracting stimuli. When these actions are meant to involve contents that are relevant to theoretical or practical conclusions one is pursuing, these actions constitute deliberation. In this way, deliberation can be a covert action that improves ND reason-responding taking the place of an overt action that would improve ND reason-responding. Of course, sometimes deliberation is a poor substitute for more vigorous action: if the kids are making a ruckus, saying "is causation always lawful?" repeatedly to oneself is probably a less effective way of dealing with distraction than sending them out to the yard. But sometimes deliberation is more effective than most overt acts available: if emotional distress is getting in the way of philosophical contemplation, it might be that mentally refocusing one's attention is more effective in reaching a theoretical conclusion than giving oneself a slap to the face and muttering "get a grip!"

Another familiar obstacle to our ND abilities to think and act for good reasons is lack of inspiration. Wit without a set of topics to organize it is challenging, and new philosophical insights are often promoted by being asked new questions. To enhance their ND abilities people will take advantage of available sources of inspiration: glance about for topics to comment on or listen to the very particular cadences of a conversational partner's speech, if one hopes to find something witty to say, or encourage a conversational partner to "never mind how other people think about the problem, just tell me whatever you think" when seeking to jump-start philosophical insight. In addition, there are acts of deliberation that can cope with a dearth of inspiration in the external world, and in this way enhance ND abilities just as overt action might. If Heather is planning to make a funny speech at a wedding and finds herself lacking for inspiration she could take overt actions that might help, such a browsing through photos of the bride and groom to be. But she might also engage in deliberative acts, such as calling to mind things that comedians often talk about, in the hope of stumbling across a topic of humor that particularly suits the people involved or the ceremonial occasion. And it might be that on a given occasion Heather would be better off turning to the world outside her head for inspiration, while on another occasion her best bet would be to turn inward and rely on deliberation.

One more example worth mentioning is found when beliefs (and perhaps also plans, desires, and the like) are not at the foreground of our awareness. If Harold's son asks him to meet in Calgary on Tuesday, Harold's thinking will tend to be most responsive to the contents of his mind that were just under discussion, and to those that are most linked (by association?) to the ideas of meeting, Calgary, and Tuesday. Harold's thinking will also tend to reflect ideas that he has dwelt on recently, especially ones he has dwelt on repeatedly. But Harold is in some danger of not taking into account facts he knows but about which he has not much thought recently in any guise. If, for instance, Harold had agreed five weeks ago to lunch with someone on the 20th, and Tuesday falls on the 20th, and going to Calgary requires departing well before lunch, this is much less likely to come to his mind than a regular Tuesday meeting of the city's Planning Council. Things one believes (plans, desires...) but is not thinking about at the moment seem less efficacious in influencing one's thoughts, even when relevant, than things equally believed (planned, desired...) but currently or recently thought about, all else being equal. Automatic use of unconscious information is clearly possible (we spontaneously use relevant facts all the time without first consciously thinking them to ourselves) but it is also clearly not perfect. Fortunately, there are a number of overt acts one can take to combat the problem: Harold can keep a day planner and consult it, for instance. However, acts of deliberation by their nature bring ideas and images into consciousness, and so are also excellent vehicles for the promotion of neglected facts. This use of deliberation will work so long as something (some ND process that guides deliberative acts) causes the act of deliberation to focus on the buried information in the first place. To make it more likely that we will recall such buried information, we use a number of techniques in deliberation: going over a conclusion or an argument again, "looking" (as we say) for potential problems. (If we are skilled deliberators, we tend to use techniques such as putting the same ideas into different "words," or approaching them from a different organizational principle or perspective, in order to enhance the probability that we will call to mind buried information).

All the deliberative acts just described would themselves be actions performed for reasons as the result of ND processes. When deliberation is brought to bear to enhance the efficacy of ND abilities to think and act for reasons, it does not do so as an alien intrusion into an ND process. Rather, deliberation is brought to bear as its own sort of action performed through ND processes that make the deliberative acts themselves more or less reasonable acts: reasonable at promoting the end of enhancing our ability to think about other things, and act in other ways, for good reasons.

We make no claim to the previously mentioned four roles for deliberation being exhaustive.[1] All four roles for deliberation illustrate something important, however. Deliberation is not something that stands apart from our capacities to think and act without deliberation. Deliberation is not something that brings some distinctive capacity—Reason—to bear. Deliberation is rather the deployment of our preexisting capacities to think and act for reasons; deployment of these capacities upon our own minds, in order to improve their operations. Considering the entirely common ways in which deliberation improves the operations of our ND capacities to think and act for reasons reveals how little deliberation is like a unique capacity for Reason, and how much it is like our ability to see what to do and do it without further comment.

2.2 How Deliberation Works

How deliberation works—the mechanisms by which deliberative acts take place—is an empirical topic about which armchair philosophy should be modest. The question is not the introspectively accessible one: What sequences of conscious thoughts and images are typical when one is engaged in deliberation? The question is the mechanistic one: How are these typical sequences of conscious thoughts and images produced when one is deliberating? And questions about the mechanisms that underlie what happens in consciousness are questions that science is typically better placed to answer than philosophy. Nonetheless, this section will sketch a speculative and partial answer to the question. The goal is not so much to answer the mechanistic question correctly as it is to show that it is *possible* to answer the mechanistic question, but of course we will also aim for correctness along the way.[2]

Consider again the story of Harold. He wishes to determine whether to agree to meet his son in Calgary. His son outlines the facts over the phone: the son will be flying into Calgary on Tuesday at noon; he would appreciate being met at the airport by his father. Harold could say, "yes, I'll meet you" right

---

[1] One more interesting role for deliberation: sometimes a person (usually a philosopher) realizes in deliberation that she has been thinking that P and that P implies Q, and it is only with the realization that her thoughts have been logically related in this way that she goes on to draw the conclusion Q. Of course, being able to do this in deliberation presupposes a nondeliberative capacity to draw conclusions on the basis of one's reasons (that one believes things entailing P is a reason to conclude P, and one must be responsive to *this* reason independently of deliberation in this case, on pain of regress). Metalevel beliefs can help bring about reasonableness in one's beliefs and actions, and deliberation is one good occasion for forming such beliefs.

[2] That is, we aim to answer the sort of "how possibly" question that Jerry Fodor made central to much of his own work.

away, or he could say, "no, I can't," or he could even say, "ducks do not lay chicken eggs." He could also throw the telephone into the sink. But he does not do any of these things. Instead, he deliberates. Why?

The short answer is that Harold desires to figure out what to do and sees deliberation as the best means to obtain this goal. None of this reaches his consciousness, however. As Philip Pettit and Michael Smith suggest,[3] desires stay "in the background" in situations like this, and so Harold does not bring to mind his desire to know what to do, or his other relevant desires: they simply influence his mental processes without being thought of. Harold wants not to break his promises, and at the moment at which his son asks about Calgary Harold is not certain about the promises he has made; he believes it to be all too likely that he has made a promise that would have to be broken if he were to meet his son in Calgary, but he is far from certain that this is the case. Somewhere in the back of his mind he knows that he has promised to attend a meeting of the city's Planning Council, and he knows the date of that meeting, and that date is the same date as the date on which his son will be in Calgary, and so on. But most of this knowledge is not effective in influencing his action at the very moment when his son asks to meet him in Calgary. It could have been—perhaps it would have been, if Harold had been looking at his plans for the month earlier in the day. And then perhaps Harold would not have deliberated, and would instead have immediately answered, "oh, no, I have a meeting of the city's Planning Council." But for whatever reason, Harold's knowledge about the meeting was not poised to influence his action immediately. Instead, Harold's belief that he *might* have a conflicting promise was poised to influence his action immediately. Harold does not have a strong practical conviction: he does not know what to do. But he desires to know what to do. Combined with his desire to not break his promises, and no doubt a number of other beliefs (that his son will not be disturbed if there is a moment of silence at this point in the phone call, and so on), Harold's belief that he does not know what to do, and his belief that deliberation might help, lead him to begin deliberation.

Notice that Harold's beginning deliberation is itself something he does not deliberate upon. It is the product of his ND capacities to act for good reasons.

Harold's deliberation is itself a complex sequence of actions, and the first of these is to hold in mind the idea (or auditory image of his saying) that his son is coming on Tuesday the 20th. Why does Harold do this, specifically? It is because he knows (without needing to bring it to mind consciously) that, if he wishes to remember what he has promised to do on a given day, it is often effective to simply hold the idea of that day vividly in mind. Under these conditions, his plans for that day, promised and otherwise, will spontaneously come to consciousness. And this recollection will greatly decrease the chance that he

---

[3] Pettit and Smith (1990).

will make a promise to his son that is in conflict with a promise he has already made to someone else. So Harold holds the idea in mind. This action, holding the idea in mind, is not a *product* of his deliberation but one of the acts that *constitute* his deliberation. It is a manifestation of Harold's ND capacities to take reasonable mental actions when he wants to determine what to do.

The result of Harold's holding the idea in mind is, suppose, that he recalls the meeting of the Planning Council. This result is something that Harold brings about through his mental activity, but it is best thought of as a *result* of this activity rather than something he directly controls, in the same way that it is best to think of launching a kite as the result of something directly controlled (running with the kite, hoisting it into the air...) along with things not directly controlled (the gusting of the wind, the shape of the kite...). Harold holds a thought in mind, and this results in him having another thought (or auditory image, or the like). Perhaps he says to himself, "oh, the Planning Council!" As he does so, his belief that he has committed to a meeting of the Planning Council on Tuesday the 20th becomes conscious, and so much more able to influence his actions than it was before when it was unconscious.

At this point, suppose, Harold takes another deliberative step. He tries to recall the time at which the Planning Council meets. Again, this deliberative step shows Harold's imperfect rationality. Harold already knows when the Planning Council is meeting, so if he were more nearly perfectly rational he would say to himself when the Planning Council meets. If he were even more nearly perfect he would skip this talking-to-himself intermediate step and simply tell his son that he has a conflicting promise and cannot meet him in Calgary. However, since Harold's knowledge of when the Planning Council meets is not effectively influencing Harold's behavior, and since Harold knows that he has this information stored in his memory, Harold has a strategy suited to imperfectly rational agents like himself: he can try to recall the time of the meeting, and this effort is likely to succeed in bringing the correct time to mind (and very unlikely to bring an incorrect time to mind). So Harold tries to recall, and is rewarded with success. The idea comes to his consciousness that the meeting is scheduled for 1 p.m.

With the meeting scheduled for 1 p.m., there is no way that Harold can be in Calgary at noon and be back in time for the meeting. And not only does Harold contain the knowledge necessary to derive this conclusion, but it also happens (we can imagine) that his knowledge is brought to bear via ND processes to derive the conclusion without further voluntary effort on Harold's part. Perhaps what happens now is that the derived belief becomes conscious: a thought occurs in Harold's mind to the effect that the Planning Council meeting conflicts with meeting his son in Calgary.

From here, perhaps, Harold, again motivated by desires that do not enter his consciousness, simply tells his son, "I would love to meet you, but unfortunately I have a meeting of the Planning Council at 1 p.m. on that day." Harold's deliberation has concluded, and he has reached a decision about what to do. But notice how much happens between Harold's last deliberative act and his utterance: Harold has incorporated his knowledge of the sequence in which he made his promises (without bringing this knowledge to consciousness), weighed his intrinsic desire to keep promises against his intrinsic desire to share his life with his son (without either of these desires affecting his consciousness), and factored in various other mundane beliefs (without any of them reaching consciousness either). All of this activity happens without the need for deliberation or any other voluntary behavior on Harold's part: he reaches his practical conclusion (and reaches the practical conclusion to tell his son, and in what words to tell him) from his final deliberative point via the influence of a number of key attitudes that all play the roles they need to play for his conclusion(s) to be reasonable.

2.3 The Moral of the Story

What deliberation does, when it enhances thinking and acting for reasons, is to act to remove barriers to the ND processes through which we normally think and act for reasons. Perhaps it is true that, as children, we first learn the value of talking to our parents, then learn the value of talking to ourselves aloud, and finally learn the value of voluntarily generating auditory images of our voices, as a means of drawing more reasonable conclusions about what to believe and do. But even if this is not true of ontogeny, it is a suitable myth for the present view. Deliberation is not the foundation of our ability to think and act for reasons but a tactic we have for enhancing our preexisting, and foundational, capacities to think and act for reasons: our ND capacities.

Because this is the role of deliberation, the value of deliberation is intermittent, contingent, and in some ways modest.

It is intermittent because sometimes we think and act for reasons without recourse to deliberation, and at other times we are better able to enhance our abilities to think and act for good reasons through turning off the noise in the background than through deliberation. Sometimes we should not deliberate about what to do, and just drive; other times, deliberation is a far better idea than just plunging forward and working out what to do "on the fly."

The value of deliberation is contingent because, so far as we can see, there is no reason in principle that we have to be designed such that blood sugar, strong emotions, ambient noise, lack of recent conscious attention, or even computational tractability is able to disrupt our ability to think and act for good reasons. There could exist creatures whose ND abilities to think and act for good reasons are flawless, or close to it. For such superhuman creatures, all deliberation would be a waste of time, in the way it would be a waste of time on our parts to deliberate on trivial, obvious topics (what is 5 plus 9? should

I brush my teeth at exactly thirteen minutes to the hour, every hour?).[4] There are animals incapable of seeing at a glance that a reaching device must be used in order to secure a certain banana, but we are capable of this feat. There are human beings among us who are capable of seeing at a glance that 39 goes into 351 nine times, while others of us are not capable of this feat. (There are also reports of savants capable of seeing at a glance that certain five-digit numbers are prime.[5] Though the power is mysterious, we see no reason to deny that these savants grasp what they do for excellent reasons, unaided by deliberation.) Why then should there not be possible creatures who can see at a glance what to do to bring the world to a just global peace, or what to think about the correspondence theory of truth? These creatures are possible, though they would be very unlike us indeed.

There could also be creatures who have all of our difficulties with ND reason-responding, but who also have trouble controlling their behavior if they start deliberating about a question. These creatures would be ones who, once started on the question of whether or not to have a precise time for brushing their teeth, would have trouble doing anything other than brushing their teeth for the rest of the afternoon. They would be like obsessive-compulsives who would be prone to developing topics of obsession and compulsion from dwelling on them in thought. These creatures are possible, if less well-adapted to a world like ours than we ourselves are.

It is only a contingent fact that the Earth is populated by neither sort of creature: neither creatures who are rationally perfect without deliberation nor creatures who are grossly impaired by it. We have great need of our powers of deliberation. But things need not have been this way; what deliberation does for us is not expressive of *its* nature so much as it is expressive of *our* nature: for others deliberation would be otiose or systematically harmful, but given the kinds of creatures we are deliberation is a tremendous boon.

Finally, the role of deliberation is modest in that deliberation can fail to respond correctly to reasons just as much as other actions can. Deliberation can fail to call to mind the neglected but vital fact, can look in worthless places for inspiration, can fail to shut out the distractions that are making it so hard to draw any conclusions at all, can take us to the wrong step in an attempt to solve a problem sequentially. It can focus our attention on certain facts that support one conclusion while diverting our attention from other, equally known, facts that support another (better supported) conclusion. Deliberation is a valuable but imperfect tool for improving our more valuable but even more imperfect abilities to think and act for reasons without it.

---

[4] These creatures might still have reasons to deliberate publicly, i.e., to reason with each other, of course.

[5] See Sacks (1985).

Insofar as deliberation was taken to be Reason, to be our distinctively non-beastly capacity to engage the world intellectually, it turns out that Reason plays a limited, contingent, and modest role in human life. Reason is not what makes it possible to think or act for reasons. Reason, rather, is a wonderful tool for enhancing our beastly abilities to think and act for reasons: our ND abilities.

{ 3 }

Thinking and Acting for Reasons

Nondeliberative, nonreflective, nonvoluntary processes *must* explain thinking and acting for reasons, but one might reasonably wonder how they *could*. Understanding these ND processes is the main project of this chapter. With an understanding of thinking and acting for reasons in hand, the chapter will end with Spare Conativism's account of acting for moral reasons.

3.1 Objective Reasons and Rationalizing Reasons

There has come to be widespread agreement in moral philosophy that reasons are, by and large, things outside of human heads.[1] Harold has a reason to call to mind his obligations in the coming days when thinking about whether or not to promise to meet his son in Calgary, and his reason to call his obligations to mind is that he might be obliged to be elsewhere that day. This possibility is the reason for Harold to deliberate as he does, not Harold's belief in the possibility of conflicting obligations. Similarly, Kiyoshi might have a reason to add salt to his soup, because the soup is unsalted. The fact that the soup is unsalted is his reason and not, say, his desire that the soup be salted. Call these sorts of reasons "objective reasons."

At the same time, acting for reasons and thinking for reasons cannot be understood by unqualified appeal to the sorts of reasons just mentioned.[2] Suppose it is true that Kiyoshi has a reason to salt the soup, because it is unsalted. But suppose that Kiyoshi does not believe that the soup is unsalted: perhaps he inattentively shook an empty saltshaker over the soup. Without the relevant belief, it seems obvious that Kiyoshi is incapable of salting the soup *for the*

---

[1] This thesis is shared in the otherwise very different views of, e.g., Dancy (2000), Scanlon (1998), and Schroeder (2008). Interestingly, things are not so straightforward in epistemology.

[2] Dancy (2000) makes the best case we know of for doing so within moral psychology. Interestingly, although Ruth Millikan has never joined this moral-psychological debate, her position on the explanation of behavior appears to put her quite close to Dancy: see Millikan (1993, chapters 7, 8, 14). But even if one denies every sort of epistemic and practical internalism, one must still acknowledge the superior qualities of a person who reasons from false premises using *modus ponens* as compared to her counterpart who reasons from the same false premises using *argumentum ad hominem*. These qualities, whether correctly called "rationality" or not, are our target of interest.

reason in question. Kiyoshi might be acting for a reason if he "further" salts his soup, but he cannot be acting for the reason that his soup is unsalted if he does not believe that the soup is unsalted. And suppose, in a complementary fashion, that Kiyoshi has no reason to salt the soup, because the soup has already been salted. Unbeknownst to him, a family member already added salt to his soup. Kiyoshi believes that his soup is unsalted. Accordingly, he salts his soup. Although we might say that he had no reason to salt his soup, it would also be odd to say that Kiyoshi acted for no reason and normal to say he acted for a *good* reason, and that he would have acted unreasonably if he did not salt his soup.

There are various ways to address Kiyoshi's situations and a common one would be to distinguish objective reasons and subjective reasons.[3] We will put the point this way: a distinction is needed between objective reasons and *rationalizing* reasons. In the first case, Kiyoshi has an objective reason but lacks a rationalizing reason; in the second case, Kiyoshi lacks an objective reason but has a rationalizing reason.

Objective epistemic reasons are determined by the facts of the world, whether or not they are believed in. Rationalizing epistemic reasons for a person are determined by what a person believes to be the facts of the world, rather than the actual facts.[4] Similarly, objective practical reasons are determined by something that prioritizes possible states of affairs (something that might be independent of desires,[5] or largely independent,[6] or identical to[7] desires) plus the facts of the world, whether or not they are believed in. And rationalizing practical reasons are determined by whatever prioritizes possible states of affairs plus what a person believes to be the facts of the world, rather than the actual facts.

One might object to the idea that there are rationalizing reasons after noting how we reason, both publicly and in private deliberation.[8] Suppose Hyacinth believes that a student of hers is probably from Goa. Asked what her reasons are for believing this, she says, "the student looks Indian but her name sounds Portuguese. That's quite rare in people who aren't from Goa." That is, she produces putative objective reasons. These putative objective reasons are putative facts about the student and Goa. They are not beliefs, though they are the referential contents of Hyacinth's beliefs (they are *what* she believes). Likewise, if she were simply thinking to herself it would be odd and out of place for her to

---

[3] The distinction between subjective and objective reasons and "oughts" is ubiquitous. See, for example, Dancy (2000), Parfit (1997), Smith (1994).

[4] And perhaps also perceptual states, if these are distinct from beliefs.

[5] We are not familiar with any view that takes such a strong position in print, but it is available in principle and has been advanced for our consideration in conversation.

[6] See, e.g., Dancy (2000), Scanlon (1998).

[7] See, e.g., Schroeder (2008).

[8] Drawing, perhaps, on Darwall (2001).

consider her beliefs rather than to consider the apparent facts, i.e., the contents of her beliefs.[9]

However, for her belief that her student is from Goa to be rationally justifiable, Hyacinth needs to have the relevant beliefs. The facts alone do not make Hyacinth's belief rational, even if they obtain: she needs to believe in the facts. If she did not have her beliefs about Goans, their names, and their looks, and if, nonetheless, knowing her student only by face and name, she developed the belief that the student must be from Goa (of all places!), she would be epistemically irrational in so believing. Developing a belief, no matter what role was played by the objective reasons themselves, *in the absence of the relevant supporting beliefs* would be developing a strong conviction for no reason at all: both colloquially and philosophically speaking.[10]

Likewise, Hyacinth's belief need not be true in order for it to be rationally justified. Her thinking is perfectly reasonable even if her student happens to have adopted a Portuguese name in an effort to shake off her past as a child movie star in Mumbai.

Thus, although people's discussions of their reasons to believe appeal to putative objective reasons, these putative objective reasons are the contents of their beliefs, and their rationality itself is dependent upon their beliefs. Hence our term "rationalizing reasons."

In the same way, an action can be rationalized by an intrinsic desire—its rationality can depend on an intrinsic desire—even if the objective reason for the action is not a desire, and even if clear-headed deliberation about what to do would never bring up the existence of that intrinsic desire. Martha's objective reason to help Nicola might simply be the fact that Nicola is in pain, but it can simultaneously be true that what makes it possible for Martha to help Nicola on the basis of that reason is, in part, her intrinsic desire that people not be in pain. The claim that Martha's intrinsic desire is a part of her rationalizing reason to help does not entail that the intrinsic desire is involved in constituting her objective reason. And likewise, Martha's deliberation need never have considered the fact that Martha intrinsically desires that people not be in pain for her desire to play its role in rationalizing her action.

Are rationalizing reasons the same as what have been called "subjective reasons"? In one sense, they clearly are. If Bernie thinks that a glass holds gin while it in fact holds petrol, Bernie has a rationalizing reason to drink the liquid

---

[9] Though occasionally one has reason to use the fact that one has a belief as a premise. Since this is a rare complication, though, we would not want to rest any argument on the phenomenon.

[10] There are complicated debates in epistemology about whether or not a person who was a reliable psychic, but who did not believe he was a reliable psychic, could have any positive epistemic status in holding his psychically derived beliefs. But we are not imagining Hyacinth to have reliable psychic access to people's places of birth. See BonJour (1985, 37f.) for one discussion of the epistemological complexities. And similarly, we set aside the complications surrounding basic perceptual beliefs.

that is in the glass because of his subjective state, and one might say that in this subjective state Bernie has a subjective reason. But there are at least two ways in which it could be misleading to call rationalizing reasons "subjective."

First, the term "subjective" suggests, if only by connotation, a sort of transparency to the thinker or actor that we reject for rationalizing reasons. A person can think and act for reasons, and so can have rationalizing reasons, even if she experiences herself as acting for no reason at all. Similarly, a person can believe she is thinking or acting for one set of reasons while actually thinking or acting for another, as we discussed back in chapter 1.

A second way in which it would be misleading to call rationalizing reasons "subjective" is tied to inference. While a false belief can be a rationalizing reason, a bad inference typically is not, even if the agent believes it to be a good one. That is, the agent's subjective stance toward her reasoning does not affect her rationalizing reasons. Suppose Hannah believes that *if* she owes taxes *then* she must submit a tax return, and believes that she does not owe taxes. If she concludes, through denying the antecedent, that she need not submit a tax return, then no amount of confidence in her inference can make Hannah into someone who believes the conclusion for a good reason.[11] In this sense, there is nothing subjective about rationalizing reasons. They might be mental states of subjects, but they rationalize what they do in virtue of their logical or probabilistic relations to one another and not in virtue of what the subject takes them to rationalize. As all-too-fallible human beings, we often think we are responding to good reasons just as we are being swayed by other forces; we think irrationally when we mistakenly think that we are rational.[12] It is possible for the belief that our reasoning is good to be part of our rationale for thinking or acting as we do, but it is rare, and certainly not compulsory. To assume otherwise is to hold Recognition, as discussed in chapter 1, and so is to make an assumption that leads straight to regresses and other problems.

3.2 Physical Properties, Contents, and Reasons

With clarifications out of the way, it is time to begin to explain thinking and acting for (rationalizing) reasons. The place to begin is with mental causation.

---

[11] There is a rich literature on the possible rationality of certain formally invalid forms of inference that we ignore here (see, e.g., Harman 1986; Stich 1990). We have no strong commitment to any particular theory of reasons to believe or reasons to act, and so we overlook this literature only for the sake of having a simple example.

[12] Hence books like Ariely's (2008) *Predictably Irrational*. These ideas are treated at length in Arpaly (2000; 2003 chapter 2).

So long as some sensible form of materialism is true, mental events[13] are found in a dense causal network located within our skulls. This causal network includes causes that are best thought of as merely physical (or chemical, or biological), causes that are best thought of as involving contents but not rationalizing reasons, and causes that are best thought of as involving rationalizing reasons.

That there are processes within us that are physical is hardly controversial. One neuron's increase in firing rate causes another neuron to increase its own rate of firing in virtue of the quantity and type of neurotransmitter reaching the second neuron from the first, and so on.

Some of these physical processes are also psychological, in that they realize mental processes. Others are *merely* physical. Perhaps Kepa learns that very few citizens of Israel speak Yiddish. Because his brain has a finite capacity to store knowledge, his learning causes him to forget something he learned long ago: that Rarotonga is the largest of the Cook Islands. The loss is caused without the content of either belief being causally efficacious in the process. Some merely physical process "pushes out" the old belief as the new one is "pushed in." (This is probably not exactly how such memories work, but the example illustrates the idea.)

Now suppose the thought of meeting her one o'clock class fills Emma with dismay. One neural event, her thinking of the class, causes another neural event, her being dismayed,[14] and it is no coincidence that the first neural event was about meeting students while the second was dismay. If Emma had thought, not about her class but about, say, frogs, her thought would not have elicited dismay. This suggests that the thought about her class elicited the dismay *because of* the thought's content.

There are a number of theories within the philosophy of mind that are especially congenial to the thesis that sometimes we feel, think, or act a certain way because of the contents of other mental events. For our purposes, all these theories are equally acceptable.[15] Theories of causation within the mind that are not obviously friendly to the relevance of mental contents can also be compatible with the modest present theoretical requirements, however.

Donald Davidson, for example, is well known for holding that it makes no sense to attribute causal powers to the properties of events. According

---

[13] Or mental states, if states are the things that stand in causal relations. We do not mean to be making a commitment one way or another on this issue. The case for events is most famously made in Davidson (1980, chapters 6 through 10).

[14] Because this is not a work in the philosophy of mind, we allow ourselves a certain shorthand for convenience, and will sometimes write about mental states as being identical to brain states when we actually prefer the view that mental states are merely realized by brain states.

[15] Theories holding that mental contents are causally significant include, but are hardly limited to, those found in Dretske (1988), Fodor (1990, chapter 5), and Jackson, Pettit, and Smith (2004, chapters 3–6).

to Davidson, only events as such stand in causal relations.[16] It might be that someone finds it helpful to explain one event by appealing to the properties of another event that caused it. But all the explainer is doing, Davidson holds, is describing the event that, in itself, has the metaphysical power to cause.[17]

It follows from Davidson's view that there is no sense to talking about whether the physical properties of a group of neurons or the content properties of those neurons caused some mental event. But there is no need for us to object. Perhaps properties do not have distinguished roles in the metaphysics of causation. Even if so, there is still some principled account of why explanatory practices in the natural and social sciences fix on certain explanations, invoking certain properties of causes, as acceptable and others as not. Something, however distant from fundamental physics or metaphysics, explains what is particularly good about putative explanations in social psychology such as *black cats tend not to be adopted because people have superstitions about them* and what is particularly bad about putative explanations such as *black cats tend not to be adopted because people have the neural configurations they do*, even though people's having the neural configurations they do is (in part) their having the superstitions they do. This principled way of preferring some property-based causal explanations over others sometimes prefers certain explanations given in terms of mental contents (since good psychology is rife with these sorts of explanations). In these cases, the contents can be counted as causally explanatory properties for our purposes: nothing more physically or metaphysically fundamental is required.[18]

Of course, every theory of causation faces certain challenges that apply, *a fortiori*, to theories of mental causation. How, for instance, does the theory distinguish between genuine causation in virtue of properties and pseudo-causation in which a demon or its natural equivalent observes one event and then brings about another because the first has the properties it does? This seems to be a perennially good and challenging question for almost every theory of causation or causal explanation. But because it is just as good a question when asked about the causation of window-breaking events by brick-tossing events as it is when asked about the causation of willing-that-P events by desiring-that-Q and thinking-P-makes-Q-likely events, it is a question that we leave to theorists of causation. The metaphysics of brick-and-window causation needs some answer to such questions, however pragmatic or nonfoundational it might be, and what brick-and-window metaphysics needs Spare Conativism can presuppose. A similar approach can also be taken to the other familiar problems in

---

[16] See, e.g., Davidson (1980, chapters 6–11).

[17] This perhaps overlooks some nuances in Davidson's thought. See Davidson (1993) and Kim (1993).

[18] A similar approach can be taken to dealing with the difficulties for causation in virtue of content raised in Kim (1998).

the theory of causation: how to understand overdetermination, preemption, causation by absence, and so on.

The causal efficacy or explanatory relevance of mental content is necessary for our ND capacities to think and act for reasons, and indeed for any capacity to think or act for reasons. Without it, it would not be true that Kenneth talked to Barbara because he wanted to visit her; it would not be true that Barbara believed that Kenneth lives in Malibu because she remembers that he told her so. So we embrace such causal efficacy or explanatory relevance.

Content is necessary, but it is not sufficient. One mental state can cause another because of its content without reasons being involved. For example, the thought that palm trees are flowering plants can make Neil think to himself that Stanford has a philosophy department, and do so simply because of an association in his memory: his mind leaps from the first thought to the second because Neil associates palm trees with Stanford. This does not appear to be a case of thinking something for a reason. Neither consciously nor unconsciously does Neil infer that Stanford has a department from the fact that palm trees are flowering plants. It is not just that this inference would be foolish, because of course Neil is quite capable of foolish inferences. It is that the process of free association by which Neil moves from the first thought to the second is not an inferential process in any sense. There is some *merely* content-based connection between the ideas of palm trees and Stanford university, generated by his past experiences, that explains the progression from one thought to the other.

It is even possible to imagine cases in which there is a reason to believe conclusion Q given premise P but the passage in the mind from P to Q is nonetheless not undertaken for that reason. Neil believes that Stanford has many palm trees on its campus and therefore, when he thinks that palm trees are flowering plants, he has a reason to conclude that Stanford has flowering plants. However, perhaps what happens to Neil when he thinks that palm trees are flowering plants is different. Palms remind him of Stanford, because he knows Stanford has many palms. With thoughts of Stanford and flowering plants on his mind he free-associates, remembers some flowers he saw at Stanford, and reaches the thought that Stanford has many flowering plants, without ever inferring it from his belief that Stanford has many palms.

What holds for beliefs holds also for actions. There are well-known situations in which bodily events are explained by the contents of mental states but not by reasons. (In these cases, the bodily event is typically not an action, precisely because of the disconnection between it and practical reasons.)[19] Crying is one such event. If the thought that he is too plain in appearance

---

[19] We suspect something can be a belief even if it is caused in a way that is 100% insensitive to reasons, while nothing can be an action if it is so caused. Perhaps this is because of the gap between immediate intentions (see later in the chapter) and bodily movements, a gap not found in the case of belief.

to be a movie star makes a man cry, it makes him cry because of its content, but thoughts about appearance do not make it reasonable to secrete heavily from one's tear ducts. One could say that the man has a reason to cry, but that would be shorthand for saying that his *sadness* is warranted, not the crying itself.[20] Similar bodily changes include stiffening with tension, trembling with anger, and becoming engorged with blood in one's sexual organs. Some facial expressions also appear responsive to the contents of beliefs and desires without being performed because of practical reasons to perform them.

There is thus a gap between thoughts and behaviors that are sensitive to the contents of mental events and thoughts believed, or actions performed, for reasons. Some, but not all, of the thoughts that are sensitive to the contents of other mental events are thought for reasons. Some, but not all, of the behaviors that are sensitive to the contents of mental events are actions performed for reasons. What, then, is the extra ingredient, in addition to being explained by mental contents, that is required to think or do something for a reason? Some, most famously Davidson,[21] would say that an action done for a reason is caused by attitudes that rationalize it, and some would say analogously that a belief that is believed for a reason is caused by attitudes that rationalize it. Is that enough? With belief, the case of Neil and the palm trees suggests that it is not.

Thomas Nagel[22] and Christine Korsgaard[23] have raised this same problem for the case of action in a particularly pointed manner. Consider a person who, having a desire for a soda, puts a coin in what he believes to be a soda machine. This is a person who appears to act for a reason, but perhaps he does not. They imagine, first, a person who has been conditioned in such a way that whenever he wants to drink and whenever he believes that the object in front of him is a pencil sharpener he puts a coin into the pencil sharpener. (The person in the example is imagined to have ordinary beliefs about pencil sharpeners. He does not, for example, have the delusion that they dispense drinks.) This person clearly does not act for a reason. But now, imagine a person who has been similarly conditioned in such a way that whenever he wants to drink and believes that the object in front of him is a soda machine he puts a coin into the soda machine. One is tempted, they say, to point to the different conceptual relation that exists between the belief that an object is a soda machine, the desire

---

[20] Warrant for emotions such as sadness is a complex topic, and one we will not investigate in depth. If emotions are, or involve, representations, beliefs, or desires then there will be straightforward explanations of at least some ascriptions of warrant to emotions. But if emotions do not involve beliefs or desires, or do not involve them in the right way to explain all of the ways in which we hold that emotions can be warranted, then things will be more complex. Compare, for example, the views found in De Sousa (1987), Green (1992), Nussbaum (2001), and Prinz (2004) to see the range of ways in which differing theories of emotions can lead to different ideas of warrant for emotions. Compare also the work of D'Arms and Jacobson (2000).

[21] Davidson (1980, chapter 1).
[22] Nagel (1970, 33–34).
[23] Korsgaard (2008).

to drink, and the instrumental desire to put a coin in the soda machine. After all, one desires to drink, one believes that by putting a coin in a soda machine one would obtain a drink, one believes the object before one is a soda machine, and so one develops the instrumental desire to put the coin in the object before one. Thus the belief that something is a soda machine and the desire to drink are related to each other in a way that the belief that something is a pencil sharpener is not related to the desire to drink. But this is not enough to explain why the soda-machine user is acting rationally and is thus distinguishable from the person who puts coins in pencil sharpeners. Pointing out that the belief and the desire of the soda-machine user have a reasonable connection does not show that a person is acting rationally on them, since the person could just as easily have been conditioned to act on the mad belief-desire pair that the pencil-sharpener user has. Thus the rationality of the soda-machine user cannot be shown by appealing to the fact that the belief and the desire caused his action nor by the fact that the belief and the desire relate to each other in a reasonable way, nor by appealing to the mere conjunction of these facts.

We agree with Nagel and Korsgaard that acting for a reason is not just a matter of being caused to do what one has reason to do by attitudes such as beliefs and desires that might be said to rationalize one's action. Yet we also deny that there can be a foundational appeal to deliberation (past, present, or possible) in explaining acting for reasons. As we showed in chapter 1, the basic explanation of what it is to think or act for a reason must appeal to something that can itself be nondeliberative and nonvoluntary, something that does not explicitly represent things as reasons but merely responds to things because they are reasons.

3.3 Because of Reasons

How can thinking and acting for reasons be a causal process, when causation by attitudes with rationalizing contents does not guarantee thinking or acting for reasons? Consider another example.

Natasha believes that cats are silly and believes that Bob is a cat. These beliefs might well produce, consciously or otherwise, the belief that Bob is silly. The contents of the two beliefs explain the formation of the third belief, but a full explanation Natasha's change in beliefs might well involve more than the mere content of her beliefs. A full explanation of how the two beliefs led to the third might well be an explanation that involves the fact that the contents of the two beliefs *entail* the content of the third. It was not a coincidence or a free-associative leap that led her to think that Bob is silly, but logic. Likewise, if Xiaoxi looks at the clock because she wants to know the time and believes that looking at the clock will tell her the time, it is not enough to say that her looking at the clock is causally explained by her believing this and desiring that. A full explanation of what Xiaoxi does in looking at the clock will in all likelihood appeal to the fact that there was a practical entailment between her attitudes and her looking at the clock: looking at the clock was practically justified, given Xiaoxi's desire and her belief, and this is relevant to explaining why Xiaoxi looked at the clock. She did not just happen to look at the clock by coincidence or by a kind of practical free-association. Her looking is explained, not only by a belief and a desire that rationalize her looking, but also by the relationship between the belief's content and the desire's content: she looks because her belief and desire rationalize her looking.

The key ingredient in thinking and acting for reasons that has so far been missing is that of being causally moved in part by the fact that one has a rationalization for so thinking or acting.

> *To think or act for a reason* is for the event of one's thinking or acting to be caused (or appropriately causally explained) by one's other attitudes in virtue of the fact that these attitudes rationalize (to some extent) the thought or action.[24]

This theory could use some elaboration. What exactly is it for some attitudes to rationalize others? And how does causation in virtue of rationalization make sense?

Consider first the nature of rationalization. There are many different theories of epistemic and practical rationalization: of the attitudes and contents that make particular beliefs and actions more or less rational. Natasha's beliefs about Bob the cat conveniently entail her conclusion about him, but a survey of theories of epistemic and practical rationality suggests that rationalization is not likely to be limited to syllogistic entailment. Most theories allow or, indeed, require more complex logical relations than syllogistic entailment.

The moral psychologist should hold that the correct (normative) theory of epistemic rationality tells us what attitudes and contents rationalize a thought, while the correct (normative) theory of practical rationality tells us what attitudes and contents rationalize an action. And it is probably best for the moral psychologist to leave the determination of the former theory to epistemologists, and the determination of the latter theory to decision theorists. Certainly, for present purposes it is not necessary to wade into confirmation theory or rational choice theory or the like and settle just what rationalization amounts to. And similarly, for present purposes it is not necessary to wade into debates about whether formal theories of rationality should be constrained by certain

---

[24] This thesis was developed in Wedgwood (2006) and Arpaly (2006). The term "causation in virtue of rationalization" is derived from Anthony (1989) who in turn acknowledges Joe Levine. See also Bill Brewer (1995). We note here that, insofar as this is a theory of believing for a reason, it is also a theory of what is called the "basing relation" in epistemology. Although there are causal theories of believing for reasons in the epistemological literature (e.g., in Moser 1989), they are not the same as the theory defended here.

normative claims, for example, that there can never be a practical rationalization for doing what one knows will bring great suffering but no compensating good. A number of alternative theories of theoretical and practical rationalization should be mentioned, though, just to suggest the range of possibilities.

With respect to beliefs, perhaps it is true that large groups of beliefs rationalize (i.e., justify) other beliefs if and only if the large group entails the new belief. Or perhaps beliefs rationalize other beliefs to the extent that the large group makes the new belief probable, or to the extent that the new belief's content is the best explanation for how all the beliefs in the large group could be true. Perhaps one belief rationalizes forming another if forming the second is heuristically a good response to the first, given a goal of efficiently produced true beliefs. Perhaps beliefs are held with variable confidence, and the explicit or implicit probabilistic relations between them are what rationalize the revision of the confidence with which other beliefs are held. Perhaps only the totality of one's beliefs can rationalize a change in one belief; perhaps it is possible for a tiny subset of one's beliefs to rationalize a change in a belief.

With respect to actions, perhaps it is true that a large group of beliefs and intrinsic desires rationalize an action to the extent that the action is the one that is associated with the greatest expected satisfaction of the intrinsic desires. (In this case, it would turn out that, contra Davidson, it is not compulsory to hold that every action is rationalized by exactly one belief and exactly one desire.) Perhaps it is true instead that only practical syllogisms rationalize actions (in which case, Davidson would be vindicated on that point).[25,26] For this specific point, it might even be true that judgments of goodness rationalize actions to the extent that the actions are judged good, though of course we will presuppose that this is not correct on independent grounds. Going forward, we will take it for granted that something akin to maximizing expected satisfaction of intrinsic desires is what rationalizes action (while recognizing that some other theory might win out in the end).

Some philosophers will object that we cannot simply embrace the idea that intrinsic desires are required to rationalize actions without further comment, given how problematic the idea has been shown to be. But we propose a two-part strategy for deferring, rather than directly answering, this challenge. The first part asks the reader for a certain patience. This work is one long discussion of the role of intrinsic desires in moral psychology, and its picture of

---

[25] Davidson (1980, chapter 1).

[26] If we have anything to contribute to all this, it is perhaps to note the value of deliberation for increasing the range of beliefs that might rationally influence belief, and for increasing the range of beliefs and desires that might rationally influence action, as discussed in chapter 2. Deliberation appears to typically increase the rationality of the thoughts and actions produced after deliberation, suggesting that perfect rationality requires more than just taking into account currently conscious or otherwise "active" attitudes.

intrinsic desires might prove to be one that is more compatible with intrinsic desires rationalizing actions than the objector thinks just now. For example, chapter 11's discussion of addiction will reveal that the intrinsic desires of addicts are not nearly as strong as they appear, and hence do not provide nearly as strong rationalizations as they appear; nothing counter-intuitive need follow from the claim that intrinsic desires rationalize actions in the case of addiction. The second part of our strategy of deferral is to refer the reader to the work of other philosophers, such as Mark Schroeder's *Slaves of the Passions*,[27] which contains what we take to be some of the best arguments in defense of the theory that desires rationalize action. But since Schroeder has done this work, we will not repeat his efforts here. Admittedly, there are more objections to answer than even this two-part strategy can claim to address. But we will save dealing with them for another occasion.

There are reasons to worry that rationalizing relations such as logical entailment or conformity to the practical syllogism cannot play the required role in causation or scientifically acceptable causal explanation. This is the second thing to clarify about the proposed theory. Does it really make sense to say that one collection of neurons caused something to happen in another collection of neurons because the former was a set of beliefs that had for their contents the premises of a good argument while the latter was a belief that had as its content the conclusion?

We do not see causation in virtue of, or explanation by appeal to, logical relations as anything more than causation or explanation in virtue of contents plus the relationship between those contents. If causation or explanation in virtue of contents is acceptable (as it must be) then so too is causation or explanation in virtue of the relations between contentful states, including relations such as probabilifying, entailing, and the like.

There are a number of more familiar models for this sort of causation or causal explanation. For instance, the fact that the objects on the left pan of a scale have a mass two times as much as the objects on the right pan of the scale can cause, or explain, the moving down of the left pan and the moving up of the right. Here a number or a proportion enters into a causal or explanatory relation. And again, the fact that the diameter of the circle circumscribing the smallest cross-section of wooden block B is 10% greater than the diameter of hole H in a child's toy causes, or explains, the failure of the child to force block B through hole H. Abstract geometrical relations can be important to causal or explanatory relations just as numbers and proportions can. In the same way, there are logical relations that can be important

---

[27] Schroeder (2008).

to causal or explanatory relations within minds. There is no difference in kind between accepting that

> the child's pushing could not get the block through the hole because the diameter of the circle circumscribing the block's smallest cross-section was 10% greater than the diameter of the hole

and accepting that

> the two beliefs caused a third because the first belief's content was of the form $P \rightarrow Q$ and the second belief's content was of the form P, and the third's was of the form Q.

How could there be an ND process by which the logical (or probabilistic) relations between the contents of mental events cause or appropriately explain thoughts or actions? It might seem that deliberation is uniquely poised to answer this question. In deliberation one can survey the logical relations that hold (or that one believes to hold) between the various contents one believes and desires. If Katie is deliberating about the grammaticality of the expression "I'm loving" and she consciously thinks to herself that, if the phrase is in common use, then it is probably now grammatical, and if she then consciously thinks of many instances of the phrase in use, then she can see that her initial principle plus her examples entail the conclusion that "I'm loving" has probably become grammatical. So in deliberation it seems clear enough how logical relations between ideas can themselves be influential. In deliberation, one can become conscious of the fact that things one believes and wants stand in certain logical relations to one another, and this conscious thought can in turn be influential.

There is a gap in this putative explanation, however. Katie thinks certain thoughts that entail a conclusion, and thinks that her thoughts entail the conclusion. But just how these contents actually lead to Katie drawing the conclusion is not yet explained. Katie has not yet been distinguished from the Neil, who free associates to a conclusion he might have reached by logical inference, or from the characters imagined by Nagel and Korsgaard, who do much the same thing in the practical realm. Deliberation makes it clear how one can think *about* logical relations, but not how those logical relations themselves might actually be causally efficacious or explanatorily relevant. Rather than solving the problem, deliberation provides just another occasion on which the problem arises.

Electronic computers provide a model of how there could be a mechanism by means of which the logical relations between representations might be involved, causally or explanatorily, in the creation of other representations. The silicon chips carrying out basic computational operations have their physical states organized so that, for example, switch A and switch B must normally both be in the "on" position in order for switch C to go from the "off" position to "on," and in this way they can carry out transformations on the basis of whether switch A *and* switch B are in the "on" position: switch C's change from "off" to "on" happens because of the logical relation between what is represented by switch A and what is represented by switch B: the relation of conjunction (and other properties and relations as well, of course, some purely physical). At higher levels, electronic computers are able to respond to much more complex logical relations between states expressing complex representational contents.

One might wonder how something as simple as a logic gate could be different from the person imagined by Nagel and Korsgaard, who is merely conditioned so that whenever he wants to drink and believes that the object in front of him is a soda machine he puts a coin into the soda machine. In their appeals to plain causal relations, there is no difference between them. But there is a key difference in the way these causal relations are related to rationalizing relations. The man imagined by Nagel and Korsgaard is conditioned so that when he is in state A and state B (the first a specific desire, the second a specific belief), he performs action C. If a logical relation plays a role in causing or causally explaining action C, it is the relation of conjunction. But conjunction is not the logical relation that rationalizes performing action C when in state A and state B. It is something like the relation of being a practical syllogism, given that state A is a desire for soda and state B is a belief that a circumstance obtains (one in which action C will satisfy the desire for a soda). So action C is perhaps caused in part by a logical relation between states A and B, but it is not caused by the logical relation that rationalizes it. On the other hand, when a computer goes from representing A and representing B to representing A&B by having states with these contents related via an AND-gate, it is the same logical relation that causes the rationalized state and that rationalizes it. That is the key difference.

Since the point is thus made in principle, we feel justified in leaving it to science to provide us with the details. But perhaps it is worth pointing out, following Donald Hebb's pioneering work in neuroscience, that neurons can also be linked to one another in the manner of logic gates.[28] That is, two neurons can be linked to a third so that the third will not become active unless both the first *and* the second are active, or linked so that the third will not become active unless either the first *or* the second is active, or one neuron can be linked to a second so that the second will only be active when the first is *not* active. Given the actual biological characteristics of neurons, it is simple enough for nature to arrange them in these sorts of ways. And if this is true, then we have a first hint as to how there might be causation in virtue of rationalization. The full answer is best left to cognitive science or computational neuroscience, not to philosophy.

So far, the discussion has been about causation in virtue of logical or mathematical (e.g., probabilistic) relations. But causation in virtue of rationalization

---

[28] Hebb (1949). For a more modern take on neural computation, see, e.g., Eliasmith and Anderson (2002).

can also be thought of as having a normative dimension that so far has not been mentioned. The fact that the contents of two beliefs are related as the two premises of a *modus ponens* argument can causally explain why a third belief is formed. Can the fact that *modus ponens* is a good, reasonable, or correct form of argument also be involved in causally explaining belief formation? If so, how? Does it even make sense to say that the goodness of reasoning with *modus ponens* causally explains events in the natural world? Addressing such questions would require an excursion into the theory of normativity as it applies to logical reasoning, and that is a topic (somewhere between meta-ethics and the philosophy of logic) that the moral psychologist should avoid when possible. So we avoid it here.[29] But it is worth noting that, in the light of the arguments from chapter 1, deliberation will do nothing to explain the kind of normativity in question, since deliberation itself is governed by, and so presupposes, the normativity that needs to be explained (and likewise for representation of reasons, i.e., Recognition). It is also worth noting that, if logical form and probabilistic weight can play causal or explanatory roles in thought and action, then it might not be much of a stretch to find a causal or explanatory role for the normativity of logical form or probabilistic weight, if this is something distinct.

3.4 Reasons, Causes, and Mountain Climbers

An obvious objection to the present theory of thinking and acting for reasons is that it requires that reasons be causes, and that this has been shown to be problematic.

The literature against the idea that rationalizing reasons are causes is large, but we find Alfred Mele's rebuttal of many of these arguments compelling (Mele 2003). So rather than survey the debate and engage it at every point, we propose to do something more limited: remind the reader of the basic case for the idea that rationalizing reasons are causes, review how the preceding arguments have made their own case for the idea that rationalizing reasons are causes, and respond to Davidson's notorious story about a mountain climber.

The simplest case for the thesis that rationalizing reasons must be causes is that there is no other way of explaining which, of multiple available rationalizing reasons for an action, was an agent's actual rationalizing reason: the reason for which she actually acted.[30] Suppose that a little girl refuses to wash her dirty hands, and that an exasperated father, Richard, then sends her to her room to sit quietly for five minutes as a punishment. Richard might well have multiple rationalizing reasons for doing exactly what he does. The punishment seems likely to promote his daughter's ladylikeness, which he might desire for

---

[29] See Schroeder (2010b) for one, very preliminary, discussion of these questions.
[30] Davidson points this out in "Actions, Reasons, and Causes." See Davidson (1980, chapter 1).

its own sake. It seems likely to promote his daughter's cleanliness, which he might also intrinsically desire, and her health. And then, it seems likely to assert his dominance over his daughter, which perhaps he also intrinsically desires (and perhaps he knows it, though he is embarrassed when he finds himself acting too overtly to assert his dominance over others merely for the sake of being in charge). Suppose that we wonder what Richard's rationalizing reasons were in acting. The punishment could just have been for his daughter's health or just to assert his authority, or some mix of two, or three, or all four. What will establish the facts here, other than the causal role played by each rationalization? Not the manner of speech or facial expression. That can be evidence to the observer, but it is only evidence, and can be misleading (a snarling facial tic might make a punishment seem to be given out of a desire for dominance when it was not). Not Richard's beliefs about the matter. Since Kant, at least, we have been aware that we do not always know our actual motives.[31] Not by holding that every rationalization available to Richard plays an equal role.[32] If it had occurred Richard five minutes earlier that his daughter will never become a doctor if her hands are forever full of germs, it would hardly follow that five minutes later the punishment was given partly in order to secure a good career for the daughter (it could have been, but that would indicate an unusual parenting style). The causal role played by his beliefs and intrinsic desires has always been the best candidate to fix such facts.

One way of resisting the idea that rationalizing reasons are causes is to hold that our reasons for action are settled by our practical reasoning (our deliberation) or our practical judgments (our beliefs about what we have most reasons to do). But as the arguments of chapter 1 showed, thinking and acting for reasons cannot be secured by these means. And the arguments of section 3.2 suggested this is because thoughts and actions are for reasons because of the *process* through which they are brought about, not because of the inputs to that process (or even inputs and outputs) alone. And if the choice is between noncausal processes and causal processes somehow bringing about thoughts and actions, causal processes are to be preferred. If rationalizing reasons are to explain thoughts and actions via ND processes, then reasons had better be causes.

[31] Kant (1991).

[32] This seems to be the position Scanlon holds in *Moral Dimensions*: "My turning up [for an evening out with a friend] would have a different meaning if I went solely out of obligation or only because I thought it would be fun (giving no weight at all to the fact that I promised). Thus, given that I see both of these considerations as reasons, there is no need, for the purposes of determining the meaning of the act, to single out one of them as *the* reason for which I act. Doing so would change, and perhaps diminish, the meaning of the act. Moreover... it is not clear what this 'singling out' could consist in unless it involved changing my mind about whether one of the considerations was a relevant reason for taking this particular action." See Scanlon (2008, 52).

One other way to resist the idea that rationalizing reasons are causes is to hold that Davidson's mountain climber shows that the idea is hopeless. This is hardly the only moral philosophers have taken from the story of the mountain climber, but it is one moral; it is also the wrong one. The story of Davidson's mountain climber seems to present a single puzzle, when in fact it presents two. The first puzzle is a puzzle for moral psychology, and it can be solved. The second puzzle is for metaphysics, not moral psychology. While this second puzzle is more resistant to solution, the moral psychologist does not need a solution before adopting a causal theory of action.

In Davidson's case (to which we add a few details, for specificity), a mountain climber and his companion are ascending a mountain together when they get into a difficult situation, and the leading climber is forced to support the weight of both climbers, something he struggles to do.[33] He sees that, if he would only release a rope, he would save himself while allowing his companion to fall to his death. Since he desires to save himself, and believes that releasing the rope would secure his safety, he has a rationalizing reason for releasing the rope. The climber, unnerved by the terrible realization that he has this rationale for killing his companion, has a spasm of shock in which his grip changes enough that he releases the rope. He thus both has a rationalizing reason for releasing the rope, and he releases the rope because of having this rationalizing reason, and yet no one holds that the climber acted for a reason in releasing the rope.

What we would like to say about Davidson's mountain climber is that, although he has a rationalization for releasing the rope, he does not release the rope in virtue of having this rationalization. That would be the explanation, on the present theory, of why the mountain climber does not act in releasing the rope. Yet it is not clear that we can say what we would like. The mountain climber releasing the rope because of his shock, which he experiences because of seeing that he has a murderous rationalization. And so it seems that he releases the rope because of his rationalization.

It will help to step back and consider a somewhat simpler but analogous case, owed to David Velleman.[34] In Velleman's case, a man believes that only by crying can he make his audience sympathetic to him, which he wants very badly, and as a result of that thought he is frustrated to the point of actually crying. Hence, it seems that the man has a belief and a desire that rationalize crying, and that cause him to cry. This might make it seem that the man's crying will have to be counted as an action, and a fairly reasonable action. But of course, it is not an action at all, and so not an action rationalized by his attitudes.

In Velleman's case, the desire to cry causes the crying by virtue of being painfully frustrating. The desire does not cause the crying by virtue of being

---

[33] Davidson (1980, 79).
[34] Velleman (2000, ch.8).

part of a rationalizing pair with the belief that by crying he can manipulate the audience in his favor. The man's attitudes do indeed form a rationalizing pair, but the process by which the man comes to cry is not one that brings about the crying in virtue of this logical relationship. Thus the crying does not count as something done for a practical reason, which is just the right result.

What, then, makes Davidson's case different from Velleman's, and more resistant to the same sort of response? What is distinctive about Davidson's case is a purely metaphysical complication. In Davidson's case, there is an observer who sees that the mountain climber's attitudes rationalize releasing the rope. And, just as a demon might observe the mass and velocity of a brick and then break a window on the basis of this observation, the observer in Davidson's case uses his observation of a rationalization for releasing the rope to bring about the release of the rope. Ingeniously, however, in Davidson's case the observer is the mountain climber himself. There is (as there must be, given the arguments of chapter 1) an ordinary means by which rationalizations bring about actions independently of being thought about by agents. But in Davidson's mountain climber, this means for bringing about actions is not used. Instead, the mountain climber realizes that he has a certain rationalization, and this thought causes the release of the rope in a way that follows a distinctive causal path, a causal path that is not the one used ordinarily when the mountain climber acts on his rationalizations. This makes Davidson's mountain climber a sort of intervening demon with respect to his own release of the rope, although his case is much more realistic than a demonic one.

Though Davidson's case is realistic, it is still true that it uses a trick that introduces a generic metaphysical problem. In any theory of causation or causal explanation in virtue of properties, one wants to distinguish the case in which a flying brick breaks a window in virtue of the brick's mass, velocity, and so on from the case in which a demon observes the mass, velocity, and so on of the brick and then breaks the window itself. In any such theory, one aims to explain why the former case is one in which the flying brick genuinely breaks the window in virtue of its mass, velocity, and so on, whereas the latter case is one in which the flying brick does *not* genuinely break the window in virtue of its mass, velocity, and so on. Solving this metaphysical problem is a perennial challenge. But it is not specific to action theory.

We think it can be taken for granted that there is a principled difference between bricks breaking windows in virtue of their masses and demonically mediated window breaking. If there is, then this principled difference can be imported to explain the difference between the rationalizing attitudes in Davidson's mountain climber causing his release of the rope in virtue of their rationalizing a release and the same attitudes causing his release of the rope via some other causal pathway that is not truly (not merely?) in virtue of the existence of the rationalization. With this difference marked, Davidson's mountain climber becomes just a version of Velleman's frustrated man: someone with a rationale for a behavior who performs the behavior in a way ultimately caused by the rationale, but not caused in virtue of the properties of the rationalizing attitudes that make them into rationalizers.

Can we justify our confidence that the metaphysical problem really has a solution, and a solution that will solve the problem not just in Davidson's case but across the board?

Consider some ordinary explanations. If a certain medication makes Julia's hair grow shiny by virtue of its chemical composition and the hair growing shiny makes her happy it is not true that the medication causes Julia to be happy in virtue of its chemical composition. There are some drugs such that using them might cause a person to be happy in virtue of the drug's chemical composition, but this is not such a drug! If Albert's seeing a man in bright sunlight causes his shooting of the man in virtue of the sun's brightness, and the man's being shot causes his family's weeping, their weeping is not in virtue of the brightness of the sun. The sun caused the family's weeping (insofar as it did) in virtue of being a cause of a family member's death.

The distinction we have been relying on, the distinction between causation that is distinctively in virtue of certain properties and causation that involves those properties but somehow more obliquely, appears to be one taken for granted in these explanations, even though these explanations that do not have troubling observer-intervener characters.

The expression "cause in virtue of" is seemingly used in the same way in the natural sciences when it is said, e.g., that the spring weather caused the deer to have many fawns in virtue its mildness, and the deer having many fawns caused the wolves to become fat, but not that the wolves became fat in virtue of the spring's mildness.

It seems as though, although causation of events is transitive (so that, if A is a cause of B and B is a cause of C then A is a cause of C), causation in virtue of properties is not. Here we are venturing deep into metaphysics, so we tread cautiously. But it does seem worth noting that the intervening observer is simply an instance of a prolonged causal chain, and that prolonged causal chains, while making it true that the final effect was caused (in part) by the initial cause, do not automatically make it true that the final effect was caused in virtue of the properties of the initial cause. (This way of looking at what is going on in Davidson's mountain climber is close to that of Markus Schlosser, except that he discusses causation in virtue of content rather than causation in virtue of rationalization.)[35]

We do not have a theory of what causation in virtue of properties is, but if it is something needed for common sense and natural science as well as for action

---

[35] See Schlosser (2007).

theory, then we are not too concerned to be positing it. Still, it would be nice to see the metaphysics of this sort of causal relationship explained.

One might see a connection between our discussion and work by Stephen Yablo.[36] In Yablo's account of the causal relevance of properties, a good causal explanation appealing to a property appeals to a property such that (1) had the cause lacked the property, the effect would not have occurred, and (2) the property is not egregiously strong or weak. An egregiously strong property is one such that there is an equally natural property, entailed by the egregiously strong property (but not entailing it), that is more closely counterfactually tied to the effect. And an egregiously weak property is one such that there is a more natural property, one entailing the presence of the weak property (but not entailed by it), that is more closely counterfactually tied to the effect.

Applying Yablo's theory to Davidson's climber, we can ask whether the climber's property of having a rationalization for releasing the rope is an egregiously strong or weak property, when explaining releasing the rope. And it appears that it counts as an egregiously strong property, because there is a weaker property (being shocked) that is entailed by having the rationalization (in that psychological context), is at least as natural, and that is also more closely counterfactually tied to releasing the rope: the actual circumstances of the climber are such that a world with a different source of shock causing a rope release is closer than a world with a murderous rationale but no shock causing a rope release.

Of course, Yablo's might not be the last word on the metaphysics of causal relevance. But so long as there must be some such account for general metaphysical and scientific purposes, then it is likely that Spare Conativism can borrow it to fill in this part of the theory.

There is, of course, much more to be said about the idea that rationalizing reasons are causes. But this will do for now. There is a respectable scientific and metaphysical framework within which one can assume that rationalizing reasons are causes or causal explainers of thought and action, and perhaps larger projects in these domains will vindicate these frameworks.

3.5 Acting for Bad Reasons

Suppose John shoots Ronald in order to win Jodie's love. John is acting for a reason. John is not, however, acting for a *good* reason (though he might be acting for better reasons than someone who, say, eats a pickle to in order to bring about world peace). One could say that he acts for a bad reason (or reasons), or one could simply say that he acts irrationally. How is this possible according to

---

[36] Yablo (2003).

a theory that holds that, to think or act for a reason, one must have a rational-izing set of attitudes cause one's thought or action?

The possibility of thinking or acting for bad reasons seems to require the existence of normative theories of epistemic and practical rationality that make sense of poor but not nonexistent rationalizations. Fortunately for present pur-poses, most normative theories seem to agree that there are things to say about agents who display neither perfect, God-like rationality nor utterly incoherent irrationality.

Two approaches seem possible. A normative theory might permit degrees of rationality, so that any thought or action with a non-zero degree of rationality is one thought or performed with *some* rationalization, however poor.[37] The attitudes both making it the case that the thought or action has the non-zero degree of rationality it does and also involved (because of their having the logi-cal or mathematical relations that establish this degree of rationality) in caus-ing the thought or action would then be the attitudes settling the bad reasons on the basis of which the thought was had or the action performed. Or the normative theory might permit no degrees of rationality, but permit the evalu-ation of the rationality of a thought or action relative to some more restricted set of attitudes, as well as some less restricted set, so that an action that is absolutely irrational (from the perspective of the less restricted set of attitudes) nonetheless can have something said in its favor: there were *pro tanto* reasons to perform it given attitudes X, Y, and Z. So long as attitudes X, Y, and Z cause or explain the thought or action in virtue of their logical or mathematical rela-tions that make them *pro tanto* reasons, they would then settle the bad reasons for which the thought was had or the action performed.

When John shoots Ronald to win Jodie's love, it is easy to imagine that his irrationality is at heart epistemic. Perhaps John grew up in an unremarkable household in an unremarkable part of the United States and had unremarkable background beliefs. Such background beliefs would strongly suggest that Jodie (like any other woman) is unlikely to love him as a result of his committing a murder. In fact, they suggest that committing the murder will make him seem reprehensible to her, or insane, which is something he does not want to happen. In other words, the belief that by shooting Ronald he would win Jodie's love is held against John's evidence. On any normative account of rational belief that takes into account attitudes not currently being thought, John probably has decisive reasons to disbelieve that killing Ronald will positively impress Jodie. Yet something, perhaps a merely physical factor, or a content efficacious one, or both, prevents his beliefs from responding to these reasons. (There might also be overwhelming practical reasons for John and everyone else to act morally,

---

[37] So long as the attitudes that cause the action (in virtue of, or in a manner explained by, their logical relation to the action) are the same ones that provide the rationale for the action.

in which case John's irrationality would be a mix of epistemic irrationality and pure practical irrationality.)

For a simple case of purely practical irrationality, suppose that Paulette smokes cigarettes, and suppose that a conventional sort of rational choice theory is the correct normative account of practical rationality, according to which a person acts rationally to the extent that she acts in a way that maximizes expected satisfaction of her intrinsic desires. Given that Paulette has many strong intrinsic desires that would be frustrated by getting lung cancer, emphysema, heart disease, and the like, given that she has other intrinsic desires that are frustrated by having an expensive habit such as smoking, and so on, and given that she only has moderate intrinsic desires satisfied by smoking (it is mildly pleasant for her; it increases mental sharpness for certain intellectual tasks; it supports her rebellious identity), and given that she knows of the various facts about how smoking relates to health, wealth, pleasure, mental sharpness, and the rest, it is rational for her to not smoke: smoking is never the action that maximizes expected intrinsic desire satisfaction for Paulette. Nonetheless, she smokes. In doing so, her action is caused, perhaps, mostly by her intrinsic desire to not suffer (something that would be caused by nicotine withdrawal) and by her intrinsic desire to be somewhat rebellious, along with the relevant beliefs. If so, then these are her reasons for smoking, and they count as her reasons because (1) they contribute to her action having more than zero practical rationality, within conventional rational choice theory, (2) they cause or explain her action, and (3) they cause or explain her action (at least in part) in virtue of the way in which they contribute to its non-zero practical rationality: because of the way smoking is a way of getting *some* expected desire satisfaction, even though it is not a way of maximizing expected desire satisfaction.[38]

To act and believe for bad reasons thus seems possible within the given framework, and all too common besides.

What about particularly hard cases? Suppose that someone affirms the consequent: does this person believe for no reason at all? Here we think it is acceptable to leave the question to normative theories of belief. Perhaps this sort of inference leaves a person with a wholly unjustified belief. But if it does not, then the source of partial justification in this sort of case (or in its practical counterpart) will also be explained by normative theory. On some heuristic-based theories of good belief formation, affirming that consequent might be a risky but weakly rationalizing inference pattern, for example. And then, what appears

---

[38] Of course, there are some who will say that, if Paulette smokes, she *must* be maximizing expected desire satisfaction at that particular moment. Though this is not something we want to argue about at the moment—we are simply seeking to illustrate practical irrationality, and our specific example is not one that needs to be fought over—we will return to the question of how intrinsic desires are related to actions in chapters 5 and 6. There, and again (in detail) in chapter 11 on addiction, we will show how it is possible to act contrary to the way in which one most intrinsically desires, or the way that would maximize expected intrinsic desire satisfaction.

to be affirming the consequent might really be something more complicated. A person who appears to be affirming the consequent might be influenced, in his inference, by his background knowledge of the range of likely explanations for the consequent: it might be that the low probability of any explanation for the consequent other than the antecedent might be influencing belief formation. And then, what appears to be affirming the consequent might really be a form of inference to the best explanation. The details of such hard cases thus need not particularly worry the moral psychologist.

3.6 Thinking and Acting for Multiple Reasons and Nonreasons

In the previous section, we did one thing and alluded to something else. What we did was explain how it was conceptually coherent for us to hold both that thinking and acting for reasons requires having a rationalization, and that people sometimes think and act foolishly. In explaining this conceptual possibility, we alluded to the idea that irrational thought and action is causally explained by appeal to merely physical and merely contentful (but not rationalizing) causal or explanatory factors that are in play along with rationalizing reasons. This idea should be examined in its own right. Is it credible? And if it is, what does it signify for moral psychology?

Thinking and acting are events and events in general happen in rich contexts, contexts in which there are many factors that are relevant to the causation or explanation of the event. The wood shavings catch fire because of the heat generated by the bow drill, but also because of the gust of oxygen-rich air blown at them by the person starting the fire, and also because of the absence of heavy rain, and so on.

Whether these explanatory factors are to be distinguished between *the cause* and *the background conditions* or are to be treated as all on a par (or to be distinguished as scientifically privileged explanatory factors versus background conditions presupposed in the privileged explanations, or...) does not matter to us, and we are happy to embrace any metaphysical position on causation and explanation compatible with our earlier, minimal commitments. There is some sense, appropriate to our purposes, in which every episode of thinking or acting for reasons is the product of multiple causal or explanatory factors, only some of which are rationalizing reasons.

Consider a case.

Chris thinks the woman sitting next to him in the coffee shop is a student. This is partially because the coffee shop is near a university and the woman is looking at papers, and these are reasons for Chris to believe what he does, so he believes in part for good reasons. But part of the story is that the woman next to Chris is wearing a scarf that, unconsciously, reminds him of a student he knew, and this unconscious association with a familiar student is also influential as a purely content-efficacious matter. And further, if Chris had already had his morning coffee, he would have noticed that the woman is reading what appears to be a stockholder's report, suggesting the woman is not a student after all. The lack of caffeine within Chris's brain appears to be a purely physical matter in influencing Chris's judgment.

Chris's story is about belief, but we can tell a similar story about action:

> Avi shouts at someone for a reason (he wants him to stop talking) but he would not have done it if he were not angry at someone else he was just talking to (a merely content-efficacious factor), which in turn would not have influenced him nearly so much if it were not for Avi's fatigue after a long day (a merely physical factor).

Chris and Avi's stories suggest ways in which all three of the factors identified in this chapter can be involved simultaneously in irrational thought and action, either as causes or as explanatory elements. Back in chapter 2, we argued that the value of deliberation is in its capacity for helping us to overcome the weaknesses in our ND capacities to think and act for good reasons. Now that there has been a discussion of the range of causal factors at play in people's minds, the point can be made this way: all believers contain ND capacities to think for good reasons, and all agents contain ND capacities to think and act for good reasons. These capacities are for rationalizing reasons to cause or causally explain thoughts and actions in virtue of the logical or mathematical properties and relations they have that make them rationalizers. But such causal or causal-explanatory capacities will, naturally, only exist within a rich web of other causal relations. Some of these causal relations will support, or ground, the exercise of ND capacities to think and act for good reasons, while others will be neutral, and still others will impair the exercise of these ND capacities. Deliberation's special value is that it can serve as a form of action that changes the causal environment within a believer or agent, changing it in a way that can (if the deliberative acts are well chosen) minimize the impact of impairing causal factors and maximize the impact of causal factors promoting or realizing ND capacities to think and act for reasons.

Does the present account give us a picture in which the brain is a battlefield between the limited forces of reason-responsiveness and the ever-present forces of irrationality, found in the form of merely physical and merely contentful causes? Far from it. Consider a variation on Chris's case:

> Chris sees a woman at a coffee shop near the university and realizes that she probably works for Advanced Micro Devices. Chris's conclusion is driven in part by the sorts of documents she is studying, but also in part is the result of a sudden connection he makes between the prominent

'AMD' logo on her briefcase and the name of the corporation—and this sudden leap is made in part because he has just been studying the Intel logo stamped onto his computer, and because Intel is a rival technology company. This associative leap is mere efficacy of content, it seems. And finally, Chris would not have been so quick to have the insight without the double espresso he consumed twenty minutes earlier. The caffeine, it seems safe to assume, plays a merely physical role in this story.

Such cases suggest that all three types of factors are involved in the development of every belief or action, whether ideally rational, deeply irrational, or somewhere in-between.

Consider the merely physical. We all like to blame "hardware" factors for our irrationalities ("I was tired," "I was drunk"...) and often we are right. Because of this, it can be tempting to think of actions that are partially the result of drinking or being tired as not really our own ("it was the liquor talking"). But if we do so we forget that a person might be rational thanks to alcohol (which allows irrational inhibitions to be overcome) or a drug such as lithium, without which the person would be a slave to mood swings. A person might be a great deliberator at a given moment in part because of the caffeine in her blood: Paul Erdős famously claimed that a mathematician is a machine for turning coffee into theorems,[39] suggesting that a merely physical influence upon our thinking such as caffeine is in fact (partly) responsible for some people reaching the highest heights of reason-responsive thought in that domain. In these cases, philosophers are not tempted by the language of the nonself. We do not dismiss the coffee drinker's brilliant theorems as not his own by saying, "it was only the coffee talking." If the person on lithium goes to the grocery store and says, "excuse me, but I'm looking for the cheese section," we feel no need to dismiss her politeness because "it's only the lithium talking," nor do we say she is irrational.[40]

We must own both sorts of actions or neither, and we prefer the idea that we own both. To own neither is to give up on too much of what we believe about the praise- and blameworthiness of ordinary people.[41] In cases in which the merely physical factors interfere with our ability to respond to reasons (as opposed to cases in which it enhances it) it sometimes happens that praise-or blameworthiness is reduced, but we will say more on this in chapter 7.

Those who are lucky enough not to need alcohol, caffeine, or lithium in order to do reasonable things owe this privilege to other merely physical factors just as much as those who need alcohol, coffee, or lithium owe their reasonableness

---

[39] This and many other wonderful Erdős anecdotes are found in Schechter (1998).

[40] Manuel Vargas makes a related point about caffeine's compatibility with thinking and acting for good reasons (Vargas 2013, 291–93).

[41] In part for reasons discussed in Arpaly and Schroeder (1999) and Schroeder and Arpaly (1999). See also Arpaly (2003).

to these specific physical factors. The (often, merely) physical factors taking the place of alcohol, coffee, or lithium (or...) in the rest of us are the factors that are corrected for by these compounds: ion channels that work efficiently, optimal genes producing proteins contributing to the capacity to learn effectively, adequate levels of blood oxygen, blood sugar, and other compounds, the survival of key neurons into adulthood, and so on. Just as oxygen is rarely mentioned when explaining the start of a fire, it generally goes without saying that one has an intact brain with adequate blood oxygen and all the rest when one's thinking and acting are being explained. It goes without saying, but this is not to say that there are no true causal or explanatory claims to be made of these sorts, any more than it is to say that the presence of oxygen has no role to play in causing or explaining fires.[42]

Now consider what is merely content efficacious, causing in virtue of content properties that do not rationalize the resulting mental state. The existence of merely content-efficacious factors means that there is no need to assume a merely physical problem has occurred every time irrationality occurs. The brain can be working normally at the level of oxygen, glucose, ions, and neurotransmitters, but this normal operation can be resulting in irrationality because some of the contents realized are influential in ways they do not rationalize: through mere association, through motivated and other forms of "hot" irrationality, and so on. These possibilities show that, just as one needs to have a biologically healthy brain in order to be likely to believe rationally, one also needs to be emotionally clear-eyed so as not to be caught, for example, in wishful thinking. To act rationally, one needs to be adequately supplied with oxygen, but one also needs to be free from psychological influences that occur when mental states affect one in a way that is out of proportion to their weights as rationalizing reasons. How this might be squared with a theory of intrinsic desire is something to which we will return in chapters 5, 6, and 11.[43]

So far in this section we have contrasted the roles of different kinds of factors in the causal web. But thinking of the mind as a complex causal web also gives us a good understanding of how to think about acting on mixed motives.

Sometimes, it seems that a person's motives are unmixed: Sean sees that the rolling log is about to strike his foot and he jerks his foot away because he intrinsically desires not to be hurt, and sees jerking his foot away as his

---

[42] In this context, it is fascinating to note some of the psychological literature that seems to show that willpower is dependent on blood sugar. See Gailliot and Baumeister (2007) for the original research; and Holton (2009, chapter 6) for a philosophical response. It strikes us as just right that Holton thinks that, when it comes to akrasia, the question is really how strength of will is possible rather than weakness.

[43] A different account of how desires can have different motivational and rationalizing forces—even from within a Humean framework—is found in Schroeder (2008). Of course, for those opposed to basing moral psychology on desires, the thesis that desires motivate disproportionately to their rationalizing weight will be less surprising.

best hope for that. The instrumental value of an intact foot for performing at tomorrow's concert was not just not in his consciousness: Sean's intrinsic desire to perform well was probably not causally efficacious at all in his movement of his foot (though this is an empirical question in the end).

On other occasions, there will be mixed motives. Richard, who punishes his daughter for refusing to wash her dirty hands, might feel his anger at her defiance while also feeling disgust at the sight of her hands, and so reasonably conclude that the punishment was probably in part a response to each of these factors: he has rationalizing reasons to assert his dominance and to keep his daughter clean, and both felt as if they were in play. The facts about the causal relations between these rationalizing reasons and his utterance of "then go to your room; you're being punished" will determine whether both rationalizations were involved in causing the action in virtue of their rationalizing relations to it. And the facts will tell the same story even if Richard is not self-conscious enough to recognize his anger at his daughter's defiance for what it is, or if Richard is in the grips of psychological egoism and believes that he is acting selfishly when he is not.

When motives are mixed there might be help from the metaphysics of causation in determining whether certain motives were predominant, whether others played a marginal role, and so on. Ordinarily we assume that these possibilities make sense: Richard might admit that his daughter's defiance influenced punishment of her, but insist that it was not "the main point—she just needs to learn to keep her hands clean." Ordinarily one assumes that either he is right or wrong, but that there is a fact of the matter. Some causal arrangements would seem to straightforwardly permit such conclusions. If the causal role played by the Richard's two rationalizations were such that the defiance-related rationalization would not have sufficed on its own for the punishment, but the cleanliness-related rationalization would have, then it seems correct to conclude that the latter was "the main reason" for which Richard acted.

Many complications seem possible: at least as many as are permitted by the literature on multiple causes. But perhaps it is worth sketching one more, somewhat complex, scenario to illustrate how useful causal thinking can be to explaining mixed motives. Staying with Richard, whose daughter defiantly refuses to wash her hands, we can imagine that there are two rationalizations playing a significant role: his defiance-based and his cleanliness-based rationalizations. And we can imagine that the former is a weaker rationalizing reason for Richard (he is not deeply committed to being the dominant personality of those around him, though he does prefer it) and that the latter is a stronger rationalizing reason (he is deeply committed to his daughter's cleanliness). From this starting point, it might seem that the latter rationalization must always be the main reason for which Richard acts, if it comes down to these two. But this is not correct. Perhaps Richard has spent the afternoon in the backyard with his daughter, drinking beer while she plays in the dirt. The effect of the alcohol, perhaps, is that it somewhat masks his underlying concern with his daughter's cleanliness while heightening his apparent (though not his actual) intrinsic desire to play the dominant role. Then, when his daughter defies his command that she wash his hands, it might be that the defiance-based rationalization plays the larger role in his issuing a punishment, even though it provides the weaker rationalizing reason. (Here we assume that alcohol typically conceals or exaggerates the effects of underlying intrinsic desires rather than changing their strengths; an indirect defense of this approach can be found in chapters 5 and 6.)

From a Kantian[44] point of view it has been said that in moral contexts, there is effectively no role for mixed motives: ultimately, either Shahnaz gives to charity for the right reasons, in which case her action has moral worth, or she does it for a tax deduction, in which case it does not. But the person who forces upon himself the disagreeable task of giving while reminding himself of the tax deduction is different from the person who, of all the ways to find a tax deduction, prefers those that have the bonus of being charitable, and then again from the person who of all ways to do good, prefers the charity that also offers a tax deduction, and so on. It is an advantage for a view to be able to account for these different shades of morally interesting motivation.

3.7 Habit and Inaction

So far we have been focused on cases of thinking and acting for reasons, but there are less central cases of thinking and acting that are performed, in part, *because* of one's reasons (and because those reasons at least weakly rationalize what one thinks or does) without being performed *for* those reasons. Habit is the central case of interest to us, and needs discussion in order to be able to talk about virtue (chapter 8) and addiction (chapter 11), but the whole class of actions discussed here is neglected and interesting.

Suppose Travis is driving to a meeting, but as he passes a crucial intersection he turns left instead of going straight. And suppose the explanation for his turning left is that this is where he would have to turn left if he were going to work, and going to work every day has given him a habit of turning left at this junction. In this situation, it seems most straightforward to say that Travis does not have a desire to turn left; he turns left simply out of blind habit (see chapter 5). But it also seems most straightforward to say that Travis *acts* out of habit—that Travis's behavior is best thought of as an action, something he does, though of course not an action of the most paradigmatic sort. We hold both of these straightforward claims to be true, but there is something of a

---

[44] See Herman (1993, chapter 1) for an argument that moral worth is ruled out by mixed motives, though not by mixed incentives.

puzzle for us in doing so. If Travis acts out of a sheer habit, how can it be true that a rationalization of his action explains what he does?

If Travis turns left simply out of habit, then his behavior is immediately caused by his perception or cognition of approaching the familiar intersection in the familiar way, along with the habit of responding to this perception or cognition with a left turn. No desire to turn left is required in order to generate the impulse to turn left: this impulse is just the characteristic effect of habit. Being influenced by a habit is a mental event, not merely a physical event, because habits are mental things. But habits are not representations or instructions, and so cannot contribute to rationalizing what is done. Hence, if there is any influence of content upon an action performed out of habit, it would appear to be the content of the perception or cognition that triggers the habit. In Travis's case, his habit is triggered by seeing himself approach a particular intersection while driving from a particular direction. This does not pin down the precise content or contents responsible for triggering the habit in him, but it gives a sense of the contents involved, and makes it clear that on no one's account of rationalization will these contents suffice to rationalize turning left at the given intersection all on their own. So it appears that Travis's action is generated by two mental events—his perceiving or conceiving of reaching the intersection in a certain way, and the triggering of his habit of turning left in such circumstances—in a way that is sensitive to content but not to the rationalization of the movement by that content. The habit itself causes or explains in virtue of certain perceptual contents, but not in virtue of a rationalization.

It is worth pointing out that not everything referred to as a habit is one in the narrow sense used here. One can say that Vlad is in the habit of going to the same coffee shop each morning and mean by it that he does it every day and without a need to think much about it. But Vlad's habit is always going to involve a large number of actions taken for reasons, and so is not a pure case of the phenomenon we have in mind. His walk involves taking actions that are not the same every time, in conditions that are not the same every time, and the details of his walk (and leaving home, and reaching the shop) will thus involve nonhabitual elements, many of which will be actions taken for reasons: smiling at a friendly stranger who passes by, waiting for a car to pass at an intersection, looking at a playful dog in a yard, and so on. Specific parts of Vlad's walk might also be the product of habit. Perhaps looking left and right before crossing the road is something Vlad is so habituated to doing that he would do it even if he were aware that no cars were present. And perhaps when he arrives at the coffee shop and is asked, "What would you like?" he is so habituated to saying, "Large decaf iced coffee" that one day, when he feels like getting a small cup of tea instead, he finds himself nonetheless saying, on cue, "large decaf iced coffee." These would be instances of acting purely out of habit, in the sense we have in mind, because they would be instances in which cognition and habit together fully generate the action Vlad performs, without supplementary rationalizing attitudes also causing the action, or causing component parts of it.[45]

Return to Travis, whose impulse to turn left comes from blind habit. If Travis's action is not performed because it is rationalized by his attitudes then we confront a difficulty. A movement that is not rationalized by the agent's attitudes cannot, by our lights, be an action done for a reason, and therefore, by the arguments of chapter 1, is not an action at all.

Some might want to embrace this conclusion. While it is true that people are treated as praiseworthy or blameworthy as a result of acting out of habit, action out of habit is a marginal kind of action, and perhaps there are ultimately better reasons to treat things done out of habits not as actions but something else. If Travis is blameworthy for being late for the meeting he was originally headed for before turning left perhaps he can be said to have "performed" an *inaction* at the crucial moment: he failed to prevent his habitual left turn, because he did not care enough about the meeting. Of course, Travis was inactive in this way without being self-conscious of it, but this does not show that Travis was not inactive on this occasion; at most, it is the beginning of an argument that Travis is less blameworthy than he might otherwise be for his inactivity.

But saying that Travis does not act might strikes one as doing a certain violence to common sense. The expression "I acted out of habit" is also a part of ordinary speech. What is more, it might well turn out that almost every action, however paradigmatic, involves habit or habit-like factors as part of its explanation.[46] If almost every action has habit or habit-like factors as part of its explanation there is reason to be cautious about dismissing as not an action everything that is contaminated by habit.

Suppose, then, that Travis acts. There are two other things that we might do here. One is to maintain that Travis acts for a reason and to revise our theory of acting for reasons. Another is to revise our idea that every action is performed for a reason.

Start by exploring the first route. For an action to be caused by, or appropriately explained by, a set of attitudes it is not necessary that these attitudes contribute a causal "oomph" to the action. There is a role in (some) accounts of causation, and in (some) accounts of scientifically acceptable explanation, for events that occur in part because other events do not occur. It is easy enough to think of examples. The bank robbers continued their spree because the police did not consider the possibility that they were using two different getaway cars; the forest fires were particularly devastating because the spring rains did not arrive; the two electrons remained entangled because they did not encounter a measurement device. There seem to be a wide range of cases in which causal

---

[45] Thus the case described by Cohon (1993) of the person who makes a sandwich for her son on a non-school night is not a case of pure habit.

[46] See, e.g., Railton (2009).

explanation by appeal to absences is correct or appropriate. And some of these cases are found in the mental realm. If there had been a fire truck parked in the intersection on Travis's left he would not have turned left. The absence of a strong rationalization *not* to turn left plays a causal role in the bringing about of Travis's left turn. The absence of a strong rationalization is not itself providing "oomph" to the process, is not doing work in the technical sense proper to physics, but it is part of the causal or explanatory picture nonetheless.[47] Thus, Travis's turn can be an action done for reasons.

A question should be raised here. Absences are cheap. Are we at risk of making it too easy for an agent to count as performing an action? For instance, suppose that Marissa has been hiking and now, utterly exhausted, collapses on the trail. But suppose that, had she desired to preserve her dignity at all costs, she would not have collapsed but instead sunk to her knees: that desire, combined with instrumental beliefs, would have sent a final jolt down the spine to the muscles allowing a more controlled process than utter collapse. Does it follow that collapsing is actually an action on Marissa's part? The correct answer seems "no." Or suppose that Yoram coughs loudly while watching a play. Had Yoram desired more strongly to not disturb others, he would have mostly suppressed the cough, and a much quieter sound would have escaped him. Does that make the loud coughing an action? Again, the answer seems to be "no."

We need there to be a difference between the cough and the collapse cases on the one hand and the case of Travis turning left out of habit on the other. And it seems such a difference exists. If Travis's car were to suddenly stop working in the middle of turning left, and Travis were to be asked what he had been doing, it would be natural for Travis to say that he had been trying to turn left. On the other hand, the coughing person was not trying to cough. A doctor might ask one to cough in order to listen to what is going on in one's lungs, and a polite person might intentionally cough to indicate her presence to someone. But most coughs are not the result of trying or, in one common bit of jargon, of immediate intentions.[48] Neither is collapsing from exhaustion.

The status of trying, immediate intention, willing, or having volitions in the theory of action has been contested. There have been many theories of action that have seen no need to postulate immediate intention (as we will call this

---

[47] One caveat that perhaps needs more than a footnote: the only absences we take to be relevant to action explanation are those that exist because, while the intrinsic desire(s) needed to rationalize the action are present, the beliefs or perceptions necessary are absent. That Travis does not intrinsically desire to kill everyone is an absence-based explanation of why he does not swerve into traffic at the intersection, but it seems wrong to appeal to this as one of Travis's reasons explaining his left turn—because Travis has no intrinsic desire.

[48] The reader will notice that this is the first occasion on which we bring up intentions of any sort. The more familiar sort of intentions, long-term intentions, play many interesting roles in the moral mind, but they are at most mechanisms through which it becomes true that people act for the right reasons, in a praiseworthy manner, or out of virtue. Long-term intentions do not replace intrinsic desires in any of these roles. So we set discussion of them to one side in this work.

attitude) as a distinct attitude with a distinct causal role. But there is both arm-chair evidence[49] and scientific evidence[50] for the existence of immediate inten-tions. To the extent that it is possible in this work we would like to avoid larger questions in the theory of action, but it seems that to explain why making an habitual left turn is an action, but collapsing out of exhaustion is not, we must venture into action theory.

We can, therefore, keep holding that Travis acts for a reason by accepting the following view:

> BDI (Belief-Desire-Intention): to act for a reason is for one's action to be caused (in the right way)[51] by an immediate intention, and for one's immediate intention to be caused or causally explained by a set of attitudes that both rationalize one's intention and cause or causally explain the intention in virtue of the fact that they rationalize it (bearing in mind that there can be causation, or causal explanation, by absence as well as by presence).

If that is so, habitual action is a form of acting for a reason. The intending that needs to be explained in Travis's case is immediately intending to turn the steering wheel to the left, and that intending is explained, in part, by the absent rationalization for doing otherwise.[52] In this way, the absent rationalization is like an absent rainstorm that explains the persistence of a forest fire. Thus we can hold that Travis acts for a reason.

But is this what we want to say? Some will find this claim a little strange. The rationalization-by-absence does not tell us what the turning left was *for*. While the absence of a fire truck in the intersection is part of the explanation of Travis's turning left, it is strange to think of its absence as a *reason* for his action. People still say "I did it for no reason, it was just habit." If it is too strange to say that the habitual action happens for reasons, we would have to revise our theory in a different way: maintain that Travis acts, but reject the assumption that all actions are for reasons.

We can keep holding that a movement is an action only if caused by an imme-diate intention that is in turn caused, by presence or absence, by rationalizing

---

[49] See, e.g., Mele (1990).

[50] See, e.g., Schroeder (2004, chapter 4).

[51] See Searle (1983) for a discussion of the issues here, though we do not mean to embrace or reject Searle's specific solution. This seems an issue best left to action theorists, as it does not directly bear on the narrow problem of acting *for reasons*.

[52] We suspect that the right way to think about immediate intentions is that they are intentions to perform what have been called "basic" or "primitive" actions such as opening a hand, utter-ing a syllable, or grasping an object one is looking at. One typically has rationalizations for such intentions because one sees the actions they command as means to, or realizers of, more complex ends that one intrinsically desires (opening a hand is one step in greeting someone; uttering a syllable at the right time is voting a certain way; gasping a particular object is a means to getting food). But we will try to avoid these details insofar as we can.

attitudes in virtue of rationalization,[53] but also hold that not all actions are performed for reasons but only those caused by present attitudes—*not* those caused by absence. The latter actions, which we can call "borderline actions," are in keeping with our reasons, they even manifest our reasons, but are not strictly speaking done *for* reasons. Travis's turn is perhaps one such borderline action.

Actions performed out of blind habit might not be the only actions that fit this description. Consider the so-called "arational actions" discussed by Rosalind Hursthouse.[54] These are actions that are expressive of emotional states without being credibly caused by rationalizing attitudes within the agent. A person who jumps for joy is a person who is apparently acting while also not apparently acting *for* a reason. Such a person, Hursthouse argues, does not act for rationalizing reasons of the standard sort, and we are inclined to agree. A typical person who jumps for joy does not jump for joy in order to show her joy, or to relieve herself of an impulse, or to savor a moment of pleasure to its fullest. Though a person might jump for any of these reasons, the typical person who jumps for joy does not jump because of any set of beliefs and desires of this sort, nor does she typically jump for the reason she has to be joyful (a successful lung transplant for your brother is a reason to be joyful, but not a practical reason to leap). Being filled with joy is the sort of mental event that tends to promote exuberant motion simply because of the attitude that it is, or because of the way it is biologically realized in creatures like us, or both. However, it still seems correct to say that jumping for joy is an action, is something one does, and not just something that happens to joyful people. This can be explained within SC if being moved by joy is like being moved by a habit: if jumping for joy is partly causally explained by the absence of reasons to not jump, just as actions out of habit are partly causally explained by the absence of reasons not to turn left (etc.). And this seems likely to be the case: jumping for joy, spontaneous as it can be, is the sort of action that is also shaped by one's reasons (it is unlikely one will jump for joy when receiving good news inside a car or standing on a frail cliff).[55]

Going back to habit: actions out of habit could, on this second approach, be (borderline) actions, caused by the absence of reasons (caused, in part, because there is only a weak rationalization or no rationalization for avoiding performing the action in question). The objection could be raised that if a movement is performed out of habit, an explanation of the movement in terms of habit is

---

[53] If the intention is not thus caused we have a tic rather than an action.

[54] Hursthouse (1991).

[55] There are other cases of arational actions that are more complex, such as cursing at a can opener. In these cases, in addition to there being an element of emotional expression, there is also an apparent element of pretending: pretending that the can opener has feelings that can be hurt by one's insults, for example. These more complex cases raise interesting issues, but issues that would be a digression from the present line of argument.

in conflict with an explanation according to which the movement is performed because it is not in conflict with a rationalization the agent has. But as the last section emphasized, there is rarely, if ever, an action with a rationalizing explanation that does not also have a nonrationalizing, merely causal explanation (at least, partial explanation) that could also be provided for it,[56] and many actions also have nonrationalizing partial explanations that involve mere content efficacy. So there is no reason to think of the two different explanations of a movement as necessarily competing. They are potentially complementary. Travis turns left in part out of habit and in part because he sees no trouble in the intersection: both explanations are correct.

One more question remains. If there exist actions that are not done *for* reasons, but only because of one's reasons, is it still true that deliberation must be done for reasons? Yes, it is. Deliberation is always done for a specific reason, namely, to determine what to think or do (as we argued in chapter 1). Reflection that is not performed for the sake of determining what to think or do is not deliberation but musing, free association, or something else.

3.8 Acting for Moral Reasons

We are now in position to address a central question for Spare Conativism: What is acting for moral reasons?

An extended example will be helpful, so imagine that Bonnie is a part-time instructor at an undistinguished private college. A student comes to her asking for an improvement in his grade so that he will pass her course, a requirement in the pre-med program. Bonnie feels a little torn. Having reviewed the student's work, it is clear that he did not cross the threshold to a passing grade. But the college for which Bonnie teaches is utterly dependent upon tuitions and the good will of its students (and their parents), and the college puts pressure on all its instructors to give passing grades to their students. It occurs to Bonnie that her reappointment for another term of work hinges on decisions such as the one she is about to make. With a sigh, she shakes her head and tells the student that, unfortunately, his work was accurately scored and so she is unable to give him a passing grade.

Grant (as seems reasonable) that failing the student is morally right: it is fair to the student and his peers, is in keeping with Bonnie's promises (explicit and implicit) on her syllabus, is truthful to those who might read the student's transcript, and is even best for social welfare (as the world hardly needs doctors unable to pass introductory-level undergraduate science courses). Factors like these will themselves be the right reasons: they will be the objective reasons

---

[56] Except, of course, for the maximal causal or explanatory account of an action, if there is one.

for Bonnie to fail the student. But of course, if Bonnie fails the student for the right reasons, then she must be in some psychological relation to these objective reasons. What relation is that?

Bonnie shakes her head and utters the words making up the sentence, "Unfortunately, your work was accurately scored, so your grade will have to remain an F." Since these movements of her body are actions, they stem from immediate intentions to make these movements, and her immediate intentions must themselves be caused by attitudes that rationalize them, and caused in virtue of the fact that they rationalize them. It is these rationalizations that have the capacity to relate Bonnie to the right objective reasons to act.

Bonnie no doubt possesses a wide variety of attitudes that rationalize shaking her head and uttering the sentence she says to the student. Perhaps the student has acted with an air of entitlement, treating Bonnie as a salesperson who for some reason does not understand how to sell him the degree for which his parents are paying so handsomely. And then Bonnie's belief that this is so, combined with an intrinsic desire she might have for status, might rationalize her putting the student in his place, which she knows failing him would accomplish. Perhaps she intrinsically desires to live free of arbitrary controls, and so resents the pressure her college puts on her to pass students regardless of actual achievement; she sees failing the student as an instance of asserting her independence of such control, and so has that rationalization for it. Perhaps she also intrinsically desires her son's welfare, and suspects that extra time with him would be in his interest, even if it might not be in Bonnie's best interest overall, and so has a rationalization to fail the student on the grounds that it might actually get her fired, and so give her more time with her son. All of these rationalizations are possible, and some complex collection of such rationalizations for failing the student are likely. But none of these rationalizations seem the relevant rationalization if Bonnie acts for moral reasons. Her moral rationalization for failing the student has to do with a specifically moral desire, a desire concerned with the right or the good moral reasons for acting. Call this desire's aptly conceptualized content "M." Her rationalization is her moral desire that M along with her belief that failing the student would achieve M (and her belief that shaking her head and uttering the key sentence will amount to failing the student). M will presumably have some relationship to the objective moral reasons just mentioned: fairness, promise-keeping, truthfulness, beneficence, and so on. Further discussion of the nature of M (or natures of various M's) we save for chapter 7, however. Here we stay focused on the rest of acting for moral reasons.

If Bonnie does the right thing for the right reason, then of all the possible causes of her immediate intentions that amount to failing the student, the actual causes include her moral desire and the relevant means-end beliefs. And these rationalizing attitudes do not only cause her immediate intentions, but cause them in virtue of the fact that they rationalize them: in virtue of the fact that they increase expected satisfaction of intrinsic desires (if that is what practical rationality amounts to) or in virtue of the fact that they form a practical syllogism (if that is what practical rationality amounts to), or something similar.

If Bonnie does the right thing for the right reason, then the actual causes of her immediate intentions *include* her moral rationalization, but the actual causes will include more than just her moral rationalization. The actual causes of her immediate intentions will include purely physical factors that have no psychological-level description: good functioning in key receptors in her neurons, or adequate oxygenation of her blood, for instance. The actual causes might also include content-related but nonrationalizing factors: if the student looks like a masculinized version of Bonnie's wayward sister (long in need of a firm correction or two from reality, Bonnie thinks) then perhaps that will lend a little extra impetus to Bonnie's immediate intention to fail the student without rationalizing it in any way: the unconscious association will make it a little easier to utter the final pronouncement failing the student.

If Bonnie does the right thing *just* for the right reasons, then there will not be another competing rationalization that also causes Bonnie to form her immediate intentions in virtue of rationalizing them.[57] But Bonnie might do the right thing in part for the right reasons and in part for reasons other than the right reasons. Perhaps two or three independently rationalizing sets of attitudes combine, with Bonnie's moral rationalization (based on her intrinsic desire that M) playing a partial role in bringing about her immediate intentions. In a certain sense, Bonnie's motives will inevitably be mixed, because some of her reasons for her immediate intentions will be absences rather than presences, and absences are always unboundedly plentiful. Bonnie says what she does in part because she does not believe that the student will burst into tears if she speaks directly; and so on. But these absent motives are rarely noted in ordinary thought, and not counted as "mixed motives" when that idea is discussed (and many of these absences would not be good candidates for scientific explanation in any event), perhaps because the contexts in which these motives would be present are too remote in some sense.

What role does deliberation have in Bonnie's case? There are various ways to imagine it, but here is one plausible one. In determining what to do, Bonnie does perform a deliberative act: she holds in mind the thought that failing the

---

[57] Here we use causation, or causal-explanatory relevance, to solve the problem of how to determine the reason(s) for which an agent acts, when she has more than one reason to immediately intend the same basic action or sequence of actions. And although we do not explore the idea, it seems we could equally use theories of causation, or causal-explanatory relevance, to determine how important different reasons were to Bonnie, or any agent, in her acting. Scanlon (2008, 52 ff.) holds that "there may be no answer to the question of which motive is predominant" (2008, 69; see 52 ff. for the argument) when multiple motives are available. But Scanlon's argument relies on not making use of causal facts in assessing the rationalizing reasons for which a person acts.

student is the sort of thing that might cost her a future appointment, given the college's priorities. This was a relevant factor to consider, but interestingly factors that Bonnie did not consciously hold in mind were much more influential in her determination of what to do. These were factors related to the sense and reference of her moral desire, such as fairness, promise-keeping, truthfulness, beneficence, and the like. For these factors to have been efficacious, we assume that representations of them in her brain must have been active in some way, and perhaps she was even vaguely conscious of their contents via the relevant concepts, but Bonnie did not focus on these factors, or deploy them in deliberation, nor did she form beliefs about their status as reasons. (Perhaps if the situation were more morally ambiguous she would have needed to deliberate about these factors, but here the right thing to do was clear enough.) Although some deliberation took place, we can imagine that it did not end up changing the reasons for which Bonnie acted.

Habit was not presented as playing a role in Bonnie's story, but it might well have done. Bonnie shakes her head "no" and tells the student that his failing grade will stand. Her utterance is very unlikely to be produced by habit, but her head-shake is another matter. It might be that Bonnie has the habit of shaking her head "no" when making negative assertions in general, or even when thinking negative thoughts in general. If so, then although she formed an immediate intention to shake her head, she perhaps did not quite do so *for* a reason, did not quite do so because it was rationalized by attitudes sending causal *oomph* to generate the needed immediate intention. It might rather have been that Bonnie's head shake was one she was aware would communicate to the student that he would be failing, and because of her moral desire M and her instrumental beliefs about how failing the student realizes or is a means to M, she lacked a strong rationalization for stopping herself from shaking her head "no." And then, having the habit of shaking her head when making negative assertions, and lacking a strong rationalization for stopping herself, she acted out of habit in shaking her head while telling the student that his failing grade would stand.

More could be said, but at this point we hope the idea is clear. Bonnie's acting for moral reasons is just a special case of her acting for reasons, which in turn is fundamentally a matter of ND processes causing her actions in the right way. According to Spare Conativism, acting for moral reasons is just this simple—and just this complex.

PART II

Desire

{ 4 }

Love and Care

This work is entitled *In Praise of Desire*, but the previous three chapters have done more to make room for desires in moral psychology than to laud them specifically. That changes beginning in the present chapter.

Having good will, and so having the ability to act for the right reasons, having the ability to be praiseworthy, and being virtuous, is just a matter of having the right intrinsic desires. This thesis is controversial in part because the nature of intrinsic desires is not well understood by philosophers. This is exemplified at many points in work in ethics and moral psychology, but nowhere more so than in the literatures on love and care.

Our immediate goal for the chapter is to argue that desires have been theoretically mistreated. Desires, it has been said, are mere drives, urges, impulses. They are tied to feelings mainly by the fleeting feelings of frustration and satisfaction afforded by them, and to our cognitive lives mainly through motivated irrationality. Or, if they play slightly broader roles than these, then they nonetheless fall short of playing the rich roles played by loving and caring. But intrinsic desires are much richer than such dismissals suggest. Intrinsic desires are tied to our emotional and cognitive lives, as well as to our motivational lives, to such an extent that they deserve a central role in theories of love and care.

The larger goal is to prepare the way for arguments for the metaphysical separation of intrinsic desires from their effects on motivation or action and on feelings (in chapter 5) and to prepare the way for a positive theory of intrinsic desire (chapter 6). In this chapter, we make a number of claims about what human lives are like as a result of our intrinsic desires. But we will not make any claims about what intrinsic desires really are in the light of these facts. Those claims will come in the two chapters that follow.

4.1 Love

A number of philosophers have advanced desire-based theories of love.[1] These are theories of what it is for a parent to love a child, for siblings to love one another, for friends to love one another, for spouses to love one another, and so on, according to

---

[1] See, e.g., Frankfurt (1999), Stump (2006), Taylor (1976), White (2001).

which what is common to all of these sorts of love is that the one who loves has the right sort of desire for the one who is loved. The simplest form of this theory holds:

For A to love B is for A to intrinsically desire B's wellbeing a great deal.

Thus, for a father to love his child is for the father to desire his child's wellbeing for the child's own sake and to desire it very much. Specific versions of the theory offer various specific complications. Harry Frankfurt's work on love, which requires higher-order conative endorsement of the first-order desire, is perhaps the best-known desire-based theory of love.[2]

There is something appealing to even the simplest version of a desire-based theory of love. People want good things for those they love: a brother who did not have a desire one way or the other about whether his sister was happy, healthy, or active could hardly be said to be a loving brother. And this desire for good things can hardly be instrumental. Nothing could be less loving than to declare, "Of course I greatly desire your wellbeing; I'm being paid a million dollars for every one-point increase your psychiatrists measure in your overall happiness!"[3] And then, while it might be that most of us intrinsically desire the wellbeing of everyone we know, it is clear that most of us intrinsically desire the wellbeing of these people only a little bit, relative to all our varied priorities; we intrinsically desire the wellbeing of those we love much more.

Desire-based theories of love might have a certain appeal, but of course there is room to criticize them. Some of these criticisms are largely internal to the desire-based approach (should the desires have this content or that? should they be supported by value judgments?) but others challenge the very idea of basing a theory of love on the attitude of desire, and these are interesting for what they reveal about contemporary thinking about desire.

In "Love as a Moral Emotion," David Velleman rejects the view that love is any type of desire, including specifically the view that love centrally involves

---

[2] Frankfurt (1999). Compare that work to, e.g., Taylor (1976), which puts constraints on the origins of the intrinsic desire, to Stump (2006), which adds further content to the desire, or Ebels-Duggan (2008), which suggest that one who loves aims at the beloved's achievement of her ends, not merely at her wellbeing.

[3] Kolodny (2003, 135) objects to Frankfurt's theory of love because "Without in fact loving Jane, one can desire to do the same things for her that her lover desires to do. For example, one can desire to help Jane out of, say, duty, or self-interest, or simply because one is seized by a brute urge." In so arguing, Kolodny forgets that Frankfurt has required—exactly for this reason—that the desires that constitute love be intrinsic desires, i.e., desires that are not derived from "duty, or self-interest." In not seeing a clear difference between an intrinsic desire for the wellbeing of Jane and being seized by a "brute urge," Kolodny comes closer to Frankfurt. Frankfurt holds that it is the right sort of second-order desire that is required to make the distinction: a person who wants to have an intrinsic desire for Jane's wellbeing, and so is disposed to take action if that desire should seem to weaken over time, is a person who does not merely have a brute urge. In this chapter and the next two, we will paint a different picture of intrinsic desires, however, on which no intrinsic desire is much like a "brute" urge as imagined here, and so not even Frankfurt's desire-friendly qualification is required.

a desire for the beloved person's wellbeing.[4] Velleman argues that, if a lover is expected to constantly strive for the beloved's wellbeing there cannot be, for example, friendship between people who choose to live in different cities, without it being true that the lover often feels impelled to travel to the city of the beloved to minister to her or his needs. Velleman also argues that, if a lover were to constantly strive for the beloved person's wellbeing, then lovers would be meddling pests, and otherwise intolerable, as the lover's attempts to maximize the beloved's flourishing sometimes fail or backfire. Since these are not the characteristics of people who love, Velleman takes there to be a serious flaw in desire-based theories.

An important implicit premise in Velleman's arguments is that a lover who desires a beloved's wellbeing is a lover who is often motivated to take actions aimed at protecting or improving the wellbeing of the beloved. Velleman presupposes that a person with a desire for an end is a person who will frequently, reliably be motivated to take the means that seem best for achieving that end. In thinking this, he is hardly alone. The idea that there is nothing more to a desire than the impulse to act in the ways that seem most likely to secure the desired end is ubiquitous.[5] But is this correct?

If an intrinsic desire is something that one can have without it creating any impulse to action, then a lover who greatly intrinsically desires the wellbeing of the beloved can love without being constantly, frequently, or even occasionally motivated to act. So this possibility needs to be considered.

Dave might be dreaming of a white Christmas: he wants there to be snow on Christmas day. Or Judy might desire that the Gators win their football games. In both cases, there exists an intrinsic desire, but in neither case is there motivation. Judy, being sane, does not spend her time trying to help her team win. She might be motivated to watch the game on television, and wear her team's colors on the day of the game, but she need be under no illusion that these activities contribute in any way to her getting this particular intrinsic desire satisfied. Likewise, Dave, being sane, does not have an impulse to try to change the weather. He might, if religious or superstitious, pray for snow, but it is hardly necessary that he do so in order for it to be true that he wants there to be snow on Christmas.

---

[4] Velleman also attacks the idea that love centrally involves a desire to be with the beloved, and in this he is right. As Velleman argues, some people who love each other can't stand to be together. Perhaps in romantic love there is a need to make a life together with one's beloved, but as romantic love is neither Velleman's target nor Frankfurt's, this is not to the point; for the agapic love that is of interest to both these theorists, it seems quite possible to love one's beloved while being quite content to not be with the beloved. See Velleman (1999).

[5] Kolodny shares this objection to desire-based theories of love, as he takes even an intrinsic desire to be a "mere urge" (Kolodny 2003, 144–146). See also, for example, Smith (1994) in ethical theory. In the philosophy of mind, see, for example, Armstrong (1980), Millikan (1989), Stalnaker (1984).

Rather than creating urges to act, Dave and Judy's desires show their presences mainly by changing emotions. Because Dave intrinsically desires snow at Christmas, he will be happy if there is snow on Christmas and a little sad if there is not. And in the days leading up to Christmas he will be hopeful if he sees that the forecast calls for below-freezing temperatures and regular flurries. This sort of news will put him in a better mood, and perhaps give him a little dose of optimism. If the forecast calls for temperatures well above freezing, though, Dave is likely to be a little glum. It might also be that Dave will feel nostalgic for the winters of his youth, when snow on December 25th was much more reliable than now, or feel a touch resentful that his career has taken him from a colder climate with snow on the ground throughout the winter months to a warmer climate that threatens to make a mockery of his simple wish for snow on Christmas day. These emotions, observed by Dave and his family, make it clear that Dave wants there to be snow on Christmas day. And likewise, Judy's desire for her team to win will make her ecstatic if the Gators win, and broken-hearted if they lose. And in fact, during the game, her emotions are likely to swing wildly from play to play and moment to moment. A badly chosen play will make Judy angry at the Gator's offensive coach, an injured Gator's quarterback will make her fearful, and signs that the quarterback has shaken off his injury will make her feel relieved. It will be evident to anyone watching her just which team Judy wants to win, without her needing to display any behavioral impulse to assist it.

In general, intrinsic desires make their subjects emotional hostages to fortune. Dave is emotionally vulnerable to the weather and Judy to the vagaries of her football team in a way that neither of them would be without his or her intrinsic desire. And so it is for all of us, independently of facts about motivation.

It might be suggested that, even in the cases of Dave and Judy, agents who intrinsically desire are always agents who are at least disposed to become motivated. Dave would feel an impulse to change the weather if he were to have the power to do so, and Judy would be motivated to cheer loudly while watching the game on television if she were to believe that her cheers would be transmitted back to the Gator's bench and provide them with encouragement. We will return to this claim in the next chapter. But note that we do not, at present, require the strong claim that it is possible for a person to intrinsically desire something without ever being inclined to pursue it. All we require is that it is often true, in ordinary people, that we intrinsically desire something and are vividly aware of how things are going with respect to what we desire, without being filled with impulses to act so as to promote the satisfaction of the desire—not even the faintest sort of impulses. Cases in which ordinary people are emotional when confronted with the weather forecast or the halftime score, without being motivated to do anything about the weather or the score, are all we require at the moment. If these sorts of cases are common, then Velleman's arguments against desire-based theories of love will be weakened, and our understanding of the range of roles played by desires will be expanded.

So far we have discussed a pair of cases in which intrinsic desires do not produce urges to act simply because there is no practical way in which the person with the intrinsic desire can make progress toward satisfying the desire. But sometimes intrinsic desires fail to motivate because they are already satisfied. Suppose that Jason has all the close friends he wants. Jason intrinsically desires a small circle of close friends, and he is lucky in that he has just what he desires. In this situation, no one would expect Jason to feel motivated to make it be the case that he has the number of close friends that he in fact has. This small circle of close friends does not require regular effort to maintain: being close friends, there is nothing special they need to do in order to preserve their friendships. While Jason is motivated to do things for his friends, to spend time with them, talk to them, and so on, he never needs to contemplate strategies specific to the goal of keeping that number of close friends. Yet it would be false to say that as soon as Jason acquired this circle of close friends he no longer desired to have a small circle of close friends. That Jason intrinsically desires to have a small close circle of friends is why he is content with his social circle: his contentment derives from having just what he desires. One could say that Jason is content because he now has what he once desired, but this is not enough to explain his present contentment. Jason might still have (in the back of his closet) the garish pajamas he desired as a boy, but having what he once wanted will not bring Jason any present contentment if he does not, at present, want what he has. The continued possession of the garish pajamas does nothing for Jason because, although having them once satisfied intrinsic desires, it no longer does so. By contrast, the continued possession of a small circle of close friends does make Jason happy, and does so precisely because he has the sort of circle of friends that he wants.

Jason's intrinsic desire for a small circle of close friends will naturally have other emotional effects too, even as it continues to play no motivational role in his life. It might contribute to Jason's being impressed by the story of a religious hermit who has gone for years with minimal human contact, for instance. On learning the story of the hermit, Jason might imaginatively experience a share of the loneliness that would be a daily oppression for him were he to live without friends, and this sense of the burden it would place on him to live as the hermit does might in turn contribute to his grasp of how momentous the hermit's decisions have been, and so to Jason's being impressed with the hermit. These sorts of emotional and cognitive effects of his desire for a small circle of friends might not be ubiquitous, but they might nonetheless be substantially more common than a specific motivation to maintain a circle of friends of appropriate size.

Consider one more way in which a person might have even strong intrinsic desires without often being motivated by them. In this sort of case, a person has an intrinsic desire and is sometimes subjected to impulses to act as a result, but these impulses are rare, because occasions on which action might increase the likelihood of the desire being satisfied are also rare.

Suppose that Gabrielle's greatest desire is to become an American citizen. She has done all she can so far to become a citizen, and she is highly committed to seeing the process through. But also suppose, as is realistic, that most of the time there is nothing she can do about her immigration status. If Gabrielle is a normal human being, when it is clear that there is nothing she can do that will materially advance her chances of getting what she so much desires, she will not have urges or impulses to take action. She might still, very naturally, be profoundly emotionally moved by her desire. Because the process of becoming an American citizen is a protracted obstacle course, Gabrielle might be tense at times and even have trouble sleeping. When her application is under review she might live an intense emotional life that swings between hope and fear as she contemplates what might go right and what might go wrong. Feeling that the stakes are high is a direct result of her desire for citizenship, and those feelings might be the predominant sign of her desire. Her impulses and actions, though another excellent sign of her desire, might be far more infrequent. Her lack of impulses need not even show that she believes it impossible to affect her candidacy for citizenship at that very moment at which all impulse is lacking. She might believe that there is a small chance that she will one day assault a particularly irritating coworker and so be arrested, and so ruin her chance to become a citizen. She might see that theoretically she could reduce the chance of this happening by taking anger management classes or by arranging to be transferred to a different job. Though in principle it might make a difference to her citizenship, the idea of her literally assaulting the coworker is far enough beyond the pale that she does not take it seriously and feels no impulse to act on it. This would not impugn the claim that she very much desires to become an American citizen.

Returning now to the topic of love: Velleman argues that if love is, at bottom, a matter of desiring something like the wellbeing of the beloved then love is a state that should be expected to generate fussing over the beloved. One would expect a person to constantly be rushing to the side of her friends when they fall sick, or suffer romantic setbacks, or have trouble folding the laundry quickly enough. Or, if not actually rushing to assist in these situations, then one would expect the loving friend to be at least motivated to do so. Velleman is right in suggesting that this is an absurd picture of what is involved when a person loves a friend, but wrong in holding that there is a problem here for a desire-based theory of love.

On the model of our first sort of case, imagine that Julian, a charming rogue, desires Veronica's wellbeing noninstrumentally (much to his surprise as a long-time rogue). But Veronica is an innocent with all the advantages in life, and Julian knows he will never lead a stable life or long remain true to any person.

(We gleefully borrow all the clichés of the romance novel for this example.) So when Veronica declares to Julian that she wishes to abandon her privileged life for the life of a rogue's lover, he decides that, for the sake of Veronica's wellbeing, he must both refuse her and must never contact her again. Without another word, he leaves for another continent, never to return. Julian never again feels any impulse to do something in order to benefit Veronica to make her better off (not even an impulse to stay away from her—traveling between continents is not typically something one needs to make an effort to avoid doing). But perhaps Julian retains a strong emotional investment in Veronica's wellbeing. He hopes that she is doing well, and would be devastated if he would somehow learn that her family had lost its fortune and been disgraced, or that she had been seriously hurt while riding her beloved horses. Thus, while he greatly intrinsically desires what is best for Veronica and has strong feelings sometimes as a result, he does nothing to improve her wellbeing, and feels no impulses to do anything, because it seems to him that there is nothing he can do.

On the model of our second sort of case, imagine that Charles was Michelle's mentor when she was an undergraduate, and that through their times spent talking together and working on some of Charles' projects Charles has come to have a sort of parental interest in Michelle's life, and he wants very much that she do well, for her own sake. Ten years later, Michelle has a wonderful life. She is an important administrator for a large hospital, an occupation well suited to her talents and interests. She is happily married to a thoughtful man who is just as smart and talented as she, and she has two daughters. She is financially secure, intellectually challenged, emotionally content. Charles could not be happier for her. But because things are going so well for Michelle, it never occurs to Charles to reach out a helping hand, or to send a supportive note, to his former protégée. He has no impulse to act for Michelle's wellbeing because she is doing just as well as Charles ever hoped she would do. His desire for her wellbeing is manifested in the delight he takes in her successes as the news trickles out to him and in the occasional few minutes he spends reminiscing about the delightful days when he could make a positive difference to her life. He need feel no impulses to act for Michelle's wellbeing to convince us that he very much desires it.

On the model of our third sort of case, imagine that Ludmilla greatly intrinsically desires the wellbeing of Lisa, but it turns out that the two of them have come to live in different cities. Each of them is very busy with her chosen profession and family. Lisa is usually doing quite well, and Ludmilla fussing over Lisa on a daily basis would be counterproductive: an annoyance to Lisa at the endless barrage of phone calls, letters, and surprise visits. It would also be a lot of effort for Ludmilla given the very modest benefit it would typically bring to Lisa. While Ludmilla very much intrinsically desires Lisa's wellbeing, she also intrinsically desires a number of other things, and like any ordinary person she distributes her efforts in part on the basis of where she can get the most of what she wants to achieve with the least effort. Occasionally, though, Ludmilla spots an object or hears a story and thinks "Lisa would like this," and then sometimes she buys the object as a birthday gift or remembers the story for the next time they will talk or exchange notes. And even more occasionally Ludmilla has a chance to make a big difference to Lisa's wellbeing: there was that time when Lisa needed all the support she could get in the wake of her mother's death. Naturally, Ludmilla had indeed felt an impulse to step in and offer her support. Such occasions to do so much for Lisa are, however, very rare in their friendship. In between them, Ludmilla's thoughts and feelings often reflect her intrinsic desire for Lisa's wellbeing, and they do so more often than her actions.

In these three scenarios, the person who loves has a strong intrinsic desire for the wellbeing of the beloved, but this desire is very rarely manifested in actions or impulses to act, and is primarily manifested in the emotions of the person with the desire. In Velleman's eyes, an emotion-based theory of love is one that contrasts with a desire-based theory of love in the way that feelings contrast with actions. But when we recall in detail what it is like desire something, and specifically to greatly desire something for its own sake, we are reminded that a desire-based theory of love predicts the emotions that we associate with people loving each other, and predicts these emotions without the need to invoke some further independent factor. The abhorrent result that to love a person is merely to have a collection of impulses to act in certain ways is one that the desire-based theory of love need not, and should not, embrace.

Velleman also underestimates the resources of a desire-based theory of love when discussing the endurance of love through changes in the beloved. He considers the idea that we love someone for her virtues or her unique quirks, but rejects it. In true love, he holds, the lover continues to love the beloved even when she loses these virtues or quirks.

Love does not always last, but even so Velleman is quite right that our love of friends, family, and spouses is not sensitive to the most ordinary ways in which superficial qualities change. A couple can talk about how they came to love each other for their beauty and graceful dancing, and still be in love long after they have ceased to be beautiful or able to dance. How can a desire-based theory of love agree?

There is no technical problem here. On the simple version of the desire-based view, to love someone is to intrinsically desire the wellbeing of that person a great deal, and the person remains the same person whether fit or shapeless, young or old, committed to modal realism or exploring solipsism. As the loved person remains the same individual, there is no reason inherent to the content of the desire for the desire to fade as the loved person's qualities change over time.

It is interesting to go beyond the technical problems, though. The phenomenon in question is not unique to love. A fan of a baseball team can remain a fan, desiring that the team be victorious, even as the staff changes, the manager changes, the owner changes, and even after the team is moved from New York to San Francisco. And similarly, a citizen can embrace her country, desiring that it be strong and free and so on, even though she admired it as a child for its justice and liberty, and even though as an adult she no longer thinks her country particularly just or free. Our attitudes toward many things, including our intrinsic desires regarding them, can persist even as our beliefs about their qualities change. Thus, the fact that it is possible to love a person after she has completely changed does not rule out a desire-based theory of love.

The couple who talks about how they first loved each other for their looks strikes us as saying something true (or something that might well be true) in a misleading way. To say that the beloved is loved for his looks suggests that the appearance of the beloved is one's sole concern. And with Frankfurt and Velleman both, we would hold that it is not possible to love someone if one's sole concern is with the person's appearance. One must be concerned with something deeper if one's attitude is to really be one of love: something like the wellbeing of the beloved. There is another way to understand "I loved him for his looks," however. It might be understood as saying that the speaker came to love someone through a causal sequence that began with liking the person's appearance, that is, as saying "I came to love him (partly) because of his looks." And on this reading, we think it is both sometimes true and also consistent with a desire-based theory of love.

It is common for desires to be transformed, so that something at first wanted instrumentally (or as a realizer) becomes intrinsically desired.[6] Cho can take a philosophy course as a means to future success in law school, yet by the end of the semester it has become true that she desires to study philosophy for its own sake. This is a very simple transformation, in which Cho at first desires something instrumentally, and then desires it intrinsically.

There is also a more complex form of this transformation. Grace might initially want to attend her college because she expects its distinguished name to help her get a job, but she might end up caring enough about it to donate money for the preservation of its historic main gate, though this does not benefit her career in any way. In this story, Grace initially wants to attend her college instrumentally. In the end, though, she is not said to want to attend her college intrinsically. Rather, she is said to want good things for her college intrinsically—things such as preservation of the historic main gate. But it is easy to imagine that, when she started college, Grace did not care one way or another about the preservation of the historic main gate. The gate's preservation was not even a means to an end for Grace, because her relationship to her college was so instrumental that only features of the college that might have affected

---

[6] The account of the phenomenon in Blackburn (1998, 206) is quite close to our own. Vargas (2013, 175–177) suggests something similar transpires in the acquisition of intrinsic desires for the right or good. Schmidtz (1994) presents a somewhat different take on very similar phenomena.

her employment prospects mattered to her, and it is easy to imagine that Grace saw no relation between the preservation of the historic main gate and her future employment prospects. Nonetheless, this sort of shift is common. What might mediate the transformation is not clear, but it seems that the transformation of people like Grace is most likely to occur when the person has a wonderful time at college, when she involves herself in the life of the college fully, and when she is somehow reminded (not in so many words) not to take the benefits of her college for granted. Under these conditions, it is easy to imagine Grace changing from a mere user of the college to someone who wants what is good for the college intrinsically.

If a transformation like the one we have imagined for Grace has been fairly described, then we have a model for how a couple can be led to love by each other's attractive appearances, even within a desire-based framework. Initially, the members of the couple want each other's presence instrumentally. It is pleasant to be in the company of an attractive person, and to hold the attention of a person to whom one is attracted. It is pleasant for those who like to dance to do so with someone who dances well, who might excite envy in one's peers, and so on. But if this instrumental partnership built out of attractive appearances and dance skills continues, it might be that the couple finds their instrumental partnership to also provide a wonderful time, that improves when they more fully involve themselves in each other's lives, and all without taking what they have for granted. And under these circumstances, it would be as expected that they come to have an intrinsic desire for what is good for one another as it would be that Grace come to have an intrinsic desire for what is good for her college.

This story, while speculative, does not go beyond the ordinary understanding we have of what desires are like.[7] As a result, while we would not claim to have demonstrated how people come to love one another, we can claim that there is nothing in the phenomenon of starting out with a superficial interest in a person's transient qualities, only to end up with a deep interest in the person's wellbeing as such, that requires us to abandon a desire-based theory of love for some other. Here as before, desires have a sufficiently complex relation to our lives as a whole that they are credible candidates to explain complex aspects of love.[8]

---

[7] The relevant empirical literature is also worth considering, of course. According to one important review (Pettigrew 1998), there is a large body of evidence supporting the idea that working together toward shared goals is one important factor in bringing people to have "affective ties" that reduce prejudice. An early study in this line found that, in the sailors of the US merchant marine after World War Two, white prejudice against blacks was diminished in those white sailors who have served on the most missions with black sailors, especially missions seeing combat (Brophy 1946), and many studies since have found similar findings.

[8] In chapter 6, we will argue that intrinsic desires in fact have the causal powers required to be what explains changes like the ones we just described, though this is still not the same thing as demonstrating that they actually cause the most familiar changes in desires of this sort.

A potential objection to our account of the growth of love out of mere instrumental desires comes from Stephen Darwall.[9] Darwall holds that the process we describe is too base a material from which to create a genuinely caring attitude, and the objection might be made equally to loving attitudes. Darwall discusses Mill's observation that some people become attached to wealth for its own sake after having pursued it for further ends, and says that surely we do not want caring for a person to come from these types of motives. But if we take the words "for its own sake" seriously, it is not clear that it matters where a desire for something for its own sake came from. Cho's desire for philosophical knowledge might have originated in her taking philosophy courses for ulterior motives, such as law school success, but now that Cho wants philosophical knowledge for its own sake, and things are such that she would continue to desire such knowledge even when it would not help her to attain anything else—in fact even if it would modestly harm her (perhaps, by decreasing her expected future earnings)—her thirst for philosophical knowledge "counts" just as much as the thirst for philosophical knowledge displayed by another person who had a desire to be a philosopher since infancy, or a third party who came to have a thirst for philosophical knowledge after being told endlessly by her philosopher parents, until she came to endorse it herself, that knowledge of truth, justice, and beauty is a great good. Similarly, once a lovelike attitude has all the features true love should have, there is no need to begrudge it its shady origins (in beauty, lust, loneliness...) any more than there is a reason to declare pearls unlovely in virtue of their origins in grit and oyster-secretion.

In addition to these arguments, there are two other characteristics of love that Velleman appeals to in order to support his theory.

There is a sense that when we love, we let go of some defensive mechanisms and leave ourselves very vulnerable, and this strikes Velleman as specific to an emotional stance toward the beloved. But when we desire something greatly we are also vulnerable as a result. Intrinsic desires for life or liberty certainly makes us vulnerable in circumstances that make it uncertain whether or not we will have what we want. More modestly, an intrinsic desire that the Gators win the championship makes one vulnerable to being tense, irritable, sad, and angry as well as hopeful and elated. The intrinsic desire for another person's wellbeing can have a similar effect.

More challenging is Velleman's observation that love involves "really looking" at the beloved and seeing him clearly. Is there any way in which an intrinsic desire for someone's wellbeing involves seeing the beloved clearly? There is probably no reasonable desire-based account of love that is compatible with the view Velleman eventually defends, according to which what we see when we see a person clearly is her autonomous, rational self. But it would still be

---

[9] Darwall (2002).

interesting to see whether the intuition that love can ever make us "see clearly" can be supported, in itself, by a desire-based account of love. It is interesting at least in part because it is a common view that love, whether it is a desire or not, mostly *interferes* with our ability to see its object clearly. A mother who loves her child more will be more likely than if she loved him less to be self-deceived about his use of illegal drugs, for example, all else being equal. But we believe that the thesis that love *sometimes* improves our epistemic access to its object is both true and supported by a desire-based account of love.

Consider how well you can tell songs that you like apart from each other and how songs from genres you dislike all sound the same: depending on what you dislike, all operas are the same screaming, all rock music is the same drum-banging, and so on. Songs from genres that you like, on the other hand, sound different. The fact that you like these songs, that is, the fact that these songs have the qualities you desire from songs you listen to, makes you "really listen" and understand them better. Similarly, if two people study a topic, the person who has an intrinsic desire to learn about the topic finds it much easier to learn about it. This happens not only because she makes more effort, but also because she has an easier time doing things such as paying attention to data and remembering them. If your object of intrinsic desire is the good of another person, then although it can cause you to be self-deceived about him, it can also create in you an epistemic sensitivity to all that concerns him. You might find yourself knowing things about him that you never made a conscious effort to know. You might find yourself reaching insights into what makes him act, feel, and think as he does, insights that elude others who perhaps have to work with him every day, but who lack your intrinsic desires (more on this and related phenomena in chapter 9).

It appears that intrinsic desires, as they are situated in ordinary human beings, can explain the phenomena of love that Velleman finds important. Intrinsic desires, as found in entirely mundane cases that have nothing to do with love, cause the general sorts of effects of interest; and intrinsic desires, as found in cases in which one person intrinsically desires the wellbeing of another very much, can be expected to cause the particular effects associated with loving. Rather than being narrowing and reductive, a desire-based theory of love can explain many of the rich emotional and cognitive features of love to which Velleman draws our attention. The more one thinks about the effects of our intrinsic desires, the more one appreciates the possibilities of a desire-based moral psychology.

4.2 Care

Caring is the second topic of this chapter, and the general thesis is parallel to that of the previous section: a number of theorists of caring have diminished or derided desire-based theories of caring, yet their grounds for doing so reflect an impoverished idea of what it is like for ordinary human beings to have intrinsic desires.

In the first two pages of *Welfare and Rational Care*, Darwall writes that caring about a person cannot possibly be a kind of desiring her wellbeing, or desiring at all.[10] According to Darwall, there are many cases in which there is a desire for someone's wellbeing without genuine care for that person. He thinks of these cases as cases in which we desire a person's good but not for his own sake. And he is right that we can imagine many cases in which one desires someone's good without caring about her. In most such scenarios, the desire is instrumental: you could want your boss to be always happy purely because it happens that when your boss is happy she is nice to you. In this case it would be natural, just as Darwall would have it, to say that you want her good but not for her sake. But of course, this observation is consistent with a desire-based theory of caring in which it is required that one intrinsically desire another's wellbeing in order to care for her.

In other cases to which Darwall draws our attention, the desire that does not suffice for caring is a realizer desire. For example, Mohandas might want Vikram be happy as part of his intrinsic desire that all people in the world be happy. Again Darwall seems correct about the particular case: Mohandas does not care for Vikram specifically. But if we are interested in a theory according to which to care about someone is to intrinsically desire her wellbeing, we will take neither instrumental nor realizer desires to ground counterexamples to the theory.

Darwall also argues against desire-based theories of caring by describing how it feels to care for someone:

> Caring for someone involves a whole complex of emotions, sensitivities, and dispositions to attend in ways that a simple desire that another be benefitted need not. If someone about whom I care is miserable and suffering, I will be disposed to emotional responses, for example, to sadness on his behalf, that cannot be explained by the mere fact that an intrinsic desire for his wellbeing is not realized. Taken by itself, all that would explain would be dissatisfaction, disappointment, or frustration.[11]

In the same vein, Agnieszka Jaworska has also argued that desires for the person one cares about are merely a small part of what it is to care about that person, and part of her evidence is likewise the idea that the rich emotions involved in caring for someone cannot be explained by a desire alone.[12]

---

[10] Darwall (2002).

[11] Darwall (2002, 2).

[12] Jaworska (1999). For a more rounded view of her take on caring, see also her (2007a; 2007b).

If we look for a moment at desires that do not involve our fellow human beings, however, we see that even they, when unfulfilled ("frustrated" in the technical sense), bring with them a wider variety of emotions. Maider has a strong desire for the survival of the Basque language. If the Basque language were to become extinct she would feel much more than "dissatisfaction, disappointment, and frustration." She would feel profound grief and, depending on the circumstances, anger. Similarly, if linguists were to announce tomorrow that the Basque language is no longer in any danger of becoming extinct, she would feel more than satisfaction, pleasant surprise, or relief (these presumably being the immediate opposites of dissatisfaction, disappointment, and frustration). She would feel genuinely happy, and, depending on the circumstances, grateful. In the current situation, in which the Basque language is endangered but has a chance of recovering, there are all kinds of complex sensitivities and dispositions in Maider as a result of her desire. The subject of the language appears in her mind quite often, in response to the smallest cues. She feels hope and fear, and a sense of duty to do her best by the Basque language and to introduce it, almost represent it, to people who have never heard of it. The sound of the language, which she has always liked, has for her taken on a tone of bittersweet longing that would not have been there if it were not for the desire for the wellbeing of the language and the ambiguous circumstances in which it exists: even funny Basque poems produce a touch of melancholy in her sometimes.

It might be objected that the example sneaks in more than a mere desire. Granting that Maider desires the wellbeing of the Basque language for its own sake, an objector might complain that the full syndrome just described goes beyond desire to something richer, namely, caring about the language.

The argument so far has been relying on the reader sharing our views about particular cases: cases in which people intrinsically desire the success of a sporting team, intrinsically desire snow at Christmas, intrinsically desire a small circle of close friends, and so on. Our contention has been that in these cases, the possession of the intrinsic desire is sufficient, in normal human beings, to generate both impulses to action (under certain conditions) and a wide variety of emotions (under somewhat different conditions), along with some cognitive effects worth noting.

If the reader has agreed, then the extension of this style of argument to the phenomenon of caring should convince the reader that caring need be no more than intrinsically desiring the right thing for the cared-for person or thing—intrinsically desiring its wellbeing, or something similar.[13] However, if the reader has not been fully convinced by previous examples, a dispute might now be coming into sharp focus. We claim that having intrinsic desires generates dispositions to a wide variety of emotions. But a theorist such as Darwall

---

[13] Which would, not surprisingly, make loving a species of caring, or else make the two attitudes close cousins. See, e.g., Frankfurt (1999) on the close relation of love to care.

or Jaworska might counter that intrinsic desires do not generate dispositions to a wide variety of emotions, and so they might hold that our previous examples have been flawed. We have claimed that our previous examples have been examples of people who merely have specific intrinsic desires: that there be snow at Christmas, and so on. But Darwall or Jaworska might claim instead that our examples have been of people who, in addition to intrinsically desiring certain things, also *cared* about those things—and it is the caring, not the intrinsically desiring, that is responsible for the emotions (and cognitive dispositions) to which we have been pointing.

To settle this possible dispute we need more evidence, especially about the relationship between intrinsic desires, caring, and emotions.[14] We also need some methodological starting points. Since the desire-centered moral psychologist holds that caring about something reduces to intrinsically desiring, it will not help the cause of a philosopher such as Darwall or Jaworska to point out that, when people are disposed to feel strongly about things, we are inclined to say that people care about them. Similarly, because Darwall and Jaworska hold that desiring is a part of caring, it will not help the cause of the desire-centered moral psychologist to demand that Darwall or Jaworska produce a case in which someone cares without desiring. The sort of case that both theorists should agree are not ruled out by hypothesis, and that would be telling, are cases in which it seems that a person intrinsically desires the wellbeing of another person or thing, but it does not seem that the person cares about that person or thing. The defender of Darwall or Jaworska seems committed to there being such cases, since desiring is only a small part of caring on those views. And the defender of a desire-based theory of caring should be willing to go looking for such cases, secure in the belief that there will be none to be found.

Are there cases in which a person intrinsically desires someone else's wellbeing without caring about it? It seems possible to think of a case that is at least fairly compelling. Suppose that Anne and Ned have known each other well enough to say "hello" in the hallway for years, but that they are not close. They work in the same place, but not as peers, and they have no real basis for a friendship. Nonetheless, Ned energetically worked to benefit Anne on an important occasion, and Anne has happily sung Ned's praises since. Ned and Anne know each other as individuals, and have very modest positive feelings about each other. They have, however, demonstrated their willingness to act so as to benefit the other in a manner that was not contingent on any expected side-benefit, and they have done so because of each other's particularities (it wasn't that Ned benefitted Anne merely as part of his larger obligations in his role, for example). So it seems that they must, to some extent, desire each

---

[14] More evidence about the relation of intrinsic desires to certain forms of learning and attending would also be valuable, but we focus here just on emotion.

other's wellbeing for each other's own sake. Yet in this situation, it might seem strained to say that they care about each other. It would be wrong to say "Ned doesn't care about Anne" or vice versa, but "caring" seems to suggest rather more than their cordial but positive relationship, in spite of the intrinsic desire for each other's wellbeing that is on display.

If the example is convincing, then it also appears to suggest a route for the desire-based theory of caring to be improved, and so not to fall prey to the example. A desire-based theory of caring should hold either of two things. The first option is to hold that to care for another person (or thing) requires that one intrinsically desire the other person's wellbeing *a great deal*. Ned and Anne, though they desire each other's wellbeing, do not desire it a great deal, and this seems a key source of reluctance to describe them as caring about each other. If they did desire each other's wellbeing a great deal, and had demonstrated it—if they had the sort of relationship that involved taking a three-day weekend to help the other one move to Tennessee, and so on—then it would be harder to sustain the claim that they do not care about each other. The second option is to hold that caring for another person (or thing) comes in degrees, with the degree of caring based on the degree of desiring: the more one intrinsically desires the wellbeing of another, the more one cares for another. The approach here would be to say that Ned and Anne care about each other a little.

If the view of Darwall or Jaworska is to make real headway against a desire-based theory of caring, it needs an example in which one person intrinsically desires the wellbeing of another person a great deal and nonetheless cannot be said to care about that other person. In our view, there is no convincing case that involves only ordinary, healthy human beings. In ordinary, healthy human beings, one who intrinsically desires the wellbeing of another a great deal is always a person who experiences a broad range of emotions surrounding that person, and is always someone who would be said to care about that other person. It is only in cases suited to textbooks in abnormal psychology that one begins to find possible divergences between intrinsically wanting another's wellbeing a great deal and caring for that person. Perhaps a person who was intrinsically motivated to help another, but who felt powerless over this inclination and who had a horror of acting on it, as a late-stage addict could feel with respect to using heroin, would be a person who intrinsically desired the wellbeing of another a great deal without caring for that person. And perhaps a person who was intrinsically motivated to help her elderly parents, but who was pathologically unable to access any emotion whatsoever in any situation, could be said to be a problem case for a desire-based theory of caring as well.

Cases from abnormal psychology are, however, problematic. Not across the board: we think there is a time and a place for the outlandish thought experiment in philosophy, and sometimes it is hard to think of a nonclinical case that illustrates the distinction between two parts of the human mind that ordinarily work in concert. But cases from abnormal psychology are problematic when there are hotly contested necessities involved at multiple points in the abnormal case. There are some who hold that desires necessarily dispose us to certain emotions upon their satisfaction, and others who hold that desires are nothing other than such dispositions.[15] There are some who hold that desires, along with appropriate beliefs, suffice for the existence of emotions in general; others hold it of some emotions but not all. And so on. Any attempt to hold that an imagined pathological case is a case in which a person has an intrinsic desire but is not disposed to enjoy its satisfaction, or is not subject to any emotions as a result of the desire, is a challenge to such theories in addition to being a challenge to a desire-based theory of caring.

We will have more to say about the cases from abnormal psychology in the next chapter. But for now we will set these possible cases to one side. It is enough for now to note that, restricting ourselves to healthy human beings, there are no obvious cases in which a person with a strong intrinsic desire for another's wellbeing appears not to care for that other, and this fact suggests (without demonstrating) that the features associated with caring—the features other than motivation, that are identified by Darwall and Jaworska—are features that are a natural consequence of possessing strong intrinsic desires.

Darwall's statement about desire frustration only producing "frustration, dissatisfaction, and disappointment" is puzzling to us, since it seems contrary to the evidence of the cases we have been discussing in this chapter. Perhaps it has something to do with a view of desire as an urge to do something, such as improve the lot of the person whose wellbeing is desired. If the wellbeing of another person is something we merely have an impulse to secure, we will be susceptible only to the sorts of emotions that impulses to act generate when the acts succeed or fail. But if intrinsic desires are more than this, as we have been urging, then there is no reason to see their emotional roles as so confined.

The following sort of question, then, persists: if Archie desires Randolph's wellbeing noninstrumentally and not merely as an instance of something else, and if that desire causes Archie to be sad when Randolph is miserable and happy when he is flourishing, what if anything is missing before we can say that Archie feels the misery and the happiness on Randolph's behalf? If Archie acts on that intrinsic desire, what is missing in his action to make it done because he cares for Randolph? Again, we are not arguing here that we have demonstrated Darwall is wrong, but rather that it is striking how quickly he dismisses desire-based explanations of the phenomena he raises. There is room for a theory of desires that grants them the rich roles they appear to play in us, and such a theory is a promising starting point for theories of love and care, and for moral psychology in general.

---

[15] See, e.g., Davis (1986), Vadas (1984), Strawson (1994).

{ 5 }

What Desires Are Not

Spare Conativism has to contend with various objections that begin from two common premises. The first is that the only essential feature of desires is that they cause actions (in conjunction with instrumental beliefs). The second common premise is that no motivational state counts as a desire in a nontrivializing sense (in a sense in which desires can be distinguished from motivating normative beliefs) unless part of its essence is to dispose the person with the desire to pleasure or displeasure (under appropriate circumstances). The first common premise lies behind arguments that denigrate desires as mere impulses to act. The second common premise lies behind arguments that denigrate desires as mere appetites.

As we saw in the previous chapter, the first common premise is one that might make a theorist wary of holding a desire-based theory of love or care, among other things. Love and care are not just motivational states but emotionally and cognitively complex states of mind. If desires are nothing but impulses to act, then desire-based theories of love and care are missing more than half of the phenomenon in each case.

The second common premise might make a theorist wary of holding a desire-based theory of moral motivation. Moral motivation often exists in spite of the fact that one is not looking forward with pleasure to the action one is motivated to take. In fact, one often dreads doing the right thing but does it anyway, acting against "what one wants to do," as people say. And then, in doing the right thing one feels miserable, and having done it one appreciates intellectually that it was good but takes no pleasure in the accomplishment. If desiring an end necessarily disposes us to pleasure in its attainment, then the experience of moral motivation suggests desires are optional.

Both common premises have a good deal to be said for them, but in the end they should be rejected. In this chapter, we argue for the separation of intrinsic desires from their familiar effects on motivation and feelings.[1] By reaching these negative conclusions, we give ourselves room to reject the common premises and so the conclusions that seem to follow from them. But the negative

---

[1] Pure theories of this form can be found in Smith (1994), where motivation is made the essence of desire and Strawson (1994), where the feeling of pleasure is made the essence of desire. A clean two-factor theory of desire is articulated and defended in Davis (1986).

conclusions raise the question of what intrinsic desires really are, if they are not essentially motivational or emotional states of mind. In chapter 6, we provide the positive theory. But this positive theory will only be plausible once the ground has been cleared for it.

5.1 Action Is Not the Essence of Desire

According to the popular action-based theory of intrinsic desire, intrinsic desires are made intrinsic desires by their effects on our actions. To intrinsically desire that P is to be in a state such that, if one believes that bringing it about that Q is a way to getP, then one is disposed (all else being equal) to bring it about that Q.[2] On this sort of theory, to intrinsically desire that one live in San Francisco is to be in a state that is disposed to cause the actions that result in living in San Francisco. If the intrinsic desire did not (tend to) cause actions that seem likely to get one to live in San Francisco, then the state in question would not be an intrinsic desire to live in San Francisco. If the intrinsic desire did not (tend to) cause actions of any sort, it would not be an intrinsic desire of any sort.

To many philosophers, the idea that intrinsic desires cause actions (necessarily, or they just would not be intrinsic desires) is an obvious one. To intrinsically desire something is just to have an impulse toward it, or to have a tendency to such impulses, they might say. The same idea has been behind a number of criticisms of the idea that intrinsic desires are the source of our reasons for action: a mere impulse to count the blades of grass on a lawn cannot provide one with a reason to count the blades of grass, as the argument goes.

In spite of how common it is, the identification of intrinsic desires with states that (tend to) cause actions is problematic, and this section is dedicated to rejecting the idea that action is the essence of intrinsic desire. Dispositions to bodily movements, however sophisticated, are neither *sufficient* nor *necessary* for the existence of desires.

Consider again the habits last discussed in chapter 3. Habits are states that tend to cause actions. If Travis is in the habit of turning left onto University Drive, then he might out of habit take just that action: turning left onto University Drive. Like intrinsic desires, habits are states that respond to one's beliefs. If Travis is in the habit of turning left onto University Drive, his habit is a state that tends to cause him to turn left onto University Drive when (but only when) he believes that he is driving, that University Drive is now on his left, and so on. Structurally, this is just the role attributed to intrinsic desires by those holding the action-based theory of intrinsic desire. But being moved

---

[2] For a particularly clear discussion see Smith (1987; 1994).

by habit is not being moved by an intrinsic desire.[3] In fact, what can often be frustrating about our habits is precisely that they operate, especially when we are inattentive, quite independently of our intrinsic desires.

To see that habits are not simply a type of intrinsic desire, consider a few lines of evidence. There is the fact that common sense distinguishes the two: it is reasonable to say "I didn't *want* to do that, I just did it out of habit" and it is unreasonable to say "you must have wanted to do it, since you did it out of habit." And common practices of offering excuses make a distinction between intrinsic desires and habits. If Travis is late because he made a wrong turn out of habit, Travis can offer "I was on autopilot and turned left on University Drive, and that really slowed me down" as at least a partial excuse. He cannot offer "I really wanted to make that left turn onto University Drive when I had the chance" as an excuse, however. These facts are not conclusive, but they are data that it would be better to capture than dismiss.

There is also the fact that habits are tied solely to behavior: they do not engage our emotions in the way we expect of intrinsic desires, nor do habits of action engage our attention or thoughts. If Travis is heading to visit Ned one evening and just happens to pass University Drive on his left, there is a danger that his habit will engage and cause him to turn left—but Travis will not get any passing enjoyment from having made his habitual left turn onto University Drive if he makes the turn while going to see Ned. Instead, he will merely be irritated at his having let habit take over when it was not helpful. And likewise, he will not have seen the approach of University Drive on his left in a positive light, nor will he have found himself contemplating possible reasons to make the left turn while on the way to visit Ned.

It might be said that habits can be distinguished from intrinsic desires on purely behavioral grounds, because when a person is in the habit of making a particular left turn (for instance) he does not go out of his way to reach the intersection with the left turn, whereas a person who intrinsically desires to savor peaches (for instance) does go out of her way to be in a position to savor peaches, by heading down to the grocery store to buy them. That is, it might be said that habits only give rise to dispositions to act under specific triggering conditions, whereas intrinsic desires give rise to dispositions to act under any condition in which a means to achieving the intrinsically desired end is grasped. And because of this, it might be said, habits present no threat to a slightly more sophisticated form of a purely action-oriented sufficient condition for (or theory of) desire.

This response does recognize something about the difference between ordinary habits and ordinary intrinsic desires. But it does not suffice to make a principled distinction. Imagine Travis has an intrinsic desire that, when he finds

---

[3] This point has been made by Rachel Cohon, though the example she gives is not an instance of pure habit. See Cohon (1993).

himself driving at the familiar intersection, with University Drive on his left, and when conditions are safe, he make the left turn. This postulated intrinsic desire's content is unusual, but Travis's habitual behavior is consistent with it. And in general, when an agent is in the habit of taking action A under conditions C, it will be possible to postulate an intrinsic desire in her to explain her habitual behaviors: an intrinsic desire to take action A when it so happens that she finds herself in conditions C. But the fact that all this is possible does nothing to increase the conviction that the postulation is reasonable. What still seems most reasonable is that habits are something quite different from intrinsic desires. The fact that habits are states that are sufficient for action when conjoined with appropriate beliefs does not show that habits are, or involve, intrinsic desires.

A different sort of objection to the action-based theory of intrinsic desire is raised by Dennis Stampe. Stampe asks us to consider the sort of case in which believing that a certain course of action will lead to a certain outcome is the self-defeating cause of just that outcome.[4] For instance, suppose a person is playing tennis, and has faulted on her first serve. It occurs to her that, if she serves just so, she will double-fault. And being anxious about double-faulting, her thought actually makes it the case that she is now disposed to serve just so and double-fault. The tennis player is in a state that, combined with her belief, disposes her to act so as to double-fault, but she does not intrinsically desire to double-fault: quite the contrary. She nonetheless satisfies the action-oriented theory's criterion for desiring to double-fault.

One possible response is to deny that the movements of the person who double-faults, or who acts out of habit, for that matter, are genuine actions at all. But this response seems to beg the question, since what it is to be a genuine action is, in part, to be caused by intrinsic desires (as we argued in chapter 3). To show that double-faults and habitual left turns are not actions requires showing that they are not caused by intrinsic desires, and so cannot presuppose that they are not.

The objections just raised attack the idea that (even belief-sensitive) dispositions to action *suffice* to make something an intrinsic desire. But there are also objections that can be raised to the idea that disposing one to action is *necessary* to a state's being an intrinsic desire.

In discussing loving and caring, we noted the range of intrinsic desires that seem to exist that also seem to have little or nothing to do with action. We intrinsically desire victories for our favorite sporting teams, but (aside from shouting encouragement at the television) rarely even feel an impulse to help our teams win, much less act on one.[5] But now, consider some cases with even

---

[4] Stampe (1986).

[5] And consider what would really help the team win. Buying team merchandise with a high mark-up is probably the easiest way to help, but it's a rare fan who even thinks of buying a cheap

weaker relations between the intrinsic desires and possible actions. Perhaps we intrinsically desire there to exist a cure for the common cold. That is, we intrinsically desire that there exist some compound such that it would, if administered, cure the common cold. Probably we intrinsically desire that someone find the cure, and that is a matter to which we might feel an impulse to contribute if it ever seemed possible to do so. But to intrinsically desire that there *exist* a cure is to intrinsically desire that the universe be such that there is some possible compound that would do the job, and that is something that we never feel an impulse toward bringing about—and we would have to be deluded in order to feel it in any case. (Mathematicians who intrinsically desire that P = NP or the like are more exotic variants on this theme.)

Also instructive are cases in which the agent wants something to happen regardless of her own efforts. For example, a person might desire that her husband love her *regardless of what she does*. It is also true that a few unfortunate ones among us intrinsically desire never to have existed, but it is certainly not the case that what they harbor is an impulse to prevent their own conceptions. These cases seem to illustrate the idea that disposing one to action is not necessary for having an intrinsic desire.

Galen Strawson has argued for the same conclusion by imagining a race of creatures known as the Weather Watchers.[6] These creatures are conscious and have rich emotional lives. But otherwise, they are just like plants: they lack any capacity for movement whatsoever, by their nature. They can perceive the weather, and they respond to it emotionally. We may imagine that the prospect of a sunny day fills them with a state phenomenologically just like hope, while the prospect of endless cloud fills them with a state just like despair. They seem, subjectively, to delight in light showers, but soon feel in a way that, in us, would count as depressed by them and then they apparently long for the sun to come back. And so on. Strawson holds that these Weather Watchers would be creatures who intrinsically desired sunny weather and a little rain, but who did not intrinsically desire (indeed, were averse to) heavy cloud and extended storms. And as biologically implausible as the Weather Watchers might be, it seems possible to imagine them being just as described, wanting various things and having their feelings pushed and pulled by events (much like fans of sports teams following their successes and defeats) without even having the capacity to be moved to action by their intrinsic desires.[7]

One might object by saying that the Weather Watchers have a disposition to act: they would perform some actions to influence the weather if they had the

---

felt pennant in order to help the team win. The fan can want very much that the team win without being much inclined to do anything practical to help.

[6] Strawson (1994). We have changed a detail or two about the case for our own purposes.

[7] For much more on the Weather Watchers, including responses to possible objections, see Strawson (1994, chapter 9) and Schroeder (2004, chapter 3).

ability to act. But weather Watchers do not act just as human beings do not photosynthesize. Saying that creatures incapable of acting have a disposition to act is as correct, and as useful, as saying that a human being has a disposition to photosynthesize because she would if she had leaves.

Some philosophers have suggested that, since the term "desire" is properly used only for those mental states that are linked to action, the attitudes of any creature like the Weather Watchers, the people who putatively desire that their husbands love them regardless of what they do and the like are more properly called "wishes."[8] Wishes, on this view, can be like intrinsic desires in every respect except that there is no necessity that one can be moved to action by a wish, while there is a necessary connection between being moved and intrinsic desires.

In our view, this suggestion falls somewhat short of capturing ordinary views about desire. "Desire" and "want" seem just the right words to talk about people who intrinsically desire that their teams win games, or people who want the facts of mathematics to be this way or that. But there is another, stronger response to make. What should we say about the person who declares, "I used to just moon about, wishing that Adam would pay attention to me, but then I thought, why not do something about it?" Or the person who declares, "I used to desperately wish that Adam would pay attention to me, and then he talked to me and I saw I might actually have a chance to get to know him"? In our ordinary way of thinking about wishes and intrinsic desires, someone making this sort of declaration is someone with one pro-attitude toward Adam. Initially, that pro-attitude is coupled with a sense that nothing can be done to attain the content of the attitude (nothing worth trying, at any rate). Then something changes, and there is the idea that something *can* be done. But if there is one attitude, and what changes is something cognitive, then the transition from wish to want is not a transition from one sort of pro-attitude to another, but a transition in the agent's optimism regarding acting to obtain the content of the attitude. In the sense that would be of interest to a theorist trying to understand how things work inside us, there is just one pro-attitude exemplified in these cases. "Wish" is a name commonly given to that attitude when one feels helpless to act so as to bring about its content, while "desire" is a name commonly given to it when one is feeling more empowered, though there are natural language variations in these patterns. And if so, then while there might be superficial reasons to distinguish wishes from intrinsic desires, there are also reasons to treat them as the same thing in underlying nature.

It seems that tending to cause movement is neither necessary nor sufficient for being an intrinsic desire. But then what is the relation between intrinsic desire and movement? Intrinsic desires are a normal cause of movement, but

---

[8] E.g., Green (1992), though note that Green does not specifically address Strawson's view.

this is a matter of metaphysical contingency. Intrinsic desires do these things, not because they must do them in order to be intrinsic desires, nor because doing these things makes something an intrinsic desire, but because these are the natural effects of intrinsic desires in minds like ours. If there is a necessity here to which we are sympathetic, it is that actions are necessarily caused or causally explained by intrinsic desires (as suggested in chapter 3). But this is to say that a movement is an action only in virtue of its relation to a rationalization, and so (in part) to an intrinsic desire, not to say that an intrinsic desire is only an intrinsic desire in virtue of its relation to action.

5.2 Feeling Is Not the Essence of Desire

It is less common to tie intrinsic desires to feelings than to actions, but it is far from *un*common. On some views, an intrinsic desire that P is a state that disposes the agent to pleasure when it seems that P, and perhaps displeasure when it seems that not-P.[9] And then there are theories on which disposing an agent to pleasure is a necessary feature of an intrinsic desire, though not sufficient.[10] These feeling-based theories of intrinsic desire improve on action-based theories in certain respects: Strawson's feeling-based theory of intrinsic desire does well with his imagined Weather Watchers, for instance, and combined action-plus-feeling theories of intrinsic desire have no trouble explaining why it is that habits are not intrinsic desires. But feeling-based theories of intrinsic desire are still problematic.

There are two opposed ways to look at the relationship between pleasure and desire. Sometimes it appears that pleasure is what we desire: for example, when we want to eat a peach we seem to do so for the sake of the pleasure it gives. At other times it appears that pleasure is what we get when we satisfy a desire. For example, sexual pleasure is not available to people who do not have sexual desires. Nonsensual pleasure often seem to be like this: you do not derive pleasure from a victory of the Red Sox unless you desire such a victory. You do not enjoy the fact that another person is happy unless you desire his or her happiness intrinsically (or as a realizer for a desire that people in general be happy, or etc.).

An important fact about the pleasure one gets from eating a peach and the pleasure one gets from the victory of a sports team is that, in the brain, they look like the same phenomenon. That is, structurally identical causal pathways from representations (of peach-caused sensory states or of victory for the Red Sox), through various neural intermediates, to pleasure appear to be used in

---

[9] Strawson (1994) offers a theory of intrinsic desire in terms of pleasure, and so (on very different grounds) does Morillo (1990).

[10] E.g., Davis (1986), Schueler (1995), Vadas (1984).

each case, differing only in the location of the starting representation.[11] Given the science, it is unlikely to be the case that some pleasures are generated independently of intrinsic desires while others are generated as a consequence of what is intrinsically desired. This science vindicates armchair arguments from philosophers such as Simon Blackburn and Butler, arguments that the "Red Sox model" applies to all pleasures.[12] If we enjoy eating a peach it is because we have intrinsic desires for certain states of affairs generated by eating a peach: for certain taste experiences, such as sweetness, for certain mouth-feel experiences, such as the soft fleshy quality of a peach, and the like. Of course, given that we already enjoy peaches we can desire them also as a means, for the sake of this enjoyment. Similarly, one often desires sex for the pleasure it brings, even though that pleasure is impossible if there is no sexual desire in the first place.

The consequence of a desire-first theory of pleasure is that pleasure would seem to be independent of intrinsic desires. Being caused by (apparently) getting what one wants, pleasure would seem to be an effect of intrinsically desiring something, not a constituent. But of course many effects are constituent effects: tending to cause harm is (part of) what makes something poisonous, and not an entirely contingent feature of poisons. So this can only be an initial observation. More is needed to separate pleasure from intrinsic desires.

Consider the creature, familiar from science-fiction, who can reason but who lacks the capacity for pleasure, displeasure, and all related feelings. Suppose that such a creature is reliably disposed to act so as to bring it about that it is fed, that its family members survive, and that justice is done. Suppose also that its attention can be drawn to the reasons to get food, to provide shelter for its family members, to pay in full for goods it receives, and so on—that its attention can be drawn to the reasons it has for pursuing its ends, in other words. Suppose even that it is born inclined to pursue food and water and the like, and that as it grows older it comes to be inclined to pursue the company of its family, to pursue the company of psychologically similar conspecifics, to pursue kindness and justice, and perhaps also the success of its kin over non-kin and the accumulation of power even at the expense of harm to others. It seems easy enough to imagine this creature. If one sort of psychological state were to underlie its patterns of action, attention, and its patterns of acquiring new such patterns, what would this psychological state be? To us, it would appear to be intrinsic desire. The imagined creature has various intrinsic desires, and though it cannot be moved by them in its feelings (since it has no feelings), it is moved in other familiar ways to act, attend, and acquire new desires.

---

[11] See Schroeder (2004, chapter 3). Chapter 6 will give the reader a sense of the kind of evidence at work.

[12] Blackburn (1998, 137–44) also argues that intrinsic desires ("concerns," in his jargon) must come before pleasure in the order of explanation. Blackburn credits Joseph Butler with an early defense of the position.

In the eyes of those philosophers who have argued that intrinsic desire is necessarily connected to pleasure, this might not yet seem convincing. To these philosophers, intrinsic desires (properly so called) are states such as having an appetite for pasta, lusting for a sexual partner, or finding the idea of a nap very tempting: desires are for states that we not only would say we are motivated (to some extent) to bring about, but that we would say we are *inclined* toward, that we *feel like* bringing about, that *appeal* to us. The contrast is with those motivational states that seem capable of resisting what we feel like doing: motivational states such as believing a course of action to be good, reasonable, right, best. As Fred Schueler puts it, if a man is torn between staying by the cozy fire to read an engaging book or venturing out into the night to attend a tedious PTA meeting, he is torn between doing what he wants and doing what he does not want, but perhaps judges more important.[13] To these philosophers, our imaginary aliens might appear to have no intrinsic desires at all. They have motivational states but not desires properly so-called.

In response, we turn from science fiction to human experience. There are drugs that substantially flatten dispositions to feel in many users: for example, high doses of the conventional anti-psychotic chlorpromazine (better known under its trade name, Thorazine). These drugs also tend to flatten impulses to act, but not in lock-step with the flattening of feelings. Someone who, on a high dose chlorpromazine, is no longer disposed to feel much of anything in response to eating, walking, or talking can nonetheless remain disposed to eat, walk, and talk. Is chlorpromazine a drug that can suppress appetitive intrinsic desires, while leaving other motivational structures intact? Clinical observation of patients on chlorpromazine have not suggested this is so. Patients on chlorpromazine are not noted for their ability to voluntarily cease smoking, for their ability to diet easily, for their ability to execute long-term plans, or anything else that would seem characteristic of a drug that suppressed appetitive intrinsic desires while letting motivating judgments of what is best go unscathed. It seems that patients on high doses of chlorpromazine retain their appetitive intrinsic desires, and insofar as they were moved by these desires before starting clorpromazine, they can be expected to be less, but still somewhat, moved by them after starting chlorpromazine. They are moved by their appetitive intrinsic desires, but no longer feel them. If this is possible, then appetitive intrinsic desires are not essentially states that make people feel excited about their contents, or find their contents appealing. The relation between affective inclination and appetitive intrinsic desires is merely causal.

One might hold that a person on chlorpromazine is disposed to feel pleasure in response to taking a walk, and simply does not feel that pleasure because of the chlorpromazine. But this gets tricky. We agree that there is an underlying

---

[13] Schueler (1995, 29f.).

structure that can be identified in the person on chlorpromazine, a structure that persists even while chlorpromazine is being used, and a structure that would, in the absence of chlorpromazine, often generate pleasure in response to taking a walk. We think of this underlying structure as the person's intrinsic desire to take walks. But does the structure dispose the person to pleasure while on chlorpromazine? This is much less obvious. Is a slice of bread disposed to get dry when it is stored in an airtight bag? The bread would dry in the open air, but it tends to stay moist in the bag. Its disposition, it seems, is contingent on its environment. (And likewise, is a slice of bread from dry Arizona disposed to dry in the open air when it is taken to humid Hawaii? Again, the disposition seems contingent on the environment.) It is far from clear to us that the bread is disposed to dry out regardless of how it is stored. Likewise with brain states that, in the absence of chlorpromazine, dispose agents to pleasure when they take walks. In the presence of chlorpromazine, there might be no tendency to pleasure. Is there still a disposition? There is the underlying structure, but a disposition to cause pleasure is not obviously present under all environmental circumstances. A defender of a feeling-based theory of intrinsic desire might say that, in people on chlorpromazine, there are dispositions *under specific conditions* to feel pleasure and displeasure. To us, this talk of dispositions under certain (normal? ideal? biologically significant?) conditions seems a frail reed upon which to be building a theory of intrinsic desire. It seems much better to hold that the intrinsic desire is the state that, under familiar conditions, is in fact responsible for the dispositions to pleasure, and for many moments of being pleased (and displeased). But the intrinsic desire is independent of this disposition (and these moments), as the case of chlorpromazine and similar drugs suggests.

Dispositions to pleasure are not, it seems, necessary for the possession of intrinsic desires. But are they sufficient? In discussing peaches and the Red Sox, we held that pleasure is evidence of intrinsic desire satisfaction. The story of the Weather Watchers also suggested that the right dispositions to pleasure and displeasure are, at the very least, powerful evidence that an intrinsic desire exists. Both lines of argument suggest that dispositions to pleasure are sufficient for the existence of intrinsic desires; we see a somewhat more complicated relationship.

Pleasure and displeasure tell us about changes in intrinsic desire satisfaction. They form a kind of sense modality: an interoceptive modality, allowing us to sense facts about what is going on inside us regarding our intrinsic desires (a sense more like our sense of limb orientation—proprioception—than like vision, in this respect). And because of this, it is probably the case that any creature capable of pleasure and displeasure is one that has intrinsic desires. But intrinsic desires are not *made up* of these feelings as a result, because the feelings *represent* facts about intrinsic desires.[14]

---

[14] See Schroeder (2004, ch.3). We will skip over many complications here. For instance: we are

Consider how common it is that pleasure and displeasure co-vary with changes in intrinsic desire satisfaction. If Ivan wants glory for Belarus and then Belarus wins an Olympic gold medal, then there is a change in Ivan's intrinsic desire satisfaction, as his intrinsic desires are more satisfied than before, and Ivan will tend to be happy. If Carmen intrinsically desires to sleep on a bed, but Carmen has been sleeping on a bed for years, then when she sleeps on a bed tonight there is no change in her intrinsic desire satisfaction and sleeping on a bed will tend not to bring her any particular pleasure (she takes it for granted, as we say). If Carmen were, to her surprise, to be deprived of a bed to sleep on tonight, she would be displeased and there would be a change, a decrease, in the satisfaction of her intrinsic desires. If she were then provided again with a bed tomorrow, there would be an increase in the satisfaction of her intrinsic desire and she would experience some pleasure. Cases like these suggest a common pattern, in which intrinsic desire satisfaction does not directly influence pleasure or displeasure, but in which *change* in intrinsic desire satisfaction does influence these feelings. More accurately, the feelings are influenced by change in intrinsic desire satisfaction relative to our visceral expectations (if you viscerally expect to sleep in a bed, i.e., take doing so for granted, or are jaded to it, then even if you intellectually grasp that you will not sleep in a bed tonight you will experience displeasure when you do not get to sleep in a bed).

It is important to remember that the view that pleasure and displeasure represent change in desire satisfaction does not imply that if Todd enjoys his first mango it is because he always intrinsically wanted a mango. More likely, Todd always wanted, like many of us, some things, such as the experience of sweetness, that a mango provides. Even if pleasure and displeasure represent change in satisfaction of intrinsic desires, one cannot immediately read the content of one's intrinsic desires off of the facts of what brings one pleasure, because every pleasure-causing event has the capacity to satisfy or frustrate a whole range of intrinsic desires.

Moving on, consider cases in which there is a failure of co-variation. In many of these cases, it appears reasonable to attribute some sort of error, or misrepresentation, to the person whose pleasure does not co-vary with changes in intrinsic desire satisfaction. A drunken Heidi can find a mishap with a carafe of wine enjoyably amusing, while a more sober onlooker asks "don't you see that you've just ruined your couch?" Heidi can comprehend it but not *feel* it, sometimes. She can intellectually grasp that something very undesired has happened, but feel as though everything is delightful. In this situation, people are

---

agnostic about whether it is in any (metaphysical) sense possible to have the sensation of pleasure independent of any sort of representational content. But if it is possible, then it is possible (in that same metaphysical sense) to have pleasure and displeasure without having intrinsic desires. Since this is not the sort of consideration we wish to make central to our argument, we merely note it in passing.

often inclined to say of the drunken woman that she is subject to a sort of error: that she "doesn't see it," "doesn't get it," "can't take it in," and so on. And the error regards Heidi's intrinsic desires: it isn't that she doesn't see the damage as damage, but that she doesn't feel how the damage is contrary to her interests. When Bill the drunken frat boy adds one more stain to a third-hand couch he is not said to fail to "get it" when he is not disturbed by the damage, because the stain does not matter to him: no substantial intrinsic desire of his is frustrated by the additional stain. Heidi, who has damaged her couch in a way she genuinely does care about, but who does not yet feel the harm she has done herself, is the one who is said to be subject to a sort of error. And likewise, Chitra, who has long wanted to professionally publish her short stories, might finally have one accepted after many rejections and find herself more stunned than delighted. In such a situation, she might well say that there is something wrong with her feelings—she *ought* to feel pleased—but she just "can't take it in," "can't believe it," "can hardly grasp that it's finally happened after so long." These are no more errors in *belief* for her than they are for Heidi who does not feel dismay at damaging her couch. Chitra believes that she has had her story accepted (the e-mail address is that of the relevant editor at the *New Yorker*, and so on) but there is some error within Chitra nonetheless. The error is precisely that she does not feel what she should feel, that there has been a change for the better in getting what she wants.

Feelings of pleasure and displeasure can be erroneous only if they are representations. Just as our sense of depth is subject to illusion (and hallucination), and so error, so too our sense of how things are going for us—our sense of change in intrinsic desire satisfaction—is subject to illusion (and hallucination), and so error. (To say that pleasure is subject to illusion is not to say that we are subject to illusions regarding whether or not we are really pleased.[15] It is to say the same sort of thing as to say that sight is subject to illusion: to say that real experiences might exist and they might misrepresent the facts.)

That pleasure and displeasure are representations of intrinsic desires is also suggested by the way we learn from them. People commonly gain insight into what they intrinsically desire by noting what they find pleasant, and what unpleasant. This is no more foolproof than other senses, of course, and pleasure is a less helpful sense modality than some. When one gets pleasure from being chatted with at a bar, one can be left uncertain whether it was the attention, the flattery, the wit, the looks, the apparent intelligence and personality, or even the pheromones of the interlocutor that made the chat so pleasant. (Likewise, when one gets pleasure while eating a novel food, one might struggle

---

[15] We might be or we might not be, but we are not talking about errors in introspecting our own pleasure. Those interested in the topic should consult Schwitzgebel (2011), where the general weakness of introspection is the central topic, and introspection of the emotions receives a little discussion.

to guess whether one intrinsically desires taste and texture experiences of those sorts, whether one was just very hungry and so mostly pleased to be eating anything at all, or whether the accompanying sake put a veil of pleasure over the whole evening, including the food.) Nonetheless, pleasure and displeasure are as useful as one would expect in such circumstances if they represent using a single dimension that expresses net change in all intrinsic desire satisfaction, as we are suggesting.

One last line of thought is worth bringing up. Pleasure and displeasure are found in a certain pattern in human beings that is like the pattern found with sensations of warmth and cold. For both, there is a single continuum along which feeling varies from one extreme (that, at least phenomenologically, seems to have no upper bound) through a neutral midpoint to the opposite extreme (that likewise seems to have no lower bound). The feelings are not compatible with one another under ordinary conditions: one cannot normally feel hot and cold at the same place at the same time, and one cannot normally feel pleased and displeased at the same time.[16] And the feelings sum together roughly the way positive and negative numbers sum together: a cold drink leaves a hot person feeling less hot, but not cold, while it leaves a cold person feeling extremely cold; a small bit of bad news leaves a pleased person a little crestfallen but still content, while it leaves an unhappy person feeling miserably as though the last straw has been placed on the camel's back.[17] There are also parallel comparative effects: the same water can feel cold to one person and warm to another depending on how cold or warm she was when she touched the water. Similarly, the same situation can be pleasant to one person and unpleasant for another who shares the relevant preference ordering, but who is "coming from" a different level of desire satisfaction: staying at an average apartment can be very pleasant for a pauper and very unpleasant for a prince even when both intrinsically desire a great deal of physical comfort, security, and so on.

In the case of feelings of warmth and coldness, there is a clear representational explanation for why the feelings work this way: warmth and cold on the skin represent something like localized changes in heat exchange with the environment: feeling warm on one's skin represents something like a net heat gain at that point, while feeling cold represents something like a net heat loss at that point, with intensity of feelings representing something like the rate

---

[16] There are exceptions. Some experience bittersweet sadness as simultaneous pleasure and displeasure, and others get such an experience from watching horror movies. But this is consistent with treating pleasure and displeasure as a sense modality, since other sense modalities also permit the simultaneous representation of inconsistent properties. There are optical illusions in which surfaces appear both red and green, and in which objects appear both moving and stationary, for instance.

[17] These are just the grossest patterns: for a much more subtle treatment of all this, see Schroeder (2004, chapter 3).

of heat gain or loss.[18] Because this is what they represent, they represent facts about the world—rates of heat exchange at points on the skin—that come on a continuum. That is why feelings of warmth and cold form a continuum. (As opposed to experiences of hue, which represent surface properties of objects that are not continuous variations along just one dimension.) And they represent facts about the world that have a neutral midpoint. This is why feelings of warmth and cold have a neutral midpoint. (As opposed to the way hearing represents loudness: with a continuum that stops at zero, just as intensities of sound waves, or object vibrations, only go down to a minimum value of zero.) And they represent facts about the world that have (approximately) unbounded limits at either end of the continuum of facts being represented. As a result, feelings of warmth and cold feel like they have no upper bound (for warmth) or lower bound (for coldness). (As opposed to darkness, which is an absolute lower bound on light intensity, and the experience of darkness, which is felt as such.) And they represent facts about the world that have a binary, exclusionary structure: heat is either being gained or lost, but not both. This is why feelings of warmth and cold cannot normally be felt for the same part of the body simultaneously (and why there is something necessarily wrong with such a feeling, if it can be created: it represents the world as being in an inconsistent state, and so necessarily misrepresents the world). And they represent facts about the world where the facts trade off in a way that is modeled by the way positive and negative numbers sum together. This is why feelings of warmth and cold normally trade off against one another. (As opposed to, e.g., experiences of light intensity and experiences of hue, which do not represent facts that are exclusionary or trade off against one another, and which are not experienced as exclusionary or trading off against each other.) And, finally, they represent facts about changes from how things were to how things are. This is why the same environment, generating different changes in two people because they come from two different prior environments, can cause one person to represent a change in the direction of heat gain while the other person represents a change in the direction of heat loss. (As opposed to, e.g., experiences of color, which do not represent such changes.)[19]

If pleasure and displeasure share all of these structural features of feelings of warmth and coldness, while not sharing structural features with other forms of

---

[18] Akins (1996) argues that feelings of warmth and cold cannot be understood as representing, because they cannot be understood as representing absolute local temperature. But her evidence for this conclusion, while fairly convincing, is also convincing support for the thesis that feelings of hot and cold represent local changes in heat transfer; hence the present formulation of their representational content. (Though note that this does not do full justice to her arguments.)

[19] Staring at a blue sky for a prolonged time before looking at a blue piece of fabric will change the experience of it, by generating a yellowish afterimage. But we take it that this is irrelevant to our example: the yellowishness here is obviously a misrepresentation, not a correct representation of change in hue.

consciousness, is it a pure coincidence? Is it credible that the structural features
of feelings of warmth and coldness are explained by the representational roles
of these features, while the same structural features of pleasure and displeasure
are a mere coincidence? Or is the commonality in the structural features of the
states of consciousness a product of the fact that pleasure and displeasure represent facts about the world that have the same structural features as the facts
about rates of heat loss and gain? To us, the latter seems the only nonmysteri-
ous explanation of the facts.

Why, then, is it sometimes quite unpleasant to do something that increases
our overall desire satisfaction? Like other modes of representation, such as our
senses, pleasure and displeasure have their limitations as reflectors of reality.
Our eyes cannot see how big the moon is and our native mathematical talents are not good at grasping the significant difference between a thirty-year
loan at 3.4% and one at 3.5%. Similarly, our visceral expectations as to levels of desire satisfaction are fairly "dumb." For example, suppose Gretchen
has a strong intrinsic desire to avoid physical pain. Going to the dentist would
increase Gretchen's overall desire satisfaction, then. Yet it would not be pleasant, as it would fail to increase Gretchen's overall desire satisfaction relative to
her visceral expectations. It is very hard for us to viscerally expect, now, pain
that might come years down the road. Gretchen, if she is not presently in pain,
viscerally expects to continue not to be in pain, in the way that a warm person
generally viscerally expects continued warmth even if she knows intellectually
that the temperature is about to change. Since Gretchen expects a continued
lack of pain, the prospect of going to the dentist does not increase her desire
satisfaction relative to her visceral expectations but decreases it. The fact that
she intellectually expects pain down the road (if she foregoes the dentist) does
not help with that. Thus, despite the connection between pleasure and desire
satisfaction, doing something that satisfies your strong desires can be unpleasant. Something similar might be happening in the case of giving up an evening
by the fire for the sake of a PTA meeting.

There is more that could be said about pleasure and displeasure, but our
purpose has been served.[20] We wanted to provide evidence that pleasure and
displeasure represent something about desires (the best candidate being change
in intrinsic desire satisfaction), and have done so. From here, we can reach the
further conclusion that intrinsic desires are independent of the feelings of pleasure and displeasure that they characteristically cause: since pleasure and displeasure represent desires, they cannot be even partially constitutive of desire
any more than a picture of Marie Curie can be even partially constitutive of

---

[20] Among the many things not discussed here are: that pleasure and displeasure are not experienced as localized, that they are specifically states of consciousness, that all pleasure is of one
kind, varying only in intensity, and that pain separates into nociception and unpleasantness. For
a full discussion of these points and more, see Schroeder (2004, chapter 3).

Marie Curie. With this final piece of evidence, we feel we have sufficient reason to reject theories of intrinsic desire that make pleasure (or dispositions to it) part of, or the whole of, the nature of intrinsic desire.

Thus, intrinsic desires are not made desires by their relations to action or pleasure. Intrinsic desires can also be separated from their cognitive effects (discussed in detail in chapter 9). Desire influences our attention patterns: if you desire to see birds you will be more likely to notice a somewhat hidden bird then another person would (and more likely to miss, due to lack of attention, the fact that the bird stands on top of a remarkable building). If you desire the victory of the Red Sox you will notice that the person a few rows from you on the airplane is wearing a Red Sox shirt. Thomas Scanlon holds that a person who has a desire to do something will notice reasons to do that thing,[21] but the phenomenon is slightly broader: one's attention is caught by all sorts of things bearing upon what one has intrinsic desires regarding. What is true of attention is also true of memory: the bird lover will remember a list of bird species better than she would remember a list of car manufacturers, other things being equal.

These effects are typical of desire, but do not constitute its essence. A person who desires to see birds but who has a severe attention disorder or is bothered by a very distracting problem still desires to see birds, and a person in whom we somehow induced a tendency to pay attention to birds is not automatically thereby induced to desire to see them. A person might notice reasons to do something as a result of habit (a person who used to have to hide while in a war zone might still notice good hiding places, for example) and a person who desires to do something might not notice reasons to do it because her desire is repressed or because of cognitive limitations.

Thus, intrinsic desires are not, in their essences, states that dispose us to actions, feelings, or cognitions. But if they are not, then what are they?

---

[21] Scanlon (1998).

{ 6 }

What Desires Are

The present work needs a theory of intrinsic desire on which is true that intrinsic desires *cause*, but are not *constituted by*, their familiar effects on motivation or pleasure (or, for that matter, cognition). This chapter describes and defends such a theory: the reward theory of desire.[1]

The reward theory of desire does not make any of the most familiar effects of desires into the essence of desire. Motivational, emotional, and familiar cognitive effects of intrinsic desires are common but inessential causal consequences of having desires on the reward theory. In healthy human beings temporarily subjected to powerful nonrationalizing, noncontent-efficacious effects on their thoughts, feelings, and actions, though, intrinsic desires can exist while failing to cause their familiar effects on motivation or feelings or thoughts, or while causing excessively strong or weak forms of their familiar effects. People who are very sleepy, overcaffeinated, drunk, and so on are people whose motivational, emotional, and cognitive states can substantially vary from what would be expected, given what they intrinsically desire, though what they intrinsically desire and how much they intrinsically desire it remains unchanged. And in unhealthy human beings, and perhaps aliens, these gaps between intrinsic desires and their usual effects can be chronic or permanent. An addict who greatly intrinsically desires things that can only be gained by ceasing to use cocaine, and who only moderately intrinsically desires things that can be gained by continuing to use cocaine, can nonetheless live for years with many of the motivational, emotional, and cognitive signs of someone with the opposite priorities (as we will show in detail in chapter 11). A clinically depressed person can fail to be motivated by her intrinsic desire for human company but still feel the displeasure that represents the intrinsic desire remaining unsatisfied. An alien who greatly intrinsically desires justice might lack the capacity to be motivated at all (like a Weather Watcher), or to feel anything at all (like an android), or both, without desiring justice any less.

---

[1] The first reward theory of desire to our knowledge is found in Dretske (1988, ch.5). For a full treatment of the idea see Schroeder (2004). Objections to Schroeder are articulated in Brook (2009), De Sousa (2009), Latham (2009), Thagard (2009), with a response by Schroeder as well (Schroeder 2009). Also compare Butler (1992) and Morillo (1990).

The theory that allows all of the foregoing to be true takes a fair bit of explaining. The way in which the reward theory of desire entails the result that desire's most familiar motivational, emotional, and cognitive signs are mere causal consequences of possessing intrinsic desires is through holding that the essence of desire is something unfamiliar. Explaining this unfamiliar essence of desire is thus the first job. Showing that this essence is nonetheless the common cause of all of the familiar effects of intrinsic desires is the second job. And the third job is to show that intrinsic desires are best thought of as the common cause of their effects: in short, that intrinsic desires are best thought of as a natural kind. Once this has been done, some benefits of the theory for the desire-centered moral psychologist will be described.

6.1 The Reward and Punishment Systems

The reward system is a system within the brain that is, in virtue of its particular states, a normal cause of overt and covert action, of positive and negative feelings, and of the cognitive effects most associated with intrinsic desires. The reward system is also the only thing in the brain that is a common cause of all of these effects (indeed, it is the only thing that is even close to a common cause of all these effects). And the reward system is a psychological natural kind.[2] The reward system's configurations are thus a reasonable starting point for a theory of intrinsic desire.

The reward system constitutes things as rewards, and we will explain in some detail what reward is in this context in just a moment. In parallel, the punishment system constitutes things as punishments. So, at least, it appears. Scientists do not understand punishment as well as reward at present, but a wealth of indirect evidence suggests that the brain has a punishment system that mirrors the operations of the much better understood reward system, just as mathematical models of reward and punishment would predict. Hence we will talk about the brain's reward and punishment systems, though most of our evidence will be drawn from what is known about the reward system.

Focusing on the reward and punishment systems could give rise to a number of different theories of intrinsic desire. We hold the following.

Reward Theory of Desire: to have an intrinsic desire regarding it being the case that P is to constitute P as a reward or a punishment.

---

[2] At least, it is by the reasonable test that it is a kind that scientists find useful, at the relevant level of investigation, for correct explanation, prediction, and control of psychological phenomena. The reward system is implemented by a biological natural kind: the brain's dopamine system. But it is still possible to distinguish the psychological natural kind (a specific sort of learning system) from the biological natural kind (the specific groups of cells and neuromodulators that implement this learning in animals like ourselves).

To have an intrinsic appetitive desire that P is to constitute P as a reward.

To have an intrinsic aversion to P is to constitute P as a punishment.[3]

To constitute a (conceivable) state of affairs P as a reward is to make it the case that P counts as a reward, in the relevant sense, and similarly for punishments. And the distinction between appetitive desires and aversions is, roughly, the familiar distinction between desiring that things be the case because we want them for their own sakes, and desiring that things not be the case because we have an aversion to them in themselves.[4] Thus, understanding the reward theory of desire is little more than understanding the relevant senses of "reward" and "punishment."

There are two sensible ways to understand each of "reward" and "punishment" in the reward theory of desire. One is the ordinary way of understanding "reward" and "punishment," according to which a child can be rewarded for sitting still at the dinner table by being granted permission to stay up late, and punished for squirming by being sent to bed early. The other is a technical way of understanding "reward" and "punishment" which is used in certain mathematical theories of learning and in certain parts of neuroscience.[5] Surprising as it might seem, the reward theory of desire is true on both understandings. However, if one is seeking a theory of desire that explains what is less basic in terms of what is more basic, then "reward" and "punishment" need to be understood in the technical, mathematical, scientific sense. This is because a full explanation of how being granted the right to stay up late can be a reward in the ordinary sense of "reward" will ultimately appeal to the technical sense of "reward."[6]

To understand the technical senses of "reward" and "punishment" it is best to start with the related notion of reward-and-punishment-based learning.[7]

Reward-and-punishment-based learning is most famously exemplified by the operant conditioning of behavior in experimental animals: by rats trained to run mazes for cheese, essentially. The association of this learning with rats and mazes is understandable but unfortunate. It is understandable because behaviorists were the first scientists to discover reward-and-punishment-based learning and give it a theoretical treatment.[8] It is unfortunate because any form of

---

[3] This theory is fully articulated in Schroeder (2004, chapter 5). For more on the distinction between appetites and aversions, see Schroeder (2004, chs. 1, 5).

[4] The evidence that this distinction is significant, and not merely terminological, is discussed in Schroeder (2004, chs. 1, 5).

[5] This technical sense is related to, but distinct from, the technical sense of "reward" long used in the theory of operant conditioning. The differences will become clear as this particular technical sense is characterized.

[6] This is fully defended in Schroeder (2004, ch.2).

[7] Also called "contingency-based learning."

[8] The investigation of operant conditioning begins with B.F. Skinner. See Skinner (1938).

learning associated with behaviorism is likely to be stigmatized as a sort of learning that, while it might explain something about rats in mazes, is not of interest to someone who wishes to understand the human mind. As the next section will show, however, the stigma is misplaced. The reward-and-punishment-based learning system is in fact the cause of many phenomena that are absolutely central to understanding the complexities of the human mind, in both some of the ways it is like the minds of other animals and some of the ways in which it is distinctive.

So what is reward-and-punishment-based learning? Human beings learn in many ways. We learn by listening, by observing others, by trying it out for ourselves, by repeatedly practicing until awkward actions become smooth, precise, and efficient. Different sorts of learning are made possible by different mechanisms. There is one mechanism that seems to underlie learning by remembering and recalling events (such as who said what at the last departmental meeting),[9] there is a different mechanism that seems to underlie learning to perform complex sequences of actions smoothly and fluently (as when a beginner gets better at riding a bicycle),[10] and so on. Reward-and-punishment-based learning is yet another sort of learning, distinct from these, and implemented by yet another mechanism.

Reward-and-punishment-based learning is a form of learning that has an opportunity to take place when one mental event participates in causing another. Such causings happen all the time: groups of edge perceptions participate in causing perceptions of squareness, thoughts that a claim is universal in scope participate in causing thoughts that surely there are exceptions, perceptions of the approach of a dance partner participate in causing efforts to take matching steps backward, and so on.[11] So there are dozens, if not hundreds, of opportunities at each moment for this sort of learning to have its effects.

In reward-and-punishment-based learning, there is the causing of one mental state by another, and then that causal sequence is followed by the unconscious release of a signal in the brain, a signal that takes one of three forms. One form causes the disposition of the first mental state to produce the second to increase (all else being equal). This sort of signal can be called a positive learning signal, though there is nothing positive about it beyond the fact that it increases the strengths of the relevant dispositions. The second form of the

[9] Episodic learning, made possible (it seems) by a process called "long-term potentiation." See, e.g., Shastri (2002).

[10] Theories of skill-learning based on back-propagation of error and recurrent decorrelation are compared in Porrill, Dean, and Stone (2004), for example.

[11] Of course, there is dispute within the philosophy of mind about mental causation. As we suggested in chapter 3, the details of this debate are not particularly important for our purposes. Since it is clear that reward learning takes place in some sense that is suitable to scientific purposes, the precise metaphysics of how it takes place can be left to other philosophers without worrying too much about the details.

signal causes no change in dispositions; this can be called a neutral learning signal. And the third form of the signal causes the disposition of the first mental
state to produce the second to decrease (all else being equal). This can be called
a negative learning signal.

Imagine Juan is trying to keep up with a more talented dance partner. He
perceives the approach of his dance partner, and this perception participates in
causing an effort to take a matching step backward.[12] If this causal sequence
is followed by a positive learning signal, then the ability of that sort of perceptual event to cause that sort of matching step backward will be strength-
ened. The probability of Juan making that sort of step backward in that sort
of situation in the future has just increased. On the other hand, if the causal
sequence is followed by a negative learning signal, then the ability of perceptions of advancing dance partners to cause Juan to take matching steps backward will be weakened. The probability that such a step will be taken in that
sort of situation in the future has just decreased. And if it is followed by a
neutral learning signal then nothing within Juan changes (at least, not through
this mechanism). If a positive learning signal appears every time Juan reacts to
his partner's approach with a matching step backwards then Juan will, in one
sense of "learn," learn to react to his partner's approach with a matching step
backwards. "Learning" here does not mean acquiring knowledge or skill; it is
learning in a different sense. Learning in this sense is analogous to (and perhaps
the same as) the sort of learning we refer to when we say "he learned to speak
more in class," or "by the time a hundred people had asked him whether as an
Irishman he liked Enya's music, he had learned to hate Enya's music."

The obvious question at this point is: what determines whether a positive, neutral, or negative learning signal will be released in a creature capable
of reward-and-punishment-based learning? There are two main parts to the
answer.

The first part is that the signal coming from the reward learning system is
influenced by how the organism perceptually and cognitively represents the
world to be. The representation of certain states of affairs causally affects the
reward system such that it directly increases the chance that a positive learning signal will be released, and this is what makes these represented states of
affairs *rewards* (technically, "positive rewards").[13] That is, this is what makes
them rewards in the sense relevant to this form of learning. To other represented states of affairs, the reward system does not directly react, and these are

---

[12] This description of things, with a perception causing an effort, is not meant to suggest that
the man does not participate "as an agent" in his movement. Even when a man takes a step backward while acting as a full-blooded agent, there is still a causal chain leading to the final mental
event that causes the movement of the leg.

[13] If a representation that p only increases the chance of a positive learning signal being
released because it causes a representation that q, then the former representation does not cause
the relevant effect directly.

neither rewards nor punishments. And a failure to represent a reward increases the chance of generating a negative learning signal. This is what makes the failure of that state of affairs to obtain a punishment (technically, a "negative punishment").

What holds for rewards holds in parallel for punishments. The representation of certain states of affairs causally affects the punishment system such that it directly increases the chance that a negative learning signal will be released, and this is what makes these represented states of affairs punishments (technically, "positive" punishments). And the punishment system responds to absent punishments by increasing the chance of generating a positive learning signal (technically, this is a "negative reward").

Note that the labels "reward" and "punishment," like "positive" and "negative," have nothing to do with feelings of pleasure or pain, self-conscious stances toward states of affairs, the intentions of would-be rewarding and punishing agents, judgments of goodness or badness, or the actual goodness or badness of any state of affairs. Within the theory of reward-and-punishment-based learning, these terms' meanings ultimately come down to variations on the strengthening and weakening of causal connections, nothing more.

Returning to Juan, recall that he perceives the approach of his partner and that this perception causally participates in causing a matching step backward on his part. Suppose that what follows this step is that Juan's partner smiles and the dance continues smoothly. This smile or smooth dancing (or what it signifies), might be a (positive) reward or a (positive) punishment in the sense relevant to reward-and-punishment-based learning, and it all depends on how Juan's brain responds. If Juan's brain responds by releasing a positive learning signal, the sort of signal that strengthens the power of the perceptual state to cause matching steps backwards, then Juan's brain has treated being smiled at (or continuing to dance smoothly)[14] as a reward. On the other hand, if Juan's brain responds by releasing a negative learning signal, one that weakens the power of the perceptual state to cause matching steps backward, then Juan's brain has treated being smiled at (or continuing to dance smoothly) as a punishment.

Most animals like ourselves respond to food (when hungry) and water (when thirsty) in the "positive" way, with the sort of reward learning that increases the strengths of just-used causal connections between mental states.[15] And most

---

[14] Or something that such states of affairs instantiate or make more likely.

[15] Actually, it is probably better to think of animals like ourselves as intrinsically desiring a state of homeostatic balance with respect to things like blood sugar, blood salinity, blood oxygen, and core body temperature—and perhaps also sex hormones or something tied to them. When we have deficiencies in these things, we have frustrated intrinsic desires for our homeostatic set points; when we have excesses of these things we also have frustrated intrinsic desires (as when one feels overfed, and there is an unpleasantness to it that goes beyond mere distension of the stomach or worry about appearance).

human beings respond to things like money, success at solving problems, our favorite music, being cooperated with, donating to charities, and seeing our loved ones with the same sort of learning.[16] Food, water, money, success, hearing "A Day in the Life" by The Beatles, being cooperated with, giving to a good cause, seeing a loved one—these are all commonly rewards, in the technical sense, for us. And similarly, most animals like ourselves respond to being deprived of food or water, or to (for instance) having their tails pinched in the "negative" way, with the sort of reward learning that decreases the strengths of just-used causal connections between mental states. Being denied supper or a turn to drink from the water fountain or being pinched are, commonly, punishments for us. And all these things are rewards or punishments because of the way representation of them disposes us to learn.

Hidden, perhaps, in the preceding description of reward-and-punishment-based learning is a fact of central importance to moral psychology: what makes a conceivable state of affairs P count as a reward or punishment for a given person (or any creature) is *constituted* by the *contingent* power of that person's representation that P to cause (more precisely, to contribute to the calculation of) a reward or punishment signal. Most of us are born constituting sweet taste experiences, full stomachs, dry bottoms, and the like as rewards: representations of these things contribute significantly to the production of reward signals, right from birth, as a result of nature's design. And most of us come to constitute the taste of chocolate, and hearing "A Day in the Life," as rewards as we get older: these representations come to have the power to promote the production of reward signals, though they were not disposed to do so from birth.[17] But there is no state of affairs that is, by its very nature, such that representing it must generate a positive or negative reward signal.[18] And there is no evidence to suggest that deliberation or other cognitive processes can, entirely on the basis of their contents, change what is constituted as a reward or punishment.[19] The little that is known about how the brain comes to treat P as a reward or punishment when it did not before suggests that this happens when P is appropriately associated with antecedent rewards or punishments. When a young child finds that she gets things that are already rewards, such as cookies

---

[16] For experimental evidence, see, e.g., Stellar and Stellar (1985), Knutson et al. (2001), Johnsrude et al. (1999), Salimpoor et al. (2011), Rilling et al. (2002), Moll et al. (2006), and Aron et al. (2005).

[17] There is some evidence that there is a specific region of orbito-frontal cortex that acts as a sort of junction box, where input from perception and cognition is either passed forward to the reward system or not, depending on the particular neural details. See, e.g., Schultz, Tremblay, and Hollerman (2000).

[18] Unless one imagines a state of affairs constituted in part by the fact that it causes this sort of response, of course.

[19] Thoughts can change whether one experiences an event as a failure to get X or an opportunity to better learn to Y, but this reframing relies on facts about whether X or Y is constituted as a reward—facts that the cognitive reframing does nothing to change.

and positive parental attention, more often when everyone is cooperative, she is unconsciously changed so that she comes to constitute cooperation as a reward also.[20] So far, no other natural mechanism for changing what is constituted as a reward is known.[21]

The second part of the explanation of how a positive, neutral, or negative learning signal is produced involves a calculation. The mere representation of a state of affairs that is a reward in the technical sense does not guarantee that a positive learning signal will be generated, and similarly for the representation of a punishment: such representations are inputs into the calculation of what is sometimes known as a "prediction error." It is easier, though, to think of what is being calculated as the difference, at each moment, between the expected amount of net reward or punishment in the world and the actual amount. Focusing just for the moment on reward: to produce reward learning, an organism must be doing three things. It must have an expectation regarding the net amount of reward to be found in the world at a given moment, it must be evaluating the actual net amount of reward found in the world at that moment, and it must be taking the latter and subtracting the former from it.[22] If the result of the calculation is positive, then a positive learning signal is released (and the more positive the result of the calculation, the stronger the positive learning signal). If the result of the calculation is zero, then a neutral learning signal is released. And if the result is negative, then a negative learning signal is produced. Thus, in reward learning:

Amount of reward learning signal = actual net rewards minus expected net rewards. Hence, Juan's partner's smile causes less reward learning in him if he expects his partner to smile at him—that is, if he takes it for granted that his partner will smile at him.

Expected net rewards are determined without a conscious reasoning process. These are expectations in the sense of the visceral expectations discussed in chapter 5 (not coincidentally; visceral expectations influence the reward system, and the reward system in turn influences feelings of pleasure). Rather than the net rewardingness of a given moment being predicted through elaborate conscious reasoning, it is produced unconsciously and with fairly modest resources: net rewardingness can be expected (rightly or wrongly, of course) on

---

[20] This is a staple of the behaviorist literature on reward learning, but on the assumption that performing a guessing task successfully is or instantiates rewards for experimental subjects the effect has also been demonstrated over the short term in an experimental context by non-behaviorists: see Johnsrude et al. (1999), where a mere statistical association between being told "you got that right" and an abstract image caused greater liking for the associated image in human subjects.

[21] It is not a coincidence, we suspect, that this process sounds reminiscent of the one we described in chapter 4 for acquiring new intrinsic desires.

[22] See, e.g., Sutton and Barto (1998) for a textbook treatment.

entirely associative grounds.[23] A group of neurons that learn purely by association can determine the net rewardingness that has been associated, in the
past, with the present perceived and conceived states of affairs, and this value
(expressed, one assumes, in the rate of firing of this group of neurons) can serve
as the viscerally expected level of net reward for that moment.[24]

The calculation of the difference between actual and expected reward or
punishment looks like an intellectually challenging mathematical task, and not
something that could be carried out unconsciously in human beings, much less
monkeys or rats, but in fact neural computations of this sort are quite tractable.
A simple subtractive calculation can be performed unconsciously by some neurons exciting one region of the brain, while other neurons inhibit activity in
that same region. Crudely, the resulting activity can be the difference between
the sum of the exciting input and the sum of the inhibiting input. When all
these states of neural activity represent magnitudes (on the same linear scale),
then the resulting level of activity in the third group of neurons can represent
a magnitude that is as great as the first magnitude minus the second. These
sorts of implicit calculations are ubiquitous in the brain, and not in themselves
problematic.

It appears that in animals like us there is one system that calculates rewards
only, and another system that calculates punishments only, with the two systems having reciprocal connections. (We have generally suppressed such details
for the sake of exposition.) The punishment system would, naturally, perform
the parallel calculation.

Visceral expectations do not by any means result in a perfectly accurate prediction of the amount of net reward that should obtain. Sometimes we know
consciously that a certain amount of net reward is coming but still expect a
different amount. It might be that, in the past, circumstances like one's current
circumstances (perhaps, sitting at a Formica countertop in a Midwestern diner)
have not been associated with tasting a perfect croissant, yet one consciously,
and rightly, expects to taste such a croissant because one knows there is a morsel
of such a croissant that one is about to pop into one's mouth. If tasting a perfect croissant is a reward for one, then one's associations will lead to a visceral
expectation of less reward than one might have predicted consciously. And this
is a kind of imperfection in the calculation of the reward signal. Nonetheless,
an unconscious, associative expectation system has substantial advantages over
a conscious expectation system. Its expectations are continuously available
without putting other cognitive activity on hold, are automatically available

---

[23] Association is not the only possible mechanism here, but deliberation is not required on
any model.
[24] See, e.g., Schultz, Dayan, and Montague (1997). The scientific investigation of these details
is continuing. The point of these speculations is simply to show that what is being described is
possible and sensible; the details might well be different from what is being suggested.

(regardless of how little one might feel like making more predictions), and can be formed using intellectual resources available to any creature capable of representing its environment and forming associations. So there are some virtues to this manner of calculating expected reward, in addition to there being faults. No doubt these virtues are responsible for the natural selection of the particular neural mechanisms we have (and share with other animals), but this particular evolutionary story is not really important to how things work inside us as we are. We will have occasion to return to discussing the unconscious, associative expectation system in chapter 11: its weaknesses play an important role in explaining aspects of addiction.

The degree to which a state of affairs is more or less rewarding or punishing is constituted by the same connections that make the states of affairs into rewards or punishments at all. A connection between representing P and the reward system might be a very strong connection, the sort that will make a large positive contribution to the calculation of net reward. This would be how P gets to count as a big reward for the creature so constructed. But the connection could always be stronger or weaker, contributing a greater or lesser value to the calculation of net reward when P is represented. And thus how much of a reward P is can range on a continuum from being barely a reward at all to being by far the number one reward possible for the creature in question.

Putting all these pieces together gives a clearer picture. Imagine an organism constantly perceiving and cognizing its environment. Through a combination of genes and environment, some of the states of affairs it perceives and conceives are constituted by one of its learning systems as greater or lesser rewards, while others are treated as neutral. The net sum of these rewards comes to some amount of net reward at each moment. At the same time, the organism also unconsciously, perhaps associatively, predicts a given amount of net reward for that moment. The net reward of the moment has subtracted from it the predicted amount of net reward, and the result is either a positive value, zero, or a negative value. If the result is a positive value, then a positive learning signal is released, and it causes certain causal connections between mental states (those causal connections that were just used) to strengthen. If the result is a negative value, then a negative learning signal is released, and it causes certain causal connections between mental states (again, those that were just used) to weaken. And if the result is zero, then a neutral learning signal is produced and nothing changes. And as with reward, so too with punishment (keeping in mind that reward signals are likely to suppress punishment signals and vice versa, when both could be released simultaneously).

The upshot of reward-and-punishment-based learning is that the mental processes—perceptual, intellectual, agentive, and so on—that lead to rewards (so defined) and the avoidance of punishments (so defined) become more dominant over time in the agents' perceptions, thoughts, and actions, while those leading to punishments and to missing rewards play a smaller role. So long as there is some nonrandom pattern to the distribution of rewards and punishments in the world of the organism, the organism will learn over time to perceive, think, and act in ways that are progressively more likely to lead to rewards and less likely to lead to punishments.[25]

Given the nature of reward and punishment, it follows that, according to the reward theory of desire, what it is to intrinsically desire that P is for the reward system to respond to representations of P in a way that directly increases the chance of a positive reward learning signal being generated. That is, Juan's brain's constituting his partner's positive regard as a reward (in the technical sense) is the same thing as Juan's desiring that his partner regard him positively. His intrinsic (appetitive) desire for the positive regard of his dance partner is his brain's responding to representations of this regard in a way that makes a positive contribution to the calculation of actual reward and, if the value of that calculation exceeds what was predicted, makes a positive contribution to the generation of a positive reward learning signal. Intrinsic aversions to it being the case that P are the mirror reflection of this arrangement in punishment instead of reward.

Given that reward learning can be stronger or weaker, there is also a simple explanation of desire strength stemming from the reward theory of desire. For an intrinsic appetite or aversion to be very strong is for the representation of its content to make a large contribution to the calculation of the overall learning signal, while for an intrinsic desire to be weak is for the representation of its content to make a very small contribution (for Juan's desire for his partner's smile to be strong, the smile has to be a "big" reward, and for it to be weak, a "small" one). The size of the contribution each representation can make to the learning signal can be compared, to generate a ranking of intrinsic desires from the strongest to the weakest, and the proportionate sizes of the contributions each representation makes to the learning signal can be compared, to generate a proportionate ranking of intrinsic desire strengths. That is, the reward theory of desire allows for there to be facts about how much more an individual intrinsically desires P than Q. Later in this work, when we refer to one desire being stronger than another, we shall have this theory in mind.

Unconsciously responding to P as a reward in the technical, learning-theoretic sense does not sound very much like intrinsically desiring that P, and responding in a manner that greatly increases the chance of one sort of unconscious learning does not sound very much like greatly intrinsically desiring that P. Although it might be true that we have the vague sense that there are unconscious learning processes, and that giving people treats (things that they intrinsically desire) can direct some of these unconscious learning processes, this is hardly the first fact about intrinsic desires that will leap to anyone's mind.

---

[25] For a more mathematical treatment of reward learning theory and contingency-based learning more generally, see, e.g., Sutton and Barto (1998).

Similarly, the combination of an explosive gas with the gas we need to breathe does not sound like water. Yet water really is a combination of hydrogen and oxygen. This is our approach to thinking about intrinsic desires. Though intrinsic desires are not familiar to us as states of the reward and punishment systems, states of the reward and punishment systems do what intrinsic desires do, and so there is good reason to have a reward theory of desire.

So far, we have said only what the reward and punishment systems are and what they do that makes them the sorts of things they are in themselves. So it is time to show that in addition to driving their own special form of learning, they also play the full range of roles associated with intrinsic desires: to show that it is states of this learning system that do what intrinsic desires do.

6.2 The Reward System Causes What Desires Cause

The reward and punishment system deserves the attention of moral psychologists because it causes what intrinsic desires cause. The system that controls reward and punishment learning causally influences actions, feelings, and (to a lesser extent) cognitions, and it is the only system that causally influences all of these in anything like the manner expected of intrinsic desires.[26]

Begin with action production. The reward system's impact on action production is both profound and very well studied, and much of what is known is very standard textbook material.[27]

The reward system sends some of its output to a key integrative structure for action production, known as the dorsal striatum. The dorsal striatum receives further input from all of the brain's sensory and cognitive regions. Finally, it receives information about what basic actions (such as opening a hand, uttering a syllable...)[28] are primed for performance at the moment. Thus, information about what is the case and what is intrinsically desired combine in the dorsal striatum with information about what basic actions are available to be performed. The output of the dorsal striatum controls the regions of the brain

---

[26] This argument is made in full in Schroeder (2004, chs. 2, 3, and 4).

[27] The impact of the punishment system on action is less well understood, and is not textbook neuroscience. However, if one line of contemporary thought is borne out and the brain's serotonin system implements its punishment system, then there is a long history of empirical study of the way that the punishment system contributes to inhibiting action and freezing movement, just as the reward system contributes to releasing action and promoting movement. See, e.g., Deakin (1983), Soubrié (1986).

[28] Though we will not explore it in this work, there is substantial empirical evidence for Danto's category of basic actions, which is essentially Davidson's category of primitive actions. See Danto (1963; 1965), Davidson (1980), and any textbook account of the neuroscience of action and, e.g., the "motor homunculus." See also Schroeder (2004, ch.4).

known as motor and pre-motor cortex.[29] These regions contain the brain's capacity to command the performance of simple bodily movements, and their activity fully dictates the voluntary bodily movements people make. The motor cortex and pre-motor cortex can be thought of as made up of many different "keys," like a multi-tiered organ keyboard, with each key capable of producing a basic bodily movement (such as opening a hand and uttering a syllable). The keys are primed by what is being thought and perceived at any given moment, but the actual "pressing" of the keys is under the control of the dorsal striatum. The dorsal striatum, you might recall, receives input from belief and perception, on the one hand, and the reward system, i.e., intrinsic desires, on the other.

The reward signal is not an optional component of action production: in its most extreme form, Parkinson disease kills all of the cells of the part of the reward system that contributes directly to action production, and the result is complete paralysis.[30] This is not to say that a *positive* reward signal is required for action: obviously, one does not need to constitute pinching one's forearm as a reward in order to pinch one's forearm. But the action production system is not designed to work independently of the reward system. If one is to pinch one's arm, the production of this action through the dorsal striatum etc. must proceed in a manner that is at least somewhat sensitive to the strengths of reward signals (positive, neutral, or negative) that are being generated. (The specific way in which cognitive input, the reward signal, and the intrinsic structure of the dorsal striatum work together to select specific actions is still being studied.) An important fact about the paralysis that can result from Parkinson disease is that it is not relieved by beliefs about what is right or good or reasonable. No such belief suffices to restore the capacity to act on its own, independently of what is constituted as a reward (i.e., intrinsically desired).

Another striking way in which the reward signal is a compulsory contributor to action is that there are known conditions that can override the output of the dorsal striatum (and hence the reward system) and create bodily movements without its help, but these movements are not actions. For instance, direct electrical stimulation of parts of the brain can override the output of the dorsal striatum, and thus the output of the reward (and punishment) system, but these movements are experienced by their makers as not their own, and most philosophers would agree: these are not actions performed by the person, but mere movements forced out of the agent by a curious neuroscientist. Tourettic tics appear to also sometimes override the normal operation of the integrative action-production structure, forcing movements (not actions) out of the person

---

[29] This skips over important sub-cortical structures (globus pallidus, substantia nigra pars reticulata, certain thalamic nuclei . . .) that are biologically important but do not change the basic causal picture.

[30] Langston and Palfreman (1995) is a sophisticated lay-account of this phenomenon.

with the disorder.[31] What happens in these cases is movement the production of which does not involve intrinsic desire.

The effect of the reward system on *mental* actions is not textbook neuroscience. Here the claim that these actions are influenced by the reward system is based on a limited number of research findings, but these are nonetheless suggestive. The best-studied mechanisms for mental action are those that are responsible for our capacities to visualize and to talk to ourselves. These mechanisms rely on distinct structures in the frontal lobes of the brain which can causally influence the same regions of the brain that are directly involved in seeing (for visualizing) and hearing (for talking to ourselves).[32] So the question arises: what controls the activity of these specialized structures in the frontal lobes of the brain? It appears to be the same combination of reward signal and cognitive information (intrinsic desire plus belief) as serves overt action. The same neural structures in the dorsal striatum that take input from belief plus desire and send output to control overt action also send output to the specialized structures in the frontal lobes just mentioned. If this output is not for the voluntary control of visualizing and talking to oneself, it would be quite a surprise.

So much for the production of actions through desire. Next, consider feelings. To keep things simple, begin with feelings of pleasure and displeasure. The evidence that increases in the activity of the reward system causes increases in feelings of pleasure is widespread and powerful, and returns us to the realm of textbook neuroscience. Many pleasure-causing drugs (including the illegal ones) are known to act directly or indirectly upon some part of the reward system,[33] electrical stimulation of parts of the reward system appears sufficient to cause pleasure under certain conditions,[34] conditions that produce subjective pleasure also produce increased activity in the reward system,[35] and so on.[36] Furthermore, expected but not actualized rewards cause drops in the reward signal,[37] and these same events cause feelings of displeasure. Evidence that increases in the activity of the punishment system causes displeasure is suggestive, though less well established.[38]

If there is room to explain feelings of pleasure and displeasure through the actions of the reward and punishment systems, then what about the wider

---

[31] Though it is important to note that Tourette syndrome is a complicated disorder, and not every Tourettic tic is involuntarily produced. See Schroeder (2005) for more on this.

[32] A lovely overview is found in Baddeley (2003).

[33] A nice pair of experiments is found in Liechti et al. (2000), Liechti and Vollenweider (2000). Schroeder (2004, ch.3) contains a review.

[34] See, e.g., Stellar and Stellar (1985).

[35] An elegant experiment showing this is reported in Salimpoor et al. (2011).

[36] For an overview, see Schroeder (2004, chapters 2 and 3).

[37] As described above.

[38] For a start, the reader might consult Lowry et al. (2008) for a review.

range of positive and negative feelings? What about feelings of fear and anger, or schadenfreude or bliss? These feelings contain pleasure and displeasure. Insofar as these are feelings, they go beyond pleasure and displeasure in how one's body feels while in their grips. Fear without the feeling of a pounding heart or hair standing on end does not feel much like fear; bliss without a feeling of muscles relaxing throughout one's body does not feel much like bliss; and so on. Not surprisingly, these bodily changes are not independent of the reward and punishment systems. There are outputs from the punishment system that reach the amygdala, a neural structure that has a famous role as the central "junction box" causing the bodily states most associated with fear and anger and disgust (it is involved in feelings linked to other emotions as well, including positive feelings).[39] Thus, the reward system (and punishment system) has causal connections of the sort required to bring about the feelings we expect to be brought about by getting, (or being denied) what one intrinsically desires (or is averse to). In chapter 4 we responded to Stephen Darwall's view that the frustration of intrinsic desires can lead only to a limited range of negative feelings (frustration, discontent...) with evidence drawn from the armchair. Our response seems correct in light of empirical evidence showing that the net frustration of intrinsic desires, relative to expectations (i.e., the release of negative learning signals), is a standard cause of a wide range of negative emotional effects.

Finally, consider the cognitive effects associated with intrinsic desires. There is evidence that these effects are also commonly generated by the reward system. Unfortunately, this evidence is the furthest from textbook-ready; it is all the product of evolving research programs. Nonetheless, it is suggestive. A little should be said about both attention and learning, the latter in both its behavioral and intellectual forms.

Insofar as the direction of attention is a voluntary (not necessarily pre-meditated) action, one would predict that it would be under the control of the dorsal striatum and hence the reward system. Evidence for this can be found by considering the deficits that people with Parkinson disease show in the voluntary direction of attention. In various experiments, it has been found that people with Parkinson disease, who share in common damage to their reward systems, have difficulty directing or redirecting their attentions when the direction of such attention is up to the person in the experiment. For instance, in one such experiment, subjects were asked to hold their eyes fixed on a particular target, but cued to pay attention ("covertly") to a location nearby the target; this voluntary direction of attention made a discrimination task easier. But people with Parkinson disease were found to not improve on

---

[39] For a review of what we know about the amygdala, see LeDoux (2000). On the connection of the punishment system to the amygdala, there are a number of works cited in Lowry et al. (2008).

the discrimination, showing that they were having trouble keeping their attentions fixed on the cued locations.[40] People with Parkinson disease thus appear to have difficulties directing their attentions where their intrinsic desires would otherwise dictate.

The particularly important roles played by the reward *learning* caused by the reward system are revealed when one compares three sorts of people: ordinary healthy people, people with deficits in reward learning caused by Parkinson disease, and people with deficits in the ability to retain any knowledge of what they consciously observed in the recent past (people with anterograde amnesia). People with anterograde amnesia and healthy people are very different in how they learn by conscious observation and recall, but they are both capable of reward learning. People with Parkinson disease and healthy people are the same in how they learn by conscious observation and recall, but because Parkinson disease attacks and degrades the reward system, people with Parkinson disease learn poorly through reward learning. Tasks that people with anterograde amnesia and healthy people both learn to perform fairly well, while people with Parkinson disease learn fairly poorly if at all, are thus revealed to be tasks that depend specifically on reward learning: on the power of our desires (specifically, our intrinsic appetites, as opposed to our intrinsic aversions) to have effects on the way we learn.[41]

In one study of such a task, people were asked to learn to solve the "Tower of Hanoi" puzzle, a simple strategic puzzle in which one must move a stack of rings from one peg via a second peg to a third one, following some simple rules that make the task somewhat intellectually challenging (though physically trivial).[42] Although it is possible to figure out how to solve the puzzle in advance of one's first move, most people do not take this approach. Most people experimentally start out with one move, then another, and so on, until it looks to them that they are getting stuck—at which point they begin again, changing something in their approach to the puzzle and seeing where the change leads, and so on. Approached in this way, it is common for a person to solve the puzzle once without being certain to solve it any faster the next time it is attempted, because the solution was reached piecemeal and through too many steps to recall each one and its significance. Thus, learning to solve the puzzle in a way that is readily repeated takes some practice and time for most people. As it happens, most healthy people learn to solve the puzzle in about the same time as most people with anterograde amnesia—in the same time as people who cannot remember

---

[40] See Sampaio et al. (2011), where every effort is made to ensure that only difficulty in controlling attention explains the experimental findings. Older work focused specifically on the voluntary direction of attention in people with Parkinson disease goes back to at least Brown and Marsden (1988), another suggestive if less controlled study with the same upshot.

[41] This presupposes that other forms of learning, such as learning of fluent motor skills, are not relevant. But this presupposition is a safe one in the context of the work described.

[42] Saint-Cyr, Taylor, and Lang (1988).

anything that they did more than a minute ago. But people with Parkinson disease, who have the same ability to consciously recall the past as healthy people but who suffer from damage to their reward systems, do far worse on this test than healthy people and people with anterograde amnesia. Learning to solve this puzzle is thus something people do, in large part, through reward learning.

In another experiment, people were given the task of using arbitrary cues to predict an associated event (both cues and events were merely displays on a computer screen; outside influences and cues were thereby eliminated).[43] Not told how the cues related to the event, people had to guess at first, and hope to improve their guesses based on the feedback they received. For some, their guesses became better over time, until they became as good as could be expected. (To make the activity nearly impossible to learn by conscious recollection alone, there was no perfect correlation between the cues and the events. The best guessing strategy was successful only 75% of the time.) For others, their guesses never improved. Here again, the people with Parkinson disease were the ones who did poorly, while healthy people and people with anterograde amnesia both did well (and similarly well). The lesson again was that the task involved reward learning much more than any other form of learning.

Although life rarely presents us with explicit puzzles for which we get feedback about whether we have done the right thing or the wrong thing, reward learning is not dependent upon how a situation is presented or how explicit or implicit the world's responses to our efforts might be. So far as reward learning systems are concerned, every moment is one in which a puzzle is being presented to us, and every following moment is one in which we are rewarded, punished, or neither for what we did in the moment prior. So at every moment, reward learning is shaping the way that mental states causally affect other mental states, with the "goal" of this learning (if it can be put this way) being to "solve" the puzzle of life: the puzzle of how to perceive, think, and act so that certain states of affairs are maximally common (the ones that are constituted as rewards, proportionally to the degree to which they are rewards) while others are minimally common (the ones that are constituted as punishments, to the degree to which they are punishments). This amounts to reward (and punishment) learning acting on us so that we perceive, think, and act in ways that are increasingly conducive to getting more of what we intrinsically (appetitively) desire, and avoiding more of that to which we are intrinsically averse, as we grow older and more experienced.

At this point, the effects of the reward and punishment systems on action, feelings, and cognitions have been canvassed, and the results have been the same. In each case, the reward and punishment systems play the roles played by intrinsic desires. Further, the reward and punishment systems are the only

---

[43] Knowlton, Mangles, and Squire (1996).

things found in the brain that play all of these roles. This negative thesis is of course an empirically risky one. However, given the current state of neuroscientific knowledge, the negative thesis is not much riskier than the structurally equivalent thesis that the heart is the sole structure in the body that pumps blood. There are human beings with tremendously impaired reward systems who are otherwise intact—people with the most severe forms of Parkinson disease. These people provide scientists with an opportunity to discover other systems capable of playing the same roles as the reward system: other systems capable of driving action even when the reward system cannot, and other systems capable of producing joy even when the reward system cannot. But no such systems have come to light. There are many important kinds of functionality spared in people with severe Parkinson disease, but no coordinated package of functions that does most or all of what is expected from intrinsic desires.

6.3 Intrinsic Desires Are a Natural Kind

Intrinsic desires play a large number of causal roles. And there is a natural psychological kind, the reward-and-punishment-based learning system, that plays these same causal roles. This suggests a natural-kind strategy for theorizing about intrinsic desires. Following this strategy, intrinsic desires should be theorized as being the natural kind that does, in fact, play all of the causal roles that intrinsic desires play.[44] And so, following this strategy, intrinsic desires are states of the reward and punishment learning systems: they are what the reward theory of desire says they are.

To treat intrinsic desire as a natural kind is to treat it as akin to, for example, water.[45] Water is that substance found in rain, in lakes, in the ocean, that is liquid, transparent, able to quench thirst, make crops grow, dissolve salt crystals. Water is not identical to, or constituted by, any of these properties or powers: it is the thing that has them. These powers might have been had by other natural kinds (some subsets of them actually are), or had by no natural kind at all, but water is the natural kind found around us that happens to be the source of these properties and powers coming together so reliably.[46]

---

[44] This strategy is described and defended in Schroeder (2004); a similar strategy for theorizing desire is articulated in Morillo (1990). Compare methodology and results to the similar investigation of the emotions in Griffiths (1997).

[45] Putnam (1975).

[46] Note that, to treat intrinsic desires as a natural kind is not necessarily to commit to the thesis that, if there is no suitable natural kind, then there are no desires (compare Churchland 1981). Consider the study of the elements: earth, air, fire, and water. Only water turned out to be a natural kind, but it was not unreasonable for early science to approach all four elements with the hypothesis that each one was a natural kind. The falsification of that hypothesis in three out of four cases did not reveal that there was no such thing as earth, air, or fire. It showed only that, whatever earth, air, and fire are, they are not the sort of thing suitable for scientific study. We take a similar approach to desire. Intrinsic desire should be approached with the hypothesis that it is

To treat intrinsic desire as a natural kind is to hold that intrinsic desires are the things, whatever they turn out to be in themselves, found in people and other animals, causing the actions, feelings, and cognitions that we associate with terms such as "desire" and "want." If they form a natural kind, then intrinsic desires need not be identical to, or constituted by, any of their most familiar effects: the natural kind can be merely the common cause of them in human beings. If intrinsic desires are a natural kind, then all of their familiar effects might in principle (and might in practice) stem from other causes in alien creatures, though intrinsic desires would be the sole common cause of these effects in us.

Why, though, should philosophers treat intrinsic desires as a natural kind? There are at least four arguments worth considering, and each has some weight.

The first argument is that, if there is a good armchair theory of intrinsic desire that reveals its essence to be something other than states of reward and punishment systems, then that theory is likely to theorize intrinsic desires in terms of action, pleasure, or both action and pleasure. But in the previous chapter, we argued at length against all such theories. From the armchair, the evidence that intrinsic desires are necessary causes of movement or pleasure, or that complexly caused movement or pleasure is a (nontrivial) sufficient condition for the existence of intrinsic desires, seems quite weak.

The weakness of this first argument is that, while chapter 5 argued against a wide class of armchair theories of intrinsic desires, it cannot be said to have argued against every possible such theory that is inconsistent with the reward theory of desire. And of course, that is where we will have to leave matters for the present.

The second argument is an entirely general argument based on the nature of thought and speech: every kind we think or talk about is best thought of as a natural kind, if there is a natural kind that is a reasonable candidate to be the extension of our concepts and the referent of our words (except for kinds introduced by stipulation, or the like). Consider air. If air had turned out to be just one kind of molecule then "air" would, like "water," be a natural kind term. The only reason "air" is not a natural kind term is that there is no natural kind that is a reasonable candidate to be the referent of "air." The air is mostly nitrogen gas, which accounts for most of the forcefulness of wind on windy days (just by being the main gas present, by a large majority) but which does not explain why we need to breathe air. The air is also made up of a lot of oxygen gas, which does explain why we need to breathe air, but it does not do

---

the natural kind, whatever it might be, that gives rise to (at least, nearly) all the phenomena we associate with intrinsic desire. If there is such a kind, then it is what intrinsic desires are. If there is not, some other hypothesis can be formed; elimination of the kind from our ontology would be rather premature, even if it would be eliminated from our science (and so, from the explanatory categories of scientific psychology).

most of the explaining of the forcefulness of the wind. So, without a reasonable candidate natural kind to refer to, "air" does not refer to a natural kind. But it could have been otherwise. From our present vantage point, "air" does not *feel* like a natural kind term, but had the facts about the atmosphere been different, and had scientists learned and widely disseminated those facts, our feelings would be different. "Desire" might be more like "water" or like "air," in that it might have a single natural kind that is a reasonable candidate for its referent, or it might not. But if there is such a natural kind, then by default one should treat "desire" as a natural kind term.

The most obvious problem with this second argument is that it relies on a controversial principle about the referential dimension of language and thought: that concepts and terms for most kinds are best understood as referring to a natural kind if there is a candidate natural kind available. And this is certainly not the place to embark on a defense of such a principle.

A third argument is that the parts of the mind studied by philosophers will, ideally, be both real and well suited to feature in ideal explanations of human thought, feeling, and action. And one good test of the reality and explanatory robustness of putative parts of the mind is that they are appealed to by our best psychological sciences,[47] or could be if only our psychologists were slightly better philosophers, and would see that their technical term X is really a term for familiar part of the mind Y. It seems likely that the psychological sciences will continue to appeal to the reward and punishment systems and make them robust parts of larger explanations of various aspects of thought, feeling, and action, for all the reasons canvassed in the previous section and many more besides. If the reward and punishment systems are going to be a staple for psychological explanations, then either philosophers will have to be able to interpret the reward system as realizing intrinsic desires, or they will have to be able to interpret the reward system as realizing some other mental state, or they will have to cede the explanation of these aspects of thought, feeling, and action to something philosophers do not study and give no role in their moral theories. This lattermost option would be intolerable, however. So insofar as the psychological sciences continue to rely on the reward and punishment systems as robustly independent causal explainers of various aspects of thought, feeling, and action, philosophers would do well to determine what mental states or events should be understood to be at work in these explanations. It seems to us

---

[47] In saying this, we at least partly accept the terms of the debate set out by well-known eliminative materialists: if intrinsic desires are more like air than water, then there will be little use in focusing on intrinsic desires in any explanation of important phenomena, though it will not be any more wrong to say that there are intrinsic desires than to say that there is air. If intrinsic desires are more like fire than water (a totally heterogeneous collection of processes, including solar fusion and high-speed highly exothermic chemical oxidation, it seems) then it will not just be sloppy or unhelpful to appeal to intrinsic desires in explanations, it will be downright embarrassing. See, e.g., Churchland (1981).

that these mental states are best thought of as intrinsic desires. And so there is a reason from scientific practice to embrace a reward theory of desire.

A problem with this third argument is that a number of philosophers, including some with substantial involvement in moral psychology, have denied that mental states need to be treated as scientifically respectable entities that enter into nontrivial, interesting causal explanations of various aspects of thought, feeling, and action. And again, while this is an interesting debate, it is not one that will be pursued in the present work.

The fourth argument for treating intrinsic desires as a natural kind is aimed solely at philosophers who are sympathetic to desire-centered moral psychology. By treating intrinsic desires as a natural kind, it is possible to go a long way toward answering many of the most damning objections to desire-centered moral psychology. This will be defended in the next section, but it has no doubt already occurred to the reader that, if intrinsic desires are not reducible to behavioral dispositions (for example), then there are many objections to desire-centered theories of acting for reasons, praiseworthiness, and the like that will be deprived of key premises. A special virtue of responding to these objections in this way is that treating intrinsic desires as a natural kind, while not uncontroversial by any means, is not controversial or defensible on grounds that are primarily moral-psychological. As a result, it does not beg any questions to strengthen one's desire-centered theory by holding that intrinsic desires are a natural kind. The debate over whether mental terms are, insofar as possible, natural kind terms is a debate in the philosophy of language, philosophy of science, and philosophy of mind, and premises about virtue, praiseworthiness, or acting for reasons are not important premises in such debates.

Of course, the four arguments just presented are far from conclusive, and are intended much more to suggest our general lines of thought than to convince the skeptic. An extended argument meant to convince the skeptic is made in Schroeder (2004, especially chapter 6), but that is far from the last word in our eyes. Nonetheless, we do find something independently appealing to the straightforward thesis that when we say "desire" we are talking about something real inside us that plays a complex set of causal roles but has an essence or nature that is not automatically transparent to us.

6.4 Solutions and Promissory Notes

Suppose, then, that intrinsic desires are identical to states of the reward and punishment systems. Intrinsic desires are causally involved in movements, feelings, and cognitions, but they could fail to be involved in any of these things, and these things can be, and routinely are, influenced by things other than desire. And intrinsic desires have strengths but, due to these influences, the strength of any given episode of motivation, emotion, or cognitive influence could be quite a bit different from the strength of the intrinsic desire being manifested.[48] What would be the importance of this for moral psychology?

If intrinsic desires are states of the reward and punishment systems, then there is room for the desire-centered moral psychologist to hold that many of the most problematic objections to her position can be answered. In this section, we show how the reward theory of desire helps to solve certain problems, and how it shows promise to solve others.

Start with love and care. We showed (in chapter 4) how to defend desire-centered theories of love and care from otherwise powerful objections by holding that intrinsic desires have a more complex role than is generally believed by their detractors. But there are ways to attack a desire-centered theory of love and care even once the richness of intrinsic desires in actual healthy human beings is recognized. It is possible to use abnormal cases and exotic thought experiments to argue that intrinsic desires are neither sufficient nor necessary for love. The reward theory of desire can help with many of these objections.

One possible objection to desire-based theories of love and care is that it is possible to imagine a person who has the theoretically demanded qualities— who intrinsically desires the wellbeing of the beloved, and so on—but who does not appear to really love or care. For instance, it is possible to imagine a person who is very strongly motivated to tend to the wellbeing of a person, but whose motivation to do so seems much more like a neurosis, a compulsion, or a tic than like true love or caring. Here the reward theory of desire can help.

The first thing to do is to be careful about the case under consideration. It is no threat to a desire-based theory of love or care to say that a person might feel alienated from her impulse to tend to Miguel's wellbeing on a given occasion, or that she might feel rueful about doing so or might do so *akratically*. In none of these circumstances need there be a temptation to deny that the act done out of an intrinsic desire for Miguel's wellbeing genuinely counts as an act done out of love: what we do out of love, all too often, is judged not to be best, is less than fully rational, and (less often, but still occasionally) provokes feelings of alienation (especially when the beloved is a socially inappropriate love object). For it to be a problem for a desire-based theory of love or care, a case needs to be one in which there is little sign of anything like genuine love or care, however conflicted or conducive to folly on a particular occasion. There must be little sign of anything like genuine love or care, while there is nonetheless a powerful motivation to act so as to do what seems to improve another's wellbeing, a motivation independent of its instrumentality to other things that might be intrinsically desired. The motivation must appear very much a sort of neurosis, compulsion, or tic.

---

[48] This is an example of the phenomenon, described in chapter 3, of mere physical and mere contentful influences on mental events.

A feature of people who seem merely neurotic, merely compelled, or merely subject to exotic behavioral tics is that these people are not, in general, made delighted or contented by the actions they neurotically, compulsively, or in tic-like fashion perform. A person who feels *merely* forced to tend to Miguel's wellbeing might feel relief that she is not prevented from acting on her compulsion, but not delight that Miguel is well or contentment that he is flourishing. But it follows from the reward theory of desire that, in human beings, getting what you intrinsically desire is a normal cause of pleasure and other positive emotions. So it seems there are two possibilities. Either the apparently compelled person is acting on what the reward theory identifies as a genuine intrinsic desire for Miguel's wellbeing, and is somehow being prevented from having the feelings that are appropriate to the satisfaction and frustration of her intrinsic desire, or the apparently compelled person is not acting on a genuine intrinsic desire for Miguel's wellbeing. If the first possibility holds, then the person who feels compelled to tend to Miguel's wellbeing is someone who, if only she were not depressed, brain-injured, associatively scarred, or otherwise damaged, would feel delight in helping Miguel. She would feel good about his flourishing whether or not she is the agent of it, and she would look forward to chances to help him out when he was in difficulties, at least, to the extent that people who love and care for others ordinarily have these feelings. And if this is how the compelled-feeling person would feel if only she were undamaged, then it seems that she does indeed love or care for Miguel, and she is simply unable to access the normal feelings that reveal love or care to us. Those feelings are *appropriate* given her desire, according to the reward theory of desire and the earlier claims about the nature of pleasure and displeasure. And if those feelings are appropriate, then it seems wrong to say that the imagined person is merely compelled, merely acting on a tic. The first possibility, in short, reveals no problem for a desire-based theory of love or care, given the reward theory of desire. But then, the second possibility does not even appeal to an intrinsic desire for Miguel's wellbeing. It appeals to some other state capable of causing the behavioral impulses imagined. And such impulses are obviously not a threat to a desire-based theory of love or care, since they are understood to not stem from intrinsic desires for Miguel's wellbeing. Thus, the specter of a compulsive wellbeing-tender who counts as loving or caring on a desire-based theory of love or care is merely apparent.

Another possible objection to desire-based theories of love and care is that it is possible to imagine a creature who lacks the theoretically demanded qualities—who does not intrinsically desire the wellbeing of the beloved—but who nonetheless appears to really love or care. By turning to thought experiments, one can imagine a person who lacks any capacity for motivation, but whose feelings (and perhaps patterns of attention) convincingly attest that she loves another—perhaps, as David Velleman might have it, by being emotionally open to the other's value as a rational agent.

Does this unmotivated person have an intrinsic desire for the wellbeing of the beloved? If the reward theory of desire is correct, then the answer might be "yes." It might be the case that the unmotivated person has an intrinsic desire in virtue of having an appropriate state of her reward system; changes in the satisfaction of this state would be represented in the person's feelings, but the state would (by the terms of the thought experiment) have no access to any mechanisms by which actions might be produced. This would still be an intrinsic desire. Furthermore, if this feeling but unmotivated being gets pleasure from the wellbeing of the beloved, and displeasure from the misfortunes of the beloved, then it can be asked whether these feelings are appropriate or not. They are appropriate, it was argued, just in case the being does intrinsically desire the wellbeing of the beloved. So the unmotivated feeler either feels about the beloved in a way that is appropriate or not. If the feelings are appropriate, then the being intrinsically desires the wellbeing of the beloved, and the reward theory of desire shows how this is possible in a creature incapable of motivation. But if the feelings are not appropriate, then it is hard to see the imagined being as genuinely loving. If one Weather Watcher feels bad at the injury another Weather Watcher suffers from a lack of sufficient water, but this feeling is not appropriate to the inner psychology of the Weather Watcher feeling it, then it can hardly be said that the first Weather Watcher loves the second since love suffices to make such feelings appropriate.

Of course, the desire-based theorist of love who holds the reward theory of desire must grant that it is possible that a person lack all capacities to act and all capacities to feel—and even all capacities for voluntarily directed attention—and yet still love. To love, that is, without showing any of the ordinary signs of love at all. But this conclusion need not be particularly problematic. When a loving creature is stripped of its capacity for emotional warmth its love will appear cold; when a loving creature is stripped of its capacity for actions expressing concern for the wellbeing of the beloved, its love will appear unconcerned. But these are just appearances. As love is stripped of more and more of its common effects, it looks less and less like love, the desire-based theorist of love can hold, because all of the *signs* of love are disappearing. Our ordinary epistemic access to that love is disappearing, but the love itself might remain. Given the reward theory of desire and our theory of pleasure, an emotionless person who putatively loves is a person for whom feelings of joy at the salvation of a putative loved one would be appropriate (i.e., an accurate representation) if the person were capable of feelings of joy. This suggests that this normal sign of love (taking joy in the salvation of the beloved) is missing, but the thing that would normally lead to the sign (that is, the love itself) is not, because what is missing is the representation (the pleasure), not the thing represented (the desire). And likewise, given the reward theory of desire and our claim in chapter 3 that all actions are manifestations (at least) of the agent's belief-and-desire-based rationalizations, an unmotivated person who putatively loves is a person for whom trying to assist the wellbeing of a loved one would be very well rationalized if the person were capable of action. Again, this normal sign of love might be missing, but the thing that would normally lead to it is still present: the act rationalized is missing, but the thing rationalizing the action exists. If intrinsic desires are things that are potentially hidden from the casual eye, then so too will be love, on a desire-based theory of love. But if it is true of a creature that it contains a state warranting the feelings we associate with love (only it cannot feel) and warranting the actions we associate with love (only it cannot act), then it seems reasonable that the creature loves: that it is love itself that warrants the feelings and rationalizes the actions.

Moving on from the topic of love: the perverse absence and the perverse presence of behavioral impulses of all sorts have been thought to be problems for desire-based moral psychology.

Begin with perverse absences. Derek Parfit has focused attention on the person who lacks any intrinsic desire to avoid pain on future Tuesdays, and on the less radical version of this person who merely strongly discounts her future pain in choosing present actions.[49] If reasons to act stem from (present) intrinsic desires, then it seems this person does not have rationalizing reasons to avoid suffering on future Tuesdays, or has much less reason to avoid tomorrow's suffering than today's. And to many, these have seemed absurdities.

We are in a position to ameliorate these problems. Begin with the harder case: that of the person who lacks any intrinsic desire to avoid pain on future Tuesdays. As Parfit is aware, pain decomposes into a potentially neutral sensory awareness of tissue damage (nociception) and the displeasure that is normally caused by it. But on the present view of the relation between intrinsic desire and displeasure, it turns out that the capacity to feel displeasure in response to nociception is the consequence of having an intrinsic aversion to nociception: pain is only possible because we intrinsically desire (via a sensory sense or mode of presentation or...) not to have our bodily tissues damaged. Hence the person who can now feel pain is a person who has an intrinsic desire that is frustrated by tissue damage, and so a person who has a practical rationalizing reason (according to Spare Conativism) to avoid tissue damage, including future damage.[50] The sort of person required for Parfit's thought experiment is a person who is not at present capable of suffering from bodily injury, though who will acquire that capacity by the coming Tuesday. For the present, she will just have to tell herself, "on Tuesday I will nocicept and find it very unpleasant, much like

---

[49] Parfit (2011, 73–82).

[50] Could a critic hold that this intrinsic desire is merely an intrinsic desire that we not suffer tissue damage *now*, with the temporal indexical a part of the desire's content (or mode of presentation...)? It is possible to imagine this, but it seems unlikely to be right. The role of this intrinsic desire in other animals (animals less given to abstract conceptualizing than human beings) would seem to include prevention of future bodily injury, a role that would not make sense if the intrinsic desire had a content that dealt only with present injury.

I find smelling a skunk to be very unpleasant." Furthermore, she must also be an unusual person in that she must not have an intrinsic aversion to feeling displeasure; most people have such an intrinsic aversion that is time-independent in the same way that we also have intrinsic desires for pleasure that are not time-dependent. Finally, she must also have no intrinsic desires at present that she can reasonably foresee will tend toward frustration given future displeasure from nociception (so, she cannot intrinsically desire to take care of friends or family members, or to go cycling, etc., since these are things one might reasonably foresee future Tuesday suffering interfering with).

For this very alien person, Spare Conativism must say that she has no present rationalizing reason to prevent her future pain. In the same way, Spare Conativism must say that a person who has a present contempt for luxury cars has no rationalizing reason to secure a future for herself in which she enjoys a luxury car (so long as she does not intrinsically desire pleasure in a time-independent way and so long as she does not foresee future lack of a luxury car potentially interfering with other things she intrinsically desires at present), even if she foresees that in the future she will intrinsically desire a luxury car and feel bad at being deprived of a luxury car. We do not find it obvious (as Parfit seems to) that in holding this position we have made an error.

As for the person who simply acts as though the future is much less valuable to her than the present, while it is true that many people act in this way, Spare Conativism can hold that most of these people act irrationally. After all, the mere fact that someone chooses a small benefit today at the cost of substantial suffering tomorrow does not show that the person has chosen what she most intrinsically desires, on the present view. There is room for merely physical and for content-efficacious but nonrationalizing factors to lead people to choose contrary to the course of action that maximizes expected intrinsic desire satisfaction.

Turning now to perverse presences: the person who has a behavioral impulse to turn on radios,[51] the person who has a behavioral impulse to count the blades of grass on squared-off lawns,[52] the person who has a sudden impulse to drown her screaming baby in its bathwater,[53] the person who has a behavioral impulse to seek out cocaine to the exclusion of all else in life, and the person who has a behavioral impulse to twitch, jerk, and shout obscenities (as happens in cases of Tourette syndrome) all seem like people who put theoretical pressure on the desire-based moral psychologist. Do these people have rationalizations for their actions? *Good* rationalizations (assuming the behavioral impulses are *very* strong)? Do these people illustrate the claim that rational action must always be action guided by Reason, not Appetite? If these people knowingly

[51] Warren Quinn (1993, 237).
[52] Rawls (1971, 432).
[53] Watson (1975, 210).

do something morally good or required as a result of their behavioral impulses, will Spare Conativism grant them moral credit? If these people knowingly do something morally bad or forbidden as a result of their behavioral impulses, will Spare Conativism call them selfish or malicious rather than victims of mental states gone awry?

These problems threaten Spare Conativism on the assumption that, if a person is behaviorally impelled to act in a coherent way that is responsive to the person's means-end beliefs, then what motivates the person must be an intrinsic desire—and if the behavioral impulse is strong, then the intrinsic desire must be a strong one. An action-based theory of desire, or some variant of it, is being presupposed. But if the reward theory of desire is correct, then there remains the possibility that in none of these cases is the person in question one who desires the end to which the person is behaviorally impelled. On the reward theory of desire, being motivated to bring it about that P is not a sufficient condition for intrinsically desiring that P, or even desiring that Q when P seems instrumental to, or a realizer of, Q. Thus, the reward theory of desire allows the possibility that the people just described do not actually desire to turn on radios or count blades of grass, drown the baby, buy cocaine, or shout obscenities; or, if they do so desire, then they might not desire these ends as much as they seem, given the strengths of their dispositions to act. The reward theory of desire leaves open the possibility that Spare Conativism need not worry about any of these cases. We will not show that all of these cases in fact come out as we would wish; that is a project for another occasion or three. But the foregoing arguments have made it clear how such arguments might proceed. We will turn to the case of the addict in chapter 11, where we show that what is in principle possible is also actual for at least one problem case, but for the moment we note just the fact that these problem cases are not automatically problems for Spare Conativism, thanks to the reward theory of desire. On the reward theory, there are many opportunities for the signs of intrinsic desires to be present or absent, strong or weak, without the underlying intrinsic desires themselves being present or absent, strong or weak.

Of course, the reward theory of desire merely leaves the possibility open. Whether or not the possibility is actual depends on the psychological details. Are the states that would bring about the kinds of radio-turning-ons, grass-countings, baby-drownings, cocaine-buyings, and obscenity-shoutings of interest to moral psychology states of the reward or punishment systems or are they not? Are they of a kind with the things that we recognize as intrinsic desires? Or are they of some distinct kind that, by being distinct from intrinsic desire, can pose no objection to Spare Conativism?

Another family of objections should also receive attention. According to these objections, it is obvious that desires cannot be the foundation of moral psychology because it is obvious that sometimes we are moved by things other than desires when acting for reasons, acting with moral worth, and so on. The case of the person who is tempted to skip the PTA meeting in order to read in front of the fire but who goes to the meeting anyway is a central sort of case here.[54] Then there is the person who helps another out of "mere inclination" (i.e., a desire to do so) standing in contrast to the person who helps another out of "duty" (i.e., a cognition of something in the domain of reasons or values).[55] Or again, there is the distinction between the person who is seduced by his desires (i.e., his Reason is persuaded to make a choice it would not otherwise have made because of the influence of desire) and the person who is overwhelmed by his desires (and so his Reason plays no part in what he does).[56]

As before, all of these problems loom for Spare Conativism because of assumptions about the nature of desire. In the first case, the idea that one does not go to the PTA out of a desire to do so is supported principally by the idea that when one acts successfully on a desire one can expect to be pleased to be getting what one wants, along with the observation that there are many cases, such as giving up an evening by the fire for a PTA meeting, in which one is motivated without there being any reasonable expectation that one will be pleased if one succeeds. (And, although the displeasure of guilt is real, it might well be that there is much more pleasure to be anticipated from skipping the tiresome PTA meeting than unpleasant feelings of guilt.) A similar line of thought might lie behind the idea that being motivated by duty is something other than (or more than) being motivated by an intrinsic desire to do the right thing (or something similar). And then, the idea that desires can seduce—the idea that seduction is an apt metaphor for the process by which desire can influence action in certain cases—strongly suggests that our experiences of pleasure are an important part of the evidence for the idea. A pleasure-based theory of desire, or some variant of it, seems to be what is behind these ideas.[57]

If the reward theory of desire is correct, then there remains the possibility that in none of the preceding cases is the feeling of pleasure a good guide to the role being played by intrinsic desires. Since, on the reward theory of desire, being pleased by improved prospects of it being the case that P is not a necessary condition for desiring that P, the reward theory of desire allows there to be a possibility that the person going to the PTA does so out of an intrinsic desire, that there is no distinction in kind between acting out of inclination and acting out of duty, and that there is no distinction in kind between motivation by reason seduced by desire and motivation by desire independently of Reason. The reward theory of desire leaves open the possibility that the desire-based theorist of moral psychologist need not worry

[54] See Schueler (1995, 29); for similar thoughts, see also Davis (1986), Vadas (1984).
[55] Obviously Immanuel Kant is the primary modern source of this idea: see Kant (1998). More recently the idea can also be found clearly expressed in, e.g., Herman (1993, ch.1).
[56] Watson (1975).
[57] Davis (1986) defends a motivation-plus-pleasure theory of desire.

about any of these cases. Perhaps, for example, the person who goes to the PTA meeting is analogous to Gretchen going to the dentist in chapter 5. Going to the PTA meeting is motivated by a desire for the long-term wellbeing of his child, say, or a desire to be liked in his community. However, while sitting by the fire, his knowledge of the hazards to his or his child's future wellbeing is purely theoretical. Comfortable as he is, without anything obviously wrong with his child or his reputation, he viscerally expects a state in which all continues to be well. As a result, going to the meeting does not provide a rise in net desire satisfaction *relative to visceral expectations* and no pleasure results. In fact, displeasure results, as the expectation that all be well runs into the chill of the night and the boring nature of the meeting. (We will go into more detail for a similar case in chapter 8.)

A stronger response is also available. If the reward theory of desire is correct and the empirical facts surrounding action are more or less as we take them to be, then it is just not possible for ordinary human beings to do things like go to PTA meetings out of a sense of duty, independently of antecedent intrinsic desires. If ordinary human beings did have this power, then they could use it to go to PTA meetings in spite of suffering from the most extreme form of Parkinson disease, in which one's reward-signaling neurons have almost all died (and so one has impaired or absent appetitive intrinsic desires). But unfortunately people do not have this power, as we discussed earlier in this chapter. People with the most extreme form of Parkinson disease are not able to become motivated to do what they grasp as their duty; they remain paralyzed. And likewise, people with less extreme forms of Parkinson disease have the same difficulties initiating actions and changing courses of action when doing what they grasp as their duty (the right, the good, the reasonable . . .) as they do when acting for pleasure or the sake of cheering on the Red Sox; so, at least, it appears from the literature, which does not hint at the disease-remediating powers of ideas of duty in people with Parkinson disease. The reward system, it seems, is compulsory for ordinary action in creatures like us. And so, if the reward theory of desire is correct, antecedently existing intrinsic desires are compulsory for ordinary action. In the previous paragraph we argued that the phenomenology of acting out of Reason rather than Appetite can be accommodated by the present theory; the empirical science of action suggests that the burden is in fact on the defenders of Reason to show that Reason really can control action independently of desire.

Although the previously mentioned potential benefits are potential benefits of holding the reward theory of desire, there are other ways of achieving these benefits too. Some of our reasons for preferring the reward theory of desire are found in the defense of the theory presented in Schroeder (2004). Others will come out as we work through the details promised for later chapters. But none of these reasons for preferring the reward theory of desire to other theories will be decisive.

Other desire-based theorists of moral psychology have taken other approaches to the sorts of problem cases we just listed. These approaches have generally taken the form of placing restrictions on the kinds of desires that a desire-centered moral psychology should be built upon. Such desires should be ones that one wholeheartedly wants to have,[58] or should be ones that could survive cognitive reflection,[59] or should be ones generated by one's beliefs about what one would intrinsically desire if one were rational,[60] or should be properly historically integrated into one's overall psyche,[61] or... Inevitably (or so it seems to us), these extra restrictions on the sorts of desires that count create additional problems for the moral psychologist.[62] One of us has written extensively about the fact that people can take foolish meta-attitudes toward their own desires, and so restrictions based on meta-attitudes (both cognitive and conative) face serious challenges: what shall we make of Ella, who disapproves of her homosexual desires? Are these desires "not truly her own?" What about Huckleberry Finn, who appears to have a virtuous heart but false moral beliefs? Restrictions based on the desires being properly historically integrated within the overall psyche face challenges from the ordinary sorts of desires, such as sexual desires, that spring themselves upon us through nonpsychological processes without being lesser partners in our moral psychological lives for all that. And restrictions based on rational acceptability are restrictions that give up too much of what one is looking for in a genuinely desire-based moral psychology.

This mention of challenges faced by other desire-based moral psychologists is not intended as a refutation of the opposing views. We merely state our reasons for staking out a different path: that of treating all intrinsic desires as equal, for purposes of moral psychology, while being more mindful than most of what intrinsic desires really are. If this path can provide solid responses to the many objections that have been leveled at desire-based

---

[58] Frankfurt comes to something like this view by his paper "Identification and Wholeheartedness," though perhaps by that time Frankfurt had also backed away from the broad moral psychological ambitions on display in "Freedom of the Will and the Concept of a Person." Compare Frankfurt (1971) to Frankfurt (1987).

[59] Tiberius (2002).

[60] Smith (1994).

[61] E.g., Fischer and Ravizza (1998).

[62] A very early expression of some of our reservations about using a restricted set of desires (or anything else) to delineate the "real" self, the motives of which are the only ones that render one apt for moral praise or blame, is found in Arpaly and Schroeder (1999). While our positive claims in that work are quite different from our present claims, we think that the negative arguments still stand.

moral psychology without subdividing intrinsic desires into those we like as theorists and those we need to push aside, then that seems a mark in favor of our theory: it is unified in its treatment of intrinsic desires. But this would only be a small mark in favor. We will rely on the overall appeal of the package of ideas presented in this book to serve as an argument, in the aggregate, for our desire-based theory.

PART III

Virtue

Credit and Blame

In Part 1, our goal was to paint a picture of Reason that left room for intrinsic desires in the theory of acting for reasons. In Part 2, our goal was to paint a new picture of intrinsic desires. Now that we have reached Part 3, our goal is to take the ideas just developed about intrinsic desires and acting for reasons and use them to paint a picture of virtue and vice.

Our starting point is the idea of good and ill will. Having good will is desiring the right or good (via the right concepts) while having ill will is desiring the wrong or bad (via the right concepts). Good will is the "moral desire" of chapter 3, on which people act when they act for the right reasons; ill will is the "immoral desire," as it were, acting on which is always acting for the wrong reasons. But, of course, there are a number of complications needed to capture the complexities. Just to start with, good will is not just a single admirable intrinsic desire, and ill will is not just a single contemptible intrinsic desire.

Once the ideas of good and ill will are made clear, Part 3 will make two main uses of it. One use will be to give a theory of being virtuous and of some particular virtues (chapters 8 and 9). But because ideas about virtue and vice are so closely linked to ideas of praise and blame, we will benefit from first presenting a theory of praise- and blameworthiness. That will be the task of the present chapter.

7.1 Attributability and Accountability

Before getting started on the theory of praise- and blameworthiness, or even on the theory of good and ill will that might serve a theory of praise- and blameworthiness, some clarifications are in order about just what sort of project is being undertaken here.

Praise and blame are not really a natural pair. Praising is an action: to praise Mohandas Gandhi for his role in Indian independence is to say (or write, or...) something nice about Gandhi. While the word "blame" can be used in a parallel way ("in his speech, Obama blamed Bush for the troubles this country is in"), this is not the main thing "blame" means. That use aside, blaming is not an action: to blame Hitler for the war is not to say (or write, or...) anything at all. Blaming is rather an attitude one takes, an attitude on the basis of which one can then act. Condemning is the true opposite of praising, since it too is an action. Crediting (as in: crediting Gandhi for his role in the peaceful transition to independence) is the true opposite of blaming, since it too is an attitude.[1] Unfortunately, "creditworthiness" has a meaning already, and one that is not the complement of "blameworthiness," so that the philosopher who wants to write in English about someone's deserving to be credited or blamed is left without any way to name this status that is both natural and precise. For convenience, we will call what we are interested in "praiseworthiness and blameworthiness," with the understanding that our interest is in being worthy of attitudes such as credit and blame, not in being the sort of person who should be praised or condemned.

Gary Watson (1996) holds there are two kinds of moral responsibility of which one might give a theory: accountability and attributability. Holding someone accountable for an action is seeing her as an appropriate candidate for certain types of treatment, such as punishment, whereas seeing an action as attributable to a person is seeing her action as speaking well or ill of her, independently of whether she should be treated in certain ways or not. On Watson's way of looking at things, Spare Conativism's theory of praise- and blameworthiness is an account of attributive praise- and blameworthiness, as will become clear.[2] Its closest intellectual neighbors are the attributive views found in Arpaly (2002; 2006), Sher (2006), and Smith (2008).

We make this clarification right at the outset because there are some who argue[3] or simply hold[4] that attributability is not any sort of responsibility, and therefore attributability-based "blame" is not really blame: it is "disesteem," say, or "dispraise." (They appear to say much less about attributability-based accounts of crediting agents, however, and so we will do the same and focus on blame for the moment.) A few things should thus be said to defend our claim to be presenting a genuine theory of (praiseworthiness and) blameworthiness.

First, we are offering an account of blameworthiness but not of blame or blaming. To grasp that someone is blameworthy for an act is not yet to blame the person. Obviously this follows if blaming is an action, as some hold. But even if blaming is an attitude, there is still a gap. On our view, Hitler is blameworthy for his actions because he acted out of ill will, but to blame Hitler for the war, it is not enough to see that Hitler acted out of ill will in playing his

---

[1] There seem to be broader and narrower senses of "credit" just as there are of "blame." The use of "credit" we have in mind is the one in which Gandhi cannot be (morally) credited for his role if he brought independence about purely by accident or purely out of a desire to spite his pro-British acquaintances.

[2] On Shoemaker's way of looking at things, many of our cases are of both attributability and answerability (Shoemaker 2011).

[3] See, for example, Neil Levy (2005).

[4] See, for example, Darwall (2006).

role in bringing the war about: one must also be against the war, and in general against the wrong or bad. Satan, as conventionally imagined, can see that Hitler is blameworthy, but Satan cannot *blame* Hitler for the war because Satan is for, and not against, the wrong or bad.[5] At least, this seems to us the correct way to think about blame and blameworthiness.

Even if one does not accept our view of blame, other accounts of blame are also consistent with attributive theories of blame*worthiness*. Thomas Scanlon holds that blame itself is inherently second-personal,[6] that it is fundamentally a mode of address to a (putatively) blameworthy person. This is not our view. But now consider Scanlon on, not blame, but blameworthiness.

> To judge an individual to be blameworthy, I am claiming, is to judge that their conduct shows something about them that indicates this kind of impairment of their relationship with others, an impairment that makes it appropriate for others to have attitudes towards them different from those that constitute the default moral relationship (2008, 141).

That is, Scanlon holds that to judge someone blameworthy is to make a purely intellectual judgment about her conduct. And what is this "relationship with others" such that demonstrating an impairment of it makes one blameworthy?

> …the kind of mutual concern that ideally we all have toward other rational beings (2008, 140).[7]

Thus, Scanlon holds that to judge someone blameworthy is to make a purely intellectual judgment about her conduct, to the effect that it displays certain features that amount to a moral failing (within Scanlon's theory of what moral failings amount to). This is attributability: the person is blameworthy for an action which, in Scanlon's words, "shows something about them"—absence of moral concern for others. Thus, Scanlon's way of thinking about blameworthiness is an attributive approach, like ours, in spite of our different approaches to blame.[8]

Second, it appears that attributability is a necessary condition for accountability: one would not want to hold a person accountable for an action if it were not attributable to the person (and not merely to chance, a tic, or the like). In addition to this appearing correct to us, it also appears to be unchallenged in

---

[5] This is a friendly amendment to Sher's theory in Sher (2006).

[6] A concept that comes from Darwall (2006).

[7] Scanlon elaborates on the nature of this concern. He explains that it implies, for example, "being disposed to be pleased when we hear of things going well for other people," as well as not to harm them, to help them when it is not too hard, and not to mislead them (2008, 140).

[8] Vargas (2013, 160–61) similarly splits being blameworthy from being accountable. As for Scanlon's position, later it will be seen that the type of concern for others that Scanlon discusses is nothing other than good will the way it would be if Scanlonian contractualism were the right view of the right and the good.

the literature making the distinction.[9] And, if this appearance is correct, then having a theory of attributability for bad acts is a necessary condition for having a full theory of blameworthiness. Thus, even for the reader who rejects any attributive theory of blameworthiness in favor of some accountability-based theory, something like the present theory is needed. For such a reader, our efforts can be read as providing a (confusingly labeled) account of this necessary attributive condition on blameworthiness.

Third, even if attributive blameworthiness is not "real" blameworthiness, it is nothing so bloodless as to be mere "disesteem," or what Scanlon calls "pointless grading" (2008, 153). It is rather the main way in which an action can be *vicious*, as will be shown in our account of virtue (in chapter 8). Some regard evaluations of the way acts reflect on agents as less important than accountability statements, which might be reasonable if one's ultimate purpose is a theory of punishment. However, viciousness in actions is something people care about, as is evident to anyone who, with some emotion, has referred to another person as an "asshole" due to his actions and their apparent motives. If one does not think what we discuss as blame should be called "blame" then one can say that, at least, it is a recognition of vice expressed in action, or of positive and negative moral worth, and that such recognition is rarely bloodless.

7.2 Good Will and Ill Will

With our preliminary clarifications out of the way, we plunge right in with theories of good and ill will. Begin with good will.

Complete good will is an intrinsic desire for the right or good, correctly conceptualized (i.e., presented via the correct sense, mode of presentation, narrow content, primary intension...; more on this in a moment).

Partial good will is an intrinsic desire for some part of the right or good, correctly conceptualized.

A person has more good will insofar as her intrinsic desire for the right or good is stronger, and less good will insofar as this intrinsic desire is weaker.

Opposing good will is ill will.

Complete ill will is an intrinsic desire for the wrong or bad, correctly conceptualized.

Partial ill will is an intrinsic desire for some part of the wrong or bad, correctly conceptualized.

---

[9] With the possible exception of Shoemaker (2011).

A person has more ill will insofar as her intrinsic desire for the wrong or bad is stronger, and less ill will insofar as this intrinsic desire is weaker.

Because every ordinary adult human being has a fair measure of both good will and ill will in her, there is also room to note individuals who are lacking good will, or who are lacking ill will. We call the former sort a person who is *morally indifferent*, and the latter sort the person who is *reverse morally indifferent*.

Moral indifference is a lack of good will. A person is more morally indifferent the less good will she has.

Reverse moral indifference is a lack of ill will. A person is more reverse morally indifferent the less ill will she has.

This could all use a certain amount of explanation.

The first thing to explain, or at least to repeat for emphasis, is our thinking about intrinsic desires. Typically, an intrinsic desire for the right or good will result in impulses to act well, feelings such as delight or relief at the thought of the right or good being done, and various cognitive effects. However, good will is absolutely not an impulse to act, nor is it a disposition to feel delight (or an occurrent feeling of delight) at the prospect of doing what is right or good. As discussed in chapters 5 and 6, intrinsic desires are the common causes of these sorts of impulses to act and feel, and various cognitive effects as well, but intrinsic desires can exist without causing these effects or even disposing one to them. The intrinsic desire is one thing, and these familiar effects of it are another, and there are many ways in which the effects can fail to be manifested. Desires are, however, the grounds of our abilities to act for reasons: both to act for reasons without antecedent deliberation, and to take the acts that make up deliberation itself (as discussed in chapters 2 and 3). They might only contingently move us to act, but they are what makes us poised to be agents in the first place.

The second thing to explain is that we have so far suppressed a complication arising from a distinction made in chapter 6. There we noted that some intrinsic desires that P are appetites for it being the case that P, while other intrinsic desires are aversions to it being the case that P. Taking this into account, we hold that good will can be both an appetite for the right or good, correctly conceived, or that it can be an aversion to the wrong or bad (again, correctly conceived). And likewise, ill will can be an appetite for the wrong or bad, but it can also be an aversion to the right or good.

The third thing to explain is the notion that, in good and ill will, the way that the right or good is conceptualized matters. Just why it matters is something to which we will turn in a moment, in our theory of praise- and blameworthiness. Here we simply wish to explain just what we mean in taking conceptualization to be important.

The reference of an intrinsic desire that counts as complete good will must, naturally, be the right or the good. But the conceptualization of that referent (that is, the sense, mode of presentation, primary intention, narrow content, etc.) is less obvious, because a given referent can be conceptualized in many different ways.

Spare Conativism holds that the sense required for perfect good will is to be determined by normative moral theory: the concepts deployed in grasping the correct normative moral theory are the concepts through which one must intrinsically desire the right or good in order to have good will. According to Kantians, the concepts deployed in perfect good will present the right as RESPECTING PERSONS (or perhaps ACTING IN A WAY EVERYONE COULD ACT, or whatever formulation of Kant strikes the reader as most apt). According to utilitarians, they present the good as HAPPINESS MAXIMIZED. Other normative theories might have it that the right or good is irreducibly plural, in which case good will would also be irreducibly plural, a matter of more than one desire (perhaps one must intrinsically desire WELFARE and also JUSTICE; perhaps one must intrinsically desire a dozen different things, some of them quite complex).

The distinction between a referent and the way it is conceptualized is a familiar one: there has to be some way of marking a distinction between what one is thinking of and how one thinks of it. This "how one thinks of it" might or might not be content, be a semantic feature of one's thought, be publicly shared, and so on, for various properties famously associated with conceptualizations, senses, modes of presentation, etc. We make no claims about these further properties, since this is really the province of philosophy of mind and language, and does not directly affect our argument. All we wish to allow ourselves is the distinction, and the convention of using block capitals to suggest the "how one thinks of it" feature of a desire along with the "what one is thinking of" feature.[10]

The potential importance of the distinction is familiar and, we take it, uncontroversial. Contemporary philosophy of language and mind has made famous possibilities such as the possibility of being desperate for water and seeing from one's instruments that there is H_2O nearby, yet failing to act—because one has a concept WATER and a concept H_2O but one does not grasp that water is H_2O.[11] For Spare Conativism, the important possibilities involve having the concept of the RIGHT or GOOD, and the concept RESPECTING PERSONS (if Kantians are right about normative theory) or MAXIMIZING HAPPINESS (if utilitarians are right; etc.), but not grasping that what is right or good is respecting persons or maximizing happiness (or etc.), and so acting

---

[10] We borrow this convention from Jerry Fodor. See, for example, Fodor (1998).
[11] See Putnam (1975), Burge (1979).

to promote what one conceives as the RIGHT while damaging what one conceives as, say, RESPECTING PERSONS (or vice versa).

Michael Smith has made a similar point in the language of desires *de re* and *de dicto*,[12] and so it is tempting to say that our point is just this: some people desire the right or good *de dicto* while others desires the right or good *de re*, and we hold that only those who desire the right or good *de re* have good will. But this jargon appears the wrong way to couch things. If Lillian's intrinsic desire is for THE RIGHT while Shamissa's is to RESPECT PERSONS, and if Kantian normative theory is correct, then on our account the following things appear to be true: Lillian intrinsically desires the right or good *de dicto*, Shamissa intrinsically desires the right or good *de re*, and only Shamissa has so far been shown to have good will. However, *both* Lillian and Shamissa intrinsically desire the good *de re*. They both have the right itself, that very thing, as the object of their desires, as the referent of their respective concepts. And if Saul were to intrinsically desire that FREGE'S FAVORITE PROPERTY be instantiated, and if Frege's favorite property were the right or good, then Saul would also intrinsically desire the right or good *de re* (if Saul treats FREGE'S FAVORITE PROPERTY as a directly referring term and not a mere description). To say that one intrinsically desires the right or good *de re* is not to say how goodness is presented by the concept(s) contained in one's desire. And it seems to us very important how goodness is presented by one's concepts. So we will prefer our way of putting the point to what one might take from Smith.

The fourth thing to explain about the theory of good and ill will is the notion that good and ill will can be either complete or partial.

Consider first ill will. If Kantians hold the correct normative theory, then complete ill will is something like an intrinsic desire to DISRESPECT PERSONS; if utilitarians hold the correct normative theory, then complete ill will is something like an intrinsic desire that HAPPINESS BE MINIMIZED; on other theories, complete ill will might be an intrinsic desire that CONSENT BE VIOLATED or that FREEDOM BE MINIMIZED. These sorts of intrinsic desires are perhaps sensible for Satan, but for actual human beings they would represent cartoonish levels of villainy. Even the worst people rarely delight in distant strangers lying or kicking their dogs. Even the worst people show little willingness to increase the rate at which such things are done just for the sake of there being more lying and suffering in the world. The worst people harbor various forms of ill will (malice towards a person or group, authoritarianism within a family or nation, and the like) but their ill will is partial rather than complete.

Turning to good will, it seems likely that there will be related phenomena. History suggests that, for most of our existence, people have been more willing

---

[12] See Smith (1994, 73ff.).

to be kind, fair, and so on to their kin and neighbors than to strangers, even with all else being equal. Yet these people who drew their circles of moral concern too narrowly still seem to have some moral credit for their kind and fair treatment of those within their circles. They had some measure of good will, but their good will was partial. Moral vegetarians would presumably want to say similar things about the partial good will of contemporary people who are concerned with suffering, freedom, and so on across all human beings, but who treat nonhuman animals quite differently.

To systematize the idea of partial good and ill will, it will help to think about *pro tanto* moral reasons. Generally, talk of *pro tanto* moral reasons is talk of considerations that always carry *some* moral weight, though that weight might be defeasible. For example, many moral philosophers hold that there is a *pro tanto* reason to relieve any given person's suffering, though they disagree about the defeaters for such reasons (and their ultimate origins). Many moral philosophers hold that there are defeasible *pro tanto* reasons to tell the truth, to keep promises, to distribute goods equally, to help people achieve their life projects, and so on.[13]

The variety of *pro tanto* reasons is constrained by the content of the correct normative theory, and by the requirement that a *pro tanto* reason be such as to always carry some moral weight. The (act) utilitarian has to hold that there is no *pro tanto* reason to keep promises, since there is not always moral weight to keeping a promise: there might be no happiness whatsoever that hangs on a given promise being kept. (There might be a *prima facie* reason to keep promises, according to the utilitarian, since it can be hard to judge the consequences for happiness of a given action. But *prima facie* reasons can turn out to be no reason at all.) The same act utilitarian might hold that there is a *pro tanto* reason to relieve the suffering of a fellow south-sider, of a Ghanaian, or of Tyrone, however. This is because relieving the suffering of someone who is a fellow south-sider, or a Ghanaian, or who is Tyrone (i.e., a particular individual) always carries some moral weight because it is, necessarily, an instance of increasing someone's utility.

Because *pro tanto* moral reasons suggest a principled way of dividing up the whole of the right or good into parts, they make an appealing basis for partial good and ill will. Partial good will can be thought of as an intrinsic desire for something that there are *pro tanto* moral reasons to bring about, while partial ill will can be thought of as an intrinsic desire for something that there are *pro tanto* moral reasons to not bring about.

A complication comes up when one considers the concepts deployed in partial good and ill will. Suppose that it is a matter of metaphysical necessity that having a certain neuroanatomically identified group of cells highly active within

---

[13] For an interesting discussion of this and related issues see Markovits (2010).

an ordinary healthy human brain (say, certain cells of the perigenual region of the anterior cingulate cortex) instantiates pleasure. And suppose that an alien neuroscientist, with no comprehension of the larger psychological workings of the human mind, is a devoted student of this specific region and comes to be fascinated by high levels of activity in the perigenual region of anterior cingulate cortex. If the alien comes to intrinsically desire that HEALTHY HUMAN BEINGS EVERYWHERE HAVE HIGH ACTIVITY IN PERIGENUAL ANTERIOR CINGULATE CORTEX then the alien has an intrinsic desire for something that, necessarily, is pleasure. But, even if it is granted that pleasure is something one has a *pro tanto* moral reason to bring about, one would not want to credit the alien with even partial good will. Nor would one fault the alien for even partial ill will if the alien were to prefer a low level of activity in this brain region, even if that necessitated (in healthy human beings) a lack of pleasure and so a state of affairs there is a *pro tanto* moral reason to avoid.

The correct response to the complication would appear to be to connect the ways in which the concepts deployed in partial good or ill will are related to the concepts deployed in complete good or ill will. For an intrinsic desire to be an instance of good or ill will the content of the desire must be something one has a *pro tanto* moral reason to do or avoid and this content must be presented by concepts that would allow the individual in question to trivially deduce that it is necessarily an instance of MAXIMIZING HAPPINESS, or RESPECTING PERSONS, or whatever the correct normative theory distinguishes as the right or good as a whole. Under this condition, it follows that if a person has a correct theory of the right or good, then the person can also readily see whether a given desire of hers, presented to her as she conceptualizes its content, is for (a part of) the right or the good, or rather for (a part of) the wrong or the bad. That strikes us as a good sign that her intrinsic desire constitutes some form of good or ill will.

The fifth and final thing to explain about good will is the idea of moral indifference, and with it reverse moral indifference. If good will is an intrinsic desire to respect others, then this intrinsic desire might be stronger or weaker in different people. If in one person the intrinsic desire to respect others is present but substantially weaker than in most other people, then the person is closer to being indifferent toward morality than most others: she displays moral indifference. Perhaps most of us can be moved, much more often than not, to tell friends and romantic partners the truth when we will likely suffer negative consequences as a result. If for Mary the intrinsic desire to respect others, even the intrinsic desire to respect Alice, Mary's spouse, is a relatively weak intrinsic desire then she will be looser with the truth, even with Alice, than most of us would. Sometimes, she will tell a lie in circumstances such that most of us would not have lied to our close friends or romantic partners in that sort of circumstance. And if Mary does so, she will be revealing a certain degree of indifference to what is right or good. Not complete indifference, of course, but a greater degree of indifference than is commonly found in people. This is a straightforward case of moral indifference.

It is worth keeping in mind that not every failure to act morally reveals an above-average degree of moral indifference. Consider the famous experiments conducted by Stanley Milgram into "obedience to authority."[14] In these experiments, participants thought they were delivering harmful, and perhaps even deadly, electrical shocks to other participants in the study. The fact that many participants did what they believed to be so harmful suggests a certain terrible moral indifference on their parts. Perhaps they did not intrinsically desire the welfare of those being shocked very much at all. But a closer look suggests practical irrationality rather than moral indifference. One of Milgram's later findings was that if participants saw another person, who also seemed to be a participant in the experiment, refuse to deliver the harmful shocks then a very large majority of the participants themselves also refused. That their refusal needed such a weak trigger—essentially, just a reminder that it could be done— strongly suggests that many participants were acting contrary to what they on balance desired in seemingly delivering the harmful shocks. And a similar conclusion is suggested by how profoundly emotionally distressing the participants found it to seemingly shock another person so painfully that he passed out or even died. It might be that, had Milgram's subjects been true moral heroes, they would not have irrationally stayed in the experiment, and so the experiment revealed them to have some very small degree of moral indifference. But even if this is so, the main explanation for their continued participation appears to be a nonrationalizing one. They are no more indifferent to morality than a person who is the victim of a psychologically sophisticated scam is indifferent to her money.

Reverse moral indifference presupposes that there is a normal level of ill will that we expect to find in people, regrettable as it might be. Perhaps most of us can be moved, more often than we would like, to say hurtful things to people who are being hurtful to us. And perhaps this willingness is not (as we might like to tell ourselves) a pure-hearted defense of ourselves as autonomous agents deserving of respect, or of others who might one day also be verbally abused if the abuser is not now confronted. Perhaps most of us act as we do in part because we have intrinsic desires to hurt anyone who attacks us. Let this all be true, and let it also be true that such an intrinsic desire is an instance of partial ill will: that mere revenge is something one has a *pro tanto* moral reason to avoid.[15] Then a person who somehow lacks this intrinsic desire, and

---

[14] See Milgram (1974) for the original research.

[15] Perhaps because revenge trivially, necessarily involves inflicting a harm, which one always has a *pro tanto* reason to avoid, and because revenge involves inflicting the harm without concern for anything that might serve as a defeater to this reason (that *I* was harmed not being a defeater itself).

so who is much harder to move to aggressive verbal outbursts simply because she lacks this common desire to avenge herself against aggressors, will tend to act a little differently. Aggressively abused by a store clerk for presenting an out of date coupon, she might calmly respond that she had not noted that the coupon had expired and is happy to pay the full price, while many others would feel the need to use a tone of voice or phrasing that would make the clerk feel bad, thereby repaying the clerk for the abuse. Of course, the abused customer's calm response could stem from good will, but perhaps it does not. Perhaps it comes simply from having much less of an intrinsic desire to return harm for harm than others have: revenge just has no appeal for her. If so, then the polite response shows a certain indifference to a common lure to immoral behavior. It shows reverse moral indifference.

In discussing moral indifference and reverse moral indifference, we assume that when determining how much a person desires something we turn to the questions of what the person cares about *more*, and *how much more*. Thus, on our view, a person who committed a crime for money and who is accused of moral indifference cannot defend himself by saying "I'm not morally indifferent because my concern for morality is very strong; it's just that my desire for money is even stronger." Prioritizing money over the right or good (presented via the correct sense) is the very nature of (some degree of) moral indifference. The more things one puts ahead of the right or the good the greater one's moral indifference.[16] (Recall that chapter 6 provides a theory of desire strength.)

So far, the goal has simply been to explain our views about good will and ill will. But these views become quite a bit more important, and call out for a full defense, when they are deployed in a theory of praise- and blameworthiness. And to this we turn next.

7.3 A Theory of Praise- and Blameworthiness

We are interested in a status people can have, that of meriting the attitudes of credit or blame for their actions in virtue of their rationalizing reasons. The

---

[16] Julia Markovits (2010) has an example of a person who would do just about anything for morality but even more for his dog. The person in question would, for example, risk his life or risk torture for the sake of the right or the good, but would not sacrifice the interests of his dog. In such a case the fact that he values the dog above morality does not make him *very* morally indifferent, because he values the dog above everything—in a mad way that is not typical even of the most avid dog lovers—and morality comes a close second. Hyperbole aside, even a person who values money a great deal does not typically value it above all—other things, such as life and the avoidance of suffering, come first. Also relevant to the degree of the greedy person's moral indifference is the extent to which he prefers money to the right and the good. (Roughly: is he a person who would commit a less serious crime for a million dollars, or a person who would commit a more serious crime for a smaller sum?)

ground of this status, we hold, is in the intrinsic desires that make up their rationalizing reasons (along with instrumental cognitive attitudes).

Praiseworthiness: a person is praiseworthy for a right action A to the extent that A manifests good will (or reverse moral indifference) through being rationalized by it.
Blameworthiness: a person is blameworthy for a wrong action A to the extent that A manifests ill will (or moral indifference) through being rationalized by it.

Kant could accept our idea of praiseworthiness if good will were not thought of as a type of desire, and so could Aristotle, as long as the good will is seen as coming from a firm and unchanging state. Thus, we see our basic theories of praise- and blameworthiness as only minimally controversial. The greater controversy begins when we understand good and ill will in the terms of the previous section. Doing so provides us with the following statements of the theories, which we take to be (metaphysically, though not epistemically) equivalent.

Praiseworthiness: a person is praiseworthy for a right action A to the extent that A manifests an intrinsic desire (or desires) for the complete or partial right or good (correctly conceptualized) or an absence of intrinsic desires for the complete or partial wrong or bad (correctly conceptualized) through being rationalized by it (or them).
Blameworthiness: a person is blameworthy for a wrong action A to the extent that A manifests an intrinsic desire (or desires) for the complete or partial wrong or bad (correctly conceptualized) or an absence of intrinsic desires for the complete or partial right or good (correctly conceptualized) through being rationalized by it (or them).

Acting on an intrinsic desire for the right or good (correctly conceptualized) is the same as acting for the right reasons. If one acts out of a correctly conceptualized intrinsic desire to INCREASE UTILITY then one performs an action for the reason that it increases utility; if increasing utility is what is right or good, then in acting to increase utility one acts for the right reason. In this way we are holding to the view that a person is praiseworthy for an action if and only if she acts for the right reasons, which are also the reasons that make the action right (Arpaly 2003).

Our theories of praise- and blameworthiness are obviously in need of defense, and we begin this defense with a quick clarification of the role of the word "rationalize" in these theories. A person who rapes someone and a person who honestly confesses "I want to commit rape" might in some sense both *manifest* the same strength of desire to rape, but only the rapist's action is *rationalized* by an intrinsic desire to violate someone sexually. For a person to be blameworthy for an action it needs to be the case that her action is actually rationalized by her ill will (or, partially, by moral indifference), in the sense of rationalization discussed back in chapter 3.

In the remainder of this chapter, we will consider four substantial objections. The first substantial objection is that our theory's reliance on intrinsic desires leaves us unable to explain what makes agents praiseworthy in acting when morality imposes side constraints on action. The second is that our theory of the correct conceptualization of the right or good leads to the wrong consequences for praise- and blameworthiness. The third is that our theory entails that too many people are praise- or blameworthy on our account, given both the ubiquity of partial good and ill will and the ease with which the absence of good or ill will can be attributed. And the fourth is an objection to giving partial moral credit to people for displays of partial good will.

7.4 Side Constraints

A problem for Spare Conativism's theory of praise- and blameworthiness arises if morality contains side-constraints, but not if morality is maximizing. Since our goal is to be (mostly) neutral about the normative content of morality, and since we have some sympathy with the idea that there are moral side-constraints on action, this possible problem needs to be addressed.

Imagine first that morality puts no constraints on the maximization of happiness, and that a person's strongest intrinsic desire, by far, is that happiness be maximized. Under these conditions, it seems straightforward how the intrinsic desire would be manifested in praiseworthy action. Wanting so much that happiness be maximized, the person would typically take the action that seemed to her to maximize happiness in her context, and in doing so she would manifest her good will and perhaps her lack of ill will. As a result, her actions would be highly praiseworthy. Of course, it might happen on occasion that this person would not actually maximize happiness: she might act irrationally, or one of her other intrinsic desires might rationally move her to neglect a small marginal difference in happiness. But it is straightforward in this person's case that it is *possible* for her to act in a way that is fully praiseworthy. And this very possibility of praiseworthy action is threatened by the notion of side constraints.

Imagine that morality does indeed impose side constraints on the maximization of happiness. Maximal happiness is still something one has a *pro tanto* moral reason to bring about, but it is absolutely forbidden to lie, even when a lie would maximize happiness. What would the mind of an optimally morally praiseworthy person look like, according to Spare Conativism?

It will not do to imagine a person whose complete good will is constituted by two simple intrinsic desires, one that happiness be maximized and the other that people not lie. For now certain trade-offs will become rational that will violate the imagined side-constraint on moral action. For instance, if Lucien foresees that either he must tell a lie or Giselle will tell a lie, then his desire that no one lie will be equally frustrated either way. Given that the desire is equally frustrated either way, it is now reasonable—on the basis of his complete good will alone—for Lucien to choose to lie, if the projected consequences will bring more happiness than if he is truthful and Giselle lies instead. This action would be an optimized expression of Lucien's complete good will, but since it leads to violating the side constraint, it cannot really be a manifestation of good will after all, or a praiseworthy action. The deontological idea is that one is not allowed to violate one person's rights even in order to prevent the violation of five people's rights; we must, as Thomas Nagel says, *avoid* murder at all costs rather than *prevent* it at all costs.[17]

An easy way to avoid this problem would be to change the content of the intrinsic desires from the universal to the personal. Rather than intrinsically desire that happiness be maximized and that lies not be told, Lucien might intrinsically desire that his actions be ones that maximize happiness and that he personally not tell lies: perhaps these two intrinsic desires could constitute complete good will. But even the individualized moral desire permits trade-offs. If Lucien intrinsically desires that he not tell lies, but he knows that—as an addict, perhaps—he is very likely to tell lies under certain conditions despite his best intentions, then he might find himself in a predicament. If he does not now tell a lie then he will be placed in a position in which surely he will tell other lies. Given that his intrinsic desire that he not tell lies will be frustrated, he will act reasonably to do the best he can to minimize his lying: he will be acting out of his putatively complete good will when he tells one lie now to prevent himself from telling five lies later. But of course this cannot be a manifestation of complete good will, if there are moral side constraints against lying under Lucien's circumstances.

Could Lucien stiffen his resolve, as it were, by making the content of his intrinsic desire more demanding? If so, the content needs to be specified carefully. Suppose that Lucien's desire is not treated as being satisfiable to greater or lesser degrees: a single lie would utterly frustrate the content of Lucien's desire, and so he cannot rationally lie now to prevent five future lies—because, by lying now, he has already lost the thing he intrinsically desired (roughly, that he *never* lie). Unfortunately, once Lucien tells a lie, this desire is permanently frustrated, and thus no longer rationalizes refraining from future lies. If his only goal is to keep his soul pristine, then once there is a single smudge on it, it does not matter how much more dirt follows. And that is not the sort of complete good will we are trying to capture.

---

[17] Nagel (1972).

A better approach would be to include the present moment in the sense (conceptualization...) of Lucien's desire. Suppose Lucien intrinsically desires that he NOT LIE RIGHT NOW, meaning that his concept NOW is deployed in desiring what he does. Then his desire can motivate him in the future even if he tells a lie in the present, and his desire will never motivate him to tell one lie to prevent more lies from being told by others or by himself on other occasions.

Unfortunately, if all that Lucien desires is that he not lie right now, then there will be nothing motivating him to prevent people from being lied to by others. More strikingly, there will be nothing to make him saddened when he reads a history of people wronged by well-intentioned lies (since his being saddened will only occur if these third-party lies are contrary to something he intrinsically desires), and nothing to makes him angry when he reads in the newspaper about lying politicians. Lucien's intrinsic desire remains personal rather than universal. To a certain, particularly tough-minded, sort of deontologist this might be an appealing picture of the agent with a perfectly good will: by far his greatest concern is proceeding rightly through life himself, and while this involves acting to dissuade second parties from wronging third parties, the deeds of the far past, causally unreachable present, or inscrutable future are not the proper concern of the perfect moral agent as such. But we have sympathy with the idea that there are side constraints on moral action, and we are not inclined to think that the ideal of the very tough-minded deontologist represents the ideal moral agent correctly. The ideal moral agent is deeply concerned with the state of the world, including the moral state of the world, even including Kant's own question of whether the crooked timber of humanity can ever be fashioned into something straight (though, as we saw discussing love and desire in chapter 4, this need not in any way imply that the agent is a busybody obsessed with correcting other people's ways). We see two ways for a deontologist to do better.

Normative theory might embrace only soft side constraints: it is wrong to kill one to save five, but if a million might die, then there might be overriding moral reason to kill the one. On this view, morality is not simply maximizing, but it is not insensitive to enormous consequences, either. If normative theory embraces soft side constraints, then the good will of the ideal moral agent will plausibly involve (at least) two intrinsic desires. One, much stronger, intrinsic desire will be the agent-centered intrinsic desire that I NOW RESPECT PERSONS, or something of this sort. The second, weaker but still very strong (in comparison to every other intrinsic desire of the agent) intrinsic desire will be that PERSONS BE RESPECTED. With these two intrinsic desires, a person will not have a rationalizing reason stemming from her good will to disrespect one to prevent five from being disrespected, but might have a rationalizing reason stemming from her good will to disrespect one to prevent one million from being disrespected (depending on the relative strengths of the two intrinsic desires). And with these two intrinsic desires, a person will typically feel worst about her own moral transgressions, but might well feel very saddened or angered when learning of distant, unalterable disrespect for persons elsewhere in the world.

Normative theory might, on the other hand, embrace hard side constraints: it is wrong to kill one innocent to save five, five million, or even five billion. For a perfect moral agent to be rationally disposed to act consistently with hard side constraints while also intrinsically desiring that third parties not be treated with disrespect is tricky, but not impossible.

The two-desire approach to the psychology of the ideal agent who respects soft side constraints cannot simply be tweaked to generate the psychology of the ideal agent who respects hard side constraints. No matter how much more a person desires that I NOW RESPECT PERSONS than that PERSONS BE RESPECTED, there will still be a number of persons being disrespected such that, at that point, the person will have a rationalizing reason, stemming from her good will, to now disrespect some person. And, almost as bad, the imagined person's emotional connection to third parties who are treated with disrespect becomes vanishingly small as the intrinsic desire that PERSONS BE RESPECTED fades to inconsequential strength in comparison to the intrinsic desire that I NOW RESPECT PERSONS.

An approach to the good will of the person who can act on that good will to respect hard side constraints can be developed, but so far as we can see it requires that the person have a single, rather complex, intrinsic desire. To explain this desire, it will help to consider how the person who respects hard side constraints ranks, in terms of their choiceworthiness, different centered possible worlds.

A centered possible world is just like a regular possible world, except that an agent, a time, and a location are singled out as privileged (as the "center" of that world). The agent so picked out is the referent of the concept ME in that world, the time so picked out is the referent of NOW, and the location so picked out is the referent of HERE. Two possible worlds that are otherwise exactly alike can be imagined with different centers, and this would correspond to imagining the same world but with a different person being "me" in that world, a different time being "now," and a different location being "here."

For the person who respects side constraints, every member of the set of all (centered) worlds in which the person now respects persons will be ranked ahead of every member of the set of all (centered) worlds in which the person now does not respect persons: this is just what it means to have a hard prohibition on ever acting, right now, in a way that disrespects persons. But within the first set of worlds, where the agent now acts respectfully, the top ranked worlds will be ones in which no person is treated with disrespect, then next will be worlds in which one person is treated with disrespect, and so on.[18]

---

[18] Perhaps the percentage of people treated with respect is more important than the raw number, and perhaps there are complications for various infinities in population size. We ignore these

Within the second set of worlds, in which the agent now acts disrespectfully to someone, the top ranked worlds will again be ones in which no one other than the person the agent himself is disrespecting gets treated with disrespect; next ranked will be those worlds in which two people are treated with disrespect, and so on.[19] This ranking of all possible (centered) worlds gives us, in principle, a well-defined sense for a single intrinsic desire. It is an intrinsic desire that is better satisfied the higher up the ranking of (centered) worlds the actual world happens to be, taking the agent at the place and time of action to be the center. Since all (centered) worlds in which the agent now acts to respect persons are higher-ranked than all (centered) worlds in which the agent now acts to disrespect persons, the intrinsic desire will never rationalize a person-disrespecting action (so long as a person-respecting action is possible; it is up to normative theory whether the hardest sorts of moral dilemmas are possible). At the same time, the same intrinsic desire rationalizes morally optional actions (if there are any) that promote person-respecting by others, and it will tend to lead to the agent feeling strongly about both her own and others' person-respecting actions, being pleased the more person-respecting there is at a time and more displeased the less there is, holding fixed whether she herself is acting to respect persons or not at that moment.

Crudely, the good will of the ideal respecter of hard side constraints will be something like an intrinsic desire that I, DEFINITELY, NOW AND EVERYONE, PREFERABLY, IN GENERAL RESPECT PERSONS. But this is not exactly a perspicuous rendering of the intrinsic desire, and it might be easiest to just think of it as an intrinsic desire generating the ranking of (centered) worlds just described.[20]

A special feature of the person who respects side constraints is that it matters to her, not just what world is instantiated, but what centered world with her, at her present time and location, is instantiated. She is not automatically indifferent between a world in which Carla respects persons while Fadheela does

---

complications, which are in any case complications that stem from particular normative commitments.

[19] Worlds without the agent are presumably ranked by the agent as just as choiceworthy as the world in the first set with the same number of people being disrespected; the person who respects hard side constraints does not think it a moral good that she personally happens to exist.

[20] Douglas Portmore has arrived at a similar idea through normative, rather than moral-psychological, considerations. Starting from the puzzle of how to square side constraints with a commitment to maximizing, Portmore reaches a picture of the content of such a normative theory that is quite close to that implicit in the psychology we imagine here. Portmore's position has been attacked by Mark Schroeder as not genuinely securing a maximization of value, and so not meeting one of its own ambitions. But, even if this is correct, it does not impugn our imagined psychology—the dispute between Portmore and Schroeder is over whether our sort of psychology exemplifies a genuine sort of consequentialism or not. See Portmore (2005; 2007) and Schroeder (2006).

not and a world in which Carla disrespects persons and Fadheela is respectful; she needs to know whether Carla or Fadheela is *her*, because *she* does not want to be the one disrespecting persons. Likewise, the person who respects side constraints is not indifferent between her now lying or her future lying, and she does not prefer a world in which she lies once now to a world in which she lies five times in the future. In this way, it matters to her when the "center" of the world is imagined to be (when is "now"). She is unwilling to choose to wrong one person even if it means that many others will escape being wronged, and she is unwilling to wrong one person now even if it means she will wrong many others later. Her agency at this very moment is the center of her moral decision-making.

In conventional decision theory, agents have preferences over possible worlds, but not over centered possible worlds. But, so far as we can see, it is impossible to capture the psychology of a person who respects side constraints using only preferences (derived from intrinsic desires) defined over uncentered possible worlds. This might appear to introduce certain decision-theoretic conundrums. The person who now respects one person, foreseeing that she will as a result later disrespect five (because she is not perfectly rational or moral), is satisfied with her choice when she makes it; she is choosing the best of the centered worlds available. But in the process of disrespecting five, later, she is in a position to wish she had disrespected the one previously, since she abhors what she is doing *now*; she sees that she is now in a centered world (the same actual world, but with a different center, a different "now" and presumably "here") that she disprefers to the world in which she then disrespected one but now respects five. Whether there are real decision-theoretic conundrums here or merely apparent ones is a question we leave to others. It is the job of the moral psychologist to say what psychology best captures a particular normative theory's commitments when it comes to acting for the right reasons, in a potentially praiseworthy manner, out of good will; it is not the job of the moral psychologist to show that every normative theory is unproblematic from the perspective of decision theory. Still, we suspect that there is nothing ultimately more problematic to the psychology of respecting side constraints than what lies on its surface: that sometimes respecting side constraints means giving up on something, something one finds tremendously morally valuable, in order not to do one wrong thing.

7.5 Conceptualization

If intrinsically desiring the right or good, correctly conceptualized, is necessary and, when acted upon, sufficient for acting in a way that is praiseworthy, then there must be two interesting sorts of cases. In the first sort, agents who think of what they are doing under the concept IMMORAL nonetheless are morally praiseworthy in acting, because they are motivated to act by intrinsic desires for the right or good correctly conceived. In the second sort, agents who think of what they are doing under the concept MORAL nonetheless are not praiseworthy in acting, because they are not motivated to act by intrinsic desires for the right or good correctly conceived.

This feature of our theory of praise- and blameworthiness is a rather controversial one.[21] But it seems to us that both sorts of cases are simple to conjure, supporting the claim that it is the right or good conceptualized in the way preferred by the correct normative theory, and not merely via the concept RIGHT or GOOD, that motivates people moved by good will.

For the first sort of case, imagine an undergraduate student, Brandon, whose moral view (greatly influenced by the writings of Ayn Rand) is that one should be selfish. Not just that selfish behavior is his moral right, but that it is his "sacred," as he would say, "moral duty." Nonetheless, Brandon often acts unselfishly. Typically he just fails to notice his failure to conform to his theoretical standards; occasionally he berates himself for his "sentimentality" when he sees that he is contributing to "weak, degenerate, socialistic" practices rather than acting selfishly and so "getting something out of" what he is doing. Imagine that a fellow student, not personally known to him, drops a pile of books and papers while leaving a building on campus, and that Brandon helps gather up the books and papers before they are ruined. Suppose that his sole substantial motivation in acting is an intrinsic desire for GENERAL HAPPINESS, or RESPECTING PERSONS, or KINDNESS CONSTRAINED BY RESPECT FOR CONSENT, or something similar—whatever constitutes the right or the good correctly conceptualized. Suppose, that is, that no ulterior motives are required to motivate him and no ulterior motives are in fact at work in him in the moment.

In this situation, Brandon acts for moral reasons even though he does not believe them to be moral reasons, and seems praiseworthy for so acting. Brandon's Ayn Rand-centered beliefs show that he is a bad philosopher, but we do not see why being a good philosopher would be necessary for one's actions to be praiseworthy. Surely most people's moral theories are poor enough to be inconsistent with morality itself at many points; Brandon's inconsistency is simply a particularly bold one. But it seems unlikely that the sad state of popular moral philosophy is sufficient to make it the case that people are rarely or never morally praiseworthy in acting. It seems obvious that a bad philosopher can be a good person, and being what is informally known as "a good person" requires being often praiseworthy for things done—things that were done for just the right reasons to do them.

---

[21] For fuller arguments in defense, see, e.g., Arpaly (2002; 2003). Markovits (2010) concurs, but with a different background theory.

The widespread acceptance of something like our line of thought also appears to be what allows people with a wide variety of ethical views to get along together: though they disagree about theory, they can sometimes (when it is true) see that, underneath the disagreements, they are all basically decent people, acting with good will. In the case of Brandon, the more morally insightful observer is inclined to call him "good hearted," "basically a good guy, when you get to know him," and other things that recognize that Brandon's will is good, in spite of his moral theory and its occasional eruptions into his behavior.

The story of Brandon does not imagine him to be thinking that his action is morally wrong at his moment of action, but this too seems possible, and seems possible without diminishing the conviction that someone so acting might genuinely act on the right reasons and be praiseworthy for so acting. We introduced this idea to the philosophical literature with our interpretation of the well-known story of Huckleberry Finn.[22] Huckleberry helps Jim escape slavery while consciously thinking that it is wrong to do so, and in fact bitterly reproaching himself at two different points for not following his "conscience." Not being an expert moral philosopher, Huckleberry can see no moral argument for helping Jim escape slavery, since Jim is (in his eyes) the legitimate property of Miss Watson, and since Miss Watson has done nothing to morally license Huckleberry's helping such a valuable piece of property to go missing. Different interpretations of the novel are possible, but one possible interpretation (not unrealistic, and one we favor) is that Huckleberry is motivated to not turn in Jim because Huckleberry intrinsically desires what is right or good via the relevant concepts, the ones that would be identified by a correct normative moral theory, and sees that this end will be promoted by Jim's escape, even as Jim's escape appears to be a blow to what Huckleberry desires in another respect: it appears to be a blow to the RIGHT. Perhaps what is moral is that every reasoning creature be treated with respect, and Huckleberry intrinsically desires this, and so wants Jim to escape slavery. That is, Huckleberry sees that Jim's life as a slave, separated from family against his will, always forced to do what another says, and never compensated for his efforts, is lived in the absence of the respect he intrinsically desires everyone to enjoy. On one interpretation of the novel, these things might all have come clearly to Huckleberry's mind, and have weighed heavily with him emotionally because of his strong intrinsic desire that everyone be treated with respect. And this might well have happened without Huckleberry ever concluding that Jim's escape from slavery would be right or good—might have happened while Huckleberry self-consciously concluded that what is right or good is to return Jim to slavery. (This version of

---

[22] The case enters the philosophical literature in Bennett (1974), and features in Arpaly (2002; 2003) and Arpaly and Schroeder (1999) as well. A critical response to the lattermost can be found in Rosner (2000).

Huckleberry Finn is rather Kantian in its presupposed normative theory, but utilitarian and other versions are also easy to imagine.)

If this version of the fiction were the true story of what moved a person in Huckleberry's situation, it would seem to us that the person would not only be doing what is right but be doing it *because* of what makes it right, and so be doing it for the right reasons. An actual Huckleberry-like person would strike us as someone fundamentally decent, if morally ignorant, who is praiseworthy for never turning Jim's counterpart in to the authorities. "Here," we might say, "is someone who cares so much for people being treated with respect that he is unable to act against it even when he thinks he should be doing something else."

For the second sort of case, in which a person with a false moral theory does what she conceives as RIGHT or GOOD but which is not a case of acting for the right reasons, and not a case of morally praiseworthy action, imagine again our undergraduate who is convinced that selfishness is the one true virtue, and that selfish actions are ultimately the only moral actions. Suppose that Brandon learns that a friend is moving from one apartment to another, and could use assistance. Brandon thinks about volunteering but, spotting a copy of Ayn Rand's *The Fountainhead* lying on his table, he checks his inclination and asks himself if there is really something in it for him. He weighs up the chances of returned favors, free beer, and exercise presented by helping the friend move, and the chances to achieve more for himself by staying at home, and decides that there is more in it for him if he helps the friend move. Concluding that helping the friend is actually selfish, Brandon judges it RIGHT to do so and acts accordingly. It is hard to see Brandon as morally praiseworthy, acting for the right reasons, or displaying any part of virtue. It would be difficult to hold him to have acted for the right reasons, in spite of the fact that his intrinsic desire to do what is right or good, conceived as RIGHT or GOOD, was a vital part of his motivation in so acting. His doing the right thing—helping the friend move—would be a lucky accident: Brandon did the "Randian" thing, and the right thing to do coincided in this case with the "Randian" thing to do.[23] If he had done the wrong thing and declined to help his friend to move, the fact that he had done so because he thought it was right (under his concept RIGHT) would not have eliminated the blame he would have deserved for being selfish with his time and energy.

Though the preceding two cases focus on separations between the concepts RIGHT or GOOD and the correct conceptualization of the right or good, similar arguments could have been given about parallel separations between the concepts WRONG or BAD and the correct conceptualization of the wrong or

---

[23] Julia Markovits reminds us that, even in a world in which a vigorous "invisible hand" made it true that acting selfishly brought about the right or good, Brandon would still not be praiseworthy. Brandom's problem is not that he brings about the right moral result by luck, but that he is not properly oriented toward the moral. See Arpaly (2002, 225–26).

bad. We will not repeat our arguments, but perhaps it is worth mentioning that sexual desires for acts that are socially forbidden and thought wrong but are not, in fact, immoral are an example here. A person can take some (conflicted) delight in doing what she conceives under her concept BAD without being the least bit blameworthy for so doing because the actions conceived as bad are inherently innocuous, and thus the intrinsic desires to perform these actions are not any sort of ill will at all.

A number of objections could be raised to the foregoing, and we will consider three.

First, Stephen Darwall has argued that conceiving a course of action as WRONG gives one a moral reason not to perform the action over and above that provided by the wrong-making features of the action precisely because the wrongness of an action is a further fact about it. Darwall is not taking aim at theories such as Spare Conativism; his concern is with the idea that the wrongness of an act provides no further reason for action above and beyond the specific wrong-making features of the act. But it is hard not to come across Darwall's position and see in it a possible objection to Spare Conativism.

Darwall writes that your right to not have your foot carelessly trodden upon "gives me a reason not to step on your foot that is additional to the fact that I would be causing you pain, suffering, and so on..."[24] Thus, there is the specific reason not to perform the act (it will cause pain and suffering) and a general reason not to perform the act (you have a right not to have pain inflicted upon you in such circumstances), and a claim that the general reason is supplementary to the specific reason.

We agree that there is an additional moral reason in Darwall's scenario, but his reasons for thinking so are consistent with Spare Conativism. A person with an intrinsic aversion to causing pain is a person with (at most) only partial good will. Complete good will requires more (even for a utilitarian). And this is just to agree with Darwall that, while there might be a *pro tanto* moral reason to not cause pain, not causing pain is not the whole of morality. Granting that there are moral reasons not yet captured by considerations such as pain does not, however, grant that these moral reasons are best conceived as making actions RIGHT or WRONG.

According to Darwall, what makes an act wrong is that it violates an obligation that anyone can legitimately demand (through the reactive attitudes) be observed.[25] So perhaps the person with complete good will intrinsically desires that she not VIOLATE AN OBLIGATION THAT ANYONE CAN LEGITIMATELY DEMAND BE OBSERVED. This would be good will if Darwall has the correct normative theory of morality. If this is what the person with complete good will intrinsically desires, though, she might nonetheless

---

[24] Darwall (2010, 152).
[25] Darwall (2010, 154).

not take this to be what is morally right or good. The person with good will might intrinsically desire to be answerable to second-person challenges in the way Darwall envisions, while thinking this is merely good manners, or morally neutral "reasonable behavior," or while imagining that what she desires is supererogatory because morality makes only a much weaker demand that she not violate contracts; and so on.

The separation between grasping an action as WRONG and grasping it as one that VIOLATES AN OBLIGATION THAT ANYONE CAN LEGITIMATELY DEMAND BE OBSERVED is possible because Darwall's is a substantive theory of the right, and so a theory that someone else might not share, even while sharing concepts such as RIGHT and WRONG. Thus, while we agree with Darwall that there is an important distinction between (as we would put it) partial and complete moral reasons for acting, and so partial and complete good will, this does not in itself show that Spare Conativism is wrong in how one should think of the sense or mode of presentation (or...) of complete good will.

A second objection comes from Gideon Rosen, who raises the question of nonculpable moral ignorance.[26] He argues that a person who has slaves in a society in which almost everyone has slaves is not blameworthy for being a slave owner, as there is no way for her to know that what she is doing is wrong. If Rosen were right, then to be blameworthy would require something more than an manifestation of ill will or lack of good will as Spare Conativism understands them. It would seem to require that the blameworthy person be motivated while believing that her action is not right or good while deploying her concept RIGHT or GOOD specifically to make this judgment.

Though we hold that that Rosen is mistaken, there is something close to the truth in his idea.

A person who lives in a sexist society can be less blameworthy for his sexism because of the inaccessibility to him of some nonmoral facts. Never having met a woman who is good at mathematics, it is forgivable that he thinks that a woman should not try to study it (if an educated person in the 18th century, our sexist might have even heard an otherwise respectable doctor say that a woman's trying to study abstract topics causes incurable damage to her reproductive organs). If he has been told that women are more childlike than men and therefore need the paternalistic care, and authority, of a husband, and the belief is taken to be true by everyone he knows, women included, he is less blameworthy for his sexism than if he did not grow up with that belief. On our view, these conclusions follow because the sexist does not need to have a lack of good will, or any ill will, in order to refuse to teach his daughter mathematics, or to insist on his authority over his wife on important matters when her

---

[26] Rosen (2004).

opinion does not strike him as particularly wise. The sexist could still be acting in a manner aimed at being fully respectful of their rational capacities, or the like, since respect requires different responses to different degrees of rational capability. On our view, the sexist would be blameworthy for these acts only if they were expressive of moral problems with his will, i.e., with the rationalizations on which he acts, and it is possible (though perhaps not systematically always the case) that a person in the wrong sort of society will have good will but be ignorant, and so act in a way with unfortunate consequences.

Slave ownership in the United States was likewise nestled in a web of false nonmoral beliefs. The enslaved people were taken to be greatly inferior in cognitive capacities, to be incapable of autonomy and self-control, and even to be less sensible to pain. A person who developed these beliefs due to their being shared by all members of his race known to him, and from whom the counter-evidence was masked to a large extent by this agreement (and lack of personal contact with ordinary, competent, pain-sensitive slaves), could be a lot less blameworthy for voting to preserve slavery than a person aware of the possibility of treating the members of the oppressed race differently through having seen it done or heard it argued for. If, however, a person is perfectly aware of the way her slave resembles her in such things as cognitive abilities, self-control, and capacity for pain and still continues to enslave her, this person is blameworthy regardless of the century in which she lives. (And in this regard, note that many Americans regard the ownership of slaves by the nation's "founding fathers" to be a horrible moral flaw that cannot be eliminated by the existence of their other virtues.) The same is true of the person who sees that women can be his equal or better in mathematics but does not treat them so: there might be a social excuse for thinking that women are not good at science in general, but failing to give a science prize to a woman who has obviously done what it takes to merit it has no such excuse.

Similar considerations apply to the case presented by Rosen of the ancient Middle-Eastern lord and his slave. The lord lives in a society in which slavery is regarded as a misfortune that can befall almost anyone rather than a race-related arrangement. In a society like that no factual excuses are available for the slaveholder, and so his only problem is moral ignorance. According to Rosen, the ancient slave owner is clearly innocent. We disagree. Consider the ancient Roman who goes to the circus because he heartily enjoys watching people thrown to the lions. We think this person is blameworthy for going to the circus. Enjoying other people's suffering in this manner speaks ill of the agent's will even if the enjoyment in question is encouraged by a corrupt and corrupting society, and even if there is no moral theory available that disagrees. Can an ancient Roman be said to be acting out of *good* will in treating his family to the amusements of the circus, thinking that they too will heartily enjoy watching people devoured by lions? We think not. The lord's treating a person as property is analogous to the Roman's enjoyment of a person's suffering.

If the slave owner sees his slave as a person like himself, equally capable of autonomous action, equally capable of suffering, equally wishing to exercise his talents and pursue his dreams—and yet grossly fails to treat him accordingly, the slave owner is blameworthy, even though he is blameworthy in a way that his society—in that respect, an evil society—endorses.

For Rosen, the potential master ought to do right by the potential slave. Ought implies can, and as the potential master cannot come up with a right conclusion as to what the right thing to do is, he cannot do so, and is therefore exempt from doing so. For us, what the potential master ought to do is not perspicuously formulated by saying that it is to do right by the potential slave. This way of putting things is technically correct but suggests the wrong concepts to be deployed. Better to say that it is the moral obligation of the slave master to respect the slave as a person (or take equal account of his happiness, or...), and the slave master can do so regardless of the century he lives in. Acting out of a failure to be moved by the obvious personhood (or capacity for happiness...) of the man before him is acting out of moral indifference, and thus blameworthy. In the same way, going to the circus in order to enjoy suffering is acting out of ill will, and thus blameworthy. (Some would like to make a distinction between the blameworthiness these agents incur for their actions and the defects they show in their characters. That will be discussed in the next chapter.)

That said, living in a society in which taking a slave, or taking your family to see Christians thrown to the lions, is looked upon by everyone as the right thing to do is can be a disorienting, confusing experience. This is true in the same way it is true that a person who is seduced by a confidence trickster who uses the sort of psychological smoke and mirrors to which no one is immune can still be regarded as imprudent even while we realize that his circumstances make his imprudence more understandable. People can be tricked into many kinds of irrational actions. A psychological study showed, for example, that if a person sees smoke coming from a nearby room but is surrounded by people who act as if they are oblivious to it she will somehow also fail to do anything about the smoke, even if it is the case that, had she sat alone, she would have alerted someone to the situation.[27] The (nonrationalizing) power of apparent peer acceptance of a practice must not be underestimated.

Suppose again that the moral thing to do is to respect persons. Consider a person who keeps slaves because he takes it to be right but who, as in Rosen's example, does not have pseudo-factual rationalizations for his behavior (such as "they are Africans, and they don't feel pain the way we do") but who just takes for granted that some unfortunate people become slaves. If the person in question has a concept RIGHT that has nothing to do with respect for persons,

---

[27] Latané and Darley (1968).

we hold that the fact that he believes having slaves to be RIGHT is no excuse for his actions. However, it might be that the person in question is generally a respecter of persons and generally takes respecting persons to be the right thing to do. Surrounded by a community that otherwise agrees with him on moral particulars, reassured by priests who otherwise give him person-respecting advice, the person in question might conclude, either unthinkingly or as a result of an effort at cognitive dissonance reduction, that taking a slave does not "count" as disrespect for persons. An agent might even explicitly advocate respect for persons or for their wishes, but upon being asked about having slaves answer "that's different," though perhaps, if pressed, be lost for an explanation as to what is different. That would not be more unusual than the behavior of some men in the United States who say that they have a lot of respect for women but, called out for addressing female (and only female) strangers as "hon," either claim honestly not to understand how it has anything to do with respect or insist that "hon" is a very respectful form of address. Like the contemporary men, the slave owners are blameworthy: they do, after all, show disrespect for persons. Their blameworthiness is mitigated by the all-too-human cognitive fog that addles their thinking and prevents them from seeing, even as they disrespect persons, that this is what they are doing, despite it being, in some ways, obvious. To the extent that such addled thinking permits an immoral action to be performed in a way that manifests very little ill will, or very little absence of good will, it reduces the blameworthiness of the actor, according to Spare Conativism. There might even be cases in which the failure of the agent has nothing to do with the quality of the agent's will, and so blameworthiness is wholly absent (we suggested this might be true in the case of the Milgram experiments' subjects) but we doubt that this is very common, both when it comes to seeing that "hon" is not a term of respect and in seeing that putting a slave in chains "counts" as disrespecting a person.

Not all factual, nonmoral errors excuse. False factual beliefs, such as the belief that Africans are not as smart as Europeans, excuse if they are reasonable for the agent to believe, if the agent makes what can be called "an honest mistake" that can be explained by the evidence available to her. In the cases just discussed we assumed that it is often (though not always) rational to believe what "everyone" believes. The contemporary person who still has such beliefs, despite counterevidence galore, is naturally taken to be vicious and blameworthy, and we agree, though we postpone the discussion for now (see chapter 9).

Our third and final puzzle comes from the role of explicitly moral concepts in self-improvement. What should we think of a young person who tries to figure out the right and the good? Is there not something admirable about simply seeking the right and the good, without having any idea what they are? We are committed to the view that if the young person's concept of RIGHT or GOOD is wide open—if he is really ready to embrace as good, right, or moral something that is far from what is truly right or good (e.g., if it is a live possibility to him that the good consists of maximizing the beauty of ducks), his search has no merit. And this too might be thought to be a serious problem resulting from our focus on the correct conception of the right or good.

In everyday life, however, the young person who looks for the right or the good is very unlikely to have such an empty, infinitely fluid idea of the right or good; as a result, the moral searching of such people is unlikely to be utterly without moral value. When we ask ourselves, pre-theoretically, what the moral thing to do is, we typically do so within some basic, broad assumptions about what morality is. We assume that morality forbids torturing babies for fun, that morality supports sharing your cookies with other children who would like them, that morality frowns on lying. We are disposed to reject theories that conflict with these assumptions. If the young person in our example, eager to find out what to do in some morally problematic situation, searches for a general theory of the right and the good with reasonable assumptions in the background as to what sorts of things they would be, his search shows good will in him but is also likely to lead to decent results—not always the right ones, but often close enough. The (perhaps partial) good will on display is his desiring not to tell lies, desiring to share, and so on: these intrinsic desires are part of what motivates his attempt to achieve a unified moral theory, since the upshot of having such a theory will be that he will be less likely to do actions that are incompatible with sharing or not lying (or ...) So motivated, he will be unlikely to reach the conclusion that Hitler had a good point about Aryan supremacy. Admittedly, it is possible, however unlikely, that he reaches conclusions that are far from the truth. He might be led, for example, to an Ayn Rand-type view through mistaken nonmoral assumptions and conceptual blunders—perhaps, generalizing from his own youthful and idealistic character, he believes that people enjoy doing such things as giving to charity or helping their friends move and therefore will do such things if they were to act selfishly; he might, being a teenager, overestimate the degree to which people want to be left alone. Perhaps, on top of that, he confuses egoism with individualism and altruism with conformity. This is compatible with his search for the right and the good having been essentially a praiseworthy undertaking, stemming from a concern for happiness, respect, or other parts (or wholes) of the right or good. On the other hand, the person who reached a version of Ayn Rand's moral theory as a result of unconsciously seeking excuses for making profits ruthlessly, whose quest is not guided initially by caring about hurt and lies, whose epistemic efforts perhaps even show some signs of motivated irrationality, with the irrationality-inducing forces being his own intrinsic desires for wealth and power and his own lack of genuine good will—this person is not engaged in a good activity, and reveals nothing but bad things about his character in the course of his quest to grasp the right or good.

What if, for innocent reasons, a person becomes convinced of the truth of a false moral theory? Perhaps one honestly wants to know what to do in some morally problematic cases. Starting with a reasonable idea of morality (that thing forbidding torturing for fun and so on), Laila embarks on a study of ethics, but her authoritative-seeming teacher is wedded to a false theory. Perhaps, for example, he is a J.J.C. Smart-style act-utilitarian, and that happens to be a false theory as it overlooks considerations of justice. Perhaps he manages to convince unsophisticated Laila that certain arguments—starting from her intuitions, though eventually contradicting some of them—show the theory to be true. Laila, now convinced, fails to respond to a consideration of moral rights when such a consideration is important and performs an immoral action—say, killing one to save five in a situation where that is morally forbidden. Is she blameworthy?

In our view, a false moral theory can corrupt a person—encourage her to reduce her good will or increase her ill will—which is why a young person who searches earnestly for the right or the good is rightly considered vulnerable. A false moral theory does not have to corrupt a person: we all know good people who are not good ethicists, and even more good people who have some incorrect moral beliefs. A false theory does, however, corrupt to the extent that the person "overcomes" her sensitivities to what are in fact good moral reasons in the name of her newfound theory (like Brandon when he quells the urge to help his friend move) or develops sensitivities to more sinister reasons. Being corrupted might be a gradual process: while Laila is blameworthy for being unresponsive to the rights of the person she kills, she might be less blameworthy the first time she does this sort of thing, when she drags herself and forces herself to kill him despite strong opposing forces in her mind, than later when her unresponsiveness to her victim's rights is unopposed by any lingering concern for justice, consent, respect, or whatever (partial?) good will initially held her back. Intrinsic desires change gradually most of the time, after all, and one would expect to see something like this pattern in a person going through a substantial shift in willingness to act for particular reasons. But once she fails to respond to her victim's rights she is fully blameworthy, and a bad person as well. Something similar would happen to Huckleberry Finn if he successfully overcame his person-respecting tendencies, as did happen to some initially innocent members of the Hitler Youth.

So far, our assumption has been that if a person is a member of contemporary society and uses terms such as "right" and "good" to express what she has in mind then that person genuinely has a concept RIGHT or GOOD, however poor her theory. It appears, though, that people's supposed beliefs about the right or good can sometimes be tied to theories or presuppositions so far from the broad parameters that make up morality that their beliefs are seemingly not about the right or the good after all, and although they use the words "right" and "good" it is wrong to attribute to them the corresponding concepts.[28] Some

---

[28] On some theories of concepts, this point comes sooner rather than later. See, e.g., Peacocke (1992).

evangelical Christians appear to hold that although only "good people" go to Heaven and only "bad people" to Hell, the importance of how one acts in this life toward people and other animals is trivial, in this calculus of goodness and badness, in comparison to whether or not one is "saved," accepting Jesus into one's life. In this system of belief, Gandhi counts as a bad person, whereas the person serving a life sentence for terrible crimes, who then accepts Jesus, is presumed to be good before he gives any other indication that he would remain a performer of good actions if released from prison. This calls into question—though does not by itself refute—the claim these people have to be thinking of, caring about, or speaking of the right or good: perhaps they have gone too far. Luckily, belonging to the religion in question does not bar one from acting on better motives, even though it discourages one from understanding the moral value of one's motives.

7.6 Too Much Credit, Too Much Blame

There are at least three ways in which our theory might be said to generate too much credit or blame. The first is through failing to explain the relative significance of acting out of ill will versus acting out of moral indifference (or good will as opposed to reverse moral indifference). The second is through the insignificant actions of agents with a great deal of good or ill will. And the third is through the ubiquity of moral indifference and reverse moral indifference.

Recall that, on our view, a praiseworthy action is an action that manifests good will or reverse moral indifference (through being motivated and rationalized by it), but not ill will or moral indifference, and a blameworthy action is an action that manifests ill will or moral indifference (through being motivated and rationalized by it), not good will or reverse moral indifference. The more good will or reverse moral indifference the action shows (through its motivation) the more praiseworthy it is; the more ill will or moral indifference the action shows (through its motivation) the more blameworthy it is. This raises the question of how one should compare the blameworthiness of acts performed out of ill will to those performed out of moral indifference. And, in parallel, how one should compare the praiseworthiness of acts performed out of good will to those performed out of reverse moral indifference.

Other things being equal, ill will is worse than mere moral indifference. To shove someone in order to get to the front of a line shows moral indifference, and is blameworthy, but to shove someone simply to see her stumble seems far more troubling. However, "all else being equal" is a key phrase: chilling moral indifference, the sort that suffices for killing a person "merely" as the most expedient way to get money, is worse than a small dose of ill will, the sort that suffices only for cruelly teasing one's colleagues just to see them squirm. Likewise, not all else is equal when one compares a person with partial ill will that is narrowly focused (for example, hatred of a particular person sufficient for one to relish harm X befalling that person) to a person with partial moral indifference that is wide-ranging (for example, indifference to anyone suffering harm X). When not all else is equal, the overall calculus of comparative blameworthiness becomes more complex. And what goes for ill will, moral indifference, and blameworthiness also seems to hold in parallel for good will, reverse moral indifference, and praiseworthiness.[29]

Turning to the second possible objection: the present theory of praiseworthiness holds that a praiseworthy action is more praiseworthy the more good will it manifests, while a blameworthy action is more blameworthy the more ill will it manifests. So imagine two people. The first person, who is quite average in the amount of good will she has, kindly helps a lost motorist reach Goodale Park. This person is presumably modestly praiseworthy. The second person is a true moral saint, with almost bottomless good will, and she also kindly helps a lost motorist reach Goodale Park. Since the second person has so much more good will than the first, it would seem that the second must on our theory be much more praiseworthy for her action than the first. But this seems wrong.

An ancestor of the present theory is indeed committed to the erroneous conclusion. In Arpaly (2002; 2003) the claim is explicitly that a praiseworthy action is more praiseworthy the stronger the moral concern that motivates it. But as Julia Markovits argues, this leads to wrong results of the sort just sketched.[30] In the present theory, however, the erroneous conclusion is avoided. The amount of good or ill will that an action manifests is not the same as the amount of good or ill will that exists and is being acted on.

A person who is reminded of a parent's death might look downcast for a few minutes, and looking this way might be a manifestation of the person's feelings of sadness. But we can imagine two very different interior lives for such a person. Perhaps the person is giving full manifestation to a delicate, haunted sadness that still affects the person these many years after the parent's peaceful death at an advanced age. But perhaps the person is holding back a tremendous flood of raw grief at the thought of the recent and violent death of the still-young parent. The very minimal manifestation of sadness that emerges in the second case is obviously not a full manifestation of the sadness being felt. Thus, we can distinguish between the degree of sadness being manifested and the degree of sadness being felt. One cannot perhaps manifest more sadness

---

[29] Markovits (2012) suggests that there might be cases of moral indifference that is worse than ill will because intrinsic desire to harm a person at least acknowledges her as something other than a mere means. We disagree. While it can be better for some to be hated than to be ignored, hating is not *morally* preferable to being indifferent, all else being equal.

[30] Markovits (2010).

than one feels (because this would violate a sort of sincerity condition on manifestation; one can only feign degrees of sadness one does not feel), but one can certainly manifest less.

What holds for sadness holds more generally for all mental states and events that vary in degree. There are few contexts in which a tremendously strong belief in an afterlife is fully manifested, since words are cheap, but volunteering for a suicide mission could be such a manifestation. So too, we hold, with strength of desire. An opportunity to assist a lost motorist is not typically an occasion for a full display of a powerful commitment to morality. Hence, the strength of desire for the right or good that is actually manifested in the two cases we imagined is the same. It is on occasions when only a person of extraordinary moral concern has a rationalization to act in a certain way that the action is one that might manifest extraordinary moral concern, and so be an action that is tremendously praiseworthy.

On this understanding of how intrinsic desires are manifested in action, it follows that there are conditions in which a good action is more praiseworthy than such actions normally are because it shows more good will than such actions normally do. It also follows that there are conditions in which a blameworthy action is less blameworthy than such actions normally are because it shows less ill will or moral indifference than such actions normally do.

An example of the first sort is provided by the person who, like Kant's sorrowing philanthropist, continues to do good works despite being in a state of great sorrow. It often takes a lot of good will to do good works when you are terribly sad, and so, assuming that a lot of good will is in fact being manifested, the sorrowing agent is more praiseworthy for her action than a person would be for doing the same good works without having to overcome the same psychological barriers. An example of the second sort is provided by the person who *does* succumb to his sadness and as a result fails to meet some moral obligation. This agent is blameworthy for his (in)action, but he is less blameworthy than he would have been if he had been in a basically cheerful frame of mind. Given his sorrow, his (in)action does not manifest as much ill will or moral indifference as it would otherwise.

Psychological barriers such as sadness show the great praiseworthiness of the sorrowing actor only insofar as they provide an occasion for manifesting a great deal of good will. The fact of overcoming internal obstacles is not, itself, a positive or negative contribution to a person's being worthy of our credit or blame. Some obstacles are easy to overcome and do not provide an occasion for manifesting great good will (the fact that one has to overcome the internal obstacle of being very slightly tired does not make one significantly more praiseworthy than one would have been if one were not very slightly tired).

Things are different when the inner obstacle to be overcome is ill will. If doing the right thing requires effort because the agent has to overcome ill will in order to do it, the agent is no more praiseworthy for that. Here we follow

Philippa Foot and Rosalind Hursthouse, to whom it matters if one's inner struggle is with a morally neutral obstacle like depression or with a morally bad obstacle such as racial hatred.[31] However, we stop short of accepting their view that a person is less praiseworthy if there is a morally bad emotion to be overcome; though this is a mark against such people's virtue, it is not clearly a mark against their actions.

We mentioned (in chapter 3) that being under the influence of alcohol can sometimes be an excusing condition. This is true because, in certain cases, an action that normally manifests a certain amount of ill will or moral indifference manifests a lesser amount; the causation or causal explanation of the action makes less of an appeal to ill will or moral indifference than it might, and more of an appeal to nonrationalizing factors induced by the alcohol. Thus, if a person is blamelessly drunk but, as a result, she states her opinion of someone in a rude manner, she can be less blameworthy than she would be if she were to commit the same rudeness while sober. It can take considerably more good will to keep your views to yourself while drunk than while sober, and so the drunken action does not show that the agent is particularly indifferent to the right or good. Rather, it shows that her normal social inhibitions (her intrinsic aversions to harming, rudeness, or the like) were not as causally efficacious as usual. If the action is the result of ill will that, it is still true that the agent might have only an amount of ill will that when sober, would not have motivated her at all—her action, in other words, manifests less ill will than an action of that type normally would.

In an interesting objection to the earlier work on which we are building, Markovits (2010) holds that a person who *only* does the good when it is difficult does not deserve the extra praise that we normally give a person if she does a good thing when it is difficult. She thinks that the praise that we give the person who does the good thing when it is hard is derivative from the thought that that if she does it when it is hard she would *a fortiori* do it when it is not hard, so her action is evidence of her being virtuous on all occasions. From which it follows that in the rare case in which the person would not have done the thing if it were easy we should not much credit the person.

We think this is either wrong or correct but in a way that vindicates the present theory. A person of the sort described is very praiseworthy provided (1) she acts for the right reasons, and not because she is the overly dramatic sort who confuses morality with heroics, and (2) doing the good thing when it is difficult for most is not actually easier for her.

Imagine that Stefanie is more likely to ride her bicycle up a mountain if it is a hard climb. Perhaps she is motivated by great challenges. The fact that the difficulty of the climb makes her more *likely* to succeed does not in fact make it

[31] See Foot (1979) and Hursthouse (1999). Note also that this is a modification of the official statement of the theory of praise- and blameworthiness.

less difficult for her to do it. It would make no sense to withhold one's admiration from the cyclist after she had just ridden up Mt. Ventoux just because, due to her particular psychology, she is only motivated fully by hard climbs.

Now consider Carla, who only does right or good things when it is hard to do so. It is not that she does them because they are hard—that would be the wrong motive—but she is set up in such a way that when things go badly wrong, nonrational factors provide less of a barrier to action. Perhaps she suffers from a low-grade depression, but can be galvanized into action by great moral challenges. The fact that things are hard at a certain moment makes it more likely that she does the right or good, but does not make it easier for her. So she should be credited as we would credit a person who does the right or good thing across the whole range of circumstances.

Compare Carla to Latta, who has particularly strong intrinsic desires for social status and attention, and who circulates mostly among people of good will with correct moral views. Latta might also be likely to take on great moral challenges while neglecting more minor moral considerations, but she is distinctly unlike Carla in that she does not act out of good will in taking on great moral challenges; she acts rather out of her intrinsic desires for status and attention. Latta strikes us as much less praiseworthy than Carla. The same sort of conclusion seems to follow for a superhero whose powers make it easy to stop violent crimes and military massacres, but make it no easier than usual to tell hard truths to loved ones. If this superhero shows the same pattern of action, taking on great moral challenges while neglecting small ones, then she is also unlike Carla. And again, she also strikes us as much less praiseworthy.

Turn now to the third problem to be considered in this section: the ubiquity of moral indifference and reverse moral indifference. Because these are cases of absent motivation, it might seem that they are utterly ubiquitous. At every moment, Henry's lack of an intrinsic desire to kill everyone would seem to be at work, explaining why he pays for his groceries calmly and drives without swerving into pedestrians. As a result, it might seem that Henry is endlessly praiseworthy for his restraint in not killing everyone, given the present theory of praiseworthiness. He seems to be displaying reverse moral indifference at every moment. And similarly, at every moment, Saravanan's lack of an extremely strong intrinsic desire to relieve suffering explains why he consistently fails to sell his mansion and many cars and send the proceeds to a highly efficient charity working in the third world to eliminate parasitic worms. As a result, it might seem that Saravanan is endlessly blameworthy for his failure to relieve suffering, given the present theory of blameworthiness. He seems to be displaying moral indifference.

We agree that there is something wrong with the idea of ubiquitous and massive praise- and blameworthiness. Fortunately, the present theory is not committed to this picture. There are two points to make.

The first is that not all claims of causation by absence, or explanations by absence, are correct, even when the claimed absence holds. The absence of a heavy truck on the bridge does not explain why the bridge stayed up when the bridge would have stayed up even if the heavy truck had been present. Likewise, the absence of an intrinsic desire to kill everyone does not always explain why Henry leaves the grocery store without blood on his hands. Perhaps, even had he intrinsically desired to kill everyone, he would have been inattentive to opportunities to kill (his mind was, after all, on what to have for lunch), or he would have on balance preferred to not kill (going to jail without first having lunch is no fun), or perhaps he would have been weak-willed (too hungry to summon the strength to leap at the cashier). And there might be much stronger conditions on causation by absence, or on good causal explanations by absence, than the simple condition that the absent cause be such as to make a difference in nearby possible worlds. We have no particular theory of causation or causal explanation to defend, but there do seem to be important differences between the putative causal facts, or causal explanations,

The crops failed because the rains did not arrive.

and

The crops failed because aliens did not bring eternal life to all creatures on Earth.

Perhaps it matters that the possible world in which Henry has an intrinsic desire to kill everyone is a very distant world. We leave it to theorists of causation and causal explanation to provide further assistance here.

The second point to make is that ideas of praiseworthiness and blameworthiness are "graded on the curve," as it were. That is, we tend to use one or more implicit contrast classes in crediting and blaming people for the things they do, rather than using an absolute scale. Suppose we were to meet two alien species, both highly intelligent. One alien species proves to be systematically more disposed toward the right or good than human beings tend to. Our moral heroes strike them as hardly above average in their love of the right or good, while their moral heroes strike us as superhumanly pure saints. They have no problem solving "tragedy of the commons" problems (the idea that these would be problems strikes them as perverse), they fight wars at about a twentieth the rate of human societies, and so on. The other alien species is systematically more disposed toward the wrong or bad than we are. Their moral heroes are the equivalent of people who win the lottery and give just half of it away to friends, family, and good causes after buying a huge mansion, a yacht, and a dozen sports cars. Their moral villains make Hitler seem merely peevish. Their whole society is perpetually at war; and so on. After meeting the two sorts of aliens, we might find ourselves vacillating in the credit and blame we feel inclined to attribute to our fellow human beings or ourselves. Someone behind you at the movie theatre was loudly eating throughout a moving drama, and you did not turn around and physically attack her. After meeting the ill-willed aliens, you might feel very good about yourself, and feel that it is to the human race's credit that we do not launch into fisticuffs over such slight irritants. You are a credit to the galaxy. But then, you did not spend your movie ticket money fighting parasitic infection in the third world, the way the good willed aliens would have all done out of "minimal decency;" perhaps you should blame yourself for your selfishness. You are a galactic disgrace. Or perhaps you compare yourself to your fellow human beings and judge that you neither to be credited nor blamed for spending a peaceful evening at the movies.

There are at least two sensible ways to take seriously the way that inclinations to credit or blame shift with the contrast class we consider. One is to hold that real praise- and blameworthiness is absolute, but that since we are mostly interested in variations within a narrow range, we typically only think about the variations, not the whole scale. The other is to hold that real praise- and blameworthiness are not absolute but are relative to a contrast class.

We do not commit to one or the other of these interpretations here, but both help to solve the problem at hand. Either way, there are ways of explaining what is wrong with giving (almost) everyone credit for not acting on powerful intrinsic desires to kill everyone, and blaming (almost) everyone for not acting on powerful intrinsic desires to relieve suffering everywhere.

On the first approach, the explanation is that apportioning credit and blame in this way is technically correct but practically infelicitous. People are not interested in thinking about how praiseworthy someone is for an action when everyone has been similarly praiseworthy for many different actions for exactly the same reasons, e.g., that none of us have powerful intrinsic desires to kill everyone, and often act in way that manifest our indifference to the potential attractions of mass murder (unlike many of the ill willed aliens). Thus, although a theorist can, in an abstract mood, correctly hold that we are all praiseworthy for our reverse moral indifference to the appeal of punching a slightly irritating person in the nose, the theorist will see that this is not really the question of interest, most of the time, when people are interested in praiseworthiness.

On the second approach, the explanation is that apportioning credit and blame in this way is not correct given the typical contrast class. Perhaps this contrast class is people of similar life circumstances, means, and so on, perhaps it is the human race as a whole, or perhaps it shifts from one occasion of evaluation to another. When the contrast class lacks people with powerful intrinsic desires to kill everyone, it is wrong to credit someone for an action that shows a lack of this desire, on this approach to praiseworthiness. Thus, it would just be wrong to hold a person praiseworthy (compared to ordinary first-world human beings, or human beings in general…) for not starting a fight in the movie theatre, because that is not a distinguished level of reverse moral indifference (compared to that contrast class).

7.7 Partial Good and Ill Will

The idea of partial ill will does not, in our experience, disturb philosophers. If a person has an intrinsic desire for something there is a *pro tanto* moral reason to avoid—an intrinsic desire to harm Clarisse or to paternalize Benjamin or to keep women "in their place" or to eliminate the Jews—it is easy for most philosophers to see the case for holding such a person blameworthy in acting on such a desire.

On the other hand, the idea of partial good will can sit poorly with the same philosophers. Partial good will can sound nice, as when one talks about wanting one's child to be successful for her own sake, something that there is indeed a *pro tanto* moral reason to promote. But partial good will can also sound far too partial, in the sense of "taking a side." Wanting one's child to be successful is wanting it more than one wants some other things. And if one wants one's own child to be successful much, much more than one wants all children to be successful in their pursuits, then this can start to seem like favoritism more than good will. More worryingly, there is a *pro tanto* reason to promote the happiness of people of European descent, but is it really good will to act out of a desire that European-descended people, specifically, be happy? This sounds more like racism than good will.

Additionally, there is a technical worry. Will it turn out that people whose wills are wholly utilitarian count as having partial good will even if Kant has the correct normative theory? Will it turn out that people whose wills are wholly Kantian count as having partial good will even if Mill has the correct normative theory? In short, will it turn out that people who whole-heartedly intrinsically desire what a credible but incorrect moral theory says one should desire count as having at least some good will?

As so often, whether someone is praise- or blameworthy for an action depends greatly on the details. There are more and less innocent cases of partiality in partial good will, but there are also cases of pure favoritism, jingoism, racism, and the like, and these cases do not, on our account, lead to praiseworthy action. Seeing the difference between the cases will take a little work. And then, the same care with cases will be required to see what to think about the praiseworthiness of people whose desires are the right ones according to the wrong moral theories.

Consider first the excessively partial moral agent. As we suggested in our initial presentation of the idea of partial good will, it seems necessary to be ready to praise this person sometimes, or it seems all too likely that no one in the history of human civilization will turn out to have been morally praiseworthy for anything. The history of morality seems to show a very slowly increasing willingness to treat every moral patient as a moral patient. It was not so long ago that almost everyone was happy to see the most terrible things done to other people so long as they were of a rival tribe, or a hated ethnicity, or a different nation, or a different race, or of the weaker sex, or a disliked sexual orientation. And perhaps the future will bring with it a similar moral perspective on the present time, for our poor treatment of the elderly, or the disabled, or third-world labor, or the people who are yet to be conceived but who will inherit the Earth we leave behind, or nonhuman animals, or other groups to which we are blind exactly because we wrongly do not care about them, or care too little. In spite of a past lack of concern for the totality of moral patients, it seems right to look back and see as praiseworthy many particular actions. And in spite of the likelihood of present moral failings, it seems right to see certain present actions as morally praiseworthy too. Since most people in the past cannot have complete good will attributed to them, and since it seems all too likely that most people in the present similarly lack complete good will, partial good will must suffice for praiseworthiness, on at least some occasions.

Taking advantage of our distinction between what is believed RIGHT and what is desired as RESPECTFUL or as MAXIMIZING HAPPINESS or DISTRIBUTING EQUALLY or the like, it could be suggested that the people in the past who were morally praiseworthy were such because they acted out of desires for the whole of the right or the good—they simply did not know what the whole of the right or the good came to. That is, although they had excessively narrow moral theories, they had some degree of complete good will, and so could be praiseworthy for manifesting it in good acts. But this suggestion is hard to believe. It is hard to believe that the people of the past had the right intrinsic desires regarding rival tribes, other ethnicities, homosexuals, and so on, but simply did not believe that satisfying these desires was what counted as RIGHT or GOOD. If people had had the right intrinsic desires, they would more often have acted correctly toward rival tribes, other ethnicities, homosexuals, and so on while simply denying that this correct treatment was required by what was RIGHT, holding that it was just optional (say). Similarly, they would have felt badly about massacres of rival tribes, the abuse of homosexuals, and so on while denying that these feelings were specifically moral feelings. This does not look much like actual history.

So it seems that the people of the past, and perhaps of the present also, must be praiseworthy for acting on their partial good wills insofar as they are praiseworthy for anything at all. But how could this make sense, given how much partial good will can look like favoritism, prejudice, and racism?

Compare three people.

Alparslan intrinsically desires that his fellow Turks are happy, or are treated with respect, or get equal shares of divided goods, or otherwise have what in fact is right or good. Since he is not a psychopath, Alparslan also intrinsically desires that people in general have these same right or good things. But he desires much more that his fellow Turks have what is right or good than that everyone have it. Alparslan is mildly pleased to learn that those "others" are doing well, justly governed, and so on, but he is not willing to do much about it unless it is easy and will not take long. He is much more devoted to the same right or good things when they are for the people he calls "us."

Isgandar also strongly intrinsically desires that his fellow Turks have what in fact is right or good. Like Alparslan, he is also not a psychopath, and so has a (weaker) intrinsic desire that everyone have what in fact is right or good. But he has a profound hatred of Kurdish people, and intrinsically desires to see Kurds harmed in natural disasters, or by political repression, and so on. This intrinsic desire is, of course, in conflict with his intrinsic desire that everyone have what is right or good, but his hatred of Kurds is strong enough that he is not moved to pity when there is news that many people were killed by an earthquake in the Kurdish part of Turkey; that sort of thing mostly delights Isgandar.

Finally, Mushin is another person of strong, tribal Turkish sympathy and (like Isgandar) strong anti-Kurdish antipathy, but his desires take a somewhat more complicated form. He greatly intrinsically desires that Turks have what is right or good *so long as it does not help any Kurds.* And similarly, he intrinsically desires (to a lesser extent) that everyone have what is right or good *except Kurds.* And finally, he, like Isgandar, greatly intrinsically desires that Kurds be harmed, ill-treated, and so on.

The present theory draws very different conclusions about the potential praiseworthiness of Alparslan, Isgander, and Mushin in acting on their various desires.

Alparslan has weak complete good will and an intrinsic desire that counts as strong partial good will. But given the weakness of his complete good will, one can also say about him that he has a potentially troubling degree of moral indifference. We might appeal to one, two, or all three of these features in explaining what he does on some occasion, in a way that determines his praise- or blameworthiness. Suppose Alparslan lives in a mostly Turkish community, and he sees a little girl fall and get scraped. His intrinsic desires that Turks have what is right or good, and that everyone have what is right or good, might both be at work in explaining why he helps the fallen girl up and dusts her off. If so, then Alparslan acts out of both complete and partial good will, and is praiseworthy. If Alparslan was quite inconvenienced by stopping, then his action will even manifest his very strong partial good will, and so be particularly praiseworthy. If, on the other hand, Alparslan sees a little girl fall while thinking that she must be Kurdish, Alparslan will obviously be less motivated to help. If he does help, then he will be showing his (weaker) complete good will, which will make him praiseworthy. He will not be likely to inconvenience himself greatly for the sake of helping because there is a limit to his (complete) good will. If he does not help, he will reveal his troubling moral indifference, and so be blameworthy (assuming not helping is in fact wrong). And then, in addition to being praiseworthy for helping or blameworthy for not helping, Alparslan might also be blameworthy for things like looking for a tell-tale ethnic marker before deciding whether to help, since this would display his lack of complete good will, and so some measure of moral indifference. Thus Alparslan can be quite praiseworthy for doing the right thing, in spite of his partiality, but his partiality limits his willingness to do the right thing, and so to act in a praiseworthy manner, in other circumstances. His partiality is also not of the most noxious sort.

Compared to Alparslan, Isgandar can be just as praiseworthy for helping what he takes to be a fallen Turkish girl, since he has the same positive attitudes and can act upon them in the same way. But if he takes the little girl before him to be Kurdish, then Isgandar will be pulled in two directions: to help, by his weak but complete good will, and to not help, by his hatred of Kurds. If he helps, this probably manifests the full measure of his weak complete good will, because—given how he hates Kurds—he would probably not have helped had his complete good will been much weaker. But this does not make him *very* praiseworthy, since "the full measure of his good will" is not that much, and furthermore, his obstacle to manifesting his complete good will is nothing but (partial) ill will, and one does not garner extra praise for having to overcome ill will. If he does not help, then he manifests both his moral indifference (the weakness of that same intrinsic desire for the whole of the right or good) and also his partial ill will toward Kurdish people. This leaves him potentially more blameworthy than Alparslan, though it depends on just how much ill will is being manifested. Isgandar might well leave a fallen little Kurdish girl alone to cry on the street with no one else around to help, when (all else being equal) Alparslan would not, just because of Isgandar's hatred for Kurds. And this is the sort of thing that would manifest his particularly objectionable partial ill will, and be a particularly blameworthy act.

Both Alparslan and Isgandar are saintly in comparison to the particularly hateful Mushin. As characterized, Mushin does not have any good will at all, neither partial nor complete, and so cannot act in a praiseworthy manner even toward fellow Turks. This is because Mushin does not have any intrinsic desire the content of which is something there is a *pro tanto* moral reason to bring about. There is no defeasible presumption in favor of helping (or treating equitably, etc.) Turks so long as no good thereby comes to Kurds. It might be true that, in some circumstance, one can see that a certain action will help a Turk and not a Kurd. And it might be true that, in that circumstance, one has a *pro tanto* moral reason to perform the act. But the consideration that no Kurd will be helped does not contribute to there being a *pro tanto* reason to perform the act! On the contrary, an intrinsic desire to provide what is right or good to Turks (or others) so long as it does not provide what is right or good to Kurds rationalizes Mushin's sometimes denying a right or good action to a person, because the right or good action would also bring something right or good to a Kurd. Such an intrinsic desire cannot constitute even partial good will. Hence, when acting on his intrinsic desires, Mushin is never morally praiseworthy. At most, he is not blameworthy in doing what is fair or kind for some fellow Turk

or fellow (non-Kurdish) human being. While Isgandar resembles the prototypi-
cal racist next door, Mushin resembles a Nazi.

This division of potentially problematic partiality into three kinds of cases
suggests to us that the present theory is sensitive to how partiality can go wrong,
as well as to how it can be less morally problematic, just as one would want.
In its least problematic guise, partiality suggests only that one's (less partial or
fully impartial) good will is less of a priority for the agent than we would hope.
In its most problematic guise, partiality is a way of having a will that is not even
partially good.

Finally, what about the more technical worry that might be raised? Will
wholehearted adherents of a credible but false moral theory count as having
any good will at all, on the present account of good will? Here, the concern is
not that partial good will is not genuinely good, but that even partial good will
might be said to be lacking in a person, simply because she holds a false moral
theory.

The first thing to say is that we expect most people not to be wholehearted
adherents of their moral theories. People might be firmly convinced, intellectually, that their theories are true, but this sort of conviction does not typically
coincide with having intrinsic desires for only those things one has *pro tanto* reason to promote according to one's theory. We are almost all raised by ordinary
people in ordinary circumstances, and so have the range of intrinsic desires one
associates with these sorts of lives, including intrinsic desires that others not
suffer, that they be happy and successful in their pursuits, that they be treated
equally under most circumstances, that we keep our promises and tell the truth
and that others do likewise, that we show respect to everyone, that we not act
contrary to someone's explicit insistence, and so on. (That we desire these ends
intrinsically is suggested not least by the fact that we flinch, both emotionally
and behaviorally, from breaking promises, causing harm, overriding someone's
refusal to consent, and so on, even when we are convinced that we are acting perfectly morally rightly in so doing.) In addition to these ordinary intrinsic desires, it might be that someone also intrinsically desires what her moral
theory says she should: that happiness be maximized, that people be afforded
maximal liberty consistent with respect for consensual agreements, that one act
selfishly, or whatever else one's moral theory might demand. Because of this
plurality of intrinsic desires, it is very likely that a person who is convinced of
a false moral theory will nonetheless have a fair bit of partial good will, and
perhaps even have complete good will, without knowing it, thus putting her in
the company of Huckleberry Finn. The person who greatly intrinsically desires
that people be afforded maximal liberty consistent with respect for consensual
agreement but who intrinsically desires absolutely nothing else of a remotely
moral cast—who can watch unmoved as a person starves to death for lack of a
consenting person willing to give him food—is very rare.

Of the person found in thought experiments who holds a particularly unsavory moral theory, and intrinsically desires nothing in the neighborhood of morality save for what the theory says makes up the moral, it might be agreed that there is no way for this person to act in a praiseworthy manner. But what about the person who holds a less unsavory, but still incorrect, theory?

Imagine a wholehearted utilitarian, whose only even approximately moral desire is an extremely strong intrinsic desire that HAPPINESS BE MAXIMIZED. And suppose that utilitarianism is not the correct normative theory of morality. Will the wholehearted utilitarian will turn out to have no claim to have even partial good will? This will be so only if it will turn out that there is no *pro tanto* moral reason to perform the action which makes as many people happy as possible. If there is such a reason, however defeasible, the wholehearted utilitarian has partial good will.

Still, there will be some moral theories such that theory A and theory B are both reasonable enough moral theories, and such that a wholehearted adherent of A (whose only even approximately moral desire is an intrinsic desire for exactly what theory A takes to be right or good) will turn out not to have even partial good will if theory B is correct. For instance, if Sun-Joo is a wholehearted Kantian who intrinsically desires to act universalizably, and if utilitarianism is the correct normative theory, so that universalizability is not a *pro tanto* moral reason to perform an action, then Sun-Joo will turn out to have not even partial good will.

Should this trouble us as theorists? Actually, it is just the right result. Sun-Joo, as imagined, is someone who has no intrinsic aversion to suffering or intrinsic desire for the happiness of other people. She is not, in short, an ordinary human being. She is a very peculiar specimen, who only cares about how her actions cause suffering or happiness insofar as she can see this to affect their universalizability—which sometimes it does, and sometimes it does not, as she correctly judges. The idea that a serious Kantian could still be praiseworthy, even if Mill was right about morality, is a reasonable idea when applied to real people.[32] But Sun-Joo is not, as imagined, a real person. She is an unfeeling oddity when it comes to suffering and happiness. She is unmoved when learning that the people of Pompeii were killed by the eruption of Vesuvius, since their suffering was not the product of any nonuniversalizable deployment of agency and since their suffering, being in the remote past, does not require her own agency to be deployed; imagining them struck down while they fled or huddled in their homes does not touch her in the slightest. So it makes sense to say that, if the only morally important thing is human happiness, she does not have any good will.

There are always more objections to consider, but we will rest here for now.

---

[32] Markovits (2010) thinks that it is not, and that therefore utilitarianism has a problem.

{ 8 }

Virtue

According to Aristotle, the virtuous person does the right thing, at the right time, in the right way, and for the right reasons. She feels what it is appropriate to feel. She does not need to use willpower in order make herself do what is just or generous, because she is already inclined to act in these ways.[1] Contemporary virtue theorists working in the Aristotelian tradition have also emphasized that the virtuous person thinks and pays attention to things in a way that reflects her virtue.[2] She is better than the rest of us when it comes to detecting morally relevant situations and has better intuitions regarding their solutions.[3] There are beliefs that no virtuous person would have, such as racist beliefs, just as there are feelings that no virtuous person would have, such as *schadenfreude*. In short, the broadly Aristotelian idea seems to be that the virtuous person's virtue is made up of a whole complex of different states and dispositions covering the whole of the person's mind and her behavior in the world.

But the virtuous person—if we understand her to be the same as the *morally* virtuous person—does not always do the right thing at the right time and in the right way. Not, at least, if that expression is understood in the most straightforward way. The right thing to do might well be to give a particular homeless man some money, but the virtuous person might nonetheless not give the money, or not at the right time or in the right way. The virtuous person could be, for example, mildly mentally retarded and so, quite innocently, take the homeless man's request for help with bus fare literally, handing him a token useable only for riding the bus rather than the money it would be much better to give. Or the virtuous person could be manic-depressive and temporarily gripped by the manic idea that simply smiling at the homeless man will literally cure all of his ills. Or the virtuous person could be so accustomed to reliance on credit cards that for her to transfer any of her wealth to the homeless man would require a complicated explanation and set of electronic transactions, and would be equally tiresomely complex for the homeless man and for the virtuous agent; to act at the right time and in the right manner would require having had cash

---

[1] Aristotle (1999), see especially book 2.
[2] See, e.g., Murdoch (1970), McDowell (1979). See also Herman (1993, 78).
[3] Some philosophers, such McDowell and Swanton, even take a cognitive disposition to perceive the requirements of morality as the heart of virtue.

on hand. None of these defects would impugn the virtuous person's kindness, generosity, or sense of justice in the slightest.

Equally, there are times when the virtuous person fails to feel the right emotions, think the right thoughts, or attend to the right things. Perhaps she cannot feel sympathy for the homeless man she meets because she is very depressed; then she might be a very kind person who is suffering from depression, not an unkind person. Perhaps she does not see that the homeless man is suffering because she is autistic; then she might be a person with a strong sense of justice who has a harder time than most identifying certain facts that are important for justly redressing inequities.[4] Perhaps she does not attend to the homeless man because she is congenitally absent-minded, and his quiet request for spare change is drowned out by her philosophical musings, which routinely pose a danger to her when she crosses a street; then she might be a very generous person who simply was not aware of an occasion for generosity. Mental retardation, mania, depression, autism, absent-mindedness, and the like are all morally neutral. Even a perfectly virtuous person can be mentally retarded, manic, depressed, autistic, or absent-minded.

Such ideas can elicit the broadly Kantian response that the various Aristotelian dispositions are unimportant, and all that is really required for virtue is good will.[5] Good actions depend to some extent on luck, and to that extent they do not reflect on a person's virtue or vice. Emotions are involuntary things, and therefore there is a deep sense in which they are morally neutral, it can seem: they have nothing to do with good will. Cognitive characteristics of people are not voluntary either, and so they too seem morally neutral in and of themselves.

The broadly Kantian response is right in its essence but wrong in its details; the broadly Aristotelian view is wrong in its essence but right in its details. Having good will is what virtue consists in, just as the broadly Kantian position would have it. But having good will is having the right sort of intrinsic desires. As a result, having good will is not divorced from the nonvoluntary qualities associated with virtue by the broadly Aristotelian approach. Having good will is the normal cause of various effects, including feeling the right things, thinking of the right things, and having one's attention caught by the right things. But it is possible for a virtuous person to be incapable of feeling the right things, or thinking the right things, or even doing the right things, without being any less virtuous for all that. Hence, there is something right in both the Kantian and Aristotelian approaches. The broadly Kantian position is right in defending a very limited theory of what virtue *is*, while the broadly Aristotelian position is right regarding what virtuous human beings, ordinarily, *are like*.

---

[4] Or a kind person who fails to identify occasions for kindness—our examples are somewhat arbitrary.

[5] Kant's own theory of virtue is another matter, of course.

8.1 A Theory of Virtue

With the theory of good will from the previous chapter in hand, Spare Conativism's theory of virtue and vice can be stated very simply.

To be virtuous is to have significant good will and lack ill will.
To be vicious is to have significant ill will or significant moral indifference.

Since having and lacking good will come in various forms, so too do virtue and vice. Good will is complete when it is instantiated by an intrinsic desire for the whole of the right or good, correctly conceptualized, and so a person possesses complete virtue when she has this sort of good will. Ill will is similarly complete when instantiated by an intrinsic desire for the whole of what is wrong or bad, correctly conceptualized, and so a person possesses complete vice when she has this sort of ill will. And then, good and ill will can also be partial rather than complete, when a person intrinsically desires what is a transparently necessary part of the right or good, or the wrong or bad, correctly conceptualized, and so a person can also have partial virtue or partial vice. Finally, good and ill will can be realized by stronger or weaker desires, and so one can have a greater or lesser share of overall virtue or vice.

Nothing prevents a person from having both complete and partial good will, or both complete and partial ill will, or any other combination of the four, and so one can have both complete and partial virtue and vice. A virtuous person might intrinsically desire the whole of the right or good, via the right concepts, a great deal—and *also* intrinsically desire various proper parts of the right or good, correctly conceptualized, to various extents. And likewise for a vicious person. An otherwise virtuous person might very slightly desire some part of, or the whole of, the wrong or bad, and so have a little partial or complete ill will, and so a little partial or complete vice, while an otherwise vicious person might very slightly desire some part of, or the whole of, the right or good, and so have a little partial or complete virtue.

This theory of what it is to be *virtuous* and *vicious* has a simple relation to theories of particular *virtues* and *vices*. A virtue is an intrinsic desire that constitutes either complete or partial good will, or perhaps a collection of such intrinsic desires, or it is a stable state of mind of an agent that manifests such a desire (in a content-efficacious but not necessarily reason-responsive way). Or, if the virtue is one in which there is an absence of ill will rather than the presence of good will, the virtue is the absence of an intrinsic desire that constitutes either complete or partial ill will, or perhaps the absence of a particular organization of intrinsic desires, or it is a stable state of mind of an agent that manifests such an absence of desire (in a content-efficacious but not necessarily reason reason-responsive way). And similarly for vices.

As with the previous chapter's theory of praise- and blameworthiness, the present theory of virtue and vice can be understood as either absolute or relational. Consideration of the virtues and vices most human beings possess, when compared to particularly decent or particularly cruel aliens, might support a theory on which all human beings possess virtues and vices in modest degrees, with only a few of us even somewhat distinguished in our virtue or vice. This would be the absolute understanding of virtue and vice. But the ways in which people often think that some human beings are tremendously virtuous, while others are tremendously vicious, might suggest rather the relational thesis that comparison groups are always implicit in a claim that someone has a virtue or a vice, and this is also something that Spare Conativism can embrace. Philippa Foot holds that virtue terms are relative to the nature of the average human being: there is a virtue of generosity because human beings are often selfish and a virtue of courage because human beings are often cowardly.[6] In holding this, she shows her commitment to a form of the relational view, and perhaps she is right to do so. In the coming pages, though, we will set this issue aside.

8.2 The Theory Applied

The present theory of virtue and vice would perhaps be clearer if illustrated. Although it would be easiest to illustrate the theory by presupposing Millian consequentialism or Kantian deontology as our working normative theory, there is also something to be said for expanding the range of examples. So consider W.D. Ross's intuitionism.

Though Ross's intuitionism is best known for its meta-ethical features, it also encompasses a plausible normative theory. According to Ross, there is an irreducible list of seven *pro tanto* moral reasons. Ross calls them *"prima facie* obligations," but we suspect *"pro tanto* reasons" comes closer to his intent, since we think that Ross intends there to be moral weight to, e.g., promise keeping even when its weight is overridden in a given context by some other moral consideration. With any needed apologies to Ross for the roughness of this interpretation, it will be our assumption for the example. Ross's irreducible *pro tanto* moral reasons are that people keep their promises, that they make reparations for any harms they have inflicted on others, that they act grateful for the benefits they have received, that they promote merited distributions of pleasure, that they promote knowledge, happiness, and virtue, that they improve themselves, and that they not harm others.[7]

---

[6] Foot (1979).

[7] This is one (admittedly unsophisticated) reading of Ross's position from *The Right and the Good*. See Ross (2002, 21ff).

The most straightforward way to combine Ross's normative theory with Spare Conativism's theory of virtue is to hold that being virtuous is possessing seven intrinsic desires: one intrinsic desire per moral reason. If Jenice is a virtuous person, then on a Ross-style normative theory her being virtuous will consist in her having one very strong intrinsic desire that she keep her promises, one very strong intrinsic aversion to harming others, another intrinsic desire that people gain knowledge, happiness, and virtue, and so on.

If a Ross-style normative theory requires specific trade-offs between moral reasons—requires that one sacrifice promises of importance I in order to avoid inflicting harms of importance J, for example—then Jenice's virtue will also consist in her intrinsic desires being weighted in the right ways: that she be sufficiently intrinsically averse to inflicting harms, relative to her intrinsic desire to keep her promises, so that she will have a rationalization for preferring to avoid inflicting a harm of importance J even when that means she must break a promise of importance I.

Since Ross's theory presents a picture of a virtuous person with seven distinct moral concerns, the virtuous person will have seven distinct complete virtues, each one constituted by intrinsically desiring the right thing (an independent part of the right and good) to the right degree (in relation to what else one intrinsically desires), under the right conceptualization (which is provided in Ross's theorizing). If Jenice is a perfectly virtuous person, it is because she has the seven complete Rossian virtues: fidelity, willingness-to-make-reparations, gratitude, justice, beneficence, commitment-to-self-improvement, and nonmaleficence.

In addition to complete virtues, there will also be many (perhaps unboundedly many) partial virtues that are possible. Ross takes not lying to be an instance of keeping one's promises (the promise kept by not lying is the implicit promise to tell the truth in ordinary forms of conversation[8]), so in addition to having the complete virtue of fidelity (as Ross calls it), constituted by her intrinsic desire that she keep her promises, Jenice might also have a partial virtue, that of truthfulness, constituted by an intrinsic aversion to lying.

The possession of complete virtues and partial virtues is, both in principle and often enough in practice, independent. A person might have the complete Rossian virtue of fidelity while lacking a distinct partial virtue of truthfulness (caring about promises while not having a distinct concern for not lying), or have the partial virtue of truthfulness while lacking the complete virtue of fidelity (caring about lies but not much caring about promises more generally), or lack both virtues, or possess both virtues.

Possessing both virtues is a striking example of the independence of complete and partial virtues on the present account, and nicely highlights just

---

[8] Ross (2002, 21).

how complicated moral life can be. Imagine that Jenice has these two intrinsic desires: one that she keep her promises, and one that she not lie. Jenice might have acquired the intrinsic desire not to lie to early in childhood, through being raised by parents who valued truthfulness. And she might have acquired the intrinsic desire to keep her promises a little later in childhood, as she started to accept responsibilities for her future conduct toward her peers (that she would bring her jump-rope tomorrow...) and parents (that she would wash the dishes after supper...). And the idea that not lying is a form of promise-keeping might have come a little later still in childhood. Now an adult, she has two distinct intrinsic desires for overlapping ends. In this circumstance, all else being equal, she will be more likely to tell the truth than she would if she had only the complete virtue of fidelity—and also be more likely to anticipate situations in which telling the truth might become difficult, more likely to attend to her own partial prevarications, and more likely to be emotionally sensitive to whether people in general lie. Because her two intrinsic desires are likely to both come into play in contexts where truthfulness is a relevant consideration, she is likely to seem to possess more of the virtue of truthfulness than it would be best to say she does. On the present theory, it would be better to say that Jenice's laudable truthfulness is reinforced by her general fidelity to her promises, and hence she appears even more truthful than she might otherwise.

The same person who shows great fidelity and truthfulness might nonetheless possess certain vices. Perhaps Jenice is a little callous.

Continuing in the Rossian framework, callousness might be something like being deficient in her intrinsic desire that people have knowledge, happiness, and virtue. Perhaps Jenice has not just one intrinsic desire for this complex, but three distinct intrinsic desires: she has an ordinary or very strong intrinsic desire that people gain knowledge, and another that people be virtuous, but perhaps she has only a distinct, and rather weak, intrinsic desire that people be happy. Not being a psychopath, Jenice has *some* intrinsic desire for the happiness of others, but perhaps it is on the regrettably low end of the normal range. Then although promises, truthfulness, the accumulation of knowledge, and so on will affect Jenice's actions, feelings, and thoughts in the ways characteristic of virtue, she will often be a little cold when it comes to her feelings about distant suffering.[9] The weakness of Jenice's desire for the happiness of others appears to be a partial vice on her part, given that in a Rossian framework the happiness of others is a part of what one cares about when one is beneficent. And a noteworthy feature of this vice is that it is realized by a weakness of an intrinsic desire with a laudable content, rather than the presence of an intrinsic desire with a lamentable content.

---

[9] That is, suffering that she has not brought about through her own agency, since suffering for which she is responsible is a matter covered by the separate Rossian virtue of non-maleficence.

The virtue of mildness will make a good final example of the present theory in action.[10] The virtues so far considered are all constituted by intrinsic desires. The virtue of mildness, on the other hand, is constituted by facts about feelings: the mild person is the person who does not easily get angered. But not just any cause of this equanimity will count as Jenice's possession of the virtue. If her mild reactions to feeling defeated or ill-used come from a steady supply of sedative drugs, or a tumor in her amygdala that prevents all such feelings,[11] Jenice does not have the virtue. Her disposition to not get needlessly angry only counts as mildness insofar as it is a manifestation of her reverse moral indifference. Perhaps Jenice tends not to get angry because she has little intrinsic desire for retribution (and a stronger intrinsic desire for retribution explains why most of us are more readily angered than she), and retribution is transparently necessarily an instance of the infliction of harm on others—an aspect of the wrong or bad, on Ross's account. Then Jenice's particularly weak desire for retribution is an absence of a common form of partial ill will, and thus is itself a partial virtue which might be called nonretributiveness. And because this partial virtue is the main causal explanation of her tendency to not be easily angered, Jenice's mildness is a stable mental state that is a manifestation of a partial virtue, and so counts as a (partial) virtue itself.

8.3 Virtues and Their Effects

To be very virtuous, we hold, it suffices to have a great deal of complete or partial good will, and to lack any substantial degree of either complete or partial ill will. But some virtue theorists believe that a virtue is a disposition to act.[12] Many others believe that virtues are complex entities that include dispositions to act but also dispositions to feel, and in some cases knowledge of the virtues, cognitive sensitivities to morally relevant matters, and more.[13] Both kinds of

---

[10] See, of course, Book 4 of *Nicomachean Ethics* for the classic treatment of this virtue.

[11] For a real example of this, see Sprengelmeyer et al. (1999).

[12] For example: J. J. Thomson likewise defines a just person as a person who is "prone" to perform just acts (1997, 280). Bernard Williams, in contending that virtue is "a disposition of character to choose or reject actions because they are of a certain ethically relevant kind" already complicates things by implying that the motivation behind the disposition is important.

[13] Julia Annas and Rosalind Hursthouse are paradigmatic proponents of rich views of virtue, in which emotions and cognitive matters are important and so are dispositions to act. The following is a sampling of views according to which virtue is more than a disposition to act but according to which there is still some type of disposition, proneness, capability or propensity as the heart of virtue: Annas talks about virtues as dispositions but "intelligent," complex dispositions, dispositions that can be educated: they, too are dispositions to feel as well as act (2011). John Rawls says that virtues are "families of dispositions and propensities regulated by a higher order desire." Owen Flanagan claims that "On every view the virtues are psychological dispositions *productive* of behavior" (1991, 282). Julia Driver talks about dispositions to "feel, behave, or act well" (1996,124) though at other times she is more action-centered. John Doris, when criticizing virtue ethics, talks about the dispositions involved in virtue as complex and as involving not

virtue theorists are likely to object to our theory. First of all, they will object to the fact we do not think of virtues as dispositions of any sort, and the latter kind of virtue theorists—those with a richer idea of virtue—will also object to our view because of the extreme parsimony of our theory.

A theory of virtue built on intrinsic desires, understood the way Spare Conativism understands intrinsic desires, is preferable to a theory merely built on dispositions to action. As Thomas Hurka argues, a person who believes strongly that acting morally is always to her advantage can have as a result a strong disposition to do the right thing, but she will not be virtuous, as her motives will be ulterior motives.[14] The categorical basis of a disposition to act should matter to the moral psychologist at least as much as the existence of the disposition itself. In addition to Hurka's case, in which the categorical basis of a disposition to act is the wrong sort of intrinsic desire, there are also cases in which the categorical basis of a disposition to act is not an intrinsic desire at all. For instance, if a person is subject to a particular behavioral tic that happens to be supportive of morally right or good ends, it would nonetheless not seem to be a part of virtue to possess the tic. We can imagine a person with Tourette syndrome who has many Tourettic tics—blinking, shrugging, grunting, and shouting vulgarities at inappropriate moments, perhaps—while also having as a tic a powerful tendency to reach out and catch those who are about to fall unintentionally. This latter tic (not a naturalistic example, but not much of a leap) would be a disposition to do what is virtuous, in part. But having such a tic is not part of having a virtue: such a tic would not, it seems to us, make up even a part of kindness or concern for others or any similar virtue. And notice that, since the tic would be triggered by the person's perception or cognition of a situation as one in which a person is stumbling or falling in a potentially harmful manner, it is not the case that the behavior is blind. It is directed in part by a perception or cognition of the situation that makes the behavior morally appropriate—but the behavior does not come from concern for the wellbeing of the stumbling or falling person. It does not come from something that is credibly even a part of good will. And that seems to be why the behavioral disposition does not suffice for even a part of virtue.

A similar conclusion should be drawn about habits that are not backed by intrinsic desires. A person who once held open doors for weak and burdened people out of genuine concern, but who now does it only out of habit, does not

---

only action but also emotional responses and even patterns of decision and deliberation (2002). Christine Swanton (2005, 1) says that virtue is "a disposition to respond to or acknowledge, in an excellent or good enough way, items in the field of the virtue." In a different vein, McDowell thinks of the virtuous person as having a "reliable sensitivity" to the requirements of morality—a cognitive capacity. It is hard to classify "reliable sensitivity" as a disposition or a non-disposition, but one way or the other we will acknowledge that a cognitive sensitivity to moral matters is one standard effect that virtue has.

[14] Hurka (2000).

seem to be someone whose disposition to act in accordance with virtue is itself any part of being virtuous. Here we agree with Kant, in *Anthropology from a Pragmatic Point of View*.

> So we cannot define *virtue* as *acquired aptitude* for free lawful actions; for then it would be a mere mechanism in the exercise of our forces. Virtue is, rather moral strength in pursuing our duty, which never becomes habit but should always spring forth, quite new and original, from our way of thinking. (1974, 26-7; emphasis in original)

Turn now to the charge of excessive parsimony that might meet a theory like SC that identifies virtue with the possession of the right intrinsic desire(s). It can first be noted that our parsimony is not uniquely ours. Robert Adams[15] and Thomas Hurka[16] have both led the way in defending similarly parsimonious theories of virtue according to which being virtuous is simply a matter have having the right pro-attitudes. For Hurka, virtue consists of loving the good and hating the bad;[17] for Adams it is excellence in "being for" the good.[18] And Richard Brandt wrote that, "[a] virtue is a relatively permanent desire or aversion (or a complex of these) directed at some action type and/or some expectable form of consequence of an action."[19] So fortunately some of the arguments we need in our defense have already been made. Others we will invent as we go.

Compare two people who are healthy adult human beings, found in ordinary situations that they understand well. The first person, imagine, has a much stronger tendency to try to improve the moral state of the world, and a much better record of actually achieving this result, all else being equal; the second person has a weaker tendency to act and a worse record of achieving good results when under comparable conditions. The first person is more passionately engaged with morally significant facts, more prone to be happy when the world is improved and more likely to be saddened or angry when the world is worsened. The first person also pays more attention to the morally significant facts, remembers them better, learns from them more quickly, and otherwise is more cognitively influenced by them. With these two people in view, it is hard to deny that the former would appear to be more virtuous.

The reader will not be surprised, at this point, by the claim that a normal, healthy human being who strongly intrinsically desires the right or good will display all of the aforementioned qualities because they are effects caused by

---

[15] Adams (2006).

[16] Hurka (2000).

[17] It is easy to see that, with a few supplementary premises invoking desire-based theories of love, Hurka's theory of virtue becomes equivalent to Spare Conativism's.

[18] Adams, however, considers pro-attitudes to have a cognitive component.

[19] Brandt (1992), however, also talks of virtues as related to dispositions to desire, which is somewhat confusing.

her intrinsic desire. Although we argued (in chapter 5) that these sorts of effects do not *make* a mental state into a desire, we also argued that intrinsic desires in fact *cause* exactly these sorts of effects (in chapter 6).

The disposition to act in accordance with virtue is the disposition that most obviously follows, in normal, healthy human beings, from having a strong intrinsic desire for the right or good. If the person of good will (in our sense) sees that her own actions are ideally poised for bringing about the right or good—or that they are required, as the case might be—then of course it will normally follow that she will be more motivated than someone else of lesser good will, all else being equal, to do the right or good thing in the circumstances. This follows from what we said about desire in chapter 6, and is in any case a commonplace.

In addition to the actions most associated with virtue, it is worth noting another sort. This is action that is a manifestation of virtue without being done from virtue (that is, without good will being part of a rationalizing reason for the action). Think of a person who knocks on wood as a matter of superstition when some improvement in the state of the world appears possible, though he is not so superstitious as to believe that knocking on wood is actually causally efficacious in bringing about good results. He does not perform a particularly good action in knocking on wood, but it still shows his good will in that it shows he is concerned enough to get nervous; the knocking on wood is an indirect manifestation of good will. Similarly, a person who writes fifty times a day on his computer the words "I want to kill Larry" has not done anything particularly wrong—his act might even be morally obligatory, if it helps him to avoid actually hurting or bothering Larry—nor is his action *rationalized* by ill will, but his act could be a manifestation of harrowing ill will, and thus vice. Dispositions to perform these sorts of actions, only obliquely connected to the right or good (or wrong or bad), can be expected from people with strong intrinsic desires for the right or good (or wrong or bad), and this seems just what one would expect from virtuous (and vicious) people.

Now consider emotions and feelings. Emotions and feelings are not voluntary, and yet the very virtuous person is expected to have very different emotions and feelings from the nonvirtuous one. She is expected, for example, to feel pleasure when she hears about decent people being fortunate, and sadness at the thought of their suffering. She is expected never to feel pernicious envy or jealousy, or unjust anger, yet reading about a serious injustice being committed is expected to make her righteously indignant.[20] On the rare occasion on which she acts badly she is expected to feel guilty. She is expected to have visceral distaste for at least some immoral people and their actions.[21] Exactly

---

[20] This expectation may be waived if we know that the person in question is unusually calm by temperament or otherwise strongly disposed not to feel anger, in which case some other affective manifestation of disapproval is expected, such as sadness.

[21] Though Kelly (2011, chapters 4, 5) cautions against taking disgust seriously in ethics.

what is true of the virtuous person's feelings depends on what moral theory is true, but in general there exist emotions and feelings or combinations of emotions and feelings that only the virtuous person is reliably subject to. There are emotions and feelings, on the other hand, that only a vicious person is expected to have on a regular basis. We have mentioned *schadenfreude*, and then there is inappropriate anger, as in the case of rage at the idea of interracial marriage, and sadistic pleasure.

All of these phenomena, and more, can be expected from the person who has strong intrinsic desires for the right or good. Given the relationship between desire satisfaction and pleasure, and between desire frustration and displeasure, it is to be expected that there will be a range of emotions that follow from having strong intrinsic desires regarding the moral realm. The phenomena of the previous paragraph went beyond pleasure and displeasure in considering anger, pernicious envy, *schadenfreude*, and so on, but this is not a problem for a desire-centered theory of virtue and vice. On any plausible theory of the emotions, all emotions involve some form of pleasure (for the "positive" emotions) or displeasure (for the "negative" emotions).[22] Hence, on any plausible theory of the emotions, emotions will be tied in some way to desires through the connection between desires and pleasure (as discussed in chapters 5 and 6). Further, on some theories of emotion, emotions are in part constituted by desires.[23] One does not count as angry that P, according to such theories, unless P is desire-frustrating for one, and one does not feel *schadenfreude* if one has no intrinsic desire that anyone suffer, and so on for the various emotions. So there is every reason to hold that having a strong intrinsic desire regarding the right or the good will suffice to dispose ordinary, healthy human beings to the emotions we expect of virtuous people, and something similar is true of the emotions we expect of vicious people (even the relatively simple intrinsic desire that the Red Sox thrive causes the person who has it to have all manner of emotions that would not be there without it).

Beliefs, too, are beyond the realm of the will, and so are most other cognitive phenomena (save for deliberation, as discussed in chapters 1 and 2). Yet some of the differences between the virtuous, the vicious, and the ordinary person involve such phenomena. The virtuous person is presumably modest, suggesting that her beliefs about her abilities are constrained in certain ways. On the other hand, the vicious person, but not the virtuous person, is the sort to believe that people of African descent are stupid and that Jews are trying to control the world. We also expect, on some occasions at least, that the virtuous person,

---

[22] The only reasonable exception is emotionally neutral surprise—i.e., surprise that is neither delightful nor shocking. But if neutral surprise is an emotion, it is not one with an important role in the theory of the virtuous or vicious person—as opposed to delighted surprise and shocked surprise, both of which are obviously tied to virtue and vice in various circumstances. So the possible exception is not theoretically important.

[23] See, e.g., Green (1992).

other things being equal, will show a certain amount of wisdom or good sense with regards to moral matters. This wisdom is supposed to be more than the average person would have. The virtuous person, it might well be thought, is not just a person who does the right thing to the extent that she perceives it, but also someone who can perceive better than the rest of us what the right thing to do is. That too does not seem a matter of one's will.

Cognitions will be discussed in detail in the next chapter, and the discussion of belief will be postponed until then. However, it is not hard to see in a preliminary way how cognitions, too, can be manifestations of good or ill will. Intrinsic desires are most famous for their bad influences upon cognition, as in motivated irrationality. But there is room for a range of influences of desire upon thought, and not all of these influences will be pernicious. A strong intrinsic desire for the right or good can help one remember that one has a meeting with activists to support gay marriage: the intrinsic desire makes it easier to remember because we better remember the things we care more about. Desires can increase one's ability to learn, understand and simply *notice* morally relevant facts. In these and many other ways, the cognitive features we associate with virtue prove to be manifestations of good will, though not actions with good will as their rationalizing reason. There is also one very intimate relation between cognition and virtue that should be mentioned: to have good will, a person needs to have the concepts necessary for good will: concepts such as EQUALITY, HARM, PAIN, WELFARE, MAXIMIZATION, or whatever normative theory requires. And of course, possessing concepts is itself a cognitive state. But this is not a manifestation of good will so much as a precondition.

Merely content-efficacious expressions of desire in feelings and cognition are not necessitated by the content of the desire but often result from it given common facts about human nature, or the nature of an individual, in a way that seems close to necessary in context. For example, a strong intrinsic desire for the good of one's child typically results in worrying about the child on various occasions, often a little more than is epistemically warranted. Can one have the intrinsic desire but not worry, even when the child is believed to be confronted with possible trouble? It seems almost beyond the capacity of ordinary and healthy human beings, but in principle there is no barrier to a person (perhaps a nonhuman person) strongly desiring what is best for a child, and knowing the child faces possible trouble, without feeling worried. The relationship between the person of good will and her virtuous actions, emotions and cognitive features is like the relationship between the loving parent and worry.

The earlier discussion of the dispositions of the virtuous person has not been meant to be comprehensive, but there are some gaps that deserve further discussion. One that is particularly interesting is that everyone but the perfectly virtuous person is susceptible to moral imperfection. How does Spare Conativism's account of virtue leave room for imperfections in acting, feeling, and thinking virtuously?

It might be helpful to start with an analogous but nonmoral case. A person with an intrinsic desire to be wealthy is more likely than others, all else being equal, to act in ways that promote his becoming richer. He is also more likely to have negative emotions at the thought of money wasted, and is more likely to pay attention to expenses and think carefully about them. But while intrinsic desires for wealth are common, managing one's money in a way conducive to getting richer is less so, for many reasons. Sometimes it is simply because the person has other intrinsic desires that motivate him more. A person whose desire for wealth is only of average strength might give up a great deal of wealth for the wellbeing of his child or for a long-distance romantic relationship. On other occasions there is irrationality. A person with a strong intrinsic desire for wealth can be influenced by physical and merely content efficacious factors in such a way as to perform irrational actions, as when endless advertising or unreflective adherence to social convention leads him to buy a new car when not doing so would make him wealthier without damaging him in any obvious way. Similarly, loving wealth does not guarantee the corresponding feelings or thoughts one might expect. The same advertising that results in the wealth-lover's buying a new car can result in his feeling warm all over when he makes the purchase (he might even *feel* richer while driving away poorer in a splendidly appointed sedan), and common cognitive fallacies might lead him to fail to grasp the cost of things (as when he pays too much for furniture because the prices pale in comparison to the price of the house he is buying and filling with that furniture).

Suppose now that Suji is a person with a great deal of good will. For her, that the right or good be done is something that she intrinsically desires very much. Does it follow that she will never tell a lie when doing so is wrong or bad? It does not. Does it follow that she will at least feel bad about such a lie, or feel good about telling the truth instead of lying? Again, it does not. All Suji's strong intrinsic desire guarantees is that she will be more likely than others with weaker intrinsic desires for the right or good to act, think, and feel in the ways that we would find characteristic of a good person, all else being equal. The fairly virtuous person can also bend to other priorities and must always contend with the possibility of irrationality.

First, consider whether Suji might knowingly tell a lie that is wrongful or bad. Even with a strong intrinsic desire that what is right or good be done, it is possible that she would tell such a lie under a number of circumstances. She might tell it irrationally, that is, while having stronger rationalizing reasons to tell the truth. She might be influenced by mere content-efficacious factors, or merely physical factors, in addition to whatever weak rationalization she might have for telling the lie, and end up lying. Perhaps she has resolved to tell a friend a painful truth that might dissolve the friendship, but she has also been watching a lot of lighthearted romantic comedies in which secrets and lies lead first to comic situations and ultimately to everyone's ending up with what they really wanted or needed all along. Though Suji knows these movies are not realistic, when the chance comes to reveal the truth to her friend, Suji fails to act because the idea (not believed, but still vivid) that everything might work out better through a lie is influential upon her. She might also tell the same lie in a way that is rationalized (assuming this is possible; we set aside meta-ethical questions about the possibility of rationalizing reasons for immorality here) by her intrinsically desiring to preserve her friendship, and being aware that doing what is right or good is likely to frustrate this other desire, which is even stronger than her good will. It might even be that Suji's intrinsic desire that what is right or good be done is stronger than her intrinsic desire that the given friendship exist, but Suji sees (correctly) that the harm done to the right or good by lying in this case, while real, is likely to be rather minor, while the harm done to the friendship by the truth in this case is likely to be enormous, and this trade-off rationalizes lying for her, in spite of her good will.

Second, consider how Suji might feel. Even with her considerable good will, Suji need not feel anything but sadness and fear as she tells the truth. It might be, for instance, that Suji's gut-level prediction is that she will normally tell the truth, even when it is difficult. She takes it for granted, in other words, that she will generally do the right thing in these circumstances. Since her feelings reflect deviations from such predicted states of affairs, telling the truth is unlikely to contribute anything to making her feel good. At the same time, telling the truth is risking a friendship Suji very much wants to maintain. That is something she is not accustomed to, if she is like most of us, because most people are not hardened to routinely losing their good friends. So the threat of a great loss is likely to make her feel sad or fearful, without being ameliorated by any delight over doing what is right but utterly expected (by her, of herself). If Suji's desire is less an appetite for the right or good and more an aversion to the wrong or bad, that might affect her feelings as well. Rather than typically feeling energized by opportunities to do what is right or good, an aversion will more typically leave her feeling inhibited at the idea of doing what is wrong or bad (which perhaps is a characteristic feeling when one has a sense of duty). And that pattern might apply to the present case, with Suji not feeling any delight at the prospect of telling the painful truth. Suji might be less rationally influenced as well: she might not be vividly conceptualizing her action as nobly bowing to her moral duty, and thinking of her action mainly in terms of its potentially sad consequences for the friendship. Under these conditions, the factors that might potentially help a person of great good will feel better about what she is doing are less vividly represented, and so less causally efficacious, than they could be, though the vividness of a representation of the facts does not itself change the facts that justify the representations, and so the feelings they warrant.

As for cognitive effects, any clarity Suji possess on moral matters can be impaired if she is, at the time of the potential lie, worried about losing her job, say, or befuddled by complete physical exhaustion.

Given the complexity of the way the reward system makes its calculations, and so of the way that intrinsic desires have their effects within us, there is room for many more ways in which Suji's acts or feelings (or thoughts) might not reflect her strong intrinsic desire for the right or good, even though it is genuinely there. The foregoing, for all its little details, is just the tip of the iceberg in this regard.

One thing desires cannot be expected to generate is a correct set of beliefs about what is right or good: general moral knowledge, in other words. And from Socrates on, many philosophers have thought that such knowledge was a key (perhaps *the* key) component of virtue. This too should receive some discussion.

An argument against the idea that virtue requires general moral knowledge has already been made possible by the arguments in the previous chapter.[24] There it was shown that general moral knowledge is not necessary for good will, or for acting in a praiseworthy manner, because having an intrinsic desire involving the concepts RIGHT, GOOD, REASONABLE, or their like is not necessary for having good will or acting in a praiseworthy manner—and if one's desires do not require these contents, then there is no need for the corresponding beliefs. A person raised to care about suffering and dignity and truthfulness and so on without ever being taught the concepts RIGHT or GOOD, or REASONABLE could see that someone was suffering needlessly and be moved to act out of kindness, could see that he had diminished someone's dignity and so feel the impulse to apologize and compensate for the act, could see that others had lied merely in order to enrich themselves and so feel saddened by their conduct and resolved to intervene to prevent its recurrence. He could, in short, do, feel, and think the right things for the right reasons, could be praiseworthy for acting well, and be fully possessed of all the virtues. Adding the concept RIGHT or GOOD or REASONABLE would not enhance his virtue. And if he does not even need the concepts to be virtuous, he certainly does not need the true beliefs one might form using these concepts. Admittedly, having the right beliefs can help a person indirectly when he wants to make himself more virtuous. The person who has the right moral theory is likely to act more wisely when he sets out to make himself more virtuous, as he would know his virtues from his vices. The person who has the wrong moral theory is in danger of being corrupted by it, as explained in the previous chapter. However, adding true ethical beliefs to a person's mind does not in itself make him more virtuous: it only makes him a better ethicist.

---

[24] And see also Arpaly (2003).

8.4 Virtue and Involuntary Attitudes: Two Alternative Views

According to Spare Conativism, stable emotions and other stable involuntary attitudes can be virtuous or vicious because involuntary attitudes, just like voluntary acts, can be manifestations of good will, ill will, moral indifference, and reverse moral indifference. One is never blameworthy or praiseworthy for such attitudes because they are not actions—they are not *rationalized* by good or ill will—but one is virtuous or vicious in having them. Other theorists have other explanations as to why people can be morally laudable or condemnable for nonvoluntary attitudes, however, and these need to be considered.

Thomas Scanlon holds that we can be laudable or condemnable for what he calls "judgment sensitive attitudes"—attitudes that reflect our judgments.[25] Angela Smith picks up the thread and provides a theory according to which we are responsible (and so, presumably, praise- or blameworthy) for an attitude if and only if the attitude reflects our judgment(s).[26] For an attitude to reflect a judgment, she says, is for it to be the case that if one has the judgment, the attitude should occur, where the "should" is the "should" of rationality. And Pamela Hieronymi offers a view in the same family, albeit with an unusual picture of our judgments.[27] The attitudes for which we are responsible, she says, embody our answers to important questions, our "take" on the world. An attitude that embodies our answer to a question can only be created or revised for reasons one takes to bear on the relevant question. We agree with Scanlon, Smith and Hieronymi about the feelings and cognitive attitudes that are virtuous or vicious, but not about why. The key difference is that Smith and Hieronymi's world is completely free of desires, and desires in Scanlon's world are cognitive attitudes rather than the noncognitive attitudes Spare Conativism takes them to be.

In developing her view, Smith goes as far as to say that the attitudes of interest follow so tightly from our judgments that if you have the judgment you would be irrational for not having the attitude as well. She draws an analogy between morally relevant emotions and the emotion of fear. She thinks that not only is it true that fear (usually) reflects our judgment that something is dangerous but that if one thinks that bulldogs are dangerous, one would be irrational not to fear them. Similarly, it is irrational not to feel guilt when you judge yourself to be guilty or otherwise make a morally relevant judgment without also having the emotion associated with it.

---

[25] Scanlon (1998) Sometimes he talks as if we are morally responsible for these attitudes and sometimes as if we are not necessarily responsible for them but they confer praise- or blameworthiness on actions that reflect them.
[26] Smith (2005).
[27] Hieronymi (2008).

One problem with this view lies with the fact that sometimes we praise or condemn someone because of involuntary attitudes that are not reason-responsive.
Consider a type of case that Smith mentions: the case of forgetfulness, as
occurs when someone misses a friend's birthday. Smith and we agree that one
is in principle legitimately criticized for such an omission. But can something
like forgetfulness ever develop, spontaneously, for a reason? Can it have logical
relations to our judgments, or to anything else? Forgetting is not an action, and
so does not happen in response to a practical reason. If Consuela forgets something because it is unimportant to her, the "because" is not there to signify a
practical reason, unless Consuela somehow *made* herself forget, but that is not
so in the forgotten birthday case. If one cannot forget for practical reasons, can
one forget for epistemic reasons? Forgetfulness, when complete, entails ceasing
to believe, and one can cease to believe for epistemic reasons. But this is not
what happens when a person forgets a friend's birthday; if Consuela forgets a
birthday, it is not that her beliefs are changing to reflect her lack of evidence for
the birthday's falling on the particular date. Our story is simple: strongly desiring the good of another person makes us better at remembering things about
her (and learning them in the first place), through content-efficacious but not
reason-responsive processes.[28] If we are not good at remembering these things,
despite having a perfectly good memory for other things, it can be a sign that
we do not much care about the person in question. The forgetfulness does not
embody or reflect our indifference in any sense more complicated than being
caused by that indifference in a content-sensitive manner.

This makes us wonder about Smith's more central cases. Grant Smith that
feeling fearful has something to do with the judgment that something is dangerous: in a typical mentally healthy person, revising the judgment that bulldogs are dangerous causes a lessening in fear of them. But is it true that if one
believes that bulldogs are dangerous, one *rationally should* fear them? Is there
something wrong, as far as rationality is concerned, with the particularly calm
person who is hard to scare and who believes dispassionately (albeit wrongly)
that bulldogs are dangerous? As far as the "should" of rationality goes, the
actual fear of bulldogs is, as it were, optional. Fear might be to a significant
extent a judgment about danger, but it is also made up of other things, things
that happen when the judgment makes contact with facts of human nature and
the nature of particular individuals. Fear as we know it includes some desire to
avoid the danger (if it does not matter to you whether or not you fail an exam,
the exam holds no fear for you). It also includes such features as increased heart
rate and shortness of breath. A creature who does not have a heart and does
not breathe and so on might not be able to feel what we call "fear," even if it
has both the judgment that the bulldog before him is dangerous and the desire

---

[28] The content-efficacy here makes the difference between forgetting from indifference and
forgetting from, say, dementia.

to avoid danger. There will be nothing irrational about that creature. Nor is it irrational for a person to be hardened to fear, as in the case of a person who, having lived through war and political imprisonment, can now face a genuinely dangerous bulldog with equanimity. Of course, it might be true that if we are talking about an ordinary human being, there is something wrong in some situations if fear is absent: if we are discussing a human being who is generally susceptible to fear the absence of fear on a particular occasion might make us suspect—or even be sure—that he did not fully accept the judgment that there is a danger. That would be a matter not of following the "should" of rationality but of taking human nature into account when judging a human being.

We have offered our own answer to the question of how attitudes can be justifiably lauded or criticized: they are virtuous or vicious in accordance with the quality of will that manifests itself in them. In contrast with both our view and the view embraced by Smith (and Scanlon, and Hieronymi), Gideon Rosen has argued that involuntary attitudes such as emotions are only laudable or condemnable insofar as they reflect good or bad voluntary actions on the part of the person lauded or condemned. According to Rosen, if someone provokes anger by enjoying human suffering the problem is that there are steps he could have taken, or could now be taking, to "manage" his sadism, and he did not take or is not taking these steps. If the sadist is doing the best he can and remains a sadist then the reasonable attitude to take is to exonerate him.[29]

Rosen treats the sadist the way it would be uncontroversial to treat a person with Tourette's syndrome. Suppose Yossi is Tourettic and suffers from involuntary coprolalia, meaning that he involuntarily curses and spouts obscenities in inappropriate contexts. Imagine also that Yossi's syndrome is (atypically) easy to treat: all he needs to do is take some pills, with no side effects to speak of, and this is enough to effect a complete remission of his symptoms for a day. If Yossi were to offend us by uttering obscenities we would disapprove of Yossi's behavior, but what we would condemn would not be his swearing itself but his failure to take his pills. Something similar would be true if, while not treatable at present, it were true that Yossi had once had an opportunity to undergo a one-time, easy course of treatment that would have prevented him from later developing the syndrome, to which he knew he was prone. If Yossi would offend people now, his guilt would lie in not having taken that step when it was still available to him.

We (and most others, we suspect) do not think ordinary sadists are best thought of as analogous to Yossi, however. If Ron is a sadistic sort of person, who takes pleasure in making the weak squirm through his little remarks and ingenious machinations in the office, and also enjoys seeing others do the same to the same sort of vulnerable, ineffectual people, we condemn Ron for enjoying

---

[29] Rosen (2004).

suffering without giving thought to his possible history of remedial efforts. We do not think that the trouble with Ron is that he is negligent—that he is failing to work through an anger-management workbook assiduously enough, or that he failed to take some metaphorical or real pills as a cruel youth—but rather that the trouble with Ron is that he is sadistic. His sadism is not a symptom of a past or present bad act, but a direct target of evaluation.

If Ron would decide to stop being such a petty sadist, and do so for moral reasons, the people who know him would mostly be happy to discover that he is not all bad, and praise him for trying to make himself a better person. But consider the idea of trying to be a better person: implicit in it is the idea that it is being a sadist—being a bad person in respect of his attitudes toward the suffering of other people—that people condemn. It is not, for instance, having made a bad decision to tease a vulnerable child back in grade 1, a decision that set off an unfortunate train of events leading to his present sadism, that is the focus of moral condemnation. And if Ron succeeds, people will say he became a better person than he was, suggesting just the same conclusion. If Ron makes an effort that fails—and it is important to remember here that successful voluntary changes of character are about as rare as successful new year's resolutions—he is still a cruel person, and will hardly be judged the equivalent of the Tourettic person for whom effective medication cannot be found. Rosalind Hursthouse has defended a similar line of thought about not sadism but racism.[30]

Rosen's approach to characters like Ron is no more convincing on less dramatic cases. Smith's birthday forgetter is not off the hook if she proves that she did all she could to remember—wrote the date down, repeated it to herself—and still forgot the birthday. Unless the reason for the forgetting is pure cognitive incapacity, the fact that she cannot remember the birthday even after making an excellent effort to do so appears to make it worse. It suggests that she really does not care at all about the person whose birthday is forgotten, and *that* is just what makes the forgetting so objectionable.

Rosen might answer by saying that someone like Ron, or the friend who forgets the birthday, has a *character defect* but is not *blameworthy* for his enjoyment of people's suffering. Technically we would agree, as we regard blameworthiness as a property people have for particular actions. Feelings, cognitions, and other mental attitudes (and events) are best thought of as virtuous or vicious rather than praise- or blameworthy. But saying that someone has a character defect—a vice—is just as much as a condemnation as saying that he is blameworthy. Hence this possible response does not put any particular pressure on the position of Spare Conativism.

---

[30] Hursthouse (1999).

8.5 Virtuous Irrationality

When the stakes are high we sometimes get emotionally engaged in a way that can breed irrationality. We mentioned, for example, that caring appropriately about one's child's wellbeing induces in many people mild irrationalities involving excessive worry. Such irrationalities are generally a manifestation of caring enough, not caring too much. Human beings are not so well designed by natural selection that they are capable of caring deeply without threat of unfortunate side-effects, it turns out. When the thing that we care about is the right or good, parallel irrationalities can be expected. And it will be worthwhile to show in some detail that such irrationalities do not impugn claims to virtue.

Consider a familiar case. Sean hits someone with his car, and the person who is hit dies. All the evidence shows that the accident was not his fault, and Sean is assured of this by his friends, by the police, and by the insurance companies. He agrees. However, Sean feels tremendous guilt,[31] has trouble sleeping, and cannot stop thinking about the accident. Sean's friends tell him to calm down, to sleep better, that it's not his fault, and so on: they recognize that he is being irrational. But they would have been terribly appalled if Sean had walked away from the scene of the accident still eager to see the funny movie he had been on his way to view with his friends, if he had slept soundly that night and awoken with nothing but a hearty breakfast on his mind, and so on. The irrational guilt is seen by Sean's friends as a manifestation of Sean's decency—of his being a person who cares about the right things to the right degree.

Susan Wolf has argued that there is a nameless virtue that consists of someone's taking a sort of responsibility for the consequences of her actions in the world.[32] If a person's nonculpable clumsiness resulted in her breaking someone's vase, the virtuous thing for her to do, even if her nonculpability is evident to everyone, would be to pay the bill. In addition to paying bills, we also owe people such things as apologies—and, Wolf says, guilt. On Wolf's view, someone like Sean might, despite his innocence, owe some compensation to the family of the accident's victim, and he also "owes" some guilt.

The idea that Sean owes guilt is puzzling. To compensate is an action, and to apologize is an action, and so it is clear enough how compensations or apologies

---

[31] Some would say that what Sean is feeling cannot be guilt, but has to be agent regret; we disagree. While it is true that paradigmatically guilt comes with a full blown belief that one has done wrong, guilt felt irrationally can persist even if one's avowed belief is that one did no wrong, in the same way that fear of flying can persist even if one's avowed belief is that flying is not dangerous. Furthermore, as noticed by Williams, even agent regret does not seem strictly speaking warranted: as we said earlier, Sean did all he could, and therefore is *deserving* of no kind of regret at all. We think there is no reason to doubt that an agent in Sean's place often feels guilt, but if you think only agent regret can be felt in this way you can continue to follow our argument substituting "agent regret" for "guilt."

[32] Wolf (2001).

might be owed. They might be actions that are right or good according to the correct normative theory of morality. Guilt, however, is a feeling. There cannot be a duty to feel guilty, or to feel anything else—or so it seems. To accept that there are duties to feel things would be to invite a type of infinite-escalation problem in which a person fails to feel guilt, and so fails to do his duty by feeling guilt. And then, since the person fails to feel guilt, he seemingly makes it true that he has done something wrong by not feeling guilt, and so has a further obligation to feel guilt at his lack of guilt. But, not having felt first-order guilt, he seems unlikely to feel second-order guilt either, and so he seems likely to break this second-order obligation, and so the wrongdoing and the lack of guilt over wrongdoing mounts up. The first failure to feel guilt seems likely to ramify into an unlimited number of distinct moral wrongs.

Even if one can have duties only to perform actions, one can have a duty to try to induce guilt in oneself, or, more realistically, fan whatever embers of guilty feeling she might have until she is appropriately tormented. But first of all, notice that there exists an Aristotelian structure here: while it is desirable to drum up guilt if one do not feel enough, the most praiseworthy agent does not need to drum up her guilt: she just feels it. There is already something wrong in an ordinary, healthy human being if, after killing someone accidentally, she needs to make a voluntary effort in order to feel appropriately bad. And then, these guilt-fanning actions have a somewhat obscure relation to moral duty. As a person who wishes to limit the damage he produces in the world, Sean can, if the situation is right, improve the lot of the victim's family by offering material compensation or by expressing regret, but what good are Sean's sleepless nights or emotional struggles going to do for them or anyone else? Conversely, if the family of the deceased are unlikely to witness his state, it does not change the fact that if his state is cheery, something is fishy about Sean.

If Sean were not to feel unwarranted guilt, one of two explanations would most likely hold. One would be that Sean is an incredibly, incredibly well-balanced person, with moral insight so precise that he never feels more than exactly the amount of guilt proportional to the blame he deserves and *never* feels guilt when agent regret is all that is appropriate (such a person would probably also be immune to any fear that is not proportional to the risk involved, any admiration that is out of proportion to the scale of the task, and so on—to be astonishingly well-balanced in his emotional life, that is). The other likely explanation for Sean's lack of guilt would be that he is simply not concerned enough with what happened. His desire to avoid causing needless harm (or whatever other intrinsic desire is relevant here) is not strong enough to bring about the sort of irrationality that usually occurs to people when such dramatic events transpire. Between these two explanations—hyper-rationality and moral coldness—that of moral coldness seems much more likely, and so it is right to find moral fault with Sean if he is unmoved by the death of the person he struck with his car.

What if Sean *were* a perfectly well-balanced person? We would have to suppress our first impressions—as one would have to do many times with an artificially intelligent robot or alien or other creature with similarly surprising emotional dispositions—and remind ourselves that in Sean's case, feeling precisely what is warranted and not one bit more is not a sign of indifference at all. If Sean experiences a nervous collapse during the days after the accident, his reaction is a manifestation (content-efficacious, but not reason-responsive) of virtue typical of an average human being—but we see no reason to hold that it is more than this.[33]

There is virtuous irrationality, in the sense that irrationality can manifest good will, but if a person is disposed to be much more nervous than average whenever the moral stakes are high, shall we regard this stable mental state as a virtue? For ordinary human beings the answer is "no." The fact that a person is more nervous than other people when the moral stakes are high does not manifest unusual amounts of good will but rather an unusually nervous temperament. This is more or less the case with people whose obsessive-compulsive disorder takes the form of "scrupulosity"—excessive worry as to whether or not they have done something morally wrong. These people have a disorder that in many others cases (and, often enough, in their own cases) causes obsessive worry about germs and about whether or not the door is unlocked. As will be discussed in the next chapter, a person who checks the door many times does not care about her property more than a person who does not check the door many times. Similarly, a person who checks her environment hundreds of times to see if she hit someone with her car is not thereby more morally concerned than a person who, due to a healthy brain, does not need to check such things more than is reasonable. This is attested to by the fact that heroes and saints, the people who display readiness to die for great moral causes and whom we hold up as moral exemplars, do not generally suffer from these neuroses.

8.6 The Unity of the Virtues

If virtue is good will, does it follow that there is necessarily only one complete virtue, namely, the virtue of intrinsically desiring the right or good, correctly conceived? Not, of course, if W.D. Ross or other pluralists are right about the right and the good. But suppose that Millian utilitarianism or Kantian deontology is the correct theory of morality. Then it would seem that, although there will be many partial virtues, there will be only one complete virtue. If Mill

---

[33] The existence of virtuous irrationality also tells further against Angela Smith's view that attitudes are laudable or condemnable only because of their logical relations with our judgments. In Sean's case there is no logical relation between his guilt and his judgment regarding what he has done, and yet it appears to be a manifestation of ordinary virtue.

is right, the sole complete virtue will be beneficence (intrinsically desiring maximal happiness); if Kant is right, the sole complete virtue will be respectfulness (intrinsically desiring that one now be respectful, roughly).

There might be no problem here at all. Perhaps those philosophers inclined to Millianism or Kantianism in their normative theorizing find nothing odd in imagining that there is just one complete virtue. But then again, there might be a real problem. For it has seemed to many virtue theorists, from Aristotle on, that there are many virtues, and that there is no one master virtue.[34] Courage, temperance, generosity, mildness, fairness—the virtue tradition has long held that each of these virtues and many others besides have an independent existence. Courage is not just a (transparently necessary) instance of generosity, fairness, or what have you, according to this tradition, and similarly for the many other virtues. We take this possible problem seriously.

A first line of response is to emphasize that it is an open question whether there is just one complete virtue or many, and that it is appropriate that this question be settled by the work of normative ethicists. It is possible that the right or good is a complicated, hybrid thing, closer to Frances Kamm's vision of it than Mill's, and thus that a long list of independent complete virtues is just what one should expect.[35] If there is a tension between Mill or Kant, as normative theorists, and Aristotle or Hume, as virtue theorists, this might well be because there is a straightforward tension between the former and the latter over just how unified or pluralistic the right or the good in fact is.

A second line of response is to point out that there is a weaker sense in which the Kantian or the Millian may hold to the plurality of the virtues, even virtues that are not merely partial virtues, derived from their relationship to some master virtue. The Kantian may, like Kant himself, say that we have a duty to develop in ourselves a cluster of inclinations that together will make us more likely to act in accordance with duty.[36] The utilitarian may, in a manner suggestive of Robert Adams or Julia Driver, defend what is sometimes called "character utilitarianism."[37] This is the view that we should develop certain types of character traits that would increase utility, either because those who have such traits will be inclined to do utility-increasing things, or because the very existence of such traits boosts utility. Both of these are approaches to virtue in a weaker sense because the so-called virtues in question are neither forms of good will nor manifestations of it. But there would still be something

---

[34] In book five of *Nicomachean Ethics*, Aristotle says that "justice" is sometimes used to name all the virtues, but not because justice, narrowly understood, is a principle from which all virtues can be derived.

[35] See Kamm (2006).

[36] See, for example, Part II of the *Metaphysics of Morals* (Kant 1991).

[37] Driver (2001) prefers the term "consequentialist" to "utilitarian" when describing her views. Adams (1976) calls the view he explores "motive utilitarianism."

to the idea that these are traits that it is good to cultivate in oneself and in one's children, and so to the idea that these traits are in some sense virtues.[38]

This second line of response is not, however, much of a response to the original concern. While a weakened sense of "virtue" might allow for a plurality of virtues so understood, it will not help to answer worries about the commitment of Millianism or Kantianism to the unity of the virtues; true virtues are more than character traits that incidentally promote acting in a morally desirable way. Virtues are such that the person who acts out of a virtue is praiseworthy when her action manifests virtue, and the virtuous agent's motives are such that she acts for the right reasons (this is true for Aristotelian virtues, at least, and it is a roughly Aristotelian notion of virtue that gives rise to the worry about unity in the first place). As a result, however interesting weak-sense virtues might be, they cannot solve a problem that was raised specifically for strong-sense virtues, and worries about unity are worries for strong-sense virtues. If the goal is to head off an unwanted commitment to the unity of the virtues, it will not help to head off commitment to a weaker thesis than the one at stake.

So perhaps SC finds itself committed to the thesis that, if (for example) Millian consequentialism or Kantian deontology is the correct normative theory, then there will be just one complete virtue. What should we make of this?

Views and intuitions about moral worth and virtue interact in various ways with views and intuitions about normative ethics. On the one hand, a view of normative ethics—say, utilitarianism—can give birth to a view of moral worth and virtue—say, the worthy person is concerned with happiness (such that virtue is ultimately the same as a strong intrinsic desire for greater happiness). But things can happen the other way around, with intuitions about moral worth giving rise to intuitions about normative ethics. For example, one powerful reason to reject ethical egoism as a normative theory of morality is that, when we imagine the person for whom his own self-interest is his main concern, we do not imagine a morally attractive person, a person whom we would be inclined to say acts for the right reasons or exemplifies virtue. The fact that selfishness does not appear virtuous is evidence that ethical egoism is an incorrect normative theory. Similarly, if there appear to be many virtues, it might be a sign that a more pluralistic view of the right or good is called for. Not just any plurality of virtues suggests that a pluralistic view of the right or good is called for, of course. As we saw earlier, a plurality of virtues that are constituted by strong but partial good will are compatible with there being just one thing that is fundamentally right or good in itself. With that caveat in place, however, it can be noted that the possibility is open that there will be apparent virtues, such as courage, temperance, generosity, or fairness, that cannot be given adequate

---

[38] We should also acknowledge the efforts of a number of Kantian theorists to develop theories of virtue in a stronger sense than that just discussed. See, for example, Korsgaard (2008), Louden (1986), Sherman (1997).

theories by reference to a single given right- or good-making feature of the world. And to the extent that such apparent virtues resist such theorizing, while nonetheless continuing to appear to be virtues, there is evidence that a more pluralistic normative theory of morality is required. In short, if there is a deep conflict between apparently correct normative theory and apparently correct moral psychology, it might be the case that the moral psychology should act as a corrective to the normative theory.

If virtues do hold separate this way, requiring the existence of irreducible distinct moral rights or goods, there is no need to jump to more radical conclusions. In particular, the conclusion that ethical particularism is true does not follow.[39] That a correct normative theory of morality cannot be stated with one simple formula such as the principle of utility or the categorical imperative is no reason to assume that there are no generalizations to make in the normative domain. The normative facts could prove to be systematic but complexly tangled: perhaps a hundred sentences are required to sum them up perspicaciously, or perhaps they are as complicated as the Basque auxiliary verb (although it is extremely regular, it has hundreds of forms).

Even absent the radical leap to ethical particularism, there might be a number of surprises in store for normative ethical theory as the nature of the virtues is investigated further. That seems a radical enough thesis for the moment.

---

[39] A clear statement of ethical particularism is found in Dancy (1983).

{ 9 }

Virtue and Cognition

The virtuous person has good will and lacks ill will. She has a strong intrinsic desire that people not suffer, or she greatly intrinsically desires that people receive in proportion to their contributions, or she intrinsically desires whatever else is right or good. But virtue is more complex than being motivated by suffering or injustice. It has a cognitive side.

Consider the kind person. She is more inclined to prevent suffering than most of us, and that is an obvious manifestation of her desire that people not suffer. She is also more inclined to feel bad about the suffering of others, and that too is an obvious manifestation of her good will. But the kind person is also going to have thoughts that are different from others' thoughts.[1] The kind person will be more likely to notice suffering: it captures her attention. The kind person will be more likely to remember that the person she met three months ago was struggling to come to terms with her brother's death: it sticks in her memory. The kind person is more likely than others to see an angry man's outburst as a product of his feeling threatened or humiliated: it seems plausible to her. And in many other ways, the kind person's cognitive life will be different from the cognitive life of the less-kind person.

Consider also the open-minded person. She might have been raised with the idea that homosexuals are degenerates, but even so she is able to see that there is nothing degenerate about her homosexual labmate. She might dislike the fashion for wearing baseball caps backwards, but she is nonetheless able to see that several such backward-capped students in her class are very talented. The open-minded person is the opposite of the prejudiced person, in other words, in her cognitive life.

How can the open-minded person have a moral virtue, if open-mindedness is a matter of good beliefs, not good will? And how can prejudice be a vice?[2] How can the kind person's patterns of attention, recollection, and interpretation be manifestations of her kindness, when these are all matters of good cognitions, not good will? And how could their absences be manifestations of vice?

---

[1] Hursthouse (1999, 115) paints a compelling portrait of the sorts of thoughts the racist has that distinguish her from the nonracist.

[2] It is easy to see how the open-minded person might have a purely epistemic virtue, if there are such things. But an epistemic virtue is not automatically a moral virtue. See Aristotle (1999), Sosa (2007) for theories of purely epistemic virtue.

Some philosophers hold that believing and other forms of cognizing are actions.[3] If these philosophers are right, then there is no puzzle here. Just as a person of good will might act to relieve suffering or right injustice, a person of good will might also form a generous interpretation of someone's angry outburst, or refuse to believe that a polite labmate is nonetheless a degenerate human being. The connection between good will and virtuous cognitions would be as straightforward as—would be the *same* as—the connection between good will and virtuous deeds. However, we do not think this cognitive voluntarism is correct. Believing is a state that can be causally induced by our actions, sometimes: in the simplest case, reading the newspaper is an action that can induce new beliefs. In itself, though, believing is no more an action than having a sunburn is an action: a person can induce a sunburn or a belief, and this induction of a state can be an action, but believing, like being sunburned, is never an action itself. So, at least, it seems to us.[4]

Because we are not cognitive voluntarists of any sort, the facts about the thoughts of the kind person and the open-minded person are facts that require a more complex explanation than facts about her actions. Virtue is a matter of having good will and lacking ill will, and vice is a matter of having ill will and lacking good will. If cognitions are not actions, then it must be explained how cognitions can be manifestations of good or ill will, and—supposing that open-mindedness is a moral virtue—it must be explained how there can be wholly cognitive moral virtues when being virtuous is just a matter of good will.

The strategy of this chapter is to explain the cognitive side of virtue as a content-efficacious but not rationalized manifestation of the good will that constitutes virtue. For the strategy to be as believable as possible in the moral case, it will be useful to begin with what is known about the manifestation of desire in cognition in the nonmoral case. This is our first topic for this chapter.

9.1 Familiar Cognitive Effects of Desire

The most obvious way in which desires influence cognition has to be through deliberation. Trying to determine what to think or do is an action that uses cognitive means (calling to mind images and ideas) to achieve its ends, and the ends of deliberation are themselves often or always cognitive. However, deliberation is not an example of the phenomenon that concerns us. Deliberation is a kind of action, and so there is no mystery to how it could be a manifestation of a desire. A person who has a strong intrinsic desire that people not suffer, for

---

[3] We are not familiar with any philosopher who holds the very strongest form of this view, but the idea that believing is a nonbasic action is defended in Steup (1988), for example.

[4] There is more to the argument, of course. For arguments in favor of doxastic voluntarism, see Steup (1988; 2008).

instance, is a person who will have a motive to deliberate when given a complex opportunity to relieve suffering (selecting a charity to which to donate can be like this). This is just as straightforward a manifestation of a desire that people not suffer as the act of donating to the charity itself.[5]

Also outside the scope of present interest is shifting the focus of attention, when this shifting is an action. Just as one can fulfill a request to deliberate about where to have supper, so too can one fulfill a request to pay attention to the next scene in a movie—or anything else in front of one. Shifts in attention are often involuntary, and such shifts will receive discussion in a moment. However, many other shifts in attention are voluntary. Though an interesting and important cognitive phenomenon, voluntarily shifting one's attention for some purpose is a manifestation of one's desires because it is an action, and so needs no further discussion here.

With voluntarily enacted cognitions excluded, there remain at least four important ways in which desires, through their contents, have effects on cognitive states even though the cognitive states affected are *not* actions, and do so without intermediating actions. These are (1) through involuntary shifts in attention, (2) through changing dispositions to learn and recall, (3) through changes in subjective confidence, and (4) through distortion by emotions and wishes. A little should be said about each in the nonmoral context, to remind the reader of just how standard these phenomena are.

The first phenomenon is the influence desires have on nonvoluntary shifts in attention. In addition to voluntary direction of attention, it is obvious that sometimes attention is directed in a manner that is not an action: rapid, nearby motion on the periphery of one's vision is typically something that grabs one's attention regardless of what one wants, and the cries of a young child are likewise almost impossible to ignore. This nonvoluntary shifting of a person's attention can be controlled by low-level properties of the stimulus (as with motion in peripheral vision), but it seems that it can also be controlled by high-level unconscious processing that represents something of interest to a person: something bearing on what a person has strong desires about.[6]

Some examples will give a sense of the phenomena we have in mind. If Christina has a passion for owls then she will be more likely than other people (all else being equal) to notice an owl's hoot, or to notice that the word "knowledge" has the string "owl" in its center. If she is in a coffee shop reading a book,

---

[5] Of course, because it is typically a less costly manifestation of good will, deliberation is typically also a less praiseworthy manifestation of good will than actually donating one's labor or money.

[6] The most famous psychological study in this regard is that performed by Neville Moray, showing that people who are paying very close attention to what they are hearing in one ear can nonetheless have their attentions captured by the sound of their own names being spoken in their other ear, while otherwise successfully ignoring everything heard in the second ear (the "cocktail party effect"). See Moray (1959).

she is more likely than others to have her attention snap from her book to the two people behind her talking about seeing an owl while hiking. And so on. Likewise, if Amanda has a passion for cars, she is more likely than other people to notice the makes and model of cars whenever she sees them. In a coffee shop, she might not find her attention wandering to a conversation about owls, but her ears will be more likely than others' to prick up when the conversation turns to restoring a 1972 Dodge Charger.

In these cases, in addition to desires shaping what captures attention, desires also shape what people end up believing. Shifts in attention can lead to the formation of reasonable beliefs that, although available (in principle) to others in the same physical circumstances, are nonetheless unlikely to be formed by others owing to their failure to attend. Christina will leave the coffee shop believing that there are owls to be seen on a nearby trail; Amanda will leave the coffee shop believing that a local person owns a vintage muscle car; a third person might leave with neither belief, even after having been equally well positioned to form both, because the third person's attention was not captured by the background conversation that "popped out" for Christina or Amanda.

Under some conditions, what makes a person better at noticing things can also make her "notice" things that are not there: the epistemic effects of our concerns on our attention are not all positive. A philosopher who thinks a great deal about causation is more likely than others to have his attention drawn to newspaper articles using the words "casual" and "Human," with the philosopher initially misreading them as "causal" and "Humean." The man who is feeling particularly sexual might have his attention caught by a pretty woman looking at him, only to realize that she is merely looking at someone in his general vicinity. And so on. So it should be noted that these effects of desire upon attention are not wholly beneficial.

Second on our list is the fact that intrinsic desires can also affect our ability to learn. What bears on that with which we are concerned is also something about which we retain knowledge more easily. For most of us, it is, all else being equal, easier to learn about a topic we love than one we do not, and easier to learn about a topic of importance for someone or something we love than to learn about a topic of no such importance. Perhaps Amanda remembers the years during which the classic Dodge Chargers were built after reading about their production history, while not remembering the dates of the 30-Years War after reading her high school history text.

There seem to be at least two explanations for how intrinsic desires affect learning, and so belief-retention, in this way. For one thing, people are diligent in doing what it takes to learn about topics that matter to them: we do our homework, and even extra homework, when the topic is important to us. This is a straightforward matter of acting for a reason, though: doing extra homework will help a person remember anything better, even the dates of the 30-Years War, and it is no surprise that a person who cares about a subject has desires that are satisfied by making sure that he retains knowledge about it, and so does what it takes to retain that knowledge.

More interesting is the apparent fact that memory works in our favor when we set ourselves to learn something that bears on our concerns. If one is really interested in the Enron financial scandal but is not interested in Rome, one can do comparable homework with equal diligence for a class about Rome and a class about Enron, yet remember a list of facts about Enron better than an otherwise similar list of facts about Rome. The facts about the famous financial scandal somehow seem to stick with one much more readily, one finds. So it goes, when one really wants to know. Outside of the classroom, similar principles apply. The person who really wants to know, who is really concerned with what is going on, is the person who is more likely to read the guide, ask questions, call ahead to see if the place is open (to actively seek out information to learn), and is more likely to then remember the phone number, remember the details of the novel, remember the courses of the expensive meal (i.e., to learn more readily). She is much more likely than her peers to develop a "feel" for her topic and understand it "instinctively."

The third phenomenon to discuss is the tendency of intrinsic desires to influence the conclusions we draw, and the feelings of confidence we have in our conclusions. People are often more cautious in drawing conclusions when the stakes are high by their lights, and often less confident in their conclusions having drawn them (at least, when the person is displaying a modicum of epistemic rationality). Concern for a topic thus seems to induce an epistemic caution or pickiness.

Consider the sort of situation often discussed in the context of epistemic contextualism.[7] Perhaps, being in the middle of a real estate transaction, it is very important to you that the bank is open tomorrow, and tomorrow is Saturday. If your friend asks you, "Is your bank open tomorrow?" you are likely to respond, "Oh, let me double-check." After all, you read only once, and on the bank's website, that the bank is open tomorrow; you feel as though you might have read the wrong line, and besides, the website could be out of date. You suspect the answer is that the bank is open, but you lack confidence and so you think you should call and ask. Whatever the truth or falsity of epistemic contextualism, as far as you are concerned you do not know yet whether the bank is open tomorrow or not. You *feel* like someone who does not know. And it is precisely the importance to you of the facts that strips you of your confidence. If you have no particular reason to be at the bank tomorrow, and you and your friend are having an anthropological discussion of an idle nature about how things in America seem never to close, as opposed to Europe where they seem keen to close as often as possible, you will be likely to say, "My bank

---

[7] What follows is not meant as a contribution to that particular debate, but a tangential observation of interest for present purposes.

is open on Saturdays," feeling sure that you know it is so. It would not occur to you that this belief of yours might be in need of double-checking, and all because the truth of your belief is not, in this context, a matter of great concern to you.[8]

The last phenomenon to mention is cognitive distortion through emotion. Emotions are infamous for more or less directly causing changes in belief that are in no way rationalized (even badly) by the emotion causing the change. Because we take emotions to either involve desires constitutively or to be typically caused by desires, we take the influence of emotion upon cognition always or typically to be the influence of desire upon cognition.

The characteristic pattern of these changes is that emotion changes belief (or patterns of thought) in whatever manner makes the belief more congruent with the emotion: in whatever manner makes the emotion more appropriate. If you are infatuated with a person you are more likely to be blind to her faults (she seems more deserving of your longing), and if you are angry at a person, you are more likely to be blind to his virtues (he seems more deserving of your anger). If you are a middle-class American woman and you are unhappy with yourself, you are more likely to overestimate your weight (you seem more deserving of your self-loathing). If you are afraid of your teacher, you are more likely to overestimate his height (he seems more deserving of your fear). If you are happy because of a baseball game, your resulting good mood can make you overly optimistic when you later reason about the likely results of the coming elections (they seem more deserving of your joy). This is has been called "belief under the influence."[9]

In addition to cases of belief being influenced by longing, anger, disgust, and the like, there are cases in which one's desire that P be true causes one to believe that P.[10] This is often known as self-deception, but one must not be misled by the fact that to deceive is to perform an action. Although it is in principle possible to intentionally install or preserve a belief in oneself by Pascal's style of self-manipulation, by direct autosuggestion, or even by taking drugs, most self-deception involves no deceptive actions at all, as Alfred Mele has argued.[11] Self-deception can happen in many other ways. An intrinsic desire that P or an intrinsic desire that would be well served if it were the case that P (but not,

---

[8] See Stanley (2005) for the epistemological side of all this.

[9] Lazar (1999).

[10] Self-deception has a rich literature, and much of it is inconsistent with the approach to the mind that we are developing in this work. Our preferred theory is that found in Mele (2001), where self-deception is theorized in terms of content-efficacious but not reason-responsive changes in belief (though Mele does not use our jargon).

[11] There are also good reasons to reject Davidson's theory according to which the self-deceptive agent knows the truth but successfully lies to herself. The scenario raises famous paradoxes—if it's me cheating myself, how come I don't catch me?—and they are plausibly avoided by explanations that do not require the subject to be acting to self-deceive, and do not require inconsistent beliefs. See Mele (2001).

generally, an instrumental desire to believe that P) can cause a belief that P. It can create a confirmation bias in favor of P as one looks at data. It can bring about selective inattention to counter-evidence to P. It can make certain data more vivid and more available than others. It can make thinking about certain things pleasant or painful and thus cause us to avoid some kinds of thinking and prefer others, thereby influencing which complex inferences get drawn and which do not, which inconsistencies get worried at and which inconsistencies go unnoticed. In all these ways intrinsic desires can skew our interpretations of our surroundings so that we end up believing that things are closer to the way we desire them to be. Other things being equal, if Charles very much desires to be a great poet, then evidence that he is not a great poet will tend less than otherwise to change Charles' beliefs in the manner that would be most epistemically rational. He will tend to continue believing he is a great poet and will develop irrational beliefs about supposed flaws in the evidence (the contemptuous peer is just feeling bitter about being surpassed; the uninterested publisher must be afraid of the profound truths in Charles' work; and so on). The precise mechanisms giving rise to these phenomena are better studied by psychologists, but the examples given seem clear enough.

9.2 The Effects of Good Will on Cognition

With the four phenomena just described now brought to mind, it will be straightforward to explain the ways in which the virtuous person is led to think and otherwise cognize as a manifestation of the intrinsic desires that establish her claim to virtue.

At the outset, we can note the mental actions that are characteristic of the virtuous person. The virtuous person sometimes deliberates about the domain of her virtue: about how to reduce human suffering the most with a charitable donation, or about whether it is fair to a much better team of Youth League soccer players to ask them to play with a handicap against a much weaker team, and so on. And likewise, the virtuous person sometimes voluntarily focuses her attention: on the rambling story told by a lonely aunt, or on the minutia of Youth League provisions for playing games under modified rules, perhaps. However, since these are kinds of actions that the virtuous person might perform, there is no specific mystery about how a theory of virtue based on good will can explain these phenomena.

More interesting are the involuntary phenomena described in the previous section. The first phenomenon, in which desires shape involuntary shifts in attention, is often found in the virtuous person. Such a person will notice, when others do not, the slightly uncomfortable body language and tone of voice that signals that someone has taken offense at a joke, or the slightly submissive body language and tone of voice that signals that a relationship has become too paternalistic. A shirt labeled "Made in Burma" will catch her attention (if she knows of the deplorable reputation of the Burmese government) and that might lead her to start deliberating about the relative exploitation of labor in different countries, and her participation in that exploitation; another person might not have registered anything as she glanced over the label. In the same way, the virtuous person cannot help being riveted by facts about injustices. Someone else might hear about the existence of CIA "black sites" for prisoner interrogation in Eastern Europe and then go on to learn about other forms of U.S. cooperation with the Czech Republic; the virtuous person's attention will be more likely to be stuck on the revelation. As a result, she will be more likely than the less-virtuous person (all else being equal) to retain this knowledge, and to reason further about it. Also, she is likely to experience the phenomenon described by Thomas Scanlon: her attention will be directed to reasons she has to act in a certain way in some situations.[12] That too can result in beliefs (in addition to actions). This is part of the moral sensitivity attributed to the virtuous person.

Enhanced learning (the second phenomenon) can also be expected from the virtuous person. The person who cares more about the right or good is a good learner of morally relevant information and skills as, in addition to the focus of her attention, she also has a greater ability to retain information. She learns better, other things being equal, the skills useful for a moral life. She learns about how to avoid causing offense, what options exist for charitable giving and which are generally better, and so on.[13] She is more likely than another person to develop a "feel" for moral matters—to have an "instinctive" sense of such things as what resolution of a conflict would be fair and what would make people happy.[14] This is the sort of thing that happens when one has learned something very well, and this too is part of the moral sensitivity of the virtuous person.

The effects of intrinsic desire on belief confidence (the third phenomenon) are also worth considering. The person who cares about the right or good will be less likely, other things being equal, to leap to an ill-supported conclusion when there is something *morally* significant at stake. While the average person will be slow to attain certainty when it concerns her own bank account, the morally concerned person will also be slow to attain certainty when it concerns

---

[12] Scanlon (1998).

[13] What, the chronically conscientious reader might ask, of cases where the agent is too sensitive—sees duties and offenses where there are none? This will be discussed later. In the meantime, the phrase "other things being equal" should be emphasized.

[14] This fact, and to some extent the previous listed effect, make the morally concerned agent somewhat similar to the virtuous agent as described, for example, in McDowell (1979). Compare also Setiya (2007).

another person's bank account. (This latter tendency, we shall see, has an important role in open-mindedness.)

Being virtuous has epistemic advantages but it also has epistemic disadvantages. Consider the fourth phenomenon: cognitive distortion through emotion. People in the grips of emotions often have their thoughts and beliefs shifted to be more congruent with their emotions, and people often believe in ways that say more about what they want to be the case than what the evidence best supports. These cognitive effects are commonly associated with virtue, too. The kind person is, other things being equal, more likely than most to feel sympathy for a bully who has just been subjected to a beating by an even bigger bully; feeling sympathy, the kind person is also more likely than most to believe that the bully is not really a hateful person so much as an anxious person who does not understand how to manage social difficulties without violence (something that, if true, would make the bully more deserving of sympathy). And the kind person is more likely than most to be persuaded that a new school anti-bullying program will be highly effective (since she will very much want it to be). Because of the desire that makes her virtuous, the kind person is prone to epistemic errors that we associate with the kind person: a tendency to see the world more optimistically than is epistemically warranted, in some respects. In other words, she is more likely than others to have the attitude of blind charity, as exemplified by Jane Bennet in *Pride and Prejudice* (which Julia Driver calls a virtue),[15] the attitude of the loving saint as described by Susan Wolf,[16] or what has been called "the virtue of hope." Other virtues open their possessors to other characteristic epistemic faults: perhaps the person who particularly hates injustice is more prone than others to find nothing but fault with the unjust person, even when the unjust person has nonmoral merits.

9.3 The Vice of Being Prejudiced

On any contemporary list of vices, one might reasonably expect to see "sexism," "homophobia," "racism," "classism" and the like. Any sort of prejudice is a vice. But how can we agree? Prejudice appears to be a matter of what one believes,[17] whereas virtue and vice are a matter of what one intrinsically desires.

No one is morally the worse for an honest mistake. If an alien who had never met any human beings were to read in an otherwise reliable guide to the solar system that Han Chinese Earthlings are by nature smarter than other

---

[15] Driver (1989).

[16] Wolf (1982).

[17] At least, we suspect, and grant for the sake of the argument, that this is the case. There is room for desire-based theories of prejudice, though we are not inclined in that direction.

Earthlings, and as a result developed that belief, the alien is not morally culpable for so believing: it would be making an honest mistake. The alien would
not be prejudiced, just misinformed.[18]

What is the difference, then, between an ordinary racist, who deserves our
condemnation, and the alien "racist," who does not?[19] One difference that
springs to mind is the fact that the Earthly racist holds his belief in, e.g., the
supremacy of the majority Chinese ethnicity against plentiful evidence that is
readily available to him. With a typical level of intelligence and with the information that is available even to rather uneducated people in the first world, he
would probably not have developed his racist beliefs if there were not something amiss with him epistemically. The run-of-the-mill racist is epistemically
irrational, as are other run-of-the-mill prejudiced people.

This conclusion might suggest that morally objectionable believing is characterized by epistemic irrationality. Yet not all irrational beliefs are morally
objectionable. The person who irrationally believes that his lottery ticket has
unusually slim chances of winning because a ticket with the same numbers won
last month is not morally vicious.

So irrationality in belief is not sufficient for moral condemnation. In fact,
there are cases in which it appears that irrationality makes a person less blameworthy. Imagine a schizophrenic who attacks another person because she takes
that person to be Satan, and takes her attack to be a desperate attempt to save
the world. The schizophrenic is not blameworthy for her attack, and her lack
of blameworthiness is in some way owed to the fact that she is so very epistemically irrational. Her belief that her victim is Satan is not held against her in the
way that an almost equally ridiculous belief in a Jewish conspiracy to enslave
the world would be held against a mentally healthy person. Instead, it serves as
a good excuse.

The key difference between the irrationality of the schizophrenic and that
of the bigot is that the bigot's irrationality is "hot" irrationality. The schizophrenic's belief are not explained by her desires.[20] When she develops her belief,
it is not because she hates the person so much that she begins to see him as
Satanic, or that the person got a job that she wanted and the only acceptable
explanation was that he is Satan. Her belief seems rather to be the product of

---

[18] Hurka (2000, 179–80) does not discuss aliens but his description of the circumstances under
which a Nazi can be regarded as praiseworthy in his desire to eliminate the Jews is friendly to our
view—it implies that for the person to be innocent he has to have about as much contact with real
life Jews as the alien has with the Chinese.

[19] Lawrence Blum holds that a racist person is not to be criticized for any racist emotions left
over after a sincere attempt to change, as these emotions are involuntary. It is interesting that he
does not do the same with beliefs. See Blum (1980, 189), quoted in Adams (1985).

[20] Or, if some aspects of the schizophrenic's beliefs are influenced by the contents of her
desires, this is clearly not the main factor explaining her schizophrenic beliefs.

processes that involve no content efficacy: some merely physical factor has gone awry.[21] On the other hand, the bigot does not reach his belief through merely physical factors gone wrong. We agree with Kwame Anthony Appiah that the racist's irrationality is motivated irrationality.[22] His thinking that the Jews are a conspiratorial people is more likely to be caused by his hatred of them, or of people who are ostentatiously "other," or to be caused by his resentment of his low social station, or the like. And the fact that the racist's belief appears to be caused by a desire opens the possibility that, however involuntary, the belief might have something to do with ill will or moral indifference.

When prejudice is a manifestation of ill will, that explains why the believer can be said to possess a vice. Perhaps there is in some prejudiced people an intrinsic desire to mistreat someone (anyone will do), or a desire to mistreat certain people in particular, or a desire to put certain people "in their places." All of these intrinsic desires are hostile to the right or good, are for things that would transparently necessarily be a part of the wrong or bad. Anyone manifesting such an intrinsic desire thus manifests a vice. Desires like these can generate negative emotional states, which can in turn deform belief-forming mechanisms (making the Jews seem dirtier, more avaricious, or more powerful than they would otherwise seem, and thus making the disgust at, contempt of, or fear of them appear more deserved). Or these desires might lead to beliefs of the wish-fulfilling sort, such as that the Jews are a cruel people, so that harsh treatment of them is justified as self-defense. The beliefs that these forms of ill will might lead to are the beliefs making up the bigot's prejudices.

Other cases of prejudice are manifestations of intrinsic desires that are not ill will. Perhaps someone believes in a Jewish conspiracy because she needs some explanation for her profound personal failures, and holding that she lost her job is because of a Jewish conspiracy is a way of holding that it is not because of her own inadequacy. Perhaps a person has a given prejudice because it is already held by peers and so holding it enables the person to fit in with her immediate group and provides her with a stronger sense of collective identity. (This is perhaps one of the common causes of schoolyard homophobia.) Perhaps one needs some way of explaining the badness in the world and a conspiracy theory serves better than an admission that the badness is random. Or perhaps one needs a scapegoat to feel better about one's own sins. There are many possible stories, all lending some credibility to Sartre's comment that had the Jew not existed, the anti-Semite would have made him up: some people, it appears, will always find some "race" about which to be racist, or otherwise some "other" against whom to be allophobic.

---

[21] If there is content efficacy in schizophrenic delusions, it is perhaps in a loose kind of free association between ideas one sometimes seems to see in unmedicated schizophrenic people. But this sort of association does not seem typically driven by wishful thinking or the like.

[22] See Appiah (1990).

The desires mentioned in the last paragraph do not constitute ill will. It is not inimical to morality to desire an explanation for one's deep failures or to fit in with one's peers or even to feel better about one's own sins. On Spare Conativism, it thus follows that, for the prejudiced beliefs described in the last paragraph to be vicious, they have to be held as a result of moral indifference. And indeed we hold that, in the modern world, given ordinary intelligence, lack of psychosis, and a normal amount of available information, an ordinary person will not be particularly prejudiced if she has enough good will. Whether or not someone is part of a conspiracy to enslave the world is a question with high moral stakes. The person who cares about the moral stakes is likely to be a "picky" believer, as most of us become when the stakes are high for us personally (as in the earlier example involving the bank's closing hours). She is not likely to accept just any story on the subject and is receptive only to solid evidence. Under such conditions, and given the typical intellectual merits of conspiracy theories, she is unlikely to be convinced.

The epistemic caution that comes with high stakes is not the only mechanism protecting the virtuous person from prejudicial beliefs. Every way in which desires influence cognition is a way in which the virtuous person can have some protection against prejudicial beliefs that others in her environment are more likely to embrace. The virtuous person will be better at remembering the morally relevant facts about the deeds of Jews and non-Jews (or whoever might be the group in question), and retaining these facts will make it harder to believe half-truths and lies that reflect badly on the group. The virtuous person will have her attention drawn to the ways in which "they" are like "us," and the ways in which "their" differences are harmless or positive, and not only to the ways in which "their" differences seem wrong-headed or ill-intentioned, because morally important facts in general will catch her attention more than they will most other people's. And the virtuous person will not want to believe that "they" are inherently bad, inferior, deserving of worse treatment—because, being kind (or otherwise beneficently inclined) she will want the world to be filled with people who are inherently good and deserve to be treated well (or who, at worst, will become deserving people when treated well). Her tendency to wishful thinking this way will, as with these other cognitive effects, tend to work as a barrier against the accumulation of prejudices.

So the possessor of bad beliefs is vicious (and his actions based on the belief blameworthy), insofar as he is, either because his beliefs are manifestations of ill will or because they are manifestations of his deficiency of good will.

Holding prejudices because of a dearth of good will needs to be distinguished from cases of culpable ignorance. A doctor who has false beliefs about medical matters because she did not keep up with developments in her field, or who has false beliefs about a patient's condition because she only briefly glanced at his chart, is guilty of culpable ignorance: she should have attended to her medicine-related beliefs and taken reasonable steps to avoid developing false ones. She should, in other words, have done her homework.

It is tempting to say that our bad beliefs are bad because they are the result of such culpable ignorance. We have an epistemic duty to "do our homework," to become informed about morally important matters, to double-check our morally relevant beliefs and do our best to make sure that they are true, and bad beliefs are bad because we reached them through a violation of this duty.

There are at least two problems with this approach.

The first is the implausibility of there being such a duty beyond certain limited cases. Although it is perhaps clear that a physician should routinely study up on the properties of certain drugs or the techniques for certain procedures, these sorts of duties cannot be a model for the majority of our lives, because we cannot in general know which of our beliefs need checking. While a competent doctor knows what journals she has to read and what charts she has to check, people do not always know where to look to avoid culpable ignorance. A person living in the U.S. today knows that race is a topic about which everyone is prone to developing prejudices and so she might be morally required to check herself for such prejudices on fraught occasions—for example, when interviewing candidates of a different race for a job. But consider June, a middle-American person living in 1995 who believes that homosexuality is a biological disorder. Suppose that June's belief is not obviously inconsistent with anything else that June knows, though she could easily learn how mistaken it is with a trip to the library (but not, in 1995, the Internet). How would she know that her belief requires scrutiny, that it is worth her while to make a trip to the library to check up on it? After all, it is not the case that she is under a moral obligation to scrutinize all of her beliefs regarding biological disorders. For all June knows, her belief about homosexuality is akin to her belief about Down Syndrome and Tourette Syndrome being biological disorders.[23]

If June deserves our condemnation, it is not because she has failed in a duty to do "due diligence" on her beliefs. The alternative we suggest is that, if June deserves our condemnation, it is because somewhere in the formation or retention of her belief there has been a manifestation of ill will or lack of good will. Perhaps the formation and retention of her belief is due to her finding homosexual behavior distasteful and "jumping to conclusions"—failing to register plenty of information that suggests that homosexuality is not a disorder. If not, then something similar is true of her, or else June's error genuinely is innocent after all, and she is not vicious. She simply has not been exposed to a lot of information, and does not know any better.

Similarly, imagine Victor, a professor who has a prejudice against students who wear their baseball caps backwards. Victor does not know he has this

[23] Gideon Rosen is aware of the relevance issue, but takes it to be supporting evidence for skepticism about moral responsibility. See Rosen (2004).

prejudice: he does not do a lot of soul-searching about his varied feelings (which seems unlikely to be a violation of his moral obligations). As Victor grades papers he tries hard to avoid racist and sexist judgments and so on, but the next paper in the stack is by a white male undergraduate of apparent middle-class means. Victor has no apparent reason to check himself for prejudice. Yet Victor might unknowingly give the student less than the grade he deserves because he remembers the student as wearing his baseball cap backwards. If he does so, it seems that we should condemn him for something other than his failure to monitor his beliefs; he has done as much to monitor his beliefs as anyone could reasonably be asked to do. If there is something to condemn, as there probably is, then it is something else: something, we hold, to do with the ill will or lack of good will that led Victor to believe worse of the student's paper than the work itself warranted.

The second problem with an approach to prejudice based on moral obligations to check one's beliefs comes from the moral insufficiency of carrying out such (putative) obligations. Performing one's belief-checking duties to the fullest does not absolve one of moral blame if one remains prejudiced in one's beliefs. A bigot can do all her homework on the subject of race—expose herself to people of the disvalued race, read about racism, reflect about it, and so on—and remain a bigot, despite believing that she has now achieved a fair and balanced view of race. In such a case, though the actions taken to improve the bigot's epistemic status might even be praiseworthy, the fact that she has taken these actions does not render her exempt from moral condemnation for her beliefs, does not absolve her from the charge of having a serious moral vice, and does not render actions taken on the basis of her beliefs morally innocent. In fact, the person who exposes herself to evidence and remains a bigot is likely to be more of a bigot than someone else, since the motivated irrationality behind her beliefs is so powerful that she retains her prejudices even in the face of prolonged contact with the facts.

When Gideon Rosen discusses culpable ignorance he refers to epistemic duties to do one's homework.[24] Some would use the term "epistemic duty" as a synonym for "requirement of epistemic rationality" or "epistemic norm." But as we take beliefs to be involuntary, we think that epistemic norms are not duties at all: duty is just not the right category here. It is true that if one believes that if P then Q and also believes that P there is a normative requirement—a requirement of rationality—that she believe that Q (or not believe one of her premises). But not all normative requirements are duties. Moral duties are the paradigmatic duties, and as a result duties have a special relationship to the will and voluntariness that epistemic requirement does not. This can be seen in the fact that in some situations, having tried excuses you from failing to do

---

[24] Rosen (2004).

something that you are obligated to do, but having tried to do your epistemic "duty" does not excuse you from it. Consider a student, Darlene. Darlene has a moral duty to return, on Monday, a book that she had borrowed from her friend in Seattle. Come Monday, Darlene fully intends to return to the book and takes it with her on her way to Seattle but the fates appear to conspire against her and her flight is delayed by an unexpected snow storm, making it impossible to arrive on Monday. In such a situation, Darlene is excused from her moral duty. When it comes to straightforward deontic requirements, one gets a grade of A for effort. Now, being a student, Darlene has an exam in a critical thinking course. Though she tries very hard to succeed in the test, she fails to draw an important conclusion that she is epistemically required to draw from her reading, and so her grade suffers, and it suffers because of her failure to fulfill an epistemic requirement. No amount of trying on Darlene's part would excuse her from her epistemic "duty." Her professor will not raise her grade even if she can prove how assiduously she studied. Not believing something that you ought to believe is not analogous, in this way, to not doing something that you ought to do.

If epistemic duties as such do not exist, and there are problems with attributing moral faults to prejudiced people for failing to do their "moral homework," then perhaps our preferred theory is correct. What is wrong with prejudice is that it is a manifestation of vice, in the form of desires that constitute ill will or moral indifference.

9.4 The Vice of Being Close-Minded

What usually goes by the name "prejudice" is far from the only kind of morally objectionable belief.

Consider Doug, who believes, against the grain of his contemporaries' opinions, that it is morally acceptable to strike his children to instill a wide variety of life lessons. It "builds their characters," he says. Doug loves his parents, who in their turn used to strike him (especially to punish crying, expressing unwarranted fear, and otherwise displaying a lack of "spine"), and his beliefs about how being struck by their father can be good for his children are sustained (in a content-efficacious but not reason-responsive manner) from his intrinsic desire to think well of his parents. There is nothing morally objectionable in Doug's intrinsic desire to think well of his parents, but it seems likely that Doug is showing a certain dearth of good will: if he cared more about people's suffering, or just about his children's suffering, he would likely see that the case for striking his children has some holes in it.

In cases like Doug's, there need be nothing that would normally go under the name of prejudice. Doug is not prejudiced against children, his own children, or other parents. Yet there is something morally objectionable in Doug's makeup. Doug is somehow impervious to the obvious idea that it is morally objectionable to strike another person without powerful justification. Though his contemporaries see the point, though magazines and talk shows return to the idea at regular intervals, though experts and dilettantes alike argue against corporal punishment for children, though even dog trainers are moving to banish the choke chain as a training aid, Doug does not come around to believing that there is anything wrong with the way he hits his children. And if the explanation is, in part, that Doug does not care enough about what is right or good then Doug is showing moral indifference and thus a vice.

If Doug has a vice, it is the vice of close-mindedness: his belief is resistant to the onslaught of counter-evidence, in a manner manifesting either a lack of good will or the presence of ill will. If this is the nature of close-mindedness, then prejudice is a special case of it: it is being close-minded with respect to something like one's negative beliefs about a group, or one's positive beliefs favoring one group over others.

Even if a person's belief has been reached rationally he can still be close-minded, because the vice is found in the way the beliefs are sustained. When Ignaz Semmelweiss was a young assistant doctor in charge of a maternity clinic at the Vienna General Hospital in the nineteenth century, he ordered his underlings to wash their hands between performing autopsies and handling patients. As a result, the incidence of fatal puerperal ("childbed") fever dropped dramatically. When Semmelweiss publicized his consequent hypothesis that the absence of hand washing was the only cause of the ubiquity of the disease, his advice was mostly ignored and he was ridiculed.

The doctors believed that they had no special reason to wash their hands between autopsies and patients, or between different patients. The creation of this belief did not necessarily involve the kind of motivated irrationality involved in prejudice, or close-mindedness, or any irrationality at all. It could easily have been a belief that they held for good reasons, up until hearing of Semmelweiss's work. But after hearing of his work with puerperal fever, their beliefs did not change. It was this failure of their beliefs to be influenced by the new evidence that is the manifestation of their vice, a vice that likely predated its manifestation.

Why did the doctors fail to see the force of Semmelweiss's evidence? Though they almost surely were prejudiced against women, their prejudice does not provide a good explanation of their behavior: it is not as if they thought the women deserved to die. An alternative explanation is this: if the doctors had admitted that Semmelweiss was right and that there is a causal relationship between failing to wash one's hands and the death of one's patients, then they would have admitted that they were responsible for the deaths of many of their patients. This would have been something, we can imagine, that these doctors would not have wanted to believe. Imagine an older colleague of Semmelweiss' who is faced with Semmelweiss' evidence for the significance of hand-washing, with its grim implication that his own actions have caused many needless deaths. It is natural for this colleague to be upset, but if he were more concerned for what is right or good he would not have rejected the evidence but rather listened, out of fear of causing more deaths and hope of saving more lives. Perhaps he would have been in tears, as Semmelweiss himself is said to have been upon his discovery. When listening to the evidence, the need to save lives would be at the forefront of his attention, rather than his own self-esteem or reputation Thus, the morally concerned colleague of Semmelweiss would not have readily concluded that there must be something wrong with Semmelweiss' observations—even though, under such conditions, there must have been a strong pull to do so. In his reaction to the young man's unusual views, the colleague would have exhibited open-mindedness.

Doctors with tremendous concern for the right or good would not have been impervious to Semmelweiss's arguments because of their sad implications, but it is possible that the doctors in question had too little moral concern and too much invested in their self-images as healers, and that their patients were greatly harmed as a result. It could be that this, rather than prejudice, was the principal explanation for the failure of his peers to heed Semmelweiss's arguments. Perhaps it was closed-mindedness that continued to kill the doctors' unfortunate patients.

9.5 The Virtue of Being Open-Minded

If closed-mindedness is a vice, then it seems open-mindedness must be a virtue. It is the virtue of so strongly intrinsically desiring the right or good that one is protected against closed-mindedness, prejudice, and the like. Open-mindedness is thus a virtue along the lines of Aristotelian courage: just as courage is having enough good will that it overrides the fear of death, open-mindedness is having enough good will to override the tendency to develop or retain beliefs in response to one's other concerns, at least when the beliefs that one would form are of moral significance. Since tendencies to motivated irrationality are so strong, open-mindedness can be a hard virtue.

The open-minded person is different from the rest of us in many epistemic situations, but she best shows her virtue when a cherished belief, whatever its source, is threatened by evidence. In such cases, many of us will be excessively shaped by our psychological needs and wishes. The open-minded person, on the other hand, is affected by her concern for the right or good in such a way that she cannot help but absorb the evidence and so come to reject her cherished belief, if that is what the evidence tells her to do.

Open-mindedness is often associated with having no opinions on certain topics, or with maintaining a skeptical view of them, and indeed, the open-minded person would on many occasions fail to form a strong opinion on a morally relevant matter, because the evidence would be so scarce and the stakes would be so high that the all-too-human tendency to jump to conclusions is overridden by moral concern. Like the person who is often unsure of her beliefs when her bank account is at stake, the open-minded person will often be somewhat unsure of her beliefs when something moral is at stake. She will very rarely, for example, form a strong opinion about a stranger's character after one or two conversations, even if the stranger took "her" parking spot or, conversely, offered her zucchini from his garden. She will often suspend judgment on new social trends, feeling she does not understand them well enough. And so on. But it is important not to confuse genuine, morally virtuous open-mindedness with other states in which a person appears to have some trouble forming opinions about morally significant matters.

Paul Feyerabend provides us with a good example of such a simulacrum of open-mindedness. In his memoir, *Killing Time*, Feyerabend discusses his youth in Nazi Austria. Everyone around him was either for or against the Nazis, but as for him, "during the Nazi period, I paid little attention to the general talk about Jews, Communism, the Bolshevik threat: I did not accept it, nor did I oppose it."[25] Feyerabend explains that he occasionally stimulated himself intellectually or provoked others by making either pro-Nazi or anti-Nazi arguments. "I was too contrarian to be loyal to anyone," he says. Even at the end of the war, as Germany surrendered, he failed to see why people so one-sidedly took it to be a good thing.

In the case of the young Feyerabend, not having an opinion does not seem to be a show of virtue. In fact, it appears scandalous. The full extent of Nazi evil might not have been available to Feyerabend, but it was certainly the case that he could see enough to make any decent person furious, and to make any decent person conclude that the Nazis were a force for evil. The oppression of Jewish students in his class, the violence in the streets on such occasions as Kristallnacht, the content of Hitler's war-mongering speeches, and many other things should have been enough for a very intelligent young man with ordinary moral concern to draw strong conclusions.

The case of young Feyerabend shows that sometimes not having an opinion is a symptom of moral indifference rather than good will. Obsessed as he was with science and art, the public affairs of Nazi Austria, including such things as the beating up of Jewish children in his school, did not interest Feyerabend enough for him to have an opinion about them, the way that a person who is not interested in golf usually has no opinion as to the relative talents of

---

[25] Feyerabend (1995, 55).

particular golfers. In his autobiography, Feyerabend unblinkingly admits his lack of moral concern at the time when he says that during "all these events" it never occurred to him to inquire further, for "the idea that the fate of any single human being was in some way connected to my own existence was entirely outside my field of vision."[26] It appears that not only did Feyerabend not possess the moral virtue of open-mindedness, but that he was led to holding no opinion by the same thing that causes some people to be closed-minded: *lack* of moral concern. There are times when, in Yeats' words, "the best lack all conviction," but there are times when those who lack conviction are clearly among the bad. In the case of young Feyerabend, we might speculate that the very same sort of thing that led certain people in similar circumstances to his to be dogmatic is exactly what led him to have no opinion, namely, an absence of concern for the moral. For Feyerabend to be truly open-minded, his lack of opinion would have to have been a manifestation of good will instead of a manifestation of moral indifference.

It is important to insert here a note on epistemic virtue. There is an epistemic virtue which shares the name "open-mindedness." On the present view, however, the person whose mind is open because of anything other than good will (or reverse moral indifference)—even if it is an otherwise plausibly laudable concern for the truth—does not have the moral virtue of open-mindedness.[27] A manifestation of concern for the truth is not always a manifestation of a concern for the right or good. Consider when the manifestation of concern is an action: the scientist who knowingly performs dangerous experiments, or the philosopher who cannot help, in the middle of a funeral, but to try to refute her host's belief in God. The truth seeker seeks the truth, but the morally concerned person qua morally concerned person need care about the truth only when the truth is morally salient, when there are moral stakes. Some will hold that the truth is always morally salient, as any false belief is capable of causing a harmful action. If that is true, the morally concerned person and the truth-concerned person would be well advised to act in the same way, and will be similarly nonvoluntarily moved in their beliefs, but even then, there will always be the question of whether it is concern for what is moral or concern for the truth (or some combination of the two) that moves the agent to act in some way.

Can there be too much good will when it comes to belief formation and revision? One might analogously ask if too much concern for self-interest can cause one to act imprudently, and it sometimes appears that it does. Suppose that George cares a fair amount about his self-interest and is also prone to being very fearful. As a result, he ends up being neurotic about things that he

---

[26] Feyerabend (1995, 41).

[27] Interestingly, if knowledge itself is a morally valuable good, an intrinsic desire for the truth is a form of good will and then the putatively epistemic virtue becomes also a moral virtue.

takes to bear on his self-interest. Very concerned about thieves, he becomes unable to leave the house without checking ten times that he has locked the door. Very concerned about money, he becomes so scared of financial ruin that he harms himself by making poor investment decisions, leaving all his money in safe deposit boxes. In this case, it might appear that if he were less concerned with his self-interest, he would also not have had his neurotic fears, and would not have compromised his self-interest in the way he does.

But the root of George's problem is not really too much concern for his self-interest. There can be people who care about theft or money more than George and yet who do not have his symptoms. George's problems arise because, with a normal amount of concern for his self-interest, he also has a tendency (still poorly understood by either scientists or philosophers) to become unnerved in high-stakes situations. Without his considerable concern for his self-interest, locking his door and taking care of his money would not have been subjectively high-stakes situations, it can be agreed, but the real problem is with his reaction to high-stakes situations, not his concern for his self-interest. It might be that the conditional *if George were less interested in his self-interest he would have fewer problems* holds true, but the truth of the conditional does not diagnose what distinguishes George as someone with a problem. And once that diagnosis is made, it appears that it would be a mistake to fault George's self-interest.

Who would be the counterpart of George with respect to the virtue of open-mindedness? Consider Trisha, who is very concerned with the moral import of her opinions (let this count as good will, for the sake of the example), and who often fails to come to a conclusion when considering moral matters. She finds herself saying things such as, "I just don't know what to think. However I make up my mind it seems that I'm condemning someone who might not deserve it, or agreeing with someone who might be in the wrong." She listens for too long to malignant rants about "welfare queens" that she should dismiss, trying for charitable interpretations, and she fears making any negative judgment at all about a member of another culture or race unless the person is as obviously bad as a self-consciously malevolent Nazi. As a result, she fails to hold the beliefs that a reasonable and judicious moral reasoner in her circumstances would hold. Trisha has a great deal of good will, and this good will appears to be manifested in her epistemic state, but it would be quite a stretch to describe her epistemic state as open-mindedness, epistemic charity, or anything else suggesting that it is an unambiguous virtue.

As with George, one might suspect that Trisha is a character who has a problem caused by an excess of concern, and if one thought Trisha suffered from an excess of concern then one might think that virtue must be something other than manifestations of strong intrinsic desires. But again, this appears to be a misdiagnosis. A person who is even more concerned with the moral than Trisha need not have her tendency to epistemic paralysis, and typically will not (if the lives of Nelson Mandela, Martin Luther King Jr., and other people of known profound moral concern are anything to judge by). The most reasonable diagnosis of Trisha's problem is that it stems from her overblown anxiety surrounding moral judgment, and not from her good will itself. As in the case of George, it might be true that the conditional *if Trisha had less good will she would reach better moral judgments* holds, but also as in the case of George, it would seem to be a mistake to read off from the truth of this conditional that her moral concern is what specifically is wrong with Trisha. As a result, it seems we can say that Trisha's irrational hesitation in making negative moral judgments does not express much of her good will: it is much more an expression of her anxious nature. And thus her irrational hesitation to judge is not a virtue.

9.6 Modesty and Immodesty

Famously, modesty raises its own questions about the moral status of involuntary mental states, as the modest person appears to be praised for a belief she has about herself—a self-deprecating belief. This deserves further investigation.

Some people think that knowledge is always good and ignorance always bad, but things are not as simple as that. If you meet a teenager who does not have an extensive knowledge of the lives of vacant-eyed celebrities, you might feel encouraged: perhaps it is a sign that she has better things to think about. If, on the other hand, you meet a person who, despite not being a lawyer, knows many things about the laws concerning bad debt, you might fear that it is a sign that she is rather irresponsible. Human memory is limited and what people put in it can be telling.

Julia Driver argues that modesty is a moral virtue and that it consists in a modicum of ignorance about one's talents and abilities.[28] At first it looks easy to resist this conclusion because ignorance, a bad thing, seems like a strange thing on which to found a moral virtue, a good thing. However, as we just suggested, this is much too simplistic a way to think about things. We agree with Driver that sometimes ignorance speaks well of a person.

From the perspective of Spare Conativism, the problem with Driver's theory is that it does not connect the virtue of modesty to the quality of the virtuous person's will: to her abundance of good will or dearth of ill will. Except in special cases, ignorance of one's talents and abilities is both a nonvoluntary, nonconative state and is not the product of any action on one's own part. In being ignorant of your talents and abilities, you are mistaken, and this seems to be neither your fault nor to your moral credit. You have an epistemic problem. In the case of modesty you have a lucky epistemic problem, but nothing more.[29]

---

[28] Driver (1989; 2001).
[29] Many people criticized Driver on this point. See Flanagan (1990), Statman (1992), and Schueler (1997).

While modesty does *paradigmatically* involve a false belief about oneself, a genuine underestimation of one's talents and virtues, ignorance is not ultimately what defines modesty. Rather, modesty is a matter of having the right sort of will. To be more precise, modesty amounts to a type of marked absence of ill will—as we have called it, reverse moral indifference. Or so we think can be shown.

Driver is a consequentialist and thinks modesty is a virtue because it promotes good outcomes. We must mention in passing that we are not sure how obvious it is that ignorance of one's abilities—which constitutes modesty according to Driver—promotes good outcomes, all in all. Utility would increase considerably if female students stopped underestimating their abilities, for example, and if Nelson Mandela had not believed in his importance as a political leader he might have given up on anything but survival while imprisoned on Robben Island. Many achievements would not have been possible if a person had not, in a few critical moments, told herself, "I can do it," even though successfully doing the "it" required a person of rare abilities. Also, while a person's underestimation of his abilities can indeed facilitate social interaction by reducing envy and excessive competitiveness, the opposite can also be true. The person who underestimates himself is prone to envy and frustration, and to the other unsavory emotions and behaviors that come with these. The pop-psychological idea of low self-esteem as the root of all evil might be ridiculous, but some people improve with a little recognition and self-recognition, becoming less envious, less bitter, and, as a result, more generous. We do not deny that something that can be aptly named "modesty" can promote good outcomes, but point out that it is far from clear.

But to many of us (including some consequentialists) it seems that the mere fact that a mental state has good consequences does not make it a virtue. Perhaps the world would greatly benefit from the addition of, say, more witty people, but that by itself would not make wit a moral virtue. Why? The short answer seems to be that witty people do not deploy their wits for moral reasons. In other words, virtuous behavior manifests good will, and most displays of wit are not such manifestations. Driver contrasts herself with Aristotelians and others who think that in order for one's action to be virtuous it is important that *one knows what one is doing*. As we argued in the previous two chapters, however, it is possible to reject the thesis that the virtuous person always knows that her virtues are indeed virtues (that she always knows what is right or good under her concept RIGHT or GOOD) without giving up on the thesis that the virtuous person characteristically does the right thing for the right reason, and so in a manner that is morally praiseworthy.

Driver holds that, with regard to meriting a certain type of visceral approval, there is something special about the person who genuinely underestimates herself, as opposed to the person who merely understates her talents and abilities when with others. It is easy to see she has a point. The second person is called "falsely modest." Driver points out that falsely modest people can be mere selfish manipulators; we think it is also important that even if a falsely modest person's actions are morally motivated—and we can imagine a person who downplays her talents with the good in mind—she would still be "falsely modest" rather than modest. False modesty performed with good motives (such as making other people feel better about themselves) is good but it is not the real thing—we will be disappointed if we discover that someone whom we thought modest is just a superbly tactful person who believes that to make the world a better place for others he ought to publicly understate his achievements, talents, and so on. While the tactful person who understates his achievements and talents in conversation does act out of good will and seems quite praiseworthy to us, Driver would be right that "modest" isn't the right word for the person in question.

What we value when we value modesty is not ignorance itself but a conative attitude that often leads to ignorance as a side effect. The attitude is, roughly speaking, that of not caring about how well you are ranked.[30]

The conative attitude involved in modesty can exist without self-underestimation, and underestimation can come without the conative attitude. Consider the following example: Krista is the best opera singer of her generation—but she does not know it, and if asked to rank herself among her peers would sincerely rank herself #10. Juana would sincerely rank herself #10 because that is what the critics say, but she is actually #20. However, as an individual to spend time with, Juana is a delight whereas Krista is impossible. Krista thinks of nothing beside how wonderful it is to be one of the ten best opera singers in the world, an extremely enviable position, especially compared to the boring stuff other people around her do. She brings up her triumphs in the middle of conversations about the weather, sports, or someone else's divorce, and she expects all manner of special treatment. Juana, on the other hand, has no such inclinations. She is interested in and thinks about all kinds of things, it would never occur to her to raise the topic of her triumphs when people are discussing someone else's divorce, and she tends toward acting as if other people should be thought of first.

Krista appears not to be modest, whereas Juana appears modest—and each is as she appears, if her inner attitudes match her outer behavior. This shows that there can be modesty without underestimation and underestimation without modesty. Now imagine a third opera singer, Renee, who is just like Juana in her behavior and outlook, except that instead of overestimating herself she assesses her talents correctly. It is just as easy to see Renee as modest as it is to

---

[30] Driver (2001, 21) holds that this is a part of modesty, but that the ignorance is a required component.

see Juana that way, which shows that modesty is not, strictly speaking, a virtue of ignorance, as it can come without any ignorance at all.

Consider the person who, like Krista, has the vice parallel to the virtue of modesty. When trying to figure out what is wrong with Krista, it is natural to come up with such phrases as "she takes herself too seriously" or "she has no sense of proportion," but as pointed out by Ty Raterman[31] it is hard to explain what it is to take yourself too seriously (after all, there are moral contexts in which taking your moral education seriously is a good thing) and, as also pointed out by Raterman, it is hard to figure out what kind of a sense of proportion one should have. Should Krista always have the vastness of the universe in mind as a comparison when she thinks of her own singing? Should Krista constantly compare her opera singing to such an endeavor as finding a cure for cancer or brokering a viable Middle East peace deal? If so, what should the successful cancer researcher or the peace maker compare herself to, if she is modest, absent a deity to compare herself to? Aaron Ben Ze'ev[32] suggests that we follow Kant and compare ourselves to the moral law, but how one compares a person to a law is not immediately clear. The ideas of over-seriousness and a sense of proportion seem to have something to them, but they need some work.

On our view, similar to the view defended by Ben Ze'ev and to Thomas Hill's view of snobbery, lacking modesty is a sort of prejudice in which the group looked down upon is everyone but oneself. Like prejudice, immodesty can be truly virulent or it can be very subtle. It is inimical to morality in the same way that prejudice is—because it makes exception to some rule that tells us that, in some sense, people are equal or deserve equal treatment: that we all matter equally, not only regardless of sex, race, or class but also regardless of our talents, abilities, and even virtues. This is what happens when Krista acts as if insulting her is somehow worse than insulting anyone else and as if listening to her is more important than listening to anyone else. When we say that Krista should have a sense of proportion about the place of opera singing in the great scheme of things, the problem we point to is not that Krista thinks opera singing is as important as curing cancer but that she acts as if being a great opera singer *or even being a great cancer researcher* has the power to grant a person the sort of special status she desires. It is hard to explain what special status it is, but this is none other than the difficulty inherent in the very idea of human equality, equality that has to be compatible with certain clear respects in which people are not equal, in their abilities as opera singers and more.

The idea that modesty and its absence have something to do with egalitarianism has been criticized. It has been suggested by Hans Maes[33] that it implies that prejudiced people such as racists cannot be modest, as they deny the

---

[31] See Raterman (2006).
[32] Ben Ze'ev (2000).
[33] Maes (2005).

equality we have mentioned. But there is no reason to think this follows from our view. A white person might have a prejudice in favor of white people and fail to have a prejudice in favor of *himself* as an individual. It has been said that the immodest person does not have to believe that she should be first in line for the life boats on a sinking ship,[34] but some arrogant people are bad enough to have such beliefs and some prejudiced people are not. As we said, prejudice can be virulent or relatively weak, and then there are complicating factors: consider the sexist man who thinks women should be *first* in line for the lifeboat but is nonetheless prejudiced against them. It is also true, and has been pointed out,[35] that a singer who says "singing is relatively unimportant, but while it does not give me a super-human status, I am the greatest singer in the world" does not sound modest, however nuanced she makes her disclaimer. It sounds incongruent because a mathematical genius who does not takes it to be important whether or not she is a mathematical genius will not insist upon her genius when it is not required by the situation, and likewise for the opera singer. She will not boast partially because of motives similar to those of the benevolent falsely modest person, that is, in order to let other people feel better about themselves and so on, but mostly in the same way that no one brings up things that seem unimportant when they are not especially relevant to the situation.

What motivates displays of immodesty? Various intrinsic desires can be at fault. Perhaps, as is often the case, one wants to compensate for a sense of worthlessness or insecurity. This desire is by itself morally neutral but it should be checked by good will, and when it is not so checked it is a sign of moral indifference. Perhaps one simply wants to be more important, or to be treated better, than other people, for its own sake. As there is (we think) a *pro tanto* moral reason to avoid this, this would be a case of ill will rather than mere moral indifference (one would intrinsically desire a certain form of injustice). It is this motivational setup, rather than simply a high opinion of one's merits, that makes a person immodest. But this motivational setup tends to *cause* a person to have a high opinion of herself. The agent who desires a special status cannot bear the thought of being ordinary, and so she tends to believe that she is exceptional in some way that could serve as an excuse, in her mind, for the special status.

What then of modesty? Given the degree to which the absence of modesty is common, it might appear that that anyone who is entirely *lacking in immodesty* deserves to be called "modest." This need not conflict with the claim that the modest person paradigmatically *underestimates* herself rather than just fails to feel superior. For human beings rarely fail to err, at least a little bit, on one side or the other, and for the person anxious not to be immodest the "safe side" on which to err is that of underestimating herself. Because she fears immodesty

---

[34] See Bommarito (2013).
[35] See Raterman (2006).

it is true that when she is epistemically "picky," she is just a little quicker to accept evidence that speaks against her than evidence that speaks in her favor. If persistent, some ignorance about her virtues is bound to result. So we are back to ignorance. But lack of ill will (and perhaps also good will of the right sort, such as an aversion to benefitting from inequality) explains how the modest person is different from the person who simply does not know her strengths, and also from the victim of depression or stereotypical low self-esteem, whose self-underestimation has nothing to do with good will or the absence of ill will. In fact, Thomas Hill might be right in that a certain type of self-deprecator—a person whose prejudice is against himself—can be morally flawed in virtue of his self-deprecation.[36]

9.7 Vicious Dreams

In "Dream Immorality,"[37] Driver argues against the view that praise and blame are primarily matters of motive rather than consequences. She does so by reviving a worry of Augustine's on the subject of dreams. She asks the following question: if the view is true, and if one dreams of committing murder, does it not follow that one is just as blameworthy as if one had committed real murder? It seems impossible to explain why we do not treat the dream-murderer in the same way unless we admit that there is something other than motive that tips our judgment of blameworthiness. The dream-murderer seems not to be blameworthy because his actions do not have consequences in the real world or because actions in dreams tend have no consequences in the real world. If we do not avail ourselves of this explanation, Driver says, we are stumped. After all, the same motive and intention are required to commit a dream-murder as are required to commit real murder.

Driver's argument poses a threat to Spare Conativism, but a threat that affords an opportunity to use some of the ideas developed in the present chapter.

It is not true that the same motives are required to commit a dream-murder as are required to commit real murder. If one were to be, in a waking and

---

[36] She is also different from the person who is servile. We agree with Thomas Hill that debasing oneself too much also conflicts with the way in which we need to look at people as equal. Just as serious overestimation of one's powers is usually the result of immodesty, serious underestimation, if it is not simply the result of major depression, can be the result of a sort of an Aristotelian opposite of the vice of immodesty, namely the vice that Hill calls "servility"—treating other people as if their moral status is higher than your own just because you are you, or just because they are not you. Prejudice against yourself is, in the sense we discussed above, still prejudice. The servile person is different from the modest person, and also from the aforementioned sufferers of depression and those innocently mistaken about their strengths.

[37] Driver (2007).

nonpsychotic life, convinced that one is committing a murder while in fact using a realistic toy gun or shooting at a hologram, one might in fact require the same amount of ill will or moral indifference as one would require for committing a real murder. However, a dream about murder does not require ill will or moral indifference at all, and when it does show such motives it oftentimes shows them in small quantities: enough ill will to lead to a real-life profanity rather than a real-life murder.

Consider, for example a person who in a vivid dream kills his father and does not feel bad about it. It might be that he would like to kill his father, but, *pace* Freud, it seems unlikely. Depending on the person, the context, and so on, this dream might have any of the following sorts of significance.

The dreamer feels very guilty about some minor misbehavior towards his father, and his dream represents it as murder.

The dreamer is struggling with his father's emotional dominance as he considers choices of which his father would not approve. Vaguely remembering the Freud that he learned in college, he represents the desirable achievement of autonomy as patricide.

The dreamer is angry at his father, although he did not quite realize this before the dream. The image of killing manifests a sort of anger that would, in waking life, likely be expressed by an angry conversation.

The dreamer is a philosopher. He has just read an article about the idea of the reactive attitudes, an idea which, for years, he has scorned with passion. After reading the article, which contains an example about killing a person, a revelation comes to him, symbolized by a story in which he "postpones his reactive attitudes" to killing his father. He wakes up with new insights.

The dreamer is a consummate stage actor who must soon play someone who kills his father; the dream reflects the actor's attempt to understand his character.

The dream-murder in the first scenario reflects the conscience of a person who feels guilty over a comparatively minor matter. Interestingly, guilt is something that one feels as a result of moral concern, so if the dream is to tell us anything about the dreamer it might be that the dreamer is not just a nonmurderer but in fact has pro-moral emotional sensitivities. The second scenario also does not reveal any kind of morally objectionable motive or character. There are even some who, like Hill, would think of such a desire for autonomy as virtuous. As for the third scenario, it is implausible that each and every person who says in anger, "if that kid touches my daughter I'm gonna kill him," or something similar, has a desire to kill anyone, even unconsciously. The third scenario shows nothing more than ordinary anger. Being angry can be bad, but it does not entail a level of ill will or moral indifference required to kill someone. And the last two scenarios are morally neutral.

In each of the cases discussed, there exists a disanalogy, as regards their inner lives, between the dreamer and a person who believes that his father is in front of him and that a weapon is available, who desires to kill his father, and who as a result attempts to commit murder. The dreamer's heart is not really filled with murderous desire: his heart is rather filled with guilt, the desire for autonomy, mundane levels of anger, a desire to act well, or philosophical wondering. He cannot be judged as if he were a person who actually tried to commit an immoral action but, luckily for his intended victim, was trapped in a virtual reality; not only that, but he cannot be judged as someone who would have committed all of these acts in reality if he were not afraid of the law or encumbered by mere social inhibitions. First of all, the act in the dream is not always something that the person wants to do. Then, even if the act were to be presented as desired, it remains true that the real world, killing your father means killing your father, whereas in the dream it often means something else.

What, Driver might ask, of the rare case in which the dream about killing father is a manifestation of a desire to kill one's father? Even Jung, whose views on symbolism in dreams most often seemed not only to defy but to mock Ockham's razor, admitted that when a fisherman dreams about fish, they might actually be fish (as opposed to Christian symbols, we presume). Surely there are cases in which a dream about killing one's father is a straightforward manifestation of what one most desires. Driver suggests at the end of her piece that her opponent might offer the view that dream immorality exists but is just very rare. Are we saying that it is?

A dream in which the desire to murder stands for the desire to murder would still not amount to what it would if it were waking life, because of the nature of sleep. The dreamer is in a peculiar state that reduces her ability to respond to reasons, both epistemic and practical. She is likely to "do" things in dreams that she would otherwise never do, such as risk her life for a nonsensical mission or move to Antarctica (note that, if she dreams of doing these things, we do not think of her as lacking in prudence or keen to live in Antarctica). Even if a dream is very realistic, it is still not like a virtual reality, as can be seen from the fact that *if* winged cats were suddenly to appear in the dream, the dreamer probably would not respond to her reasons to think it strange, which shows that she is not fully responsive to her epistemic reasons even when she does not actually dream of seeing any winged cats. Similarly, even if a dreamer seemingly helps a person in a dream because it increases utility it is still true that if winged cats had appeared she might have (for instance) gone on a shooting spree instead, without feeling any conflict. An action that is an exercise of good or ill will has to manifest some intrinsic desire concerning some at least *pro tanto* moral reason, and responding to such reasons is at best very erratically achieved in a dream state. And so a dream action is still not generally a manifestation of good will, ill will, moral indifference, or reverse moral indifference in the way that a real life action is: divorced from reasons, it is not clearly an action at all.

A dream can, nonetheless, be a manifestation of good will, ill will, moral indifference, or reverse moral indifference. After all, in the examples in which the dreams are not manifestations of murderous motives, they *are* manifestations of other things, such as an intrinsic aversion to acting wrongly or an intrinsic desire for autonomy. A great deal of epistemic caution would be needed in drawing any conclusion about particular dreams, but in principle this point is correct. A malicious or benevolent dream is not a vice or virtue, because it is merely a transient mental event, not a stable state of mind. But it can, on occasion, be a display of vice or virtue.

So far we have been talking about dreams. What, however, about fantasies and daydreams in which the agent has some conscious control of what happens? The first thing to notice is that what a person does in a fantasy cannot be considered as just a "muted" blameworthy or praiseworthy action because, unlike the actually acting agent or the dreamer, the fantasist's beliefs include that the fantasy is imaginary and that the fantasist is in charge. Whether or not it takes ill will to imagine killing someone, it does not generally take as much ill will as actually killing. In fact, some people who daydream about killing will say to themselves, "alright, this is a fantasy, I am not hurting anything, so of course I can do this. Thank goodness for fantasies." That type of thought process can easily be the result of their moral concern. The fantasist is blowing off harmless steam instead of acting in a hostile way.

This makes fantasies in themselves unimportant to someone like Driver, as no one is suggesting that people can be blameworthy or praiseworthy for imaginary actions (except insofar as they might be nurturing ideas of actually performing good or bad acts, or the like). However, a suspicion that fantasies can be manifestations of good or ill will cannot be this easily dismissed. While one has considerable control over one's imaginings, one has no control over an important factor: one cannot directly control what gives one pleasure or displeasure. It is a bad sign—and apparently a symptom of the deepest moral indifference—if a child enjoys causing pain to animals. It is widely considered a sign of a child who might grow up to become a psychopath or have "antisocial personality disorder."[38] Is it not then a bad sign if a child enjoys vividly imagining that he causes pain to animals? What gives us pleasure, after all, depends on what we want and what we care about.

What do fantasies say about what we want? One domain in which much ordinary (as opposed to philosophical) thinking is found concerns sexual desires. Suppose we have a person who fantasizes about being a captive of an exacting queen and being grossly mistreated by her. It would be ridiculous to

---

[38] Lockwood and Ascione (1998).

assume that this is in fact something he wants. Stereotypically, the person might enjoy an enactment of his fantasy with a cooperative partner, a situation as different from being a royal captive as could be. If we take our lead from how we understand this sexual fantasy scenario when we try to assess the person who ordinarily fantasizes, in a nonsexual way, about doing bad things to others, we might expect something similar to be true of her: that she fantasizes about killing someone usually does not mean she would enjoy killing him.

Still, we disagree with Thomas Hurka who treats fantasies as desire-independent unless they are what Cherry (1988) calls "surrogate fantasies," fantasies in which one really wants something and makes do with a fantasy of the very same thing. There are ways for a fantasy to reveal desires that are not as obvious, just as with dreams. On our view, a fantasy is related to a desire (or desires) so long as we feel pleasure or displeasure at it, so perhaps it is more accurate to say that not fantasy itself but pleasure or displeasure in a fantasy is a manifestation of desires. If one enjoys sexual fantasies at all, one probably has sexual desires. If a person constantly fantasizes about his own death, it is generally wrong to jump to the conclusion that he is suicidal, but it is likely that he suffers from depression. And if we encounter someone who regularly enjoys fantasizing vividly and in detail about doing atrocious things to people who have done her no wrong, or even simply imagines horrible suffering befalling people, we worry, especially if the enjoyment is acute. Though such fantasies might not be blameworthy themselves, there is ill will on display nonetheless, and thus the pleasure of these fantasies is a manifestation of vice.

Which raises a common question: what about those video games in which one essentially fantasizes about committing acts of violence? Are they related to anything genuinely bad in the heart of the person who plays them?

It is important here to distinguish two questions. One question is whether playing such games for long periods of time can do any harm to a person's moral character, especially if the person is young. This is an empirical question and we shall not try to answer it here. A second question is whether simple attraction to such games reveals something bad about the moral concerns of the one attracted. This can be the case regardless of the empirical facts about the first question.

We take it that enjoying other people's suffering per se is inherently bad, a symptom of ill will. While accepting our premise, an advocate for violent computer games might argue that this need not be the sort of enjoyment offered by these games. There is competition and skill, there is the satisfaction of fighting and defeating evil (monsters or Nazis), and there are outlets for anger (one can even express one's disgust with pop culture, as with a past computer game in which one killed Smurfs). In other words, the pleasures offered by the games are not bad the way enjoying the suffering of fictitious people for its own sake would be.

Whether enjoying violent games manifests ill will appears to be related to how we think about the moral status of some basic violent and competitive urges that most of us have. Many of us have some fantasy or another involving somehow outdoing, outsmarting, or just overcoming a competitor or someone who provokes anger. Some people, perhaps also drawn to certain types of feminism, would say that such competitive urges are expressions of intrinsic desires for ends (dominance, destruction, or the like) that we have *pro tanto* moral reason to avoid, and so are ill will. Others would think that such urges can be inherently morally neutral, the way sexual urges are, and likewise the cause of good or of bad, depending on circumstance. If one accepts the latter view, certain types of violent fantasy need not incriminate their possessors at all.

Of course, the enjoyment of the suffering of fictional people is a lot more complicated a matter than we can sum up in this section—what about enjoying reading *Hamlet?*—and so we shall leave full discussion of it to those who try to understand moral imagination.

{ PART IV }

Puzzles

{ 10 }

Inner Struggle

Inner struggle appears to present us with Reason at war with Appetite, while Spare Conativism appears to make no room for such bellicosity. If reason is the slave of the passions, and can never pretend to any other office than to serve and obey them,[1] then how is an apparent slave revolt even possible? When there is inner struggle, what is the struggle between?

There is room for inner struggle because, even if rationality is nothing but doing what best satisfies one's desires given one's beliefs, we do not automatically take the most rational course of action. Any number of merely physical or merely content-efficacious factors can interfere, as shown in chapter 3. Nor do we automatically take what we *think* is the best or most rational course of action, nor are we automatically pleased at the thought of the best or most rational course of action (as explained in chapter 6, more desire satisfaction does not automatically entail more pleasure). Gaps such as these give us many opportunities to feel torn, as this chapter will attempt to show.

10.1 *Akrasia*

Inner struggle is not the same thing as acting against one's judgment of what it would be best to do, that is, *akrasia*.[2] This is most obvious in that there is inner struggle that results in action in accordance with one's best judgment (i.e., *enkratic* action), and so inner struggle that involves no *akrasia*. But it might be pointed out that situations in which one is merely *enkratic* are situations in which *akrasia* was a live possibility, so the separation between inner struggle and *akrasia* is not yet clear. A stronger piece of evidence for the separation is that there can be *akrasia* without inner struggle. A smoker who is attempting to quit cigarettes might, on some occasion, judge that it is best to decline a cigarette that is politely offered to her, only to find herself immediately contravening her judgment and accepting the cigarette and smoking it, without having any sense of struggle. One could call

---

[1] As Hume suggests in the *Treatise*. See Hume (2000).
[2] There are other ways to think about weakness of will, such as the one suggested by Richard Holton (1999). We shall not discuss them here.

this story one of inner struggle, but it would be an odd bit of jargon. We prefer to reserve the phrase for cases in which there is something recognizable from the inside as struggle in part for clarity but also in part because what we identify as inner struggle is a puzzle for the present theory, whereas simple *akrasia* is not.

On the present theory, a person who believes that, all things considered, it is best to go to the gym and lift weights is merely a person who has a belief. This belief is poised to engage with her intrinsic desire to do what is best, an intrinsic desire involving her concept BEST,[3] so as to lead her to do what appears best—in this case, to go weightlifting. Irrational *akratic* action will happen when the course of action that a person believes to be best is the same as the course of action that is best rationalized for her, and yet (because of a failure of ND capacities to act for reasons) the person does not do what is best rationalized, and does something else. The *akratic* course of action will be rationalized to some lesser extent, and will involve beliefs and desires causing it in virtue (in part) of their own (lesser, but non-zero) rationalizing relations to the immediate intention acted upon. Nothing about believing some course of action best will automatically suffice to overcome any failures in ND capacities; there is no causal magic brought about by this belief.

In other cases of *akrasia* the agent acts more rationally then she would have acted if she were to stick to her best judgment. These are cases in which the course of action desired as BEST is not, in fact, the course of action maximally rationalized by the agent's beliefs and desires, and the agent takes a course of action that would appear to satisfy or make progress toward satisfying other intrinsic desires with a combined strength in excess of the strength of the intrinsic desire to do what is BEST. In these situations, so long as all the beliefs and desires influence action production proportionally to the extent to which they rationalize action production, the person will believe it is best to go weightlifting but do something else instead. She will thus be *akratic*, but act more rationally then she would have if she were *enkratic*: she will be a person who is being more reasonable than she thinks she is.[4]

The ease with which *akratic* action is possible according to the present theory is a virtue. Since Socrates, philosophers have noted the seeming ubiquity of actions contrary to what one judges best, and since Socrates there have been philosophers whose theories of action were in tension, or inconsistent, with this seeming ubiquity: philosophers who have thus been moved to hold that *akrasia* is impossible,[5] or that last-ditch *akrasia* is impossible,[6] or that it is at least a great puzzle how *akrasia* is possible.[7] If it seems that a person has

---

[3] Assuming she has such a desire—but if people can acquire intrinsic desires for the victory of the Montreal Canadiens, why not for doing what is best?

[4] See Arpaly (2000).

[5] See, for example, Hare (1963).

[6] See, for example, Blackburn (1998).

[7] Aristotle's discussion of *akrasia* certainly does not suggest that it is readily explained, for instance (Aristotle 1999, book 7). Davidson (1980, chapter 2) provides a more recent tortured explanation of the phenomenon.

judged it best to not eat the cake, smoke the cigarette, dispute the truth of theism with relatives over Thanksgiving, or deliberate upon what to do in the event of being denied tenure, and the person nonetheless eats, smokes, disputes, or deliberates, the present theory has the resources to accept the apparent facts at face value.

Interestingly, what turns out to be a bit of a puzzle is not how *akrasia* is possible but how it happens that we so often do what we believe to be best. After all, when the belief that something is best is held to be just one belief, engaging just one intrinsic desire out of many, the fact that we often do what we believe to be best comes as a bit of a surprise. Given all the things that we intrinsically desire, and all of the possible actions that they can rationalize and cause, it so happens that we often perform the action that we also believe best. Why?

One possible explanation could come from the referential content of the concept BEST. If what it is best to do is what it is most practically rational to do, a fairly regular correlation between a belief that an action is the best and the performance of that action could be expected. After all, such a correlation would hold when one's belief was correct—when the action believed best was indeed the action that was most practically rational—and when one's action was the rational action. And it can hardly be a surprise when a person both has true beliefs and performs rational actions.

It is not obvious that this is the best, or only, way to understand how common *enkrateia*[8] is from within the present theoretical framework. We leave further investigation for another time, however, and return to the main topic at hand: not *akrasia* as such, but inner struggle.

10.2 The Experience of Inner Struggle

Imagine Maggie is torn between going to work one evening and calling in sick to spend the evening with friends. She feels pulled in both directions, and needs to take steps to resolve the conflict. But she finds that, even after taking what seem reasonable steps to resolve the conflict, the conflict persists. Whichever decision[9] she has made, whichever course of action she has judged best, whichever intention she has formed, whichever overt actions she has already taken

---

[8] Here we mean something broad by *"enkrateia,"* namely, action that conforms to an agent's belief about what it is best to do. We do not mean to be saying that the mere *enkrateia* discussed at length by Aristotle (1999), in which one overcomes lack of virtue or inner struggle in order to do what one believes best, is especially common.

[9] We do not endorse any specific theory of decision here, but of course we need it to be compatible with our larger needs in the theory of action. Perhaps decisions are a kind of intention formation, or a kind of belief formation (about what it is best to do), or a change in dispositions regarding future volitions. What they cannot be, for our purposes, are things such as motivationally efficacious cognitive states, or causally independent sources of motivation not affected by intrinsic desires.

toward acting in the one way rather than the other, she feels pulls and barriers inside her that make it difficult to do what she has decided, judged best, intended, or started doing.

Maggie's sense of inner struggle is likely to have five distinct aspects.

First, Maggie is likely to feel her struggle as happening between her "self" and recalcitrant aspects of her own mind, and so she is likely to feel more identified with some aspects of her mind during her inner struggle and more alienated from others. Call this the *identificational* aspect of her inner struggle. If she is truly undecided, her sense of self might shift with the vacillations in her opinion as to what to do. At one moment her self might seem to be the part that wants to go to work (the other part being just laziness that has to be overcome) and at another moment her self might seem to be the part that wants to be with friends (the other part being just irrational guilt that has to be overcome). When she decides, her sense of self settles on one "side"—say, the side of going to work.

Second, she might feel, for example, gloomy at the prospect of going in to work, and feel a thrill of delight when she imagines calling in sick. Call these the *hedonic* aspects. Inner struggle often and saliently involves pleasure and dis-pleasure in various guises, sometimes tied up with strong emotions that include much more than just the hedonic tone in question, as with a person confronting the fear of doing one thing and the prospective humiliation of failing to do it, for example. At other times inner struggle involves pleasure and displeasure in a barer way, and one simply finds that the prospect of doing one thing is pleas-ant, while the prospect of doing the other is unpleasant (or perhaps both are unpleasant, or both pleasant, to similar or different degrees).

Third, Maggie might, for example, find it difficult to put on her work clothes, in that the movements required to go to her closet and select the relevant slacks and t-shirt seem somehow unavailable to her. Maggie might feel that she can easily choose between peeling an orange, putting on some music, playing a game on her computer, and so on, while feeling that the option of going to the closet and getting on the work clothes is somehow missing from the menu. Call these aspects of her inner struggle the *motivational* aspects. Feeling that certain actions are available to be performed, if one would so choose, while others are not, is an interesting part of the phenomenology of acting that is not much dis-cussed by philosophers. However, it seems to us an entirely common aspect of the experience of action generally. A person standing on a balcony might not be in the least inclined or disposed to leap off the balcony, in the sense that it is a very distant possibility for the person: there is no nearby possible world in which the person leaps (as can be seen from the statistical frequency of leaping in people with this feeling). Yet the same person might feel that the act of leap-ing is an available option for her. (This fact itself can be unnerving; it appears central to what Sartre calls 'vertigo'.)[10] Or she might feel that the act of leaping

---

[10] Sartre (1948).

is not an available option for her. (And this might be reassuring.) And whether she feels that leaping is or is not an option for her might be different on different occasions, quite independently of any desire to commit suicide or demonstrate her radical freedom. In cases of inner struggle, it sometimes happens that one side of the struggle requires an action that feels phenomenologically unavailable; other times, it happens that one side of the struggle requires an action that feels all too readily available.

Fourth, Maggie might, for example, rehearse her reasons to go to work and to not call in sick but find them not yet efficacious in bringing about the actions required to actually go to work. Call these the *reflective* aspects. Technically, these mental actions might not be acts of deliberation, because they might be aimed not at determining what to do (as practical deliberation must be; see chapter 1) but at causing an already settled-upon action.[11] However, they are mental actions that involve calling to consciousness (apparent) reasons. If Maggie is struggling with herself over whether or not to call in sick to work and she reminds herself of the fact that it is hard to earn enough to pay the rent every month, and so she needs all the hours she can get, then Maggie is calling to mind a fact that is (apparently) a practical reason to go to work, and so doing something she might well have done in deliberation.

Fifth, Maggie might find herself in some way trying to force herself to, for example, get up and go to her closet. Call this the *volitional* aspect of her inner struggle. She might exhort herself, talking to herself using her auditory imagination. Perhaps she says to herself, "just go to the closet and put the shirt on. Go on! Time to go! Get moving!" Maggie might also simply "will" herself to go to her closet and so to begin the process of going to work, where phenomenologically this willing can be just a matter of having a sense of mental effort and having an idea of the end toward which the effort is being directed. On other occasions, willing that one get up seems to involve a proprioceptive image of oneself getting up (or performing whatever other action one might be willing oneself to take), along with a sense of effort.

Of course, the sense of inner struggle is more than a feeling at a moment, even a complex of the five kinds of feelings just described. Inner struggle is dynamic. In it, one feels that one's actions—possibly even one's mental actions—are contested by *oneself* on one side and by *opposing forces* on the other. On the one hand, it seems that the issue of what to do is settled. There is a decision, judgment of what is best, intention, or initial overt action that is clear on what to do.[12] On the other

---

[11] If the conclusion of practical deliberation is a volition or action, however, then these will still count as deliberative acts, since then the person facing inner struggle has not yet reached a practical conclusion about what to do.

[12] As this makes clear, we are not discussing difficult deliberations, in which one feels pulled in different directions, but at the end of which one feels wholeheartedly resolved. Our previous discussion of deliberation (chapters 1 and 2) seems sufficient for this purpose, perhaps supplemented by some of the discussion in this chapter.

hand, this sense of the issue being resolved does not lead directly to action. There is a constant inner threat to the performance of the action decided upon, judged best, intended, or initiated. And there are actions, both covert and overt, that the struggling person can perform that might lead to winning or losing the struggle.

Return to Maggie, who has settled in some way upon going to work this evening, but who is struggling with herself because she feels she is in danger of calling in sick instead, so that she can spend the evening with friends. The dynamics of her struggle could take various forms.

Maggie might take overt actions to resolve her inner struggle. She might, for instance, ask her housemate for a ride to work. Doing so, she might find that she feels more committed and resolved. She is still unhappy at the prospect of going to work, perhaps, but now she feels tied to the mast, and this makes an end of the inner struggle. Other overt actions she can take to end her inner struggle might include getting some coffee (perhaps she tells herself that she just needs to wake up a little and then her resolve will stiffen) and looking at her bank balance (seeing exactly, to the penny, how badly she needs each day of work might spur her on).

Maggie might also take overt actions that resolve her inner struggle by changing which "side" she is on. She might send a quick message to her friends, asking them if they think she should call in sick, and their reply that she should might make her decide to call in sick, and that itself might resolve her inner struggle. (Or it might not, of course.) Or she might procrastinate until it is too late to show up to work on time, and then feel resolved to instead call in sick at the last second. But if this is how she resolves her inner struggle, then she will not typically take these actions while consciously thinking to herself that she is taking them in order to change her mind about what to do. After all, in the example, Maggie sees her decision, judgment of what is best, intention, or even her current course of action to be one settled on going in to work, however reluctantly. That is the side of "her," in her struggle against "herself."

Inner struggle is even more commonly thought of as involving covert actions, that is, mental actions. Maggie might well start by reviewing her reasons to go to work, then proceed to exhorting herself. Taking a leaf from William James's observations about the difficulties of getting out of bed on a cold day,[13] she might try to stop deliberating and just go to her closet, where her work clothes are found. She might bargain with herself, contemplating some plan that involves going to work now but doing something nice after work.

As with overt actions, Maggie might also take covert actions that end up changing her mind about what to do, without seeing that this is what she is doing. She might review everything that she will be missing by not seeing her friends and become convinced that she really ought to skip work after all. (And

---

[13] James (1890).

perhaps still be torn, and have a new inner struggle against an impulse to go to work nonetheless.) She might ask herself what her sister (a seeming model of *eudaimonia*) would do, with the answer being that of course she would skip work, and this might resolve the tension in favor of skipping work. And so on.

10.3 Inner Struggle Explained

With the resources we have, we need to explain how there can be a sense of one-self struggling against opposing forces for control of one's actions, a struggle involving the five phenomenological aspects described in the previous section. We need to explain how inner struggle is manifested in the sorts of overt and covert behaviors we imagined for Maggie. We need to explain how inner struggle results sometimes in rational, and sometimes in irrational, action. And we need to do it all without appealing to anything like a distinction between Reason and Appetite, or even appealing to a distinction between kinds of intrinsic desires.

Begin with the first aspect, the very feeling of struggling against part of oneself. To feel that it is self on one side and not-self on the other side of one's struggles is itself a puzzling matter, since in ordinary cases it is the self on both sides of the struggle. "Losing" an inner struggle might lead to irrational action in many cases, but it does not typically lead to nonagency. (A person with Tourette syndrome struggling against a tic might sometimes be in this position, but it is certainly not the norm.) How is this sense of self in the struggle to be understood?

The simplest way of thinking about this is to recognize that feelings of agency and alienation are, first and foremost, *feelings*.[14] They tell us that certain of our acts are our own and that others are not. These feelings are useful for recognizing when we move our own bodies as opposed to when other people, strong winds, shifting rocks, and so on move us. This is perhaps their sole function from the perspective of natural selection. But these feelings also usefully distinguish "the disease" from "me" in people with Tourette syndrome, it seems.[15] As mere feelings, however, feelings of agency and alienation can go wrong. For example, one theory of schizophrenics holds that a key problem they suffer from is not feeling themselves to be the agents of their own inner speech, and so identifying it as thought insertion ("voices in my head").[16] If our feelings tell us that we are the agents of our overt or covert actions directed at getting us to work, then we will feel that "we" are trying to get to work, and that whatever opposes our getting to work is not our doing, and perhaps not even "us." If our feelings tell us that we are not the agents of our overt or covert

---

[14] We discuss alienation more fully in Schroeder and Arpaly (1999).
[15] See Schroeder (2005).
[16] Gallagher (2000).

actions directed at getting us to skip work, then we will feel that "we" are being overridden by something that is not "us," though if we are not suffering from Tourette syndrome we are probably wrong to feel this way. If the decisive inner or outer actions happen after what feels like a struggle, then it will feel that "we" have won or lost the struggle, as the case may be, though in either case we will be the ones acting.

For many people, feelings of agency track conscious beliefs about rationality in action. Their feelings of agency are strongest when they believe themselves to be acting reasonably, and the more unreasonably they believe themselves to be acting the more likely they are to feel alienated from their actions. So, for many people, the courses of action that they consciously think of as most rational will be the courses of action that they experience as "theirs," the ones "they" are struggling to carry out against inner forces. But there is no necessity to this. Some people have lived with procrastination, fear, and depression all their lives, and have integrated these forms of irrationality into their senses of agency. When prescribed a drug that allows them to be efficient, unafraid, and not sad, they will sometimes experience their newly reasonable actions as alien, as somehow fake or not really their own. (Others with the same problems and the same drugs will feel that their actions are finally truly their own; people, it seems, are just different in this regard.) These people, presumably, will not always feel their inner struggles as ones in which "they" are on the sides of the courses of action they believe most reasonable. Likewise, an anorectic might experience her resolve not to eat as her "self" and her desire to eat as an external obstacle. Feelings of selfhood do not always track what we feel to be the rational part of ourselves, nor do they always track rationality itself, or a faculty of Reason.

With the relevant caveats, however, it seems many people will experience themselves as the agent working on behalf of the course of action consciously believed to be most reasonable. This gives us a starting point. But it does not yet give us the possibility of struggle. After all, it could have been that human beings were designed to always immediately execute actions, so that, while we might feel the owners of some actions and alienated from others, we would in neither case struggle.

To experience inner struggle, one has to conceive of some future (perhaps very near future) course of action without yet acting in a way that decisively embraces or rejects that future. One has to make a decision, draw a conclusion about what it would be best to do, form an intention, start to carry out the action (without yet having completed it), or something similar, and then, while the ultimate fate of the course of action contemplated is still open, experience one or more of the four remaining aspects of inner struggle described in the previous section.

The hedonic aspect of inner struggle is straightforward to explain within Spare Conativism. A person struggling with herself will have a number of intrinsic desires that will be served by each of the courses of action being conceived. When one course of action is decided upon, believed best, intended, or initiated, this does nothing to change the strengths of the intrinsic desires that are now going to be frustrated by the selected course of action. So there will be some opportunity for pleasure here (at the prospect of performing the selected action, since it will be expected to bring about states of affairs that will satisfy some intrinsic desires) and some opportunity for displeasure (at the prospect of foregoing other states of affairs, ones that would have satisfied other desires). As discussed in chapter 5, though, pleasure and displeasure normally fluctuate with change in net satisfaction of intrinsic desires relative to gut-level expectations. There is room for abnormal feelings (as when one is hedonically insulated by the effects of alcohol) and there is room for feelings that are more strongly affected by expectations than by intrinsic desire satisfaction. Finally, there is room (mentioned also in chapter 8) for the differences between appetitive desires and aversions to play a role in affecting feelings.

If Maggie takes her job and income for granted, then the prospect of getting paid will not be much of a delight to her, even though it satisfies or is a means to satisfying a number of her intrinsic desires. If Maggie is not hardened to the experience of turning down visits with her friends (that is, if she did not come to viscerally expect turning down visits from her friends) then she will feel the full force of disappointment at the prospect of doing so. This will be true even if Maggie's intrinsic desires are, on balance, likely (given her beliefs) to be much better satisfied by her going to work than by her calling in sick to see her friends: the effects of expectations will make the prospect of work on balance unpleasant even though it is the more desire-satisfying course of action. Thus, even if Maggie selects the course of action that is practically rational, she might not feel good about pursuing it, she might feel bitterly disappointed at the thought of what she is giving up, and she will get prospective pleasure from contemplating skipping work to see her friends. These feelings will, of course, be sensitive to how Maggie frames her thinking. If she is not hardened to losing jobs, then if she thinks about calling in sick as risking her job, she might feel bad (perhaps fearful) about the idea of doing it; likewise if she is not hardened to lying and sees calling in sick as lying (though perhaps she feels exploited, and so could see her lying as permissible self-defense). And also, if Maggie has an appetite to see her friends but an aversion to lying (or being poor, after being fired) then that too might shape the way she feels about her options. Aversions provide opportunities to feel relief (when the aversive state of affairs is avoided) but they seem to have less direct pathways to inducing delight and excitement than do appetitive desires, and so the idea of not lying about being sick might feel less exiting than the idea of seeing her friends, even though her intrinsic aversions to dishonesty and poverty might outweigh her intrinsic appetites served by seeing her friends.

The motivational aspect of inner struggle is the sense that certain physically possible courses of action are open or closed for one at a given moment. Here some science is relevant to the phenomenon. Action production in the brain is a complex process, as discussed in chapter 6. Part of that process involves parts of the brain that can command immediate bodily movements. These parts of the brain are stimulated in part by how the world is being perceived and conceived at a given moment: these experiences and thoughts promote certain (perhaps merely associated) immediate bodily movements. All of these possible commands for immediate bodily movements are inhibited globally and only selectively released, through a process sensitive to what is believed and desired.[17] But inhibited commands for immediate bodily movements still exist, and have effects. These effects include phenomenological ones: through feed-forward signaling, commands (even inhibited ones) for immediate bodily movements cause feelings related to carrying out the movements that are most available—the movements for which the commands to produce them are most strongly stimulated, even if held in abeyance. This appears to be what is responsible for the felt availability of jumping from a balcony, when that feeling exists: the motor command for vaulting the railing (or the like) is promoted, perhaps purely on associative grounds, by the sight of the balcony, or the direction of the conversation, or the noting of the height as a danger, or the like. Of course, in those who are not suicidal, this motor command is solidly inhibited, in a way that is not likely to change. For the nonsuicidal, the beliefs and desires that cause selected available actions to be released are very unlikely to release the action of vaulting the railing, given how obviously desire-frustrating the consequences are. But while inhibited, the command for vaulting the railing is still active, and so it can cause its feed-forward effects on bodily consciousness, and one has a somatosensory and proprioceptive image readily available of the movements involved in vaulting the railing. If the command for vaulting the railing is highly stimulated in context (perhaps one keeps thinking about this very action, out of morbid fascination with one's own response), it will tend to cause a very vivid image of the action. And hence the sense of availability. If some action requires a movement that, for whatever reason, is not being made available (the structure that would issue the needed motor command is not being stimulated), then that action is not available to be performed at that moment (there is nothing for the combined effects of beliefs and desires to release) and it is not likely to feel available (because it will not be sending its feed-forward signals to somatosensory or proprioceptive perceptual centers).

In Maggie's case, it might be that she can picture herself going to the closet, but that this does not (for some reason) promote the relevant motor commands, and so the actions required to get her work clothes on do not feel available to her. And it might be that other actions, such as picking up her phone to tell her friends that she will see them tonight, feel vividly available to her: the relevant

---

[17] A process that is also sensitive to purely contentful factors (such as habit) and to purely physical factors (such as fatigue), of course.

motor commands are not yet being acted upon, but they are highly excited—perhaps because Maggie is thinking a lot about how wonderful it would be to see her friends tonight and not go to work.

The fourth aspect of inner struggle is the reflective one: the person who is struggling with herself brings to mind her reasons to act in the way she has selected, and perhaps also brings to mind reasons to change her mind. The basic mechanisms of reflection were discussed in the context of deliberation in chapter 2, but inner struggle raises a question not previously asked: what would cause one to bring (apparent) reasons to mind when one has already settled on a course of action—when one has decided, concluded what is best, intended, or even initiated an action?

Maggie's story provides a good opportunity to consider the possibilities. The first is that Maggie's selected course of action—to go to work—is the rational one. Though it is the rational course of action, and is believed to be so, Maggie knows that she does not always do what it is rational to do. Sometimes, as the result of nonrationalizing influences upon thought and action, Maggie does what is foolish. But Maggie has learned that she can sometimes increase the chance of rational action by repeating to herself her reasons for performing the rational action, or avoiding the irrational action, or both. Her approach works, insofar as it does, because reflection in general, like deliberation, is a useful tool for enhancing our capacity to act via ND processes. But, one might wonder, why is it that Maggie is capable of taking rational mental actions (reminding herself of her reasons to go to work) when she is in danger of taking irrational nonmental actions (calling in sick)?[18] The answer here is speculative, but it does not seem that interference with reason-responsiveness is always uniform and global. On the contrary. The fact that Maggie is not doing what she must soon do to work (put on her work clothes) might be a manifestation of irrationality in action on her part, but there is no reason that the interference in her acting for reasons in this action needs to carry over to generate equal interference with her acting for reasons in the case of a mental action, such as reviewing reasons for going to work. But note that, just as this rational action in reflection is possible, it is not guaranteed either. Maggie might instead call to mind her reasons to call in sick. Doing this might be irrational, but irrational action is always possible, even irrational reflective action. If Maggie is vividly aware that it is irrational for her to call to mind the reasons to not do what it is rational to do, she might feel alienated from her mental actions, but it would be more common for her to take these actions without seeing them as a threat to her rationality. It would be more common for her to see herself as just wistfully thinking about what could have been. And then, it might even be rational for Maggie to reflect in this way, since it might be rational to keep turning the facts over in her mind

---

[18] Wallace (1999, 225) asks a similar question in arguing against the present sort of view.

in the hope that some forgotten fact (she has a coworker who owes her a shift's worth of work as a favor, perhaps) will come to mind that will allow her to have everything that she wants, and sacrifice nothing.

The second possibility to consider in Maggie's scenario is that her selected course of action is actually the irrational one. Although it seems best to her to work tonight, she is in fact terribly exploited, owes her employer nothing, would be better off getting almost any other job, is unlikely to be fired in any event (perhaps she is the only person who reliably shows up for work sober), and the friends she would see include people she loves but will not see again for a long time (perhaps two are leaving to work on development projects in Nigeria). If Maggie nonetheless believes it is best to go to work, then she might still bring to mind the reasons she has to go to work. Doing so would, however, be irrational—she would, effectively, be taking actions likely to decrease the chance that she will see her friends, when it is seeing the friends that is best rationalized by her attitudes. However, irrational action is possible, and she might carry it out here. Or, in parallel with the previous case, she might do what seems to her foolish or merely wistful and bring to mind all the reasons to see her friends—rationally doing so, without grasping that this pattern of considering reasons is rational. And here no special explanation is required, since Maggie is simply taking a (mental) action that is well rationalized. The only thing odd is that Maggie herself, foolishly, does not believe that it is.

The fifth aspect of inner struggle mentioned in the previous section is that of willing oneself to do what seems rational (or perhaps, alienatingly, what seems irrational). Inner exhortation is a straightforward matter—it is just talking to oneself (deploying verbal imagery and the like) in the imperative mood. But willing that one do things might also be a matter of fixing one's attention on the idea of the action one needs to perform and holding one's attention there, an effortful mental behavior that might promote action (for instance, by promoting activity in the relevant brain structure issuing commands for immediate action, or by decreasing activity in brain structures promoting competing actions). Or it might be a matter of silencing one's mental imagery, as meditative practice encourages, so as to shift from contemplation to action. Such mental actions seem more or less phenomenologically familiar, and as actions they are all, like acts of deliberation, capable of being carried out for better or worse reasons, consistently or inconsistently with what one has already decided, concluded is best, intended, or begun doing.

The present theory thus has the resources to explain how it is that the aspects of inner struggle exist and get experienced by ordinary people. How does it explain the dynamics of inner struggle?

The dynamics of inner struggle will be different in different cases, of course, but Maggie will again serve as a useful example. Perhaps her struggle begins when she learns that her friends are holding a party tonight and that she is invited. Remembering that she is committed to working an evening shift,

Maggie decides she cannot go (judges it best, intends not to go, or perhaps begins to compose a reply sending her regrets). But now Maggie finds she just cannot send her response in which she declines the invitation. She knows how to do so, and can imagine herself doing it, but she is stuck getting from imagination to action. So she tells herself "oh, just tell them you can't go." This fails to lead to her sending her response. She starts reviewing her reasons to go to work, bringing to mind how she needs the money, how she agreed to this shift long ago, and so on. But then perhaps she also starts reviewing her reasons to call in sick instead, and see her friends. She reminds herself that she will not see two of these people again for a whole year, and that she is unlikely to be fired even if she does call in sick. Then she recognizes that these thoughts are weakening her resolve, and she tells herself "don't be silly." She makes an effort to stop deliberating. But finds herself still stuck, failing to take any action at all. So she tells herself, "just get up and put on your work clothes." And then she does so. Having done so, she finds it easier now to send the response declining the invitation, and she sends it with a feeling of deep regret.

In this version of Maggie's story, the dynamic aspect of her struggle is brought out; but with the previous discussion of the five aspects of inner struggle already outlined, it is clear enough how these dynamic aspects will be explained by Spare Conativism. Suppose, just for convenience (it could be otherwise), that Maggie acts on her best rationalization in going to work. Then she believes, not inevitably but also not surprisingly, that this course of action is indeed the rational one, and so feels identified with it. When she finds herself failing to take an obvious step toward going to work, namely, declining the invitation to see her friends, she experiences the failure as an inner obstacle to her legitimate agency. The source of her reluctance is perhaps just the desires that she is going to frustrate by declining the invitation, being more causally efficacious than they rationalize, blocking her from closing off the course of action that they rationalize. Experiencing herself as internally blocked, and having learned to use exhortations in this context, she says to herself, "oh, just tell them you can't go." But inner exhortation is not particularly effective in this case, which seems typical; perhaps one reason it is easy to exhort oneself when one is in the grips of motivated irrationality is exactly that, by being a not very efficacious strategy for generating rational action, it is also not particularly likely to be inhibited by the desires generating the motivated irrationality in the first place. Whatever the reason, it is evident to Maggie that she is still being irrational, so she needs to do something else. She takes a new action: rehearsing reasons to go to work (and so to decline the invitation). It is a rationalized course of action for her, since it seems likely to increase the chance that she will in fact decline the invitation, and that is the best rationalized course of action for her. But in the process of deliberating, Maggie's strong intrinsic desires to be part of her friends' lives, intrinsic desires that (poorly) rationalize thinking instead about the reasons to call in sick and not go to work, cause her to act irrationally in reflection and shift from thinking of reasons to go to work to thinking of reasons to call in sick. But Maggie soon recognizes the irrational drift of her reflections, and this recognition helps her to stop reflecting in this manner (perhaps her intrinsic desire to not act irrationally, or to make sense to herself,[19] comes to bear here given her explicit recognition that her reasoning is going wrong). She first exhorts herself again, in terms that maximally engage her intrinsic desire to be reasonable: "don't be silly." Having found reflection to be an unsafe strategy for generating the rational overt action just now, Maggie takes a different course of mental action, and stops herself from further reflection. Her effort to do this might have failed, of course, because irrational action is always possible, but given that it is a fairly modest rational action (one that does not directly get her to decline the evening with her friends) it is not a surprise that it is successful even though so far Maggie's efforts to overtly decline the invitation have failed. Now, having silenced her reflective processes, she notices that she is still not doing what she needs to do, eventually, in order to ultimately get to work and decline the invitation to see her friends. She takes a new mental action, telling herself to put on her work clothes. This new exhortation does not come out of a deliberative process, but it seems fairly ingeniously related to her rationalizing reasons. The exhortation is to do something that does not directly reject the invitation, and so it does not require a direct clash with the intrinsic desires that have so far prevented and subverted rational action. But the exhortation is also something that, if carried out, increases the chance that Maggie will ultimately do what is rational; taking a means often increases the chance that we will rationally (or irrationally) take the end to which it is a means. Maggie would show herself more practically rational by not needing to exhort herself at this point, and simply putting on her work clothes, but of course she is not particularly practically rational at this point, hence the need for all of the mental maneuvering. As it happens, the exhortation works. Maggie does something rational, and having done it, she is less vulnerable to the previous irrationality. This seems to be a matter more of content efficacy than acting for reasons—the mere fact that Maggie has her familiar work clothes on is hardly a significant reason, in itself, for her to go to work. But it also seems to be effective enough as a means for Maggie's ends. Now she finds herself unblocked; when she goes to reply to her friends, declining their invitation, she is able to do so. She feels regret, because the opportunity to see the friends is less taken for granted than the opportunity to go to work, and so more influential upon her feelings, especially given that the intrinsic desires in question were quite strong on both sides. But this regret is not an effective barrier to her rational action, which now goes ahead straightforwardly. Maggie's struggle is over.

---

[19] An intrinsic desire given a much more prominent role in Velleman (1992), but one we agree many people are likely to have.

Even if the foregoing example is found convincing in outline, it might be wondered just what the mechanisms are by which intrinsic desires are sometimes more efficacious and sometimes less efficacious at bringing about the actions that they intrinsically rationalize. Attention to relevant factors is one factor with influence, and the extent to which a course of action goes contrary to gut-level expectations is another. But the foregoing has been silent on the exact mechanisms by which irrationality is made possible. This has been intentional. The philosopher can note from the armchair that certain patterns are highly suggestive, but it is really the job of the cognitive scientist to give the fuller explanations of the mechanisms by which irrationality is made possible, with the relative importance of various factors measured and compared under various conditions. No doubt it is possible to go a little further than the present discussion while remaining safely in the armchair, but an armchair does not present a good vantage point from which to see what results are going to show up on the lab bench, and the philosopher should be happy at some point to hand off certain explanatory projects to her colleagues in the sciences. We hope to have got at least reasonably close to that point.

Addiction

In David Carr's addiction memoir, *The Night of the Gun*, there is the story of how, one cold November night in Minneapolis, Carr put his infant twin girls into snowsuits, bundled them into his car, and drove to a house that specialized in dealing cocaine for intravenous use.

> I could not bear to leave them home, but I was equally unable to stay put, to do the right thing. So here we were, one big, happy family, parked outside the dope house. It was late, past midnight.
>
> Then came the junkie math; addled moral calculation woven with towering need. If I went inside the house, I could get what I needed, or very much wanted. Five minutes, ten minutes tops...
>
> Sitting there in the gloom of the front seat, the car making settling noises against the chill, the math still loomed. Need. Danger. A sudden tumbling? Naw. Nothing to it, really. In that pool of darkness, I decided that my teeny twin girls would be safe. It was cold, but not *really* cold. Surely God would look after them while I did not.[1]

Carr ends up leaving the girls in the car for hours. When he returns they are still alive, sleeping peacefully. Though he gets lucky, it is obvious that his leaving them was a terrible act. Anyone should agree, with Carr himself, that he is blameworthy for what he did. At the same time, it needs to be acknowledged that what Carr did he did because of his addiction to cocaine. Back when he was familiar with the pleasures of cocaine but not addicted, he would not have acted in this way.

11.1 The Puzzle

It is easy for Spare Conativism to account for Carr's blameworthiness. But it is challenging to explain how that blameworthiness is mitigated by the fact of addiction.

An intrinsic desire to use cocaine, or to have a particular experience characteristic of cocaine use, is Carr's main positive motivation to go into the house.

---

[1] Carr (2008, chapter 28).

This desire, we take it, is not a form of ill will. There are possible situations in which the satisfaction of this desire is entirely morally permissible. However, in leaving his daughters behind and entering the house, Carr acts wrongly. And he acts wrongly because of a deficiency of moral concern: he does not intrinsically desire his daughters' happiness, or their treatment as ends in themselves (or...), as much as he might, and his deficiency is part of the explanation of why he acts wrongly. Had he cared enough, he would not have left his daughters behind in order to consume cocaine. Hence Carr displays moral indifference, and is blameworthy.[2]

Our difficulty in discussing the case comes in accounting for the fact that addiction is a mitigating factor when considering Carr's blameworthiness. Yes, Carr demonstrates a certain amount of indifference to something of tremendous moral importance, but he would not have abandoned his daughters in order to see the Minnesota Vikings play football, or to finish work that might be important for his career. His addiction is something that has a special hold upon him, and in assessing the way in which he is blameworthy the addiction should be recognized. Within our desire-centered moral psychology, however, doing so appears to be difficult. Spare Conativism is focused entirely upon the intrinsic desires of people who are blameworthy. Do they intrinsically desire what is right or good, or are they conatively indifferent to it? This is the only question SC asks about people like Carr. It does not ask about the origin of his desire for cocaine,[3] it does not ask about the ease with which he might resist his desire,[4] it does not ask about his attitude toward his desire for cocaine.[5] It does not, in other words, take into consideration the various facts that other desire-centered moral psychologists have appealed to in explaining what is special about people who do what is wrong because they are addicts. As a consequence, our theory appears unable to make a distinction between the case of David Carr and the case of the imaginary fan of the Minnesota Vikings who faces a parallel situation and who makes the parallel choice. The fan who leaves his infant children alone in the cold car in order to see some football, and who does so with as clear a vision of the stakes as Carr seems to have, strikes us as horrifyingly indifferent to his children's fate. His moral indifference is grotesque: he is willing to leave his children to risk death by exposure just in order to watch a football game. And because he is not (by stipulation) an addict or otherwise psychologically disturbed with respect to his enthusiasm for the Vikings, he has no excuse for his behavior, not even a partial excuse. He is simply a man who loves his football team far more than he loves his children, to

---

[2] Perhaps Carr is also blameworthy for being indifferent to the law, or to the enrichment of criminals, but we set these issues to one side. They complicate, but do not fundamentally change, the assessment of Carr's blameworthiness.

[3] E.g., Fischer and Ravizza (1998).

[4] E.g., Fischer and Ravizza (1998).

[5] E.g., Frankfurt (1971).

an extent that renders him nearly indifferent to the children, and that is not an excuse but an explanation of what is morally wrong with the man: his priorities are morally unacceptable. Carr deserves a partial excuse, because his behavior is driven by addiction, while the fan of the Vikings does not. But if we look only at the desires that explain their actions, it is hard to see how a principled difference could be found from within our theoretical perspective. Carr seems to desire cocaine much more than he desires what is right or good regarding his daughters, and from our perspective this would seem to make him just the same as the football fan who desires to see football much more than he desires what he ought regarding his daughters.

What our theory needs is for the fact of Carr's addiction to make a difference to his desires, and so to the verdict of moral indifference. This needs to be a difference that distinguishes Carr from the fan of the Vikings who performs parallel acts because he really wants to see his team play and does not much care about his daughters' lives. But this cannot be found within our theory of blameworthiness. If it is to be found anywhere, it will be in the theory of addiction. And so we now turn to addiction.

11.2 The Science of Addiction

Early research on addiction in human beings focused on phenomena such as dependency, withdrawal, and tolerance.[6] However, in more recent years scientific thought has been redirected toward other phenomena.[7] A striking fact about addiction is that the condition persists even once use has stopped, dependency has ended, withdrawal is over, and tolerance is gone. The abstinent addict who has ceased to show these signs of addiction nonetheless remains extremely vulnerable to poor decisions to return to using the addictive good, and this vulnerability decreases only very slowly as abstinence continues over the years.[8]

If addiction were to end with the end of withdrawal or the like, then the treatment of addiction would be a simple matter: hospitalize people until their withdrawal symptoms end, then send them off cured.[9] As recognition has grown that this is not a successful method of treating addiction, theoretical work on the nature of addiction has come to focus on the condition that exists both in actively using addicts and in abstinent addicts. This is work on addiction itself.

---

[6] This can be seen in, e.g., the lingering focus on these issues in the psychiatric diagnostic criteria for addiction-type disorders in the *Diagnostic and Statistical Manual of Mental Disorders*, and is commented upon in Hyman (2005).

[7] Representative scientific papers illustrating this include Robinson and Berridge (2002), Hyman (2005), and Schultz (2011).

[8] One nice discussion of the theoretical importance of the abstinent addict is found in Gjelsvik (1999).

[9] This point is made succinctly by Hyman (2005, 1414), whom we paraphrase here.

Research on addiction has come to focus on the way that addictive goods "hijack"[10] the reward system. This hijacking affects the reward system in a way that other, nonaddictive, goods do not. There are long-term effects of this hijacking, and several have been identified as central to the persistence of addiction beyond withdrawal and into even prolonged abstinence. We will say a little about this research on its own terms in this section. In the next, we will consider what it means for a philosophical theory of addiction.

To understand the science of addiction, return to the topic of the reward system.[11] Recall that the reward system is, at bottom, a learning system.[12] For the purpose of understanding addiction it is useful to note that the reward system's distinctive compound carrying the positive learning signal is called "dopamine." The release of dopamine causes reward learning, the sort of learning described in chapter 6 as that in which the ability of one mental event to cause another is increased when one instance of the first mental event causing the second is immediately followed by an increase in the amount of dopamine received.[13]

Ordinarily, increases in the release of dopamine, that is, positive learning signals, are generated by perceiving and thinking about the world and representing the world as containing more intrinsically desired things than (unconsciously, "viscerally") expected. A monkey perceiving a sudden burst of sweet juice in its mouth during an experiment has an increase of dopamine release in its brain,[14] and a human being who realizes that she will be getting money for what she has just done in an experiment also has an increase in the dopamine released in her brain.[15]

What is special about addictive drugs is that they all promote dopamine release, or promote dopamine reception, or simulate the immediate effects of dopamine release. And they do this independently of perception and cognition,

---

[10] We take this apt expression from a philosophical work written in response to the neuroscience: Elster (1999), but it can also be found in use by scientists, e.g., in the abstract for Schultz (2011).

[11] Another valuable discussion of the neuroscience of the reward system and addiction—one that is perhaps more accessible to philosophers than some others, while still being more technical than what follows—can be found in Gardner and David (1999). Other discussions of the reward system by philosophers—to more conventionally philosophical ends—can be found in Morillo (1990) and Schroeder (2004). This section and the next receive an extended treatment on their own in Schroeder (2010a).

[12] For our full argument to this effect, see Schroeder (2004, chapter 2). For key experiments, see Romo and Schultz (1990), Schultz and Romo (1990), and Bao, Chan, and Merzenich (2001). Theoretical papers sharing this position include Schultz, Dayan, and Montague (1997), Dayan, Montague, and Sejnowski (1996), and many of the papers in Houk, Davis, and Beiser (1995).

[13] A lucid scientific presentation of reward learning can be found in White and Milner (1992).

[14] Schultz and Romo (1990). It should be noted that, of all the findings described in this list, this is the only very direct observation; for the rest the finding that it is dopamine release that is being observed is more inferential. But the inferences have been widely accepted within neuroscience.

[15] Knutson et al. (2001).

independently of the representation of things that are intrinsically desired. They work directly on the dopamine-releasing cells, or on other neurons that are directly causally connected to these cells. This is where the metaphor of hijacking comes from. There is a normal process by which dopamine release leads to reward learning, and that process goes via perceiving or conceiving things that have come (through natural development or through learning) to be promoters of dopamine release—that have come to be intrinsically desired things. States of affairs are perceived or grasped cognitively, and if those represented are ones that are intrinsically desired, and are in excess of expectations, there is an increase in dopamine release, leading to unconscious reward learning. Addictive drugs circumvent this process. They promote unconscious learning, and all of its consequences, regardless of how their use is perceived or conceived, regardless of whether or not using them satisfies any intrinsic desires, regardless of expectations. A person who hates Imelda will not have dopamine release promoted in her by seeing Imelda. But a person who hates cocaine in just the same way, with just the same neural connections between the idea of cocaine and the reward system as her counterpart has between the idea of Imelda and the reward system, will nonetheless get a strong surge of dopamine-type effects if that person consumes cocaine. This is the way in which addictive drugs hijack the reward system.[16]

Cocaine and other addictive drugs thus stimulate the same effects as things that are intrinsically desired—sporting victories, trips to Hawaii, finally winning the love of one's beloved—regardless of how the drugs themselves satisfy or frustrate one's intrinsic desires. This is a key step in explaining addiction. This is the hijacking.

In and of itself, hijacking is not sufficient to explain addiction. People can feel and act as though they very much want trips to Hawaii without feeling and acting as though they are addicted to trips to Hawaii. Why is it that the immediate effects of cocaine, which are like the immediate effects of going to Hawaii, lead to addiction?

To understand what is most distinctive about addictive drugs, it is necessary to pay attention to the role of expectations in computing the reward signal. These expectations, which leave us still surprised by things we might

---

[16] It should be noted that different addictive drugs fit this pattern more or less well. The connection between cocaine, amphetamines, and MDMA ("ecstasy") are all much as one would think from the preceding description. The route by which opiates (including heroin) affect the reward system appears to be a little more indirect, and perhaps also involves a hijacking of a parallel punishment system, though this has not been substantiated. Nicotine, alcohol, and THC (marijuana's active ingredient) have all been demonstrated to have purely chemical effects on the reward system (i.e., not mediated by perception or cognition of one's ingestion of these compounds), but the ways in which these effects are related to addiction appear to require further study. At this point, however, scientists generally hold out hopes for reward system-based explanations of addictions to all these substances.

consciously expect but have not yet got used to, and which leave us jaded to things we have experienced so often we take them for granted, are a part of every calculation made by the reward system. However, they are circumvented by addictive drugs.

The way in which unconscious prediction features in generating an increase in dopamine release is worth going over carefully, because it is the key to our account of addiction. In a well-known experiment that is the foundation of recent work on the brain's reward system, a monkey was given a sip of sweet juice one second after a light turned on.[17] Initially, the turning on of the light had no effect on the monkey, but the arrival of the juice had a strong effect, and greatly increased the release of dopamine (for a moment; the effect is in general a very short-term one). As the light continued to be paired, after a one-second delay, with the juice, the release of dopamine started to change in the monkey. Soon the turning on of the light caused the same strong increase in dopamine release that the juice had initially, while the juice itself caused no change in dopamine release. The monkey had come to predict (unconsciously, "viscerally") that the juice would follow one second after the light. Now it was the light that brought the news that something satisfying an intrinsic desire (namely, the juice's arrival) was to happen; the juice itself added nothing unpredicted: the monkey "took for granted" that there would be juice one second after the light came on. Finally, the experimenters turned on the light, but did not deliver any juice. When the light was perceived dopamine release increased in the monkey's brain. One second later, when the unconsciously predicted juice was not received, dopamine release in the monkey dramatically *decreased*. The absence of what was intrinsically desired but "taken for granted" caused a drop in reward signaling.

These experiments illustrate the pattern that conforms to what would be expected on a theoretical basis from a system that implements reward-based learning. While representations of intrinsically desired states of affairs always contribute to the calculation of a reward signal, these contributions are sometimes balanced out by gut-level expectations, so that the net result is a neutral learning signal, even when a creature represents getting what it intrinsically desires.

The reason to have a reward learning signal express only the difference between what is actual and what is unconsciously predicted is illuminating: it is required to prevent overlearning of connections between kinds of mental events. Imagine a creature that gets water when it performs a certain action under certain conditions. The first time the creature performs the action, its getting water is unpredicted, and so it undergoes some reward learning and its propensity to perform the action under the conditions will go up. But at a

---

[17] See Schultz and Romo (1990) and Romo and Schultz (1990), published back-to-back, which brought a new level of precision and insight to research on dopamine and reward learning.

certain point, the action will be bringing about a fully predicted result—getting water—when it is performed under the relevant conditions. When this point is reached, it would actually be harmful to continue the behavioral learning further. At this point, further behavioral learning will make the action more and more likely to be performed under the given conditions, even though all that will be gained is a set amount of water. As this disposition to take this one action increases in strength, the creature will lose the ability to look for food, explore, or flee predators under the water-related conditions, because its behavior will be totally dominated by the tendency, when in those conditions, to perform the water-securing action. The creature will have overlearned, have become excessively likely to perform one action, because its unconscious link between perceiving the conditions and performing that action was forced to grow stronger and stronger without limit.

What goes for our imagined creature goes also for human beings. Tim intrinsically desires that his father be healthy. If every occasion on which Tim asked after his father's health, and on which he received the desired news, were an occasion on which he would undergo unconscious reward learning, then soon he would do little other than ask after his father's health (so long as that health remained good). Regardless of what else Tim could be doing, the power of his idea of asking after his father's health to cause that action—asking after his health—would be so great that whenever Tim thought of his father's health he would be very unlikely to do anything other than ask after it. And since many things can make Tim think of his father's health, many things would lead to this particular behavior. Tim's day would be dominated by asking after his father's health. It is for this sort of reason that there are natural limits to reward learning, implemented through unconscious predictions of intrinsically appetitive and aversive states of affairs.

Return now to addictive drugs. Because they hijack the reward system, addictive drugs can keep producing powerful reward learning effects long after trips to Hawaii, sips of water, news of good familial health, and the like would have produced weaker reward signals and eventually stopped producing them at all. Because these drugs hijack the reward system, the reward system always reacts to them as though more strongly intrinsically desired things happened than were unconsciously predicted—no matter how satisfying of intrinsic desires the unconscious prediction system was predicting consumption of the addictive drug to be. The result is very close to the preceding imagined scenarios in which nothing can shut off the reward learning caused by one kind of event.[18] The result of consuming addictive drugs is that they generate reward learning

---

[18] It appears that the brain has mechanisms that adapt, to some extent, to the continually overpowering reward learning generated by the addictive drugs, but this amounts to only weak resistance to the effects of the hijacking. Some tolerance effects would be an example of the action of such mechanisms.

in a pattern that would only be appropriate if addictive drugs were intrinsically desired to an infinite extent, that is, if, no matter how satisfying of intrinsic desires the reward system predicted cocaine consumption to be, cocaine consumption would be more satisfying of intrinsic desires than that. This is the source of the problems. The natural activators of the reward system slowly diminish in their power to generate more reward learning until their power reaches (at the limit) zero; the hijackers of the reward system never do, because they circumvent the normal process by which a reward signal is generated.

The immediate effects of a sharp increase in dopamine release are, most saliently, pleasure and motivation (to do what seems needed to secure the intrinsically desired thing, if there is something still to be done; if not, then the motivation might be expressed by just bouncing around excitedly, talking a mile a minute, and so on—a case of mere content efficacy, in other words). These effects, in themselves, would not have to be problematic. After a health scare, Tim will at first be pleased and motivated by news that his father's health is improving, but eventually (with luck) he will come to take it for granted again, and this sort of news will not be particularly pleasing or motivating. But it would not be a disaster for Tim if he continued to get pleasure from this news every time, and to find it invigorating (both an impetus to maintain that good health, when possible, and to just bounce along excitedly when not). The characteristic effect of addictive drugs is that one never becomes fully jaded to their effects, because they cause these effects by hijacking the reward system. But in itself, this would not have to be any more problematic than Tim never taking his father's health for granted. But of course, the problems quickly begin to accumulate.

The problem is that the immediate effects of an increase in dopamine release, that is, pleasure and motivation, are accompanied by the long term effect on unconscious learning. And this long term effect on learning appears to be the main source of the central phenomena of addiction. It is the source of the phenomena in common between addicts who are still using and abstinent addicts, and also between people who wholeheartedly hate the drugs they abuse and people who wholeheartedly love these same drugs.[19]

The first important effect caused by the runaway reward learning that addictive drugs induce is an effect on unconscious behavioral dispositions—on habits and their relatives. Habits and related unthinking behavioral tendencies appear to be realized in a region of the brain that is crucial in action production, and that is an important recipient of dopamine (the dorsal striatum). Runaway reward learning induces increasingly strong habits and related unthinking behavioral dispositions. Long-time smokers often report smoking cigarettes unthinkingly, even when they have already consumed so much nicotine that

---

[19] To pick up a Frankfurtean theme (Frankfurt 1987).

more nicotine will make them feel ill. This appears to be the result of the strong habits and habit-like behavioral dispositions inculcated through the effects of reward learning upon the smoker.

It is easy to denigrate the importance of habits and their relatives. After all, it seems easy enough to override habits when one is paying attention. But this is a mistake.

For one thing, it is possible to exaggerate how easy it is to override habits. For some habits, it only takes a little attention to override them, but for others it can be extremely difficult to do so. An informant reports to us an experience of being trained to throw grenades in the Israeli armed forces. An important part of grenade-throwing technique is not to watch whether the grenade falls where one has thrown it, since this leaves the thrower open to injury. Trainees were lined up with mock grenades, and required to take turns lobbing the mock grenades at mock targets. A menacing instructor stood over the trainees and threatened to hit them with a stick if they should watch where the mock grenades fell. And many trainees were struck on the first try. Our informant reports that he focused his mind on the task, so that he would not be humiliated or hit with the stick when his turn came—but, sure enough, when his turn came he threw his grenade, watched it fly, and got hit with the stick.

For another, it is possible to exaggerate how easy it is to pay attention to whether or not one is acting on an unfortunate habit at any given moment. It can be easy enough for a drug addict to not use the drug on any one given occasion, but abstinence requires not using the drug on every occasion. And insofar as not using requires not being subject to temptation, abstinence also requires never going anywhere out of habit, never talking to anyone out of habit, never agreeing to do something out of habit—if doing so might lead to temptation. People rely on their unconscious, habit-derived behavioral dispositions to guide them successfully through routine parts of the day; we do not constantly monitor ourselves. But many of a would-be abstinent addict's unconscious, habit-derived behavioral dispositions have become untrustworthy, and these actions need to be monitored, or the abstinent addict will do things without thinking about them at the time, only to find a difficult situation arising. "Why did I agree to go to that party where everyone will be using?" "Why did I turn down this street that leads me close to the dealers, and not down the next street?" "Why did I end up calling my old drug buddy when I was bored?" Questions like these are often answered by an addict's unconscious, habit-derived behavioral tendencies. While we all have these tendencies, in the addict the effect of the addictive drug has been to strengthen the drug-associated tendencies out of all proportion.

We also have habits of thought, and there is strong evidence that dopamine release, and so reward learning, is important to shaping habits of thought just as it is important to shaping habits of action, as was discussed in chapter 6.[20]

---

[20] See also, e.g., Greenspoon (1955), Saint-Cyr, Taylor, and Lang (1988).

We are not aware of the effect being documented in addicts, but would not be surprised to learn that Carr's "junkie math," and the thinking of addicts in general, was influenced by habits of considering certain things, habits of rehearsing certain excuses, habits of avoiding thinking about things in terms likely to lead to not using, and so on. These would be mental habits developed and powerfully reinforced by prolonged addicted drug use. And, if habits of action are difficult to monitor, how much more so for habits of thought! Is dwelling on the difficulties of sober life an aspect of accepting a difficult reality, or is it a pattern of thought one learned while using because such thoughts promoted drug consumption and so got reinforced as addiction-supporting habits? These are the sorts of questions it is very difficult to answer as an addict struggling not to use, and yet without such answers the advice to "be vigilant" against habits of thought that lead back to drug use is not very helpful advice, illustrating just how challenging it can be to cope with badly formed habits. It is a commonplace in, for example, Alcoholics Anonymous that there is a sense in which an addict cannot trust his or her own mind, and must be particularly vigilant against certain patterns of thinking that lead back to consumption of alcohol or other addictive goods. We suspect that the habits of thought built specifically by use of addictive goods are one basis for such observations.

The second important effect caused by the runaway reward learning induced by addictive drugs is the effect on the unconscious prediction system. Because addictive goods induce runaway reward learning in this system, the system responds to perceptual and cognitive signs of coming cocaine (or whatever the addictive drug of choice might be) by predicting that the world will soon contain enormous satisfaction of intrinsic desires. If the addict consumes the addictive drug, then the predicted nature of the next moment is apparently confirmed (and exceeded) given how the reward system responds to the drug. But suppose the addict does not consume the drug. There will be a sudden drop in the release of dopamine: the predicted satisfaction of intrinsic desires is missing. This affects the addict's feelings and motivations in just the way having any "positive" (desired) thing snatched from a person would affect her. The addict feels tremendously denied, restless, motivated to find some way to still attain the predicted reward: and there is the unconsumed drug, right there, in front of the addict.

It might be thought that this problem of absent but unconsciously predicted reward events would at least be restricted to situations in which the addictive drug is right in front of the addict but not consumed. But the unconscious predictive system, though not tied to the sorts of evidence recognized in conscious reasoning, is still much more sophisticated than this. Just as a light came to be a predictor of juice for a monkey, so too do things associated with addictive drugs come to be predictors of the event that generates the reward learning signal, that is, the acquisition of the drug. Anything substantially statistically associated with the addictive drug should come to cause unconscious prediction of drug acquisition, given what is known about the unconscious predictive system. The abstinent addict who can talk to an old friend who was also a drug buddy will, on seeing the old friend or thinking about the opportunity to talk to her, unconsciously predict possible future consumption of the addictive drug, and feel motivated to reach out. To go on to talk to the friend keeps the world looking as good as predicted (it unconsciously "looks" like the addictive drug is still coming), but to not talk to the friend feels disappointing, de-motivating, feels like a problem in need of a solution. It does so because this is how it feels when one experiences a sudden drop in dopamine release generated by suddenly abandoning an unconsciously predicted reward-associated event. Thus, the addict feels good about talking to the old drug buddy, and motivated to do so, and actions to prevent this interaction feel bad and induce motivation to find some way around this decision. Under these circumstances, it is no surprise that abstinent addicts often unwisely get in touch with old drug buddies, even before habits are taken into account. And what goes for talking to friends goes also for visiting old hangouts, listening to music that is strongly drug-associated, going to drug-associated sorts of events, going to places where drugs will be available, and so on.

In addition, all of these effects can be generated (probably, to a lesser degree) by mere perception or cognition of things that are merely fictional or imaginary instances of things associated with addictive drug consumption. Watching someone pretend to inhale cocaine on television is something that elicits strong feelings in cocaine addicts, even though the act is known to be fictional and even though there is no change in the availability of cocaine.[21] The unconscious prediction system does not seem to typically make sophisticated discriminations between what is merely depicted or imagined and what is real. As a result, the effects on feelings and motivations that can be generated by the presence of the addictive drug, or a friend or a place associated with that drug, can also be generated (perhaps more weakly) by pictures of these things, people, places; by talking about them, by seeing films and television programs reminiscent of them, and so on. For the abstinent addict, these feelings and motivations are often just around the corner. And because the immediate trigger need only be something associated with the addictive drug, it need not be obvious to the addict what the ultimate source is of her longing to talk to this person, or of her disappointment at missing that event, or the like.

The effects just described are sometimes called "cravings" or "cue-conditioned cravings" by scientists working on addiction.[22] Cravings, in this literature, are negative feelings experienced when an addict is exposed to cues—things and images of things—associated with past consumption of addictive drugs. While anything one imagines having but is denied can cause a craving in the ordinary

---

[21] One experiment relying on this effect is Berger et al. (1996).
[22] E.g., Lowenstein (1999), Berger et al. (1996).

sense of the term, drug addicts are particularly vulnerable to particularly strong and persistent cravings felt in the presence of even modest cues associated with former addictive drug use, all because of the runaway reward learning to which they have been subjected. Cue-conditioned cravings in addicts are associated with motivations to consume the addictive good, or take steps (not necessarily regarded as such) toward such consumption.

The generation of powerful behavioral tendencies and habits, on the one hand, and powerful cravings, on the other, are two effects generated by the runaway reward learning generated by addictive drugs. In the absence of these effects, abstinent addicts would be much harder to distinguish from nonaddicts who are merely familiar with the effects of the addictive drugs.

11.3 The Philosophy of Addiction

The previous section describes how the reward system induces problematic effects in drug addicts. For a moral psychologist, the next thing to do is to understand these problematic effects in terms that have some meaning in moral psychology. And for our purposes, what this amounts to is trying to understand how these problematic effects are related to desires.[23]

Consider the two effects in turn.

First, there is the effect on unthinking behavioral tendencies and habits. Addictive drugs strongly inculcate behavioral tendencies and habits that lead to increased probabilities of drug consumption by addicts. How should this be understood?

One way in which to interpret the phenomenon is to say that this effect is a matter of the addictive drugs inducing very strong desires to do the things that drug addicts are inclined to do. After all, strong behavioral tendencies sound, almost by definition, like strong desires. However, we have already argued extensively against this line of thought back in chapter 5. What is done out of habit is not done out of a desire to do it.

If part of what is distinctive in the motivation of addicts is habit, then that part of what is distinctive does not entail that addicts have unreasonably strong desires for the drugs to which they are addicted. An addict with a moderately strong desire for an addictive drug might nonetheless be extremely strongly motivated to act to get that drug, if the required action is also one that is habitual (or one that involves habitual components), because the behavioral force of the unusually strong habits generated by addictive drug use would in those circumstances combine with the desire for the addictive drug to generate a much stronger behavioral inclination to use the drug than would exist if the desire

---

[23] For a longer discussion along similar lines, see Schroeder (2010a).

alone existed, or if the desire and a habit of strength appropriate to the desire were to exist.

Second, there is the effect that addictive drugs have on unconscious prediction of how much intrinsic desire satisfaction the world is about to have. Since we characterized this as amounting to how addictive drugs generate cravings for those drugs, this would seem to be an obvious point at which desires enter the picture. But again the picture is more complicated than that.

Consider first the unconscious prediction system, and its proclivity for predicting extremely desire-satisfying events upon being presented with cues (real or imagined) that are statistically associated with consuming addictive drugs. Insofar as it is correct to treat it as a *predictive* system, it is impossible to see it as instantiating desires. Predictions are true or false; they make claims about how the world will be. Desires are neither true nor false, and they make no claims about how the world will be. And given that the unconscious prediction system is required to have a predictive role within the computational models of the reward system that form our basis for understanding it, we assume we are on safe ground in holding that the unconscious predictive system does not, itself, instantiate desires.

The unconscious prediction system gives rise, in addicts, to cue-conditioned cravings. These cravings are states in which the addict feels bad (deprived or denied) and is highly motivated to do something that will redress the apparent state of deprivation or denial. Are cue-conditioned cravings desires? Is this where desires distinctive of addiction can be found?

Cue-conditioned cravings appear to be very like desires. A person who has a cue-conditioned craving to go to a familiar old bar where she used to get drunk, or to go into the house dealing cocaine while his daughters wait in the car, appears to be a person with a strong desire. The person in this situation feels highly motivated, feels good about the prospect of doing the thing in question and bad about the prospect of not doing it, and would describe herself as very much wanting to do what she craves doing.

To address cue-conditioned cravings, we need to return to the reward theory of desire. If we interpret the reward system as realizing intrinsic desires, then this affects how we think about intrinsic desire strength, and this is where these general considerations once again make contact with the moral psychology of addiction. If a state of affairs is treated as "positive" to a certain degree by the reward system—representations of that state of affairs contribute to the calculation of reward learning with this weight or that weight, more or less than most other representations in the system—then that is the best candidate for how much a state of affairs is intrinsically desired. If a strongly intrinsically desired state of affairs fails to have a strong motivational or emotional effect on a given occasion, it might be because the individual is jaded, but this would not diminish the claim that the state of affairs was strongly desired. Tim can strongly desire that his father be healthy but be rather jaded about it and so not typically feel strongly about his father's health, nor be much motivated (in the moment) to act to protect that health. And similarly with a weakly desired state of affairs having a strong effect on motivations or feelings on a given occasion: a soda might be only weakly desired, but if one was fully expecting a soda only to be denied it at the last second, one can feel strongly about it anyway, and motivated to rectify the situation (while acknowledging that "it's only a soda," perhaps). And, in addition to these normal ways in which the strength of a desire might not match the strength of its effects on motivation or feelings, there might be abnormal ways in which there might be a mismatch. Perhaps extreme sleep deprivation can reduce the motivational and felt impact of a desire without thereby changing the strength of the desire or the jadedness of the person who desires, for example.

If this is credible, then the same should be said about desires for addictive drugs. Addicts desire to consume the drugs to which they are addicted, but do they desire them as much as one would think given how strongly they feel about them and are motivated by them? Given, that is, how strongly they crave them? Following the preceding reasoning, the answer has to be "no." The cravings addicts have are not proportional to the strength of the addicts' desires for their drugs. This will be true because these cravings follow (largely or entirely) from the unconscious prediction of a very "positive" event when the addict sees or thinks about things associated with the addictive drug, and as we saw in the previous section, it is a distinctive feature of addictive drugs that the unconscious prediction will always become excessively "positive." Regardless of how positively the reward system responds to the idea of cocaine, the consumption of cocaine will always "teach" the reward system that it should have predicted that the event would be more positive than that. Thus, the effects of the unconscious predictive system—the cravings—will be effects that are out of proportion to how positively the reward system treats the addictive drug (that is, out of proportion to how strong the connection is between representations of consuming the drug and promotion of reward learning, independently of the drug's actual effects). And thus, the cravings will have effects out of proportion to how much the addictive drug is desired.

11.4 The Blameworthiness of Addicts

Given the present discussion of addiction and the previous discussion of blameworthiness (from chapter 7), we can now give a full account of the blameworthiness of an addict who does something wrong or bad because of the addiction.

Return to the case of David Carr. Carr left his infant daughters in his car in the November cold of Minneapolis in order to consume cocaine. His motive—the consumption of cocaine—is not ill will. But to act on that motive in that

circumstance is to act wrongly in part because of an absence of needed good
will. It is to act with moral indifference. And this is the source of Carr's blameworthiness. This far we got at the outset. But what puzzled us was the explanation of how Carr's blameworthiness is reduced or mitigated in some way by the
fact that he did what he did because of his addiction. He is not the cold-hearted
monster who could abandon his children for hours in order to see a football
game. He does not deserve the same blame that such a monster would deserve.
Carr was gripped by an addiction to cocaine, and that matters.

After the previous section, we can say what is special about an addiction to
cocaine or to any other drug. Carr's addiction appears to be instantiated in an
extremely strong desire for cocaine. He very powerfully craves cocaine at the
moment at which he makes his terrible decision, and this craving is a key part
of the explanation of his action. But this is only half right. It is true that, if
he had not experienced his lack of cocaine as a "towering need" for more, he
does not seem like the sort who would have left his daughters alone in the car
in the cold. His craving, and perhaps also certain habits of thought and action,
are a key part of the explanation of his behavior. But the "towering need," the
immense craving, is not indicative that there is an equally towering desire for
cocaine motivating Carr. There is a desire—a strong one, perhaps—that is having enormously outsized effects on Carr's feelings and motivations.

As a result, Carr's leaving his daughters is not a manifestation of the mon-
strous moral indifference we might have thought—the sort we would have
rightly attributed to him if he had done the same thing in order to watch football. Carr credibly cares for his daughters as much as he should, prioritizing
them appropriately relative to his intrinsic desires for career, cocaine, romance,
and other ends. But caring as much as any decent parent should, while desiring
cocaine no more than any fan of a sports team desires his team to win, does
not lead to Carr doing the right thing, as it would in the responsible sports fan.
And this is because there is, in an addict like Carr, a motivational force to the
idea of cocaine out of proportion to how much it is intrinsically desired. This
motivational force, added to the force that is proper to the intrinsic desire given
that it is (presumably) a strong one, leads Carr to do something terrible. And
given that there is no question about his understanding of the situation, this
makes him a suitable candidate for blame. But Carr does not manifest mon-
strous moral indifference in his act. He demonstrates something lesser. A true
moral hero, a parent of colossal concern, would have done otherwise in the circumstances. So Carr appears to demonstrate that he is much less than perfect
in his desire for what is right and good in the circumstances. A true paragon
would have seen that the bottom was hit before getting out of the car; the transformation that eventually takes root in Carr and leads to his breaking free of
cocaine would have flowered right there. But Carr is not this paragon, and his
action shows it. In doing what is wrong he shows he is to some degree less than
perfectly concerned with the right and the good, and since he acts wrongly he is

blameworthy. But all his action shows is that he is less than a paragon. It does not show that he is less than an ordinary parent; it does not show that he is a cold-hearted monster. And for this reason, Carr is less blameworthy than he might have been, had this strength of motivation come from something other than his addiction.

11.5 Addiction in Moral Psychology

The larger moral of Carr's story is a moral about any desire-based moral psychology. Addiction has often seemed to be a problem case for desire-based moral psychological theories, because addiction presents the appearance of people being moved by intrinsic desires that do not rationalize their actions, desires that do not render them apt candidates for being blamed for their unfortunate acts, desires that do not raise the question of whether the person has a vice, but instead suggest that the person has a disease. That is, addiction has often seemed to be a phenomenon revealing that intrinsic desires, stripped bare, cannot be taken seriously as the core of moral psychological theorizing. But this chapter has argued that these conclusions were premature. Although addicts no doubt have strong intrinsic desires served by using their addictive goods, addicts also act, feel, and think in ways that suggest much stronger intrinsic desires than they actually possess. Addiction is a fascinating phenomenon, but it does not reveal desires as a problem. Rather, scientific investigation of addiction reveals that the real problem lies with the hijacking of the neural systems implementing intrinsic desires. This hijacking generates effects that suggest the existence of powerful intrinsic desires without actually generating these desires. Thus, scientific investigation of addiction reveals that the real problems faced by addicts are problems generated by things in their minds that prevent them from feeling and acting upon their actual intrinsic desires.

Conclusion

Conclusions are a time for taking stock and looking forward. We conclude with a little of each.

C.1 Taking Stock

According to Spare Conativism, the heart of moral psychology is an intrinsic desire with both the right sense and the right reference. It is an intrinsic desire for the right or good (its referential content) grasped through the concepts privileged by the correct normative theory of the right or good (its sense). Having this intrinsic desire is what makes a person good-hearted, or possessed of complete good will. This is good will not in Kant's technical sense, but in the pre-theoretic sense Kant sought to illuminate.

Other intrinsic desires approximate complete good will by having referential contents that are *pro tanto* moral reasons, presented via the concepts that the correct normative theory would pick out for such reasons. These intrinsic desires make up partial good will. They play large roles in the moral-psychological lives of most people. Unless the correct normative moral theory is surprisingly simple, most of us are likely to possess stronger intrinsic desires for parts of the right or good than for the right or good, complete and unadulterated, in itself. We intrinsically desire that others not suffer, that we keep our explicit promises, that no one strike our children needlessly, and so on, more strongly— more *fiercely*, even, in some cases—than we intrinsically desire that happiness be maximized, that all persons be respected, that welfare be promoted within the bounds of consent, or whatever it is that morality actually requires.

Lying at the heart of moral psychology, complete and partial good will explain a good deal of what is most central to the moral mind. Perhaps there is more to moral psychology that has claim to being a part of its "heart" (not being moral anatomists, we deploy the term cautiously) but according to Spare Conativism at least three answers to three canonical questions in moral psychology rely centrally upon good will.

First, paradigmatic acting for right reasons is acting out of good will. Acting for the right reasons, according to SC, is a matter of one's action manifesting one's good will. In the simplest case, this is a matter of one's action being caused by one's good will (and associated means-end beliefs), and caused in virtue of the fact that one's good will (along with beliefs) rationalizes the immediate intention upon which one acts.

Second, paradigmatic praiseworthy action is right action taken out of good will. Being praiseworthy for a right act, according to SC, is a matter of one's right act manifesting either one's good will or one's marked dearth of ill will, though the former is the paradigmatic case.

Third, paradigmatic virtue is just the possession of a great deal of good will. Other stable states of mind, manifesting the presence of good will or the absence of ill will, count as virtues too, but only through their connections to good will and the absence of ill will.

To defend these three claims, we independently defended theses about thinking and acting for reasons, on the one hand, and intrinsic desires, on the other.

Since deliberation is an action, taken for better or worse reasons, we argued that thinking and acting for reasons must be something prior to deliberation, rather than dependent upon it. One could say: deliberation does not *solve* the problem of thinking and acting for reasons, because it *exemplifies* it. Some nondeliberative, nonvoluntary, nonreflective process has to explain thinking and acting for reasons. And while this does not compel the theorist to accept our version of a causal theory of acting for reasons, it makes room for this sort of theory. Also making room for such a theory was the demonstration that the problem of "deviant causation" of actions by rationalizing reasons can be reduced to the problem of explaining how properties, even purely physical properties in purely physical contexts, can be relevant to causation (or causal explanation) in general.

As for intrinsic desires, we observed both the richness of their actual causal roles and the difficulty of finding their necessary features among the most familiar of those causal roles. So we suggested a way forward: to treat intrinsic desires as the independently existing causes of their most familiar effects, that is, to treat them as belonging to a natural kind. As it turns out, there is a unique psychological natural kind that stands apart from, but causes, all the effects most commonly associated with intrinsic desires. A natural kind, in short, that is suitable for identifying with intrinsic desire. Theorizing desires in this way allows for a separation between how motivated one is at a given moment, or how strongly one feels at a given moment, and how much one intrinsically desires at that same moment. Once established, this separation allowed for the claim that intrinsic desires are (along with means-end cognitive attitudes) rationalizing reasons, and the claim that selected intrinsic desires are good will and so (along with means-end cognitive attitudes) rationalizing moral reasons, to be defended against a number of challenges.

Two such challenges were systematic and difficult enough to warrant their own chapters for discussion. In those chapters, we showed that, by embracing our theses about reasons and desires, Spare Conativism has the resources to explain inner struggle in ordinary people and irrational choice in addicts.

Inner struggle is not between a faculty of Reason and a faculty of Appetite. Instead, we argued, inner struggle is a matter of the agent taking mental actions aimed either at promoting one course of action in light of the agent's sense that she is otherwise likely to take some other course of action, or taking mental actions aimed alternately at two (or more) different and opposing courses of action. And, in these struggles, the role of intrinsic desires is both monolithic and complex. It is monolithic in that we always tend, typically and insofar as we are healthy, to take the mental actions that seem to promise progress toward getting things we intrinsically desire. It is complex in that intrinsic desires are not the only forces that can move us, they do not always move us with a force appropriate to their strength as intrinsic desires, and as attention shifts to different facts the intrinsic desires that are most causally effective upon our actions change without their status as rationalizers changing. Because of the complexity of the role of intrinsic desires in shaping deliberation and overt action, it can give rise to the sorts of inner struggle that everyone experiences while still being a single, monolithic mental state.

Addiction is likewise not a struggle between a faculty of Reason and a faculty of Appetite, even in those addicts who have resolved, and now struggle, to stop using their addictive goods. Rather, addiction is a phenomenon in which habits (of thought as well as of action) and in which cravings (generated by disordered gut-level expectations) disrupt the influence of intrinsic desires upon action, leading addicts to choose what they intrinsically desire less strongly over what they intrinsically desire more strongly. Rather than being a case in which a person's intrinsic desires are out of control, calling into question the idea that intrinsic desires can rationalize actions, addiction illustrates how rational action requires the unadulterated, unimpeded influence of our intrinsic desires on our actions.

C.2 Looking Forward

Inevitably, the longer the philosophical work, the more questions seem to be left unanswered. Here we note a few questions that particularly caught our attention, starting with our discussion of reasons.

The nature of deliberation seems to be in tension with certain projects in meta-ethics, and it would be interesting to know whether this tension is remediable. According to the meta-ethical constructivist, moral reasons are constructed by deliberation. That is, moral reasons exist in virtue of past, present, or possible acts of deliberation. The arguments of chapter 1 seem to show that not all reasons for action can be constructed in this way. But is there a way of extending the arguments to show that moral reasons for action cannot be constructed by deliberation? Consider the relationship between deliberation and moral reasons. There can be moral reasons to deliberate: to make sure an otherwise innocent decision does not do environmental damage, for instance.

And this moral reason must exist prior to a person's deliberating in this way for this reason, given the arguments of chapter 1. However, the moral reason might have been constructed by prior or present deliberation (or by facts about possible deliberation) that was not conducted for moral reasons. The possibility of a regress exists only if the deliberations that are said to construct moral reasons are themselves conducted for moral reasons. And so it would appear that constructivism is untouched by our arguments so long as it allows for there to be nonmoral practical reasons for deliberation prior to there being moral reasons, and so long as these nonmoral practical reasons are the source of the reasons for past, present, or possible deliberations that in turn construct moral reasons. This is not the path taken by some well-known constructivist projects, however.[1] And perhaps this is an accident, or perhaps it stems from deeper features of constructivism in the moral domain.

From meta-ethics to epistemology: over the last few decades, epistemologists have been working on "the basing relation." They want to know what it is to believe that P based on one's previous belief that Q implies P and one's having just learned that Q; and so on. Believing P based on these other beliefs is not just believing P while holding the other beliefs, because one might hold P just coincidentally and so not, in the ordinary sense, based on the other beliefs. It is also not just to be caused to believe P by these other beliefs, because one might be caused to believe P by them in the wrong way. But then what is it? This puzzle about the basing relation appears to be the puzzle about what it is to believe for rationalizing reasons. A natural question to ask, then, is whether the epistemological question has different features from the practical question, or whether the two are strictly parallel. Either way, there seem to be a number of opportunities for engagement between the view on thinking for reasons developed in chapter 3 and epistemological work on the basing relation.

Thinking and acting for reasons in Spare Conativism is a matter of being caused to think or immediately intend (and so act) by attitudes that rationalize the thinking or immediate intending, and to be caused (or causally explained) in virtue of the fact that these attitudes rationalize (at least in part) what they cause. As we argued in chapter 3, this causation (or causal explanation) has to involve the attitudes, their contents, and the logical or perhaps mathematical relations between them. But, as we also noted in chapter 3, this apparently leaves out the normativity of rationalizing reasons. Can the normativity of rationalizing reasons itself be a further cause, or causal explainer, of a thought or immediate intention (and so action)? If so, how? It is easy to imagine a crude account that makes such causation possible. It might be that the normativity of rationalizing reasons rests, ultimately, upon an irreducibly normative nonnatural property instantiated when one has rationalizing reasons, and

---

[1] Korsgaard (1996).

this property might cause (or causally explain) thought and immediate intentions as an empirically detectable supplement to the natural order of cause and effect. This crude account is easy to imagine, but too crude to believe. It is also easy to imagine an account of the normativity of reasons that would make it impossible for the normativity to be given a role in the immediate causation of thought or immediate intentions. It might be that the normativity of rationalizing reasons rests on the biological functions of the brain, which in turn derive from natural selection. If so, then while the normativity of rationalizing reasons would have a ground, it would be one that would be based on facts in the distant past, and so facts cut off from doing present work in causing (or causally explaining) thought or immediate intentions. This crude account is as easy to imagine as the previous, but also as easy to reject. What is wanted is something in between: an account of the normativity of rationalizing reasons that also makes it understandable how this property is capable of playing a role in the causation of thoughts and immediate intentions. Whether what is wanted is *possible* is another matter.

Next consider the nature of intrinsic desires.

An odd feature of the reward theory of desire is that it recognizes a deep distinction between appetitive desires and aversions: between desires based on reward and desires based on punishment. There is a good neuroscientific basis for this distinction, but is there anything that can be said from the armchair in favor of it? Superficially, it can seem that there are a number of points in favor of the distinction. Sometimes desiring seems to pull us to approach; other times it pushes us to avoid. Sometime it makes a prospect tantalizing; sometimes it makes a prospect repellent. But on closer inspection, it can seem that one and the same content can be tied to approach, when it seems we can get it, and avoidance, when we might pursue something else to the detriment of getting the first thing. Likewise, the wanted thing can be tantalizing and the prospect of losing the wanted thing can be repellent. So perhaps the neuroscientific distinction has no impact on phenomenology after all. Still, it would be odd for there to be a deep neural distinction that has no reflection in ordinary experience. The deep neural distinctions between the various things called memory (remembering an event, a fact, a person's face, remembering to go to the store for milk, remembering how to ride a bike...) are reflected in our ordinary understanding that these different memories have different features: a person can be good at remembering facts but not faces, a person who gets amnesia will still remember how to ride a bicycle, and so on. What, then, is the experienced dimension of the distinction between reward and punishment, and so between differently oriented intrinsic desires?

A larger controversy upon which the reward theory of desire bears is the nature of love and care. In chapter 4, we stated minimal theories of love and care. These theories are in the spirit of Spare Conativism, but were not defended as correct. The point of articulating them was not to show that they are correct but to show that they are not vulnerable to some thoughtful criticisms of them, on account of the complexity of intrinsic desires within ordinary human lives. And this claimed complexity was itself support for, and supported by, the reward theory of desire. But, after the debate over the roles played by actual intrinsic desires is over, one can return to the theories of love and care. Would a minimal theory of these states, one just in terms of strong intrinsic desires with the right contents, survive? One interesting further question to raise about love and care can be found lurking in chapter 7, and its discussion of the sense and reference of the good will. The idea that love involves intrinsically desiring what is best for the beloved is an appealing idea, but what is the conceptualization (or sense, or narrow content, or mode of presentation, or...) of "what is best" here? On the one hand, it seems compatible with loving one's child that one want what is best so conceived while having a false theory of what is best: out of love, a father can press his son to develop sporting talents that the son does not really possess and does not value, it would seem. On the other hand, if one intrinsically desires health, intellectual achievement, and love for one's child, but has an odd theory of what is best and sees oneself as akratically promoting what is less good for one's child in promoting her health, achievement, and attainment of love, then one also appears a loving parent.

One other lingering question about the reward theory of desire stands out for us: is there some way of re-interpreting the reward system as realizing valuing attitudes rather than intrinsic desires? Gideon Yaffe has proposed such an interpretation,[2] and insofar as one wishes to hold a cognition-of-value-based motivational psychology such an interpretation of the reward system seems particularly promising. After all, if valuing attitudes (or beliefs about reasons, for that matter) are to be at the center of a motivational psychology then they must be realized by the neural system that controls action, and that system prominently features reward (and punishment) signals. In favor of this value-based interpretation of the reward system is the fact that the brain does not come with labels: reward learning itself is not clearly a matter of intrinsic desires as opposed to beliefs about values, from the perspective of the armchair theorist. Also in favor are all the arguments that beliefs about (or perceptions of) value (or reasons) must be at the center of motivational psychology. Against the value-based interpretation are certain more puzzling considerations derived from the larger role of the reward (and punishment) system. The system does not appear to be required for, or to realize, ordinary thinking about values: people whose actions are impaired by Parkinson disease do not express different values, although they are experiencing changes in their reward systems, for example. And it has not often been thought that simply valuing something disposes one to pleasure at its coming to be the case, or that a hungry person's

---

[2] Yaffe (in preparation).

inability to keep her attention off of a chocolate bar is a sign of her valuing eating the chocolate bar. But these are just first thoughts in what might prove to be a very interesting debate.

Moving on to good will and virtue, there are again some lingering questions. Some of these questions concern the relation between Spare Conativism and normative moral theory. According to SC, all morally praiseworthy actions are performed from rationalizing attitudes that include intrinsic desires with a sense and reference that is intimately related to the correct normative theory of morality. If SC is right, then one ought to be able to infer from morally praiseworthy motives—ideas about what counts as at least partial good will—to the content of normative theories. Perhaps, for example, one way to approach the question, "Can it be true that the moral thing to do is the thing that leads the agent to eudaemonia?" is to ask, "If we meet a person whose reason for refraining from murder is a desire for THE GOOD LIFE or HAPPINESS, do we regard him as praiseworthy?" If we regard him as too self-centered to be virtuous then perhaps eudaemonia is not the root of moral reasons.[3] Similarly, perhaps one way to approach the question of whether a certain form of Kantianism is correct is by asking whether the person who follows that kind of Kantianism will seem virtuous (as opposed to, say, overly obsessed with laws or overly concerned with her own actions). The question of what moral psychology can teach us about normative ethics is an interesting one.

Another question one might raise has to do with situationism.[4] If people's morally relevant courses of action depend on such factors as whether or not they happened to have found loose change that morning or whether the product they were selecting was to their left or to their right, their patterns of behavior would appear too fragmented to be explained by the idea of robust character traits. How are theories that relate praise- and blameworthiness in actions to the desires that cause the actions to deal with these data? On the one hand, it might appear that intrinsic desires, diverse as they are, can explain the diversity of people's behaviors much better than less diverse and more coarse-grained character traits. It might be argued that people are not consistently honest across contexts because they have differently strong intrinsic desires regarding telling the truth, copying schoolwork, getting songs without paying for them, and so on, and as a result have different rationalizations for acting in different contexts related to honesty. On the other hand, even diverse collections of intrinsic desires seem unlikely to rationalize acting more generously after finding loose change, or choosing to buy a product one finds on one's right-hand side.

Finally, we closed *In Praise of Desire* with two puzzle cases, but of course left many more puzzles for others.

---

[3] At least not in such a simple way. The virtuous agent does not act for the sake of eudaemonia but rather for the sake of the fine, according to Aristotle.
[4] See Doris (2002), Harman (1999).

Discussing addiction reminds us of the many other mental conditions that need to be discussed in the context of desire, moral reasons, credit, and virtue. What shall we say about the blameworthiness of a kleptomaniac, for example? What about other impulse-control disorders? What about obsessive-compulsive disorder? Tourette syndrome?[5] All these cases of deviant motivation need explaining, with the help of empirical science. What, for that matter, is the connection between desire and depression? It might look to some as if depressed people lose many of their desires. To us it appears more likely that depressed people, due to cognitive and emotional distortions, are less inclined to do things that they intrinsically desire. Similarly, they are less likely to feel desires that they have, and then the failure to satisfy these desires contributes to the displeasure that comes with depression. But here, again, more explanation is required and more debate is sure to ensue. Similar questions arise about other deviant mental states, such as mania.

Our larger goal throughout this work has been to show that desire-based theories in moral psychology deserve philosophers' attention. This seemed best done by articulating and defending a specific desire-based moral psychology: Spare Conativism. But in addition to our larger goal, and the related one of sparking additional discussion on the general question of the role of desire, we also aim to spark rival desire-based theories, spark responses from defenders of the desire-based theories that we rejected here, and spark criticisms of SC that are internal to its fundamental assumptions about the roles of intrinsic desires in moral psychology. Spare Conativism is not what we imagine an ideal theory in moral psychology will look like. But it is the point from which we hope such a theory will start.

---

[5] Tourette syndrome is discussed in Schroeder (2005).

{ WORKS CITED }

Adams, R. 1976. "Motive Utilitarianism." *Journal of Philosophy* 73, 467–81.

Adams, R. 1985. "Involuntary Sins." *Philosophical Review* 94, 3–31.

Adams, R. 2006. *A Theory of Virtue: Excellence in being for the good.* New York: Oxford University Press.

Akins, K. 1996. "Of Sensory Systems and the 'Aboutness' of Mental States." *Journal of Philosophy* 93, 337–72.

Annas, Julia. 2011. *Intelligent Virtue.* New York: Oxford University Press.

Anscombe, G.E.M. *Intention.* 2000. Cambridge, MA: Harvard University Press.

Anthony, L. 1989. "Anomalous Monism and the Problem of Explanatory Force." *Philosophical Review* 98, 153–87.

Appiah, A. 1990. "'But Would That Still Be Me?' Notes on gender, 'race', ethnicity, as sources of 'identity'." *Journal of Philosophy* 87, 493–99.

Ariely, D. 2008. *Predictably Irrational: The hidden forces that shape our decisions.* New York: Harper.

Aristotle. 1999. *Nicomachean Ethics.* Irwin, T. (trans.) Indianapolis: Hackett.

Armstrong, D. 1980. *The Nature of Mind.* St. Lucia, Queensland: University of Queensland Press.

Aron, A., Fisher, H., Mashek, D., Strong, G., Li, H., and Brown, L. 2005. "Reward, Motivation, and Emotion Systems Associated with Early-Stage Intense Romantic Love." *Journal of Neurophysiology* 94, 327–37.

Arpaly, N. 2000. "On Acting Reasonably Against One's Best Judgment." *Ethics* 110, 488–513.

Arpaly, N. 2002. "Moral Worth." *Journal of Philosophy* 99, 223–45.

Arpaly, N. 2003. *Unprincipled Virtue.* New York: Oxford University Press.

Arpaly, N. 2006. *Merit, Meaning, and Human Bondage.* Princeton, NJ: Princeton University Press.

Arpaly, N. and Schroeder, T. 1999. "Praise, Blame, and the Whole Self." *Philosophical Studies* 93, 161–88.

Baddeley, A. 2003. "Working Memory: Looking back and looking forward." *Nature Reviews: Neuroscience* 4, 829–39.

Bao, S., Chan, V., and Merzenich, M. 2001. "Cortical Remodelling Induced by Activity of Ventral Tegmental Dopamine Neurons." *Nature* 412, 79–83.

Barry, M. 2007. "Realism, Rational Action, and the Humean Theory of Motivation." *Ethical Theory and Moral Practice* 10, 231–42.

Batson, C. and Shaw, L. 1991. "Evidence for Altruism: Toward a Pluralism of Prosocial Motives." *Psychological Inquiry* 2, 107–22.

Beaney, M. (ed.) 1997. *A Frege Reader.* Oxford: Blackwell.

Ben Ze'ev, A. 2000. *The Subtlety of Emotions.* Cambridge, MA: MIT Press.

Bennett, J. 1974. "The Conscience of Huckleberry Finn." *Philosophy* 49, 123–34.

Berger, S., Hall, S., Mickalian, J., Reid, M., Crawford, C., Delucchi, K., Carr, K., and Hall, S. 1996. "Haloperidol Antagonism of Cue-Elicited Cocaine Craving." *The Lancet* 347, 504–8.

Blackburn, S. 1998. *Ruling Passions: A theory of practical reasoning*. Oxford: Oxford University Press.

Blum, L. 1980. *Friendship, Altruism, and Morality*. London: Routledge and Kegan Paul.

Bommarito, N. 2013. "Modesty as a Virtue of Attention". *Philosophical Review* 122, 93–117.

BonJour, L. 1985. *The Structure of Empirical Knowledge*. Cambridge, MA: MIT Press.

Brandt, R. 1979. *A Theory of the Good and the Right*. Oxford: Oxford University Press.

Brandt, R. 1992. "The Structure of Virtue." In *Morality, Utilitarianism, and Rights*. New York: Cambridge University Press. 284–314.

Brewer, W. 1995. "Mental Causation: Compulsion by Reason." *Proceedings of the Aristotelian Society Supplementary Volume* 69, 237–53.

Brook, A. 2009. "Desire, Reward, Feeling: Commentary on *Three Faces of Desire*." *Dialogue* 45, 157–64.

Brophy, I. 1946. "The Luxury of Anti-Negro Prejudice." *The Public Opinion Quarterly* 9, 456–66.

Brown, R. and Marsden, C. 1988. "Internal Versus External Cues and the Control of Attention in Parkinson's Disease." *Brain* 111, 323–45.

Burge, T. 1979. "Individualism and the Mental." *Midwest Studies in the Philosophy* 4, 73–121.

Butler, K. 1992. "The Physiology of Desire." *Journal of Mind and Behavior* 13, 69–88.

Carr, D. 2008. *The Night of the Gun: A reporter investigates the darkest story of his life—his own*. New York: Simon and Schuster.

Carroll, L. 1895. "What the Tortoise Said to Achilles." *Mind* 4, 278–80.

Chan, D. 1995. "Non-Intentional Actions." *American Philosophical Quarterly* 32, 139–51.

Churchland, P. 1981. "Eliminative Materialism and the Propositional Attitudes." *Journal of Philosophy* 78, 67–90.

Clark, A. and Chalmers, D. 1998. "The Extended Mind." *Analysis* 58, 10–23.

Cohon, R. 1993. "Internalism about Reasons for Action." *Pacific Philosophical Quarterly* 74, 265–88.

Dancy, J. 1983. "Ethical Particularism and Morally Relevant Properties." *Mind* 92, 530–47.

Dancy, J. 2000. *Practical Reality*. New York: Oxford University Press.

Danto, A. 1963. "What We Can Do." *Journal of Philosophy* 60, 435–45.

Danto, A. 1965. "Basic Actions." *American Philosophical Quarterly* 2, 141–8.

D'Arms, J. and Jacobson, D. 2000. "The Moralistic Fallacy: On the 'appropriateness' of the emotions." *Philosophy and Phenomenological Research* 61, 65–90.

Darwall, S. 2001. "Because I Want It." *Social Philosophy and Policy* 18, 129–53.

Darwall, S. 2002. *Welfare and Rational Care*. Princeton, NJ: Princeton University Press.

Darwall, S. 2006. *The Second-Person Standpoint: Morality, respect, and accountability*. Cambridge, MA: Harvard University Press.

Darwall, S. 2010. "Because It Would Be Wrong." *Social Philosophy and Policy* 27, 135–57.

Davidson, D. 1980. *Actions, Reasons, and Causes*. Oxford: Oxford University Press.

Davidson, D. 1993. "Thinking Causes." In Heil, J. and Mele, A. (eds.) *Mental Causation*. Oxford: Clarendon. 3–17.

Davis, W. 1986. "The Two Senses of Desire." In Marks, J. (ed.) *The Ways of Desire: New essays in philosophical psychology on the concept of wanting*. Chicago: Precedent. 63–82.

Dayan, P., Montague, P., and Sejnowski, T. 1996. "A Framework for Mesencephalic Dopamine Systems Based on Predictive Hebbian Learning." *The Journal of Neuroscience* 16, 1936–47.

Deakin, J. 1983. "Role of Serotonergic Systems in Escape, Avoidance, and Other Behaviours." In Cooper, S. (ed.) *Theory in Psychopharmacology, Volume 2*. New York: Academic. 149–93.

Dennett, D. 1978. *Brainstorms: Philosophical Essays on Mind and Psychology*. Cambridge, MA: MIT Press.

De Sousa, R. 1987. *The Rationality of Emotion*. Cambridge, MA: MIT Press.

De Sousa, R. 2009. "Dust, Ashes, and Vice: On Tim Schroeder's theory of desire." *Dialogue* 45, 139–50.

Doris, J. 2002. *Lack of Character: Personality and Moral Behavior*. New York: Cambridge University Press.

Dovidio, J., Piliavin, J., Schroeder, D., and Penner, L. 2006. *The Social Psychology of Prosocial Behavior*. Mahwah, NJ: Lawrence Ehrlbaum Associates.

Dreier, J. 2001. "Humean Doubts about Categorical Imperatives." In E. Millgram (ed.) *Varieties of Practical Reasoning*. Cambridge, MA: MIT Press. 27–49.

Dretske, F. 1988. *Explaining Behavior: Reasons in a world of causes*. Cambridge, MA: MIT Press.

Driver, J. 1989. "Virtues of Ignorance." *Journal of Philosophy* 86, 373–84.

Driver, J. 2001. *Uneasy Virtue*. New York: Cambridge University Press.

Driver, J. 2007. "Dream Immorality." *Philosophy* 82, 5–22.

Ebels-Duggan, Kyla. 2008. "Against Beneficence: A normative account of love." *Ethics* 119, 142–70.

Eliasmith, C. and Anderson, C. 2002. *Neural Engineering: Computation, Representation, and Dynamics in Neurobiological Systems*. Cambridge, MA: MIT Press.

Elster, J. 1999. *Strong Feelings: Emotion, Addiction, and Human Behavior*. Cambridge, MA: MIT Press.

Festinger, L. and Carlsmith, J. 1959. "Cognitive Consequences of Forced Compliance." *Journal of Abnormal and Social Psychology* 58, 203–210.

Feyerabend, P. 1995. *Killing Time: The autobiography of Paul Feyerabend*. Chicago: University of Chicago Press.

Fischer, J. and Ravizza, M. 1998. *Responsibility and Control: A Theory of Moral Responsibility*. New York: Cambridge University Press.

Flanagan, O. 1990. "Virtues and Ignorance." *Journal of Philosophy* 87, 420–80.

Flanagan, O. 1991. *Varieties of Moral Personality*. Cambridge: Harvard University Press.

Fodor, J. 1990. *A Theory of Content: And other essays*. Cambridge, MA: MIT Press.

Fodor, J. 1998. *Concepts: Where Cognitive Science Went Wrong*. New York: Oxford University Press.

Foot, P. 1979. *Virtues and Vices: And Other Essays in Moral Philosophy*. Oxford: Blackwell.

Foot, P. 2001. *Natural Goodness*. New York: Oxford University Press.

Frankfurt, H. 1971. "Freedom of the Will and the Concept of a Person." *Journal of Philosophy* 68, 5–20.

Frankfurt, H. 1976. "Identification and Externality." In Frankfurt, H. 1988. *The Importance of What We Care About*. New York: Cambridge University Press. 58–68.

Frankfurt, H. 1987. "Identification and Wholeheartedness." In Frankfurt, H. 1988. *The Importance of What We Care About*. New York: Cambridge University Press. 159–76.

Frankfurt, H. 1999. "Autonomy, Necessity, and Love." In *Necessity, Volition, and Love*. New York: Cambridge University Press. 129–41.

Gailliot, M., and Baumeister, R. 2007. "The Physiology of Willpower: Linking blood-glucose to self-control." *Personality and Social Psychology Review* 11, 303–27.

Gallagher, S. 2000. "Self-Reference and Schizophrenia: A cognitive model of immunity to error through misidentification." In D. Zahavi (ed.) *Exploring the Self: Philosophical and Psychopathological Perspectives on Self-Experience*. Amsterdam: John Benjamins. 203–39.

Gardner, E. and David, J. 1999. "The Neurobiology of Chemical Addiction." In J. Elster and O. Skog, eds. *Getting Hooked: Rationality and Addiction*. Cambridge: Cambridge University Press. 93–136.

Gjelsvik, O. 1999. "Addiction, Weakness of the Will, and Relapse." In J. Elster and O. Skog, eds. *Getting Hooked: Rationality and Addiction*. Cambridge: Cambridge University Press. 47–64.

Glock, H. 2009. "Can Animals Act for Reasons?" *Inquiry* 52, 232–54.

Green, O. 1992. *The Emotions: A Philosophical Theory*. Dordrecht: Kluwer.

Greenspoon, J. 1955. "The Reinforcing Effect of Two Spoken Sounds on the Frequency of Two Responses." *American Journal of Psychology* 68, 409–16.

Griffiths, P. 1997. *What Emotions Really Are: The Problem of Psychological Categories*. Chicago: University of Chicago Press.

Hacker, P. 2007. *Human Nature: The Categorical Framework*. Oxford: Blackwell.

Hardcastle, V. 1999. *The Myth of Pain*. Cambridge, MA: MIT Press.

Hare, R. 1963. *Freedom and Reason*. Oxford: Clarendon Press.

Harman, G. 1986. *Change in View: Principles of reasoning*. Cambridge, MA: MIT Press.

Hebb, D. 1949. *The Organization of Behavior: A neuropsychological theory*. Hoboken, NJ: Wiley.

Herman, B. 1993. *The Practice of Moral Judgment*. Cambridge, MA: Harvard University Press.

Hieronymi, P. 2008. "Responsibility for Believing." *Synthese* 161, 357–73.

Hobbes, T. 1994. *Leviathan: With Selected Variants from the Latin Edition of 1668*. Indianapolis, IN: Hackett.

Holton, R. 1999. "Intention and Weakness of Will." *Journal of Philosophy* 96, 241–62.

Holton, R. 2009. *Willing, Wanting, Waiting*. New York: Oxford University Press.

Hookway, C. 1999. "Epistemic Norms and Theoretical Deliberation." *Ratio* 12, 380–97.

Houk, J., Davis, J., and Beiser, D. 1995. *Models of Information Processing in the Basal Ganglia*. Cambridge, MA: MIT Press.

Hubin, D. 2001. "The Groundless Normativity of Instrumental Rationality." *Journal of Philosophy* 98, 445–68.

Hubin, D. 2003. "Desires, Whims and Values." *The Journal of Ethics* 7, 315–35.

Hume, D. 2000. *A Treatise of Human Nature*. David Fate Norton and Mary J. Norton (eds.) Oxford: Oxford University Press.

Hurka, T. 2000. *Virtue, Vice, and Value*. New York: Oxford University Press.

Hursthouse, R. 1991. "Arational Actions." *Journal of Philosophy* 88, 57–68.

Hursthouse, R. 1999. *On Virtue Ethics*. New York: Oxford University Press.

Hyman, S. 2005. "Addiction: A Disease of Learning and Memory." *American Journal of Psychiatry* 162, 1414–22.

Jackson, F., Pettit, P., and Smith, M. 2004. *Mind, Morality, and Explanation: Selected collaborations*. New York: Oxford University Press.

James, W. 1890. *Principles of Psychology*. New York: Henry Holt & Co.

Jaworska, A. 1999. "Respecting the Margins of Agency: Alzheimer's patients and the capacity to value." *Philosophy and Public Affairs* 28, 105–38.

Jaworska, A. 2007a. "Caring and Full Moral Standing." *Ethics* 117, 460–97.

Jaworska, A. 2007b. "Caring and Internality." *Philosophy and Phenomenological Research* 74, 529–68.

Johnson, A. and Redish, A. 2007. "Neural Ensembles in CA3 Transiently Encode Paths Forward of the Animal at a Decision Point." *Journal of Neuroscience* 27, 12176–89.

Johnsrude, I., Owen, A., Zhao, W., and White, N. 1999. "Conditioned Preference in Humans: A novel experimental approach." *Learning and Motivation* 30, 250–64.

Kamm, F. 2006. *Intricate Ethics: Rights, responsibilities, and permissible harm*. New York: Oxford University Press.

Kant, I. 1991. *The Metaphysics of Morals*. Gregor, M. (trans.) New York: Cambridge University Press.

Kant, I. 1998. *Groundwork of the Metaphysics of Morals*. Gregor, M. (trans.) New York: Cambridge University Press.

Kelly, D. 2011. *Yuck! The nature and moral significance of disgust*. Cambridge, MA: MIT Press.

Kim, J. "Can Supervenience and 'Not-Strict Laws' Save Anomalous Monism?" In Heil, J. and Mele, A. (eds.) *Mental Causation*. Oxford: Clarendon. 19–26.

Kim, J. 1998. *Mind in a Physical World: An essay on the mind-body problem and mental causation*. Cambridge, MA: MIT Press.

Knowlton, B., Mangles, J., and Squire, L. 1996. "A Neostriatal Habit Learning System in Humans." *Science* 273, 1399–1402.

Knutson, B., Adams, C., Fong, G., and Hommer, D. 2001. "Anticipation of Increasing Monetary Reward Selectively Recruits Nucleus Accumbens." *Journal of Neuroscience* 21, 1–5.

Kolodny, N. 2003. "Love as a Valuing Relationship." *Philosophical Review* 112, 135–89.

Kolodny, N. 2005. "Why Be Rational?" *Mind* 114, 509–63.

Korsgaard, C. 1986. "Skepticism about Practical Reason." *Journal of Philosophy* 83, 5–25.

Korsgaard, C. 1996. *Sources of Normativity*. New York: Cambridge University Press.

Korsgaard, C. 1997. "The Normativity of Instrumental Reason." In G. Cullity and B. Gaut (eds.) *Ethics and Practical Reason*. Oxford: Oxford University Press. 215–54.

Korsgaard, C. 2008. *The Constitution of Agency: Essays on Practical Reason and Moral Psychology*. New York: Oxford University Press.

Korsgaard, C. 2009. "The Activity of Reason." *Proceedings and Addresses of the American Philosophical Association* 83, 27–47.

Langston, J. and Palfreman, J. 1995. *The Case of the Frozen Addicts*. New York: Pantheon.

Latané, B. and Darley, J. 1968. "Group Inhibition of Bystander Intervention in Emergencies." *Journal of Personality and Social Psychology* 10, 308–24.

Latham, N. 2009. "Three Compatible Theories of Desire." *Dialogue* 45, 131–8.

Lazar, A. 1999. "Deceiving Oneself or Self-Deceived? On the Formation of Beliefs Under the Influence." *Mind* 108, 265–90.

LeDoux, J. 2000. "Emotional Circuits in the Brain." *Annual Review of Neuroscience* 23, 155–84.

Levy, N. 2005. "The Good, the Bad and the Blameworthy." *Journal of Ethics and Social Philosophy* 1, 2–16.

Liechti, M., Saur, M., Gamma, A., Hell, D., and Vollenweider, F. 2000. "Psychological and Physiological Effects of MDMA ('Ecstasy') After Pretreatment with the 5-HT$_2$ Antagonist Ketanserin in Healthy Humans." *Neuropsychopharmacology* 23, 396–404.

Liechti, M. and Vollenweider, F. 2000. "Acute Psychological and Physiological Effects of MDMA ('Ecstasy') After Haloperidol Pretreatment in Healthy Humans." *European Neuropsychopharmacology* 10, 289–95.

Lockwood, R. and Ascione, F. 1998. *Cruelty to Animals and Interpersonal Violence*. West Lafayette, IN: Purdue University Press

Louden, R. 1986. "Kant's Virtue Ethics." *Philosophy* 61, 473–89.

Lowenstein, G. 1999. "A Visceral Account of Addiction." In J. Elster and O. Skog, eds. *Getting Hooked: Rationality and addiction*. Cambridge: Cambridge University Press. 235–64.

Lowry, C., Hale, M., Evans, A., Heerkens, J., Staub, D., Gasser, P., and Shekhar, A. 2008. "Serotonergic Systems, Anxiety, and Affective Disorder." *Annals of the New York Academy of Sciences* 1148, 86–94.

Maes, H. 2005. "Modesty, Asymmetry, and Hypocrisy." *The Journal of Value Inquiry* 38, 485–97.

Markovits, J. 2010. "Acting for the Right Reasons." *Philosophical Review* 119, 201–42.

Markovits, J. 2012. "Saints, Heroes, Sages, and Villains." *Philosophical Studies* 158, 289–311.

McDowell, J. 1979. "Virtue and Reason." *The Monist* 62, 331–50.

McGeer, T. and Pettit, P. 2002. "The Self-Regulating Mind." *Language and Communication* 22, 281–99.

Mele, A. 1990. "He Wants to Try." *Analysis* 50, 251–3.

Mele, A. 2001. *Self-Deception Unmasked*. Princeton, NJ: Princeton University Press.

Mele, A. 2003. *Motivation and Agency*. New York: Oxford University Press.

Milgram, S. 1974. *Obedience to Authority: an Experimental View*. New York: Harper Collins.

Millikan, R. 1989. "Biosemantics." *Journal of Philosophy* 86, 281–97.

Millikan, R. 1993. *White Queen Psychology and Other Essays for Alice*. Cambridge, MA: MIT Press.

Moll, J., Krueger, F., Zahn, R., Pardini, M., Oliveira-Souza, R., and Grafman, J. 2006. "Human Fronto-mesolimbic Networks Guide Decisions about Charitable Donation." *Proceedings of the National Academy of Sciences* 103, 15623–28.

Moray, N. 1959. "Attention in Dichotic Listening: Affective cues and the influence of instructions." *The Quarterly Journal of Experimental Psychology* 11, 56–60.

Morillo, C. 1990. "The Reward Event and Motivation." *Journal of Philosophy* 87, 169–86.

Moser, P. 1989. *Knowledge and Evidence*. New York: Cambridge University Press.

Murdoch, I. 1970. *The Sovereignty of Good*. London: Routledge and Kegan Paul.

Nagel, T. 1970. *The Possibility of Altruism*. Oxford: Oxford University Press.

Works Cited   305

Nagel, T. 1972. "War and Massacre." *Philosophy and Public Affairs* 1, 123–44.

Nozick, R. 1974. *Anarchy, State, and Utopia*. New York: Basic Books.

Nussbaum, M. 2001. *Upheavals of Thought: The intelligence of emotions*. Cambridge: Cambridge University Press.

Oddie, G. 2005. *Value, Reality, and Desire*. New York: Oxford University Press.

Parfit, D. 1997. "Reasons and Motivation." *Proceedings of the Aristotelian Society, Supplementary Volumes* 71, 99–130.

Parfit, D. 2011. *On What Matters*. Oxford: Oxford University Press.

Peacocke, C. 1983. *Sense and Content: Experience, Thought, and Their Relations*. New York: Oxford University Press.

Peacocke, C. 1992. *A Study of Concepts*. Cambridge, MA: MIT Press.

Pettigrew, T. 1998. "Intergroup Contact Theory." *Annual Review of Psychology* 49, 65–85.

Pettit, P. and Smith, M. 1990. "Backgrounding Desire." *Philosophical Review* 99, 565–92.

Piliavin, J. and Charng, H. 1990. "Altruism: A review of recent theory and research." *Annual Review of Sociology* 16, 27–65.

Porrill, J., Dean, P., and Stone, J. 2004. "Recurrent Cerebellar Architecture Solves the Motor-Error Problem." *Proceedings of the Royal Society B: Biological sciences* 271, 789–96.

Portmore, D. 2005. "Combining Teleological Ethics with Evaluator Relativism: A promising result." *Pacific Philosophical Quarterly* 86, 95–113.

Portmore, D. 2007. "Consequentializing Moral Theories." *Pacific Philosophical Quarterly* 88, 39–73.

Prinz, J. 2004. *Gut Reactions: A perceptual theory of emotion*. New York: Oxford University Press.

Putnam, H. 1975. "The Meaning of 'Meaning.'" *Minnesota Studies in the Philosophy of Science* 7, 131–93.

Quinn, W. 1993. *Morality and Action*. New York: Cambridge University Press.

Railton, P. 1988. "Alienation, Consequentialism, and the Demands of Morality." In Scheffler, S. (ed.) *Consequentialism and Its Critics*. Oxford: Oxford University Press. 93–133.

Railton, P. 2003. *Facts, Values, and Norms: Essays toward a morality of consequence*. New York: Cambridge University Press.

Railton, P. 2004. "How to Engage Reason: The Problem of Regress." In J. Wallace, P. Pettit, S. Scheffler, and M. Smith (eds.) *Reason and Value: Themes from the moral philosophy of Joseph Raz*. Oxford: Clarendon. 176–201.

Railton, P. 2009. "Practical Competence and Fluent Agency." In D. Sobel and S. Wall (eds.) *Reasons for Action*. New York: Cambridge University Press. 81–115.

Raterman, T. 2006. "On Modesty: Being Good and Knowing It Without Flaunting It." *American Philosophical Quarterly* 43, 221–34.

Rawls, J. 1971. *A Theory of Justice*. Cambridge, MA: Harvard University Press.

Raz, J. 1999. *Engaging Reason: On the theory of value and action*. Oxford: Oxford University Press.

Rilling, J., Gutman, D., Zeh, T., Pagnoni, G., Berns, G., and Kilts, C. 2002. "A Neural Basis for Social Cooperation." *Neuron* 35, 395–405.

Robinson, T. and Berridge, K. 2002. "The Psychology and Neurobiology of Addiction: An incentive-sensitization view." *Addiction* 95, 91–117.

Romo, R. and Schultz, W. 1990. "Dopamine Neurons of the Monkey Midbrain: Contingencies of responses to active touch during self-initiated arm movements." *Journal of Neurophysiology* 63, 592–606.

Rosen, G. 2004. "Skepticism about Moral Responsibility." *Philosophical Perspectives* 18, 295–313.

Rosner, J. 2000. "Reflective Endorsement and the Self: A response to Arpaly and Schroeder." *Philosophical Studies* 101, 107–12.

Ross, W. 2002. *The Right and the Good*. Philip Stratton-Lake (ed.) New York: Oxford University Press.

Sacks, O. 1985. *The Man Who Mistook His Wife for a Hat: And other clinical tales*. New York: Touchstone Books.

Saint-Cyr, J., Taylor, A., and Lang, A. 1988. "Procedural Learning and Neostyrial Dysfunction in Man." *Brain* 111, 941–60.

Salimpoor, V., Benovoy, M., Larcher, K., Dagher, A., and Zatorre, R. 2011. "Anatomically Distinct Dopamine Release During Anticipation and Experience of Peak Emotion to Music." *Nature Neuroscience* 14, 257–62.

Sampaio, J., Bobrowicz-Campos, E., André, R., Almeida, I., Faria, P., Januário, C., Freire, A., and Castelo-Branco, M. 2011. "Specific Impairment of Visual Spatial Covert Attention Mechanisms in Parkinson's Disease." *Neuropsychologia* 49, 34–42.

Sartre, J.-P. 1948. *Being and Nothingness*. H. Barnes (trans.) New York: Philosophical Library.

Scanlon, T. 1998. *What We Owe to Each Other*. Cambridge, MA: Harvard University Press.

Scanlon, T. 2008. *Moral Dimensions: Permissibility, meaning, blame*. Cambridge, MA: Harvard University Press.

Schechter, B. 1998. *My Brain Is Open: The mathematical journeys of Paul Erdős*. New York: Simon and Schuster.

Schlosser, M. 2007. "Basic Deviance Reconsidered." *Analysis* 67, 186–94.

Schmidtz, D. 1994. "Choosing Ends." *Ethics* 104, 226–51.

Schroeder, M. 2006. "Not So Promising After All: Evaluator-relative teleology and common-sense morality." *Pacific Philosophical Quarterly* 87, 348–56.

Schroeder, M. 2008. *Slaves of the Passions*. New York: Oxford University Press.

Schroeder, T. 2004. *Three Faces of Desire*. New York: Oxford University Press.

Schroeder, T. 2005. "Tourette Syndrome and Moral Responsibility." *Philosophy and Phenomenological Research* 71, 106–23.

Schroeder, T. 2006. "Reply to Critics." *Dialogue* 45, 165–74.

Schroeder, T. 2010a. "Irrational Action and Addiction." In D. Ross, H. Kincaid, D. Spurrett, and P. Collins (eds.) *What is Addiction?* Cambridge, MA: MIT Press.

Schroeder, T. 2010b. "Practical Rationality is a Problem in the Philosophy of Mind." *Philosophical Issues* 20, 394–409.

Schroeder, T. and Arpaly, N. 1999. "Alienation and Externality." *Canadian Journal of Philosophy* 29, 371–87.

Schueler, G. 1995. *Desire: Its Role in Practical Reason and the Explanation of Action*. Cambridge, MA: MIT Press.

Schueler, G. 1997. "Why Modesty Is a Virtue." *Ethics* 107, 467–48.

Schultz, W. 2011. "Potential Vulnerabilities of Neuronal Reward, Risk, and Decision Mechanisms to Addictive Drugs." *Neuron* 69, 603–17.

Schultz, W., Dayan, P., and Montague, P. 1997. "A Neural Substrate of Prediction and Reward." *Science* 275, 1593–99.

Schultz, W. and Romo, R. 1990. "Dopamine Neurons of the Monkey Midbrain: Contingencies of responses to stimuli eliciting immediate behavioral reactions." *Journal of Neurophysiology* 63, 607–24.

Schultz, W., Tremblay, L., and Hollerman, J. 2000. *Cerebral Cortex* 10, 272–83.

Schwitzgebel, E. 2011. *Perplexities of Consciousness*. Cambridge, MA: MIT Press.

Searle, J. 1983. *Intentionality: An essay in the philosophy of mind*. New York: Cambridge University Press.

Seidman, J. 2008. "Caring and the Boundary-Driven Structure of Practical Deliberation." *Journal of Ethics and Social Philosophy* 3, 1–36.

Setiya, K. 2007. *Reasons without Rationalism*. Princeton, NJ: Princeton University Press.

Sher, G. 2006. *In Praise of Blame*. New York: Oxford University Press.

Sherman, N. 1997. *Making a Necessity of Virtue: Aristotle and Kant on virtue*. New York: Cambridge University Press.

Skinner, B. 1938. *The Behavior of Organisms*. New York: Appleton-Century-Crofts.

Shastri, L. 2002. "Episodic Memory and Cortico-Hippocampal Interactions." *Trends in Cognitive Sciences* 6, 162–68.

Shoemaker, D. 2011. "Attributability, Answerability, and Accountability: Toward a Wider Theory of Moral Responsibility." *Ethics* 121, 602–32.

Smith, A. 2005. "Responsibility for Attitudes: Activity and passivity in mental life." *Ethics* 115, 236–71.

Smith, M. 1987. "The Humean Theory of Motivation." *Mind* 96, 36–61.

Smith, M. 1994. *The Moral Problem*. Oxford: Blackwell.

Sosa, E. 2007. *A Virtue Epistemology: Apt belief and reflective knowledge, Volume 1*. New York: Oxford University Press.

Soubrié, P. 1986. "Reconciling the Role of Central Serotonin Neurons in Human and Animal Behavior." *Behavioral and Brain Sciences* 9, 319–64.

Sprengelmeyer, R., Young, A., Schroeder, U., Grossenbacher, P., Federlein, J., Büttner, T., and Przuntek, H. 1999. "Knowing No Fear." *Proceedings of the Royal Society of London B: Biological Sciences* 266, 2451–6.

Stalnaker, R. 1984. *Inquiry*. Cambridge, MA: MIT Press.

Stampe, D. 1986. "Defining Desire." In Marks, J. (ed.) *Ways of Desire: New Essays in Philosophical Psychology on the Concept of Wanting*. Chicago: Precedent. 149–73.

Stanley, J. 2005. *Knowledge and Practical Interests*. New York: Oxford University Press.

Statman, D. 1992. "Modesty, Pride, and Realistic Self-Assessment" *Philosophical Quarterly* 42, 420–38.

Stellar, J. and Stellar, E. 1985. *The Neurobiology of Motivation and Reward*. New York: Springer-Verlag.

Steup, M. 1988. "The Deontic Conception of Epistemic Justification." *Philosophical Studies* 53, 65–84.

Steup, M. 2008. "Doxastic Freedom." *Synthese* 161, 375–92.

Stich, S. 1990. *The Fragmentation of Reason: Preface to a pragmatic theory of cognitive evaluation*. Cambridge, MA: MIT Press.

Stich, S., Doris, J., and Roedder, E. 2010. "Altruism." In J. Doris and the Moral Psychology Research Group (ed.) *The Moral Psychology Handbook*. New York: Oxford University Press. 147–205.

Strawson, G. 1994. *Mental Realilty*. Cambridge, MA: MIT Press.

Stump, E. 2006. "Love by All Accounts." *Proceedings and Addresses of the American Philosophical Association* 80, 25–43.

Sutton, R. and Barto, A. 1998. *Reinforcement Learning: An introduction*. Cambridge, MA: MIT Press.

Swanton, C. 2005. *Virtue Ethics: A pluralistic view*. New York: Oxford University Press.

Taylor, A., Hunt, G., Holzhaider, J., and Gray, R. 2007. "Spontaneous Metatool Use by New Caledonian Crows." *Current Biology* 17, 1504–7.

Taylor, G. 1976. "Love." *Proceedings of the Aristotelian Society* 76, 147–64.

Thagard, P. 2009. "Desires Are Not Propositional Attitudes." *Dialogue* 45, 151–56.

Thomson, J. 1997. "The Right and the Good." *Journal of Philosophy* 94, 273–98.

Tiberius, V. 2002. "Practical Reason and the Stability Standard." *Ethical Theory and Moral Practice* 5, 339–53.

Tye, M. 1995. *Ten Problems of Consciousness*. Cambridge, MA: MIT Press.

Vadas, M. 1984. "Affective and Non-Affective Desire." *Philosophy and Phenomenological Research* 45, 273–80.

Vargas, M. 2013. *Building Better Beings: A theory of moral responsibility*. New York: Oxford University Press.

Velleman, D. 1992. "What Happens When Someone Acts?" *Mind* 101, 461–81.

Velleman, D. 1999. "Love as a Moral Emotion." *Ethics* 109, 338–74.

Velleman, D. 2000. *The Possibility of Practical Reason*. New York: Oxford University Press.

Wallace, R. 1999. "Three Conceptions of Rational Agency." *Ethical Theory and Moral Practice* 2, 217–42.

Watson, G. 1975. "Free Agency." *Journal of Philosophy* 72, 205–20.

Watson, G. 1996. "Two Faces of Responsibility." *Philosophical Topics* 24, 227–48.

Wedgwood, R. 2006. "The Normative Force of Reasoning." *Noûs* 40, 660–86.

White, N. and Milner, P. 1992. "The Psychobiology of Reinforcers." *Annual Review of Psychology* 43, 443–71.

White, R. 2001. *Love's Philosophy*. Lanham, MD: Rowman and Littlefield.

Wolf, S. 1982. "Moral Saints." *Journal of Philosophy* 79, 419–39.

Wolf, S. 2001. "The Moral of Moral Luck." *Philosophic Exchange* 31, 4–19.

Yablo, S. 2003. "Causal Relevance." *Philosophical Issues* 13, 316–28.

{EXAMPLE INDEX}

RICK tries to be the life of the party on a whim, 11–13

REBECCA is not rational to deliberate while driving in swift-moving traffic, 26

RON is a blameworthy sadist even if he tried to improve his character in the past, 217–18

SARAVANAN lacks an extremely strong intrinsic desire to relieve suffering, without seeming blameworthy, 191

SATAN cannot blame Hitler for the war because Satan is in favor of the wrong or bad, 161

SAUL intrinsically desires the right via the concept FREGE'S FAVORITE PROPERTY, 165

SEAN has various motives for moving his foot out of the path of a log, but does not act on all, 78–79; blamelessly hits someone with his car and then feels bad, 219–21

SHAHNAZ either gives to a charity for the right reasons or does not, 80

SHAMISSA intrinsically desires the right via the concept RESPECT PERSONS, 165

STEFANIE is only fully motivated by hard bike rides, 190–1

SUJI has a great deal of good will but can still act, feel, and think like a less virtuous person on occasion, 212–14

SUN-JOO is a wholehearted Kantian, while utilitarianism is the correct normative theory, 199

TIM has intrinsic desires that give rise to instrumental and realizer desires while visiting family, 7–10; would act irrationally if learning of his father's good health always generated a reward signal in him, 280; could get pleasure from learning of his father's good health without harmful consequences, 281; can be jaded to his father's good health, 281, 286–7

TODD might enjoy a mango without having an intrinsic desire to eat mangoes, 120

TRAVIS turns left out of habit, 80–86; might be said to be inactive when "acting" out of habit, 82; might rather be said to be acting for a reason, 82–83; might rather be said to be acting in keeping with his reasons, 84–86; shows that motivation does not suffice for desiring, 111–13

TRISHA is slow to form negative moral judgments because of fear, not good will, 244–5

VICTOR does not know he is prejudiced against students who wear baseball caps backwards 237–8

VLAD goes to the same coffee shop each morning, but not from pure habit, 81–82

XIAOXI looks at a clock because her belief and desire rationalize her looking, 61–62

YOSSI is blameworthy only for his past acts permitting tics, not the tics themselves, if they cause harm, 217

YORAM could have suppressed his cough, but his coughing is not an action, 83

{SUBJECT INDEX}

actions: "arational," 85; borderline, 85–86; dorsal striatum has a role in, 137–8; and immediate intentions, 83–84, 87–88; and inaction, 82; motor and pre-motor cortices have a role in, 138; are for reasons, 28

Adams, R., 208, 222

addiction, 274–97; blameworthiness diminished in, 287–9; cue-conditioned cravings in, 283–5; dependency in, 276; and desires, 285–7; and dopamine, 277–8; habits created by, 281–3; hijacking of the reward system in, 278–81; reward learning in, 277–85; tolerance in, 276; withdrawal in, 276

affirming the consequent, 75

agent-relative reasons. *See* side-constraints

Akrasia, 259–61

alcohol: and addiction, 278n16, 283; disappearance of desires for, 9; enables whimsical actions, 14; excusing condition created by, 190; and hedonic misrepresentation, 120–1; and irrational inhibitions, 77–8; and nonrational influence on action, 77–80; and whimsical actions, 14

appetite. *See* reason and appetite

Aristotle, 1–2, 200–1

attention: and addiction, 282; and deliberation, 43–5, 51; and inner struggle, 270, 273; and intrinsic desires, 104; and self-deception, 231; and good will, 201, 208; and intrinsic desires, 117; intrinsic desires influence nonvoluntary, 125; reward signals influence, 140–1; and virtuous people, 225, 227–8, 231–2, 236

Ben Ze'ev, A., 248

blaming and crediting, 159–60

blameworthiness and praiseworthiness. *See also* good and ill will; and accountability, 160; acting for the right or wrong reasons constitutes, 170; and agents who wholeheartedly hold false moral theories, 198–9; and aliens with different amounts of good will, 192–3; and attributability, 160–2; concepts RIGHT or GOOD not required for, 176–87; contrast classes in, 192–3; and effort, 190–91; and favoritism or partiality, 194–8; good philosophy not required

for, 177; and nonculpable ignorance, 181–6; relative weight of ill will and moral indifference in, 187–8; sensitivity of them to amount of good will being manifested, 189–91; and the sorrowing philanthropist, 189; theories of, 170

Brandt, R., 208

Butler, J., 117

care, 104–9; degrees of, 107–8; distinguished from merely instrumental or realizer attitudes, 105; and the reward theory of desire, 147–50

causation: by absence, 82–83, 192; computers as an example of, 65–66; and demonic interveners, 58, 70

by logical or mathematical relations, 56, 62, 64–66; metaphysics of, 57–59, 70–72; by properties, 70–72; and neuroscience, 66; by the normative status of logical or mathematical relations, 66–67; and scientific explanation, 58

chlorpromazine, 118–19

cocaine: role in blameworthy action, 275–6, 287–8; hijacks the reward system, 278–81; and pressured speech, 14; and desire strength, 126

cognitive voluntarism, 226

concepts. *See* good and ill will, conceptualization of

Darwall, S.: and care, 105–9; and development of intrinsic desires, 103; and moral reasons for action, 180–1; neuroscientific response to, 140; rejects attributability-based theory of blameworthiness, 161n6

Davidson, D., 69–72, 230n11

deliberation, 19–52. *See also* recognition; and action, 22–23; no algorithms for, 28; and alienation, 23; in birds and rats, 4n9; does not change what is constituted as a reward or punishment, 132; component parts of, 25–26; and compounded insights, 43–44; constitutive end of, 23–24, 86; and distractions, 45; foolish views of, 33–36; for good reasons, 33–36; and imagery, 24–25; and inner struggle, 263–4; and inspiration,